AL-FIQH AL-ISLĀMĪ

الفقه الإسلامي

AL-FIQH AL-ISLĀMĪ

ACCORDING TO THE ḤANAFĪ MADHHAB

VOLUME 1

PURIFICATION, PRAYERS, AND FUNERALS

SHAYKH MOHAMMAD AKRAM NADWI

AL-FIQH AL-ISLĀMĪ

ISBN: 978-0-9555779-0-1

British Library Cataloguing in Publication Data
A catalogue record of this book is available from The British Library

Editors: Susanne Thackray, Dr Jamil Qureshi, Syed Tohel Ahmed, Junaid Ahmed, Shafiur Rahman.

Cover Design: Syed Nuh

Printed by: Imak Offset Print, Istanbul, Turkey
Typsetting: Abdassamad Clarke

Angelwing Media
www.angelwingmedia.net

بسم الله الرحمن الرحيم

CONTENTS

Dedication from the Author and Publisher

We dedicate this book to our respective parents (Hafiz Tajammul Husain & Munawwar Jahan, Taiyabur Rahman & Rabia Khanom, Bashir Uddin & Anwara Begum and Syed Abdul Latif & Renwara Khanam). It was our parents who firmly laid the foundation of Imān in our hearts. May Allāh forgive them for any shortcomings and envelope them in His Infinite Mercy.

"Your Lord has decreed that you worship none but Him, and that you be kind to parents. Whether one or more attain old age in your life, say not to them a word of contempt, nor repel them, but address them in terms of honour. And out of kindness, lower to them the wing of humility, and say, "my Lord! Bestow on them Your Mercy, even as they cherished me in childhood." (*Isrā'*: 23–24)

Publisher's acknowledgement

We would like to express our sincerest gratitude to all those who made the publication of this book possible. To Shaykh Mohammad Akram Nadwi for giving us the opportunity to publish this brilliant and unique work – we have indeed been honoured to work with him; Dr Jamil Qureshi for all his guidance; Dr Yeasmin Mortuza and Usamah Ward for their suggestions and finally our gratitude goes to the source from which flows immense joy and happiness – our families. May Allāh reward them all abundantly.

PREFACE

ALL PRAISE IS OWED TO ALLĀH; blessings be upon His slave and messenger, the seal of the Prophets, Muḥammad and on his family, his Companions and all those who follow the guidance that came through him.

The idea of writing this book occurred at an *ifṭār* meeting during Ramaḍān 1425, when some friends identified the need for a manual of Ḥanafī *Fiqh* with all the necessary references from the Qur'ān, and earliest legal sources. The idea was strengthened in *Dhū al-Ḥijjah* of last year, when brothers Junaid Ahmed, Shafiur Rahman and Syed Tohel Ahmed visited me and expressed their willingness to publish the work. I then became convinced of the need to give priority to this project, ahead of my other commitments.

Over the last two years, I have taught several parts of the book at different institutions and *madrasahs,* and discussed it at various lectures. My thanks to those who organised these occasions and to all who attended and made helpful comments.

My thanks also to my colleague Dr Jamil Qureshi for his careful reading of this work with a copy-editor's eye. I am especially grateful to my daughters Husna, Sumaiya and Mohsina for their help in reading the manuscript, testing the explanation of legal issues, and making helpful suggestions. May Allāh reward them all.

I hope this book will provide English-speaking readers with a comprehensive guide to a Muslim's essential religious duties and obligations, together with a clear understanding of the sources upon which it is based.

May Allāh accept this humble effort, forgive our mistakes and sins, and may He guide me and my readers to true worship of Him and obedience to His commands.

Mohammad Akram Nadwi
Oxford
9th Rabīᶜ al-Awwal 1427

KEY TO TRANSLITERATION

ا	*alif*
ب	*bā*
ت	*tā*
ث	*thā*
ج	*jīm*
ح	*ḥā*
خ	*khā*
د	*dāl*
ذ	*dhāl*
ر	*rā*
ز	*zā*
س	*sīn*
ش	*shīn*
ص	*ṣād*
ض	*ḍād*
ط	*ṭā*
ظ	*ẓā*
ع	*ʿayn* (indicated with a ʿ)
غ	*ghayn*
ف	*fā*
ق	*qāf*
ك	*kāf*
ل	*lām*
م	*mīm*
ن	*nūn*
ه	*hā*
و	*waw*
ي	*yā*
ء	*hamzah* (indicated with a ')

Longer vowels are indicated by a stroke over the letter, e.g. *ā, ī, ū* and *Ā, Ī, Ū*.

INTRODUCTION

ISLAM IS A WAY FOR PEOPLE TO LIVE IN THIS WORLD. This way derives from, and also enables, a conviction that living in this world is a test and trial, preparing believers for their everlasting home in the life Hereafter. In its details, Islam consists of faith, practice, law, spirituality, ethics and manners. The present work is devoted to understanding the laws of Islam related to the practice of rites, personal relationships, contracts and other aspects of everyday life.

LAW

Islamic Law, which is called Sharīʿah in Arabic, covers all aspects of Muslim life in relation to individuals, societies and states. The exclusive right to form law belongs to Allāh alone. It is He Who determines what man should and should not do; how society should and should not operate: "*Whoever judges not by that which Allāh has revealed: such are disbelievers*",[1] "*Whoever judges not by that which Allāh has revealed: such are wrongdoers*",[2] and "*Whoever judges not by that which Allāh has revealed: such are evildoers*".[3] "*The decision is for Allāh only*".[4] Allāh and Allāh alone is the indisputable Commander and Law Giver.

Commitment to Islam entails, as well as having the right mind or intent to obey and serve Allāh, having sufficient understanding of the actions

[1] *al-Māʾidah* 44.
[2] Ibid., 45.
[3] Ibid., 47.
[4] *al-Anʿām* 57.

that are commanded or prohibited by Him, and sufficient understanding of general and particular conduct that is pleasing to Him or displeasing to Him. The technical term for such 'sufficient understanding' is *fiqh*. One who is proficient in this is called a *faqīh* (pl. *fuqahā'*).

The *faqīh* is not a priest of some sort. Indeed, he is far from it. The *faqīh* does not have some private or mysterious relationship with Allāh from which other believers are excluded. Rather, the *faqīh* is one of the believers, neither more nor less. A person is not saved by knowing a *faqīh*, or by having some piece of *fiqh* dispensed by the *faqīh*, like a sort of medicine or a sort of sacrament. Rather, a person is saved according to their own actions and their own intentions and endeavours, their own deeds and their own inner disposition, as directly judged by Allāh.

What the *faqīh* knows can be taught to others and learnt by them; it can be understood and discussed; it can be agreed or disagreed with. All that the *faqīh* has by way of authority is dependent upon sources which are public – the Book of Allāh, the Qur'ān; the Sunnah of Allāh's Messenger ﷺ, which is the paraphrase and exposition of the meaning of the Qur'ān for everyday life, and the ideal practical embodiment of that meaning; and the Sunnah of the Messenger's noble Companions, whose dispositions and deeds were educated in the presence of Allāh's Messenger ﷺ, and who, after his death, dedicated their lives to preserving and spreading the knowledge they had learnt from him. These are the sources of the knowledge upon which the authority of any *fiqh* depends, and all of them are in the public domain.

SOURCES OF LAW

There are, primarily, four sources through which we can know Allāh's will and command. They are the Qur'ān, the Sunnah, a consensus of juristic opinion (*Ijmā*ᶜ), and disciplined reasoning by analogy (*Qiyās*).

The Qur'ān

The Qur'ān is the Book of Allāh sent through Muḥammad ﷺ, the last of the Prophets. It contains knowledge imparted by Allāh for the guidance for humankind. It provides a code of conduct for every believer. It is the commandment and a warrant for the believer, providing solutions to every situation that the believer may encounter until the Hereafter.

The Sunnah

The second source for Sharīʿah is the Sunnah of the Prophet ﷺ. Every judgement, statement, and action by the Prophet ﷺ is normative. Even actions he approved of in others are implicitly normative. He never spoke from his own imagination or desire, but imparted only what Allāh had revealed to him. The Qur'ān bears witness to this fact: "*By the Star when it sets, your comrade errs not, nor is deceived, nor does he speak of his own desire, it is naught save an inspiration that is inspired.*"[5] Again, the Qur'ān asserts the position of the Prophet ﷺ: "*No, by your Lord, they will not believe in truth until they make you judge of what is in dispute between them and find within themselves no dislike of that which you decide, and submit with full submission*".[6]

The Sunnah supplements the Qur'ān as a source of Islamic law. Believers are asked always to turn to both sources for answers to the problems and difficulties facing them, and they inspire regulations for every aspect of their lives: "*O believers, obey Allāh, and obey the Messenger and those of you who are in authority; and if you have a dispute concerning any matter, refer it to Allāh and the Messenger if you are (in truth) believers in Allāh and the Last Day. That is better and more seemly in the end*".[7]

After the death of the Prophet ﷺ every case that came up before the Companions and the generations that followed had to be referred to the Qur'ān, then to the judgements, sayings and actions of the Prophet ﷺ. There are a large number of cases on record in which a right was claimed based on a judgement, saying or action of the Prophet ﷺ.

Imām al-Bukhārī narrated that Fāṭimah and ʿAbbās came to Abū Bakr, seeking their share from the property of Allāh's Apostle ﷺ. Abū Bakr said to them: "I heard Allāh's Apostle ﷺ saying: 'We Prophets do not inherit nor leave an estate for an inheritance. Whatever we leave is a charity'."[8] Here we see that the claim was rejected based on a ḥadīth. This ḥadīth was cited by Abū Bakr and was not questioned by anyone.

Being the second source of Sharīʿah, later on the Sunnah of the Prophet ﷺ was collected very carefully by his Companions and the

[5] *al-Najm* 1-4.

[6] *al-Nisā'* 65.

[7] Ibid., 59.

[8] al-Bukhārī, *k. al-farā'iḍ, b. qawl al-nabī ṣallallāhu ʿalayhi wa sallam lā nūrathu mā taraknā ṣadaqatun.*

people of succeeding generations. Among the most famous and reliable collections of Sunnah are: *al-Muwaṭṭa'*, by Imām Mālik (d. 179), *al-Jāmiᶜ al-Ṣaḥīḥ*, by Imām al-Bukhārī (d. 256), *al-Jāmiᶜ al-Ṣaḥīḥ*, by Imām Muslim (d. 261), *al-Jāmiᶜ al-Ṣaḥīḥ* by Imām al-Tirmidhī (d. 279), *al-Sunan* by Imām Abū Dāwūd (d. 275), *al-Sunan*, by Imām al-Nasā'ī (d. 303), *al-Sunan* by Imām Ibn Mājah (d. 273) and *al-Musnad* by Imām Aḥmad ibn Ḥanbal (d. 241).

Ijmāᶜ

Ijmāᶜ is the consensus of qualified legal scholars in a given generation on any legal regulation. This, then, is the third source of legal opinion. The validity of *ijmāᶜ* as a source of law is based on the Qur'ān and the Sunnah. Allāh says in His Last Book: "*And whoever opposes the Messenger after the guidance (of Allāh) has been manifested unto him, and follows other than the believers' way, We appoint for him that unto which he himself has turned, and expose him unto Hell – a hapless journey's end*".[9]

The Prophet ﷺ said: "My people will never all agree upon error".[10] An example of this is the *ijmāᶜ* of the Companions on the *khilāfah* of Abū Bakr, then the *khilāfah* of ᶜUmar.

Qiyās

Qiyās means analogy and has been defined in different ways; the most popular meaning is: to carry the principle of one issue to a comparable issue based on a legal cause (*ᶜillah*) for judgement common to both issues.

Analogy as a source of law is supported by a number of Qur'ānic verses and Sunnah. The following ḥadīth is often quoted: "On the appointment of Muᶜādh ibn Jabal as a judge and governor of Yemen, the Prophet ﷺ asked him: 'According to what will you judge?' He replied: 'According to the Book of Allāh'. The Prophet ﷺ asked: 'And if you do not find it in the Book of Allāh?' Muᶜādh said: 'Then I will judge on the basis of the Sunnah of His Prophet ﷺ'. The Prophet ﷺ asked him: 'If you do not find it in both the Qur'ān and the Sunnah?' Then Muᶜādh said: 'I will exert myself to form my own judgement'. To this, the Prophet ﷺ said: 'Praise is

[9] *al-Nisā'* 115.

[10] al-Tirmidhī, *k. al-fitan, b. mā jā'a fī luzūm al-jamāᶜah;* Ibn Mājah, *k. al-fitan.*

to Allāh who has guided the messenger of His Messenger to that which pleases Him'."[11]

Below, a few examples of analogical extension from Qur'ānic verses are given:

1. The Qur'ān says: "*Give not the wealth of the foolish which is in your keeping, and which Allāh has given you to maintain, to them; rather, feed and clothe them from it and speak kindly to them. Test orphans till they reach marriageable age; then, if you find them of sound judgement, deliver over to them their fortune*".[12]

This Qur'ānic verse forbids guardians to deliver property to those orphans who are weak of understanding, but it makes it permissible to give them their property when they reach an age of understanding and maturity. From this verse, a law has been derived by analogy that all transactions of a child are invalid without the guardian's permission. The legal cause (*ʿillah)* behind this being immaturity of understanding.

2. The Qur'ān says: "*O you who believe, strong drink and games of chance and idols and divining arrows are only an infamy of Satan's handiwork. Leave them aside in order that you may succeed*".[13]

Drinking wine is forbidden according to this verse. Beer and other such drinks, which intoxicate, are also unlawful on the basis of analogy. Drugs such as heroin, cocaine and marijuana, etc., are also unlawful on this same principle.

3. The Qur'ān says: *"O you who believe, when the call for the Jumuah Salah is proclaimed, hasten to the remembrance of Allah, and leave off business. That is better for you if you did but know*".[14]

According to this verse, commercial transactions are forbidden after the call to Friday *Ṣalāh*. From the analogy based on this injunction, all kinds of business, such as hiring, borrowing, working in factories and offices and other similar engagements that prevent a person from offering Friday *Ṣalāh* are forbidden.

DEVELOPMENT OF THE LAW

During his lifetime, the Prophet ﷺ entrusted a number of his Companions to teach Islam and to act as judges and give legal rulings for the people

[11] Abū Dāwūd, *k. al-aqḍiyah, b. ijtihād al-ra'y fī al-qaḍā'.*

[12] *al-Nisā'* 5-6.

[13] *al-Mā'idah* 90.

[14] *al-Jumuʿah* 9.

on his behalf. Their legal dicta are quoted and preserved in compilations of ḥadīth; in particular, the judgements of the first four caliphs were accorded practically the same status as the Sunnah of the Prophet ﷺ himself. The qualities that the Prophet ﷺ found and approved of in these men were the qualities that, in later generations, Muslims looked for in those whom they would call *imāms*, men worthy to be followed. Men who had dedication in their personal bearing and conduct in their relationship with Allāh (piety) and well-being in relation to people (righteousness) – combined with the necessary intellectual competence to distinguish and pursue Islamic values within the realties of this world without becoming so distracted or distressed by its demands as to betray those values.

After the Prophet's death ﷺ, the territories to which the law had to be extended expanded rapidly. Many of the Companions left Madīnah and settled in other cities to teach, and to give rulings and judgements to order people's affairs. ʿUmar took particular care to appoint in every city learned Companions who were competent to teach the Qur'ān and the Sunnah, and to uphold the law. The most eminent among those appointed by him were Abū al-Dardā' in Syria and ʿAbdullāh ibn Masʿūd in Kufah.

The Kufan School

Kufah was founded at the command of ʿUmar. More of the Companions settled there than in any city except Makkah and Madīnah. ʿAbdullāh ibn Masʿūd and ʿAlī ibn Abī Ṭālib were the most influential in developing *fiqh* in Kufah. ʿAbdullāh ibn Masʿūd moved to Kufah in 17 AH, the year it was founded, and remained there until the last period of ʿUthmān's caliphate. He devoted his time to teaching the Qur'ān, Sunnah and *fiqh*. About 4,000 people learnt *fiqh* directly from him or from his students. When ʿAlī moved to Kufah during his caliphate, he was pleased to see the abundance of jurists in the city.

Among the prominent scholars trained by Ibn Masʿūd were ʿAlqamah ibn Qays al-Nakhaʿī (d. 62) and al-Aswad (d. 75). Their teachers also included ʿUmar, ʿUthmān, ʿĀ'ishah, ʿAbdullāh ibn ʿAbbās, ʿAbdullāh ibn ʿUmar and many other Companions. In this way, the *fiqh* developed by ʿAlqamah and al-Aswad in Kufah also contained and reflected the knowledge of the major scholars of other cities.

Among ʿAlqamah and al-Aswad's students, the most prominent was Ibrāhīm ibn Yazīd al-Nakhaʿī, who succeeded them as the principal teacher in Kufah. For his extraordinary contribution to knowledge of the law, he earned the title of *Faqīh al-ʿIrāq*. Al-Nakhaʿī died in 96 AH. and was succeeded by Ḥammād ibn Abī Sulaymān (d. 120). ʿAbd al-Malik ibn Iyās al-Shaybānī said: "I asked Ibrāhīm, 'To whom will we put questions after you?' He replied: 'Ḥammād'." A leading Kufan scholar, Mughīrah, said: "We called on Ibrāhīm during his illness. He said to us 'stick close to Ḥammād; he has asked me about all that the people have asked me'."[15]

Abū Ḥanīfah

Ḥammād ibn Abī Sulaymān was succeeded by his best student, Abū Ḥanīfah Nuʿmān ibn Thābit (d. 150) who was one of the first to employ the recognised methods of legal reasoning in a systematic way, and to gather the legal judgements and dicta of his time into an organised corpus. This is why Imām Shāfiʿī (d. 204) famously said about him: "In the matter of *fiqh* people are dependent on Abū Ḥanīfah". Abū Ḥanīfah learnt *fiqh* from Ḥammād and remained close to him for eighteen years until his death in 120 AH. Abū Ḥanīfah also travelled many times to Makkah and Madīnah. During the Hajj season, the *Ḥarāmayn* served as a focal point for scholars from different parts of the Islamic world. Abū Ḥanīfah made good use of these occasions to meet scholars, exchange ideas and learn from them. He brought to that knowledge, intelligence unequalled in his field for its clarity, rigour and organising power. He knew from his extensive experience in trade, as well as from the scores of legal queries that were addressed to the scholars of Kufah, himself in particular, of the community's need for a systematically arranged body of laws.

The sheer multitude of transactions and relationships now subject to the rule of Islam, the growing distance from the generation of senior Companions, on whose judgements one could justifiably depend, the growing volume of divergent (sometimes conflicting) legal opinions that were circulating, along with individual reports of the dicta of the Prophet ﷺ or the Companions, the context and legal implications

[15] al-Dhahabī, *Siyar aʿlām al-nubalāʾ*, v. 232.

of which were not always fully understood – all impressed upon Abū Ḥanīfah the need for a systematic compilation of the law. Abū Ḥanīfah fully understood the scale of the project he was undertaking. It would have been neither proper nor practicable for him to undertake this on his own. He therefore formed a committee of forty of his best students, all of whom had established reputations in special areas relevant to jurisprudence.

This committee met daily and their work proceeded through free discussion and debate. Abū Ḥanīfah would listen to the discussion, summarise it, and then offer his conclusions and opinion. According to the sources, his opinion was generally so well balanced and well argued that the other members of the committee usually accepted it.[16] The aim was always to proceed by unanimity and consensus. However, if differences of opinion could not be reconciled all such different opinions were recorded. The work was completed over about 30 years, between 121 and 150 AH, the year of Abū Ḥanīfah's death. It had even continued through the years that Abū Ḥanīfah spent in prison. Over those 30 years, literally thousands of cases were decided by this consultative committee based on the legal queries submitted to it. Its particular decisions and its general methods of reasoning were communicated to every city in the Islamic world by the hundreds of students of the Kufan School appointed to judicial posts throughout the ʿAbbāsid dominions. The committee also enjoyed a more or less official status in that functionaries and officials of the state regularly consulted it.

Abū Ḥanīfah was very concerned to distinguish between abrogating and abrogated *aḥādīth*. He followed a ḥadīth when it was proven to be from the Prophet ﷺ and his Companions. He was also very knowledgeable about the *aḥādīth* of the people of Kufah and their *fiqh*; via all the reports that reached his city, Abū Ḥanīfah knew by heart the last practice of the Messenger of Allāh ﷺ (i.e. the Sunnah) on which he died.[17]

Abū Ḥanīfah's students

Few teachers in history can have been so blessed in their students as Abū Ḥanīfah. Among those students, three were generally recognised

[16] Shiblī, *al-Nuʿmān* 181.

[17] On Abū Ḥanīfah, see al-Dhahabī, *Siyar aʿlām al-nubalā', vi.* 390-403.

as being the most outstanding, and were regarded as Abū Ḥanīfah's successors in the Kufan School of *fiqh*. They were Zufar ibn al-Hudhayl (110–158 AH), Abū Yūsuf and Muḥammad ibn al-Ḥasan al-Shaybānī (135–189 AH).

Zufar ibn al-Hudhayl ibn Qays's first interest was ḥadīth, but once he turned to *fiqh* he remained committed to it for the rest of his life; indeed he held the post of *qāḍī* (judge). He was particularly skilled in analogical reasoning, and Abū Ḥanīfah called him the greatest of his companions in this respect. Wakīʿ ibn al-Jarrāḥ used to consult him.[18]

Yaʿqūb ibn Ibrāhīm ibn Ḥabīb al-Anṣārī, widely known as *Qāḍī* Abū Yūsuf, was born in Kufah in 113 or 117 AH. He heard *aḥādīth* from al-Aʿmash, Hishām ibn ʿUrwah, Sulaymān al-Taymī, Yaḥyā ibn Saʿīd al-Anṣārī and others, and was known as a master of the field. He stayed in Abū Ḥanīfah's class until he became the most prominent of all his students. After Abū Ḥanīfah's death, the ʿAbbāsid Caliph Mahdī appointed him as *qāḍī* in 166 AH. Mahdī's successor, Hādī, retained him in this post. Subsequently, Hārūn al-Rashīd, on learning of his attainments, appointed him *Qāḍī al-quḍāh* (Chief Justice) for the whole realm, a post which he was the first to hold in Islamic history. He died in 182 AH.[19]

Muḥammad ibn al-Ḥasan al-Shaybānī heard *ḥadīth* from Misʿar ibn Kidām, al-Awzāʿī, Sufyān al-Thawrī, Mālik ibn Anas and others. He is one of the twin pillars of Ḥanafī *Fiqh*, the other being Abū Yūsuf. For about two years he attended Abū Ḥanīfah's lectures, and after the latter's death completed his education under Abū Yūsuf. He was accompanying Hārūn al-Rashīd on a visit to Rayy in 189 AH, when he died.[20]

Major sources in Ḥanafī Fiqh

Imām Muḥammad al-Shaybānī's books are considered the basic source of Ḥanafī *Fiqh*. He left a vast corpus of writings (Ibn al-Nadīm lists 66 titles under his name) which became standard works in the curricula of the Ḥanafī School. His books are divided into two categories:

1) *kutub ẓāhir al-riwāyah:* books narrated from him through well-known chains and reliable narrators. Six books can be listed here: *al-Mabsūṭ,*

[18] On Zufar, see al-Dhahabī, *Siyar aʿlām al-nubalāʾ, viii.* 38-41.

[19] On Abū Yūsuf, see al-Dhahabī, *Siyar aʿlām al-nubalāʾ, viii.* 535-9.

[20] On Muḥammad al-Shaybānī, see al-Dhahabī, *Siyar aʿlām al-nubalāʾ, ix.* 134-6.

al-Ziyādāt, al-Jāmiʿ al-ṣaghīr, al-Jāmiʿ al-kabīr, al-Siyar al-ṣaghīr, al-Siyar al-kabīr. Together they are called *al-uṣūl.* To them are also attached *Kitāb al-āthār,* and *al-Ḥujjah ʿalā ahl al-madīnah.*

2) *Kutub ghayr ẓāhir al-riwāyah:* books narrated from him through less known chains of narrators. These books, alongside Abū Yūsuf's *al-Amālī* and the books of Ḥasan ibn Ziyād, are called *al-nawādir* ('less popular').

Imām Muḥammad's works provided the foundation for all later writings. Below, those jurists who developed this school in one or other way are identified.

Imām Abū Jaʿfar al-Ṭaḥāwī's (d. 321) most enduring contribution in the area of practical law are his formularies, of which three were much mentioned: *al-Shurūṭ al-kabīr, al-Shurūṭ al-awsaṭ* and *al-Shurūṭ al-ṣaghīr.* Much of this material was incorporated in later works of the Ḥanafī School, especially *al-Hidāyah* of al-Marghinānī, and the *al-Fatāwā al-hindiyyah.* Al-Ṭaḥāwī produced two important and widely admired works on the *fiqh* of ḥadīth, the *Sharḥ Mushkil al-āthār* and *Sharḥ maʿānī al-āthār.*[21]

Abū al-Layth al-Samarqandī (d. 375), was a prolific writer on *fiqh* and other branches of religious sciences. His most notable works are *Khizānat al-fiqh,* a handbook of Ḥanafī Law, *Mukhtalif al-riwāyah* on divergent doctrines among the earliest Ḥanafī authorities, and *al-Muqaddimah fi al-ṣalāh* on the duty of *ṣalāh,* with many commentaries.[22]

Al-Qudūrī's (d. 428) *Mukhtaṣar* enjoyed a scholarly renown and reverence comparable to the *Risālah* of al-Qayrawānī among the Mālikīs, and the *Mukhtaṣar* of al-Muzanī among the Shāfiʿīs. It is a concise legal manual on all the chapters of *fiqh* starting with purification and ending with the law of inheritance. It inspired a great many commentaries, including for example *al-Jawharah al-nayyirah* of Abū Bakr ibn ʿAlī al-ʿAbbādī and *al-Lubāb fi sharḥ al-kitāb* of ʿAbd al-Ghanī al-Maydānī.[23]

Al-Sarakhsī's (d. 483) *al-Mabsūṭ,* a commentary on al-Ḥākim al-Shahīd's *al-Kāfī,* marks the transition to a more logical and systematic

[21] See al-Dhahabī, *Siyar aʿlām al-nubalā', xv.* 27-32; N. Calder, *EI* art., al-Ṭaḥāwī.

[22] See al-Dhahabī, ibid., *xvi.* 322-3; J. Schacht, *EI* art., Abū al-Layth.

[23] See al-Dhahabī, ibid., *xvii.* 574-5; M. Ben Cheneb, *EI* art., al-Qudūrī.

arrangement of the subject-matter within chapters. Al-Sarakhsī lived and worked in Transoxania, inheriting and developing its juristic tradition. He produced a number of works, the most important being the *Mabsūṭ, Sharḥ al-Siyar al-kabīr* and *Uṣūl al-fiqh.*[24]

This was followed by al-Kāsānī's (d. 587) *Badā'iʿ al-ṣanā'iʿ*, which has a strictly systematic arrangement. In a process common to all the schools of the law, the older works mentioned above were gradually ousted by later handbooks and their commentaries. One of the most important of these is al-Marghinānī's (d. 593) *al-Hidāyah.* His principal work was the legal compendium *Kitāb Bidāyat al-mubtadī*, based on al-Qudūrī's *al-Mukhtaṣar* and al-Shaybānī's *al-Jāmiʿ al-ṣaghīr.* He himself wrote a multi-volume commentary on this compendium, *Kifāyat al-muntahī.* Before he completed it, however, he decided it was too diffuse and wrote a second commentary, the celebrated *al-Hidāyah.* Later writers repeatedly edited and annotated it, providing a great many commentaries. Burhān al-dīn Maḥmūd al-Maḥbūbī (fl. seventh century) produced a synopsis of it which he called *Wiqāyat al-riwāyah.* Another of the literary offspring of *al-Hidāyah* is of al-Quhistānī's (d. 950) *Jāmiʿ al-rumūz*, which enjoyed great authority in Transoxania.[25]

A second and important later work is the *Kanz al-daqā'iq* of Abū al-Barakāt al-Nasafī (d. 710), again with numerous commentaries: for example *Tabyīn al-ḥaqā'iq* by al-Zaylaʿī (d. 743) and *al-Baḥr al-rā'iq* by Ibn Nujaym (d. 970). The same Ibn Nujaym wrote *Kitāb al-Ashbāh wa-l-naẓā'ir,* a treatise on the systematic structure of positive law. In the Ottoman Empire, the *Durar al-ḥukkām* of Mullā Khusraw (d. 885), a commentary on his own *Ghurar al-aḥkām*, gained particular authority. *Multaqā al-abḥur* of Ibrāhīm al-Ḥalabī (d. 956), which is based on Qudūrī's *al-Mukhtaṣar,* Buldājī's (d. 683) *al-Mukhtār,* al-Nasafī's *Kanz al-daqā'iq* and *Wiqāyat al-riwāyah,* has two very popular commentaries on it namely Shaykhzāde's (d. 1078) *Majmaʿ al-anhur* and al-Ḥaṣkafī (d. 1088) *Durr al-muntaqā.* The same al-Ḥaṣkafī is the author of *al-Durr al-mukhtār,* on which Ibn ʿĀbidīn (d. 1252) wrote a commentary called *Radd al-muḥtār,* a highly esteemed work paying particular attention to the problems of the contemporary world. The latest exposition of the Ḥanafī doctrine

[24] See al-Dhahabī, ibid., *ixx.* 147; N. Calder, *EI* art., al-Sarakhsī.

[25] See al-Dhahabī, ibid., *xxi.* 232; W. Heffening, *EI* art., al-Marghinānī.

in the traditional style is the *Hukuki islamiyye ve istilahati fikhiyye kamusu* by Ömer Nasuhi Bilmen, *Muftī* of Istanbul.[26]

The most authoritative handbook of traditional Ḥanafī doctrine in India, after *al-Hidāyah*, has been *al-Fatāwā al-hindiyyah*, which is not a collection of *fatwās* but rather a voluminous compilation of extracts from the authoritative works of the school, made at the order of the Mughal Emperor Awrangzīb ʿĀlamgīr (1067–1118).[27]

Among the more important collections of Ḥanafī *fatwās* are those by Burhān al-dīn ibn Māza (d. about 570), called *Dhakhīrat al-fatāwā*, Qāḍī Khān (d. 592), Sirāj al-dīn al-Sajāwandī (end of the sixth century) who is also the author of a very popular treatise on the law of inheritance, al-Bazzāzī al-Kardarī (d. 827), Abū al-Suʿūd (d. 982), and al-Anqarawī (d. 1098).[28]

GOALS AND METHOD OF THIS BOOK

This book presents the norms and rulings of the *fiqh* of the Ḥanafī School, together with the sources – verses of the Qur'ān, reports of the Sunnah of Allāh's Messenger (*aḥādīth*) and records of the proofs and practices of his Companions (*āthār*) – from which those norms and rulings are drawn.

Accompanying each ruling are brief explanatory notes, full references to the source texts and, in most cases a full or abridged translation of the relevant parts of those texts.

Regarding the sources used for this book, I refer to those that are authoritative. Among the *aḥādīth*, I have chosen those that specifically relate to the point and which are central to the arguments according to the *madhhab* (school) of Abū Ḥanīfah.

I do not seek to demonstrate that Abū Ḥanīfah was right and those who differed from him were wrong. I seek refuge in Allāh from any such intent. I have the deepest respect for all the imāms, jurists and traditionists of Islam, and believe that they all served the religion of Allāh with sincerity and great sacrifice – love and respect for them bring one closer to Allāh. I mean to demonstrate only that Abū Ḥanīfah had evidences from the sources just as the other imāms and jurists did.

[26] See W. Heffening, *EI* art., al-Ḥanafiyyah.

[27] Ibid.

[28] Ibid.

Abū Ḥanīfah is one of many jurists that Islam has produced. Anyone who follows any of them with sincerity and love and fear of Allāh in their heart, may hope for Allāh's forgiveness and mercy. On the Day of Judgement, we are not going to be questioned about whether we followed Abū Ḥanīfah, Mālik, Shāfiʿī or Aḥmad ibn Ḥanbal, may Allāh bestow His mercy on all of them. Rather, Allāh will look at those who did not follow their own desires, but who made their effort to follow the guidance. May Allāh make us among those.

Arrangement of the material

The present work is arranged according to the traditional subdivision and ordering of topics. Later volumes will cover contracts and other elements of the law. The first three volumes deal with:

I: *ʿIbādāt: ṭahārah, ṣalāh, janāʾiz.*
II: *ʿIbādāt: zakāh, ṣawm* and *ḥajj.*
III: Muslim personal law.

كتاب الطهارة

THE BOOK OF PURIFICATION

Introduction

AL-ṬAHĀRAH (RITUAL PURITY) is a basic condition of worship; *ṣalāh* is invalid without it. Allāh says: "*Allāh loves the repenters and the purified*".[29] The Prophet ﷺ said: "Purification is half of the faith".[30] "The key to *ṣalāh* is purification".[31]

The soundness of the outward aspect of human life is called *ṭahārah* (purification); its opposite is *najāsah* (filth). The soundness of the inward aspect of human life is called *taqwā* (piety); its opposite is *ithm* (sin). Since Islam is a combination of both outward and inward soundness, *ṭahārah* holds an important place, and is considered half of faith. It elevates the believer from base instincts, and enables him to receive divine mercy. *Najāsah,* on the other hand, degrades one, and renders one vulnerable to evil influences. Hence, in the verse cited above, those who repent and those who purify themselves are mentioned together as pleasing Allāh.

As a term of law, *al-ṭahārah* means: 1. removing dirt and filth; its opposite is *najāsah;* 2. washing specific parts of the body; its opposite is *ḥadath* (impurity). The first type of purification is achieved by removing

[29] *al-Baqarah* 222.

[30] Muslim, *k. al-ṭahārah, b. faḍl al-wuḍū'.*

[31] al-Tirmidhī, *k. al-ṭahārah, b. mā jā'a anna miftāḥ al-ṣalāti al-ṭuhūr.*

the *najāsah* using water or other pure liquid, or by using clean, dry solid matter such as soil, stone or paper. The second type of purification is achieved by *wuḍū'*, *ghusl*, or *tayammum* if the use of water is difficult.

Since water is the major means of purification, I will start by discussing different types of water and related issues, explain different types of *najāsah* and how to be purified and cleaned of them, and then discuss *wuḍū'*, *ghusl*, *tayammum* and the issues related to *ḥadath*.

Chapter 1: Types of water

Water is the essential means for all kinds of purification. It is divided into three types: 1. *ṭahūr* (purifying); 2. *ṭāhir* (pure) and 3. *najis* (impure). We shall now discuss each of these separately.

ṬAHŪR

Ṭahūr is pure water, and is qualified to purify other things. It is considered pure because of its inherent purity and, as such, it can be used by an individual for *wuḍū'* and *ghusl*. This kind of water is called *muṭlaq* (absolute). It consists of the following sub categories:

Rainwater

Rainwater is purifying, because Allāh says: "*And We sent down purifying water from the sky*".[32] and "*He causes water to descend on you from the sky to purify you*".[33]

Similarly snow and hail are also purifying. Abū Hurayrah reported a supplication of the Messenger of Allāh ﷺ in which he said: "O Allāh, wash my sins from me with snow, water and hail".[34] This ḥadīth indicates that snow and hail purify as well as water. Jābir said: "I asked ᶜĀmir al-Shaᶜbī and al-Ḥakam about snow. Both of them said: 'One may do *wuḍū'* with it'."[35] While doing *wuḍū'* with snow or hail one should make sure that one is washing, not just wiping. Jurists require that, by way of a sign that water has flowed, two or more drops should fall off the body.[36] Shuᶜbah said: 'I asked Ḥakam about *wuḍū'* and *ghusl* with snow. He said: 'One breaks the snow into pieces then does *wuḍū'* and *ghusl* with it'."[37]

Sea water

It has been narrated that the Messenger of Allāh ﷺ was asked about sea

[32] *al-Furqān* 48.

[33] *al-Anfāl* 11.

[34] al-Bukhārī, *k. al-adhān, b. mā yaqūlu baᶜda al-takbīr.*

[35] ᶜAbd al-Razzāq, *al-Muṣannaf, i.* 243.

[36] al-Kāsānī, *Badā'iᶜ al-ṣanā'iᶜ, i.* 92.

[37] Ibn Abī Shaybah, *al-Muṣannaf, i.* 161.

water. The Messenger of Allāh ﷺ said: "Its water is purifying".[38] Abū al-Ṭufayl narrated that Abū Bakr al-Ṣiddīq was asked: "Can one do *wuḍū'* with sea water?" He said: "Sea water is purifying".[39] On being asked about sea water, ʿUmar said: "Which water is purer than sea water?"[40] Ibrāhīm al-Nakhaʿī said: "Sea water suffices, though fresh water is more beloved by me".[41]

River water

River water like sea water is purifying. It is narrated from ʿAbdullāh ibn ʿAbbās that he said: "There is no harm in doing *wuḍū'* with either sea water, or water from the Euphrates river".[42]

Pond and well water are also purifying. The Prophet ﷺ and his Companions relied on well water in Makkah and Madīnah, and when they travelled, they used pond water. ʿAlī ibn Abī Ṭālib narrated that the Messenger of Allāh ﷺ called for a bucket that contained water from the Well of *Zamzam*. He drank from the bucket, then did *wuḍū'* with its water.[43] The Prophet ﷺ was asked about rain water that collected in a field. He said: "It is purifying and can be used for drinking".[44] Abū al-Zubayr narrated that Jābir ibn ʿAbdullāh was asked what a person in a state of *janābah* (a state of impurity when *ghusl* is compulsory) was to do if they found a pond along their path. He said: "He should bathe in a corner of it".[45]

Piped water supply

Piped water as supplied in most urbanised parts of the world for drinking or washing is *muṭlaq* water. It can be used for *wuḍū'* or *ghusl* or any cleaning purpose. Similarly, water supplied by pipe or canal for

[38] Abū Dāwūd, *k. al-ṭahārah, b. al-wuḍū' bi mā' al-baḥr;* al-Tirmidhī, *k. al-ṭahārah, b. mā jā'a fī mā' al-baḥr annahu ṭahūr;* al-Nasā'ī, *k. al-ṭahārah, b. mā' al-baḥr;* Ibn Mājah, *k. al-ṭahārah, b. al-wuḍū' bi mā' al-baḥr.*

[39] Ibn Abī Shaybah, *al-Muṣannaf, i.* 121.

[40] ʿAbd al-Razzāq. *al-Muṣannaf, i.* 95.

[41] Ibn Abī Shaybah, *al-Muṣannaf, i.* 122.

[42] Ibid., i. 121

[43] Aḥmad, *al-Musnad* 564.

[44] Ibn Mājah, *k. al-ṭahārah, b. al-ḥiyāḍ.*

[45] Ibn Abī Shaybah, *al-Muṣannaf,* i. 130.

irrigation purposes, though perhaps unfit for drinking, may be used for purification and cleaning.

Mixed and leftover water

Water that has been mixed with pure substances like flood, or water mixed with milk, saffron or soap is purifying as long as it has not been mixed with so much of the other substances that one can no longer call it water. If this is the case, the water is still considered pure, but it cannot be used for *wuḍū'* or *ghusl.* Umm ʿAṭiyyah narrated that the Messenger of Allāh ﷺ entered his house after the death of his daughter Zaynab and said: "Wash her three times or five, or more, if you see fit to do so; with water and lote tree leaves".[46] Umm Hānī narrated that the Messenger of Allāh ﷺ and his wife Maymūnah had a bath from the same container that had a trace of dough in it.[47] In both of these *aḥādīth,* we find that the water was mixed with another substance, but since the other substance was not dominant, it remained fit for use in purification.

As regards leftover water, i.e. water that remains in a pot after some of it has been drunk, the following types remain purifying. The leftover water of a human being is pure regardless of whether the one who drank from the pot was in a state of purity or impurity, a Muslim or non-Muslim, except the leftover water of someone who has just eaten or drunk any forbidden thing (like pork or wine).[48] ʿĀ'ishah said: "I would eat flesh from a bone when I was menstruating, then hand it over to the Prophet ﷺ and he would put his mouth where I had put my mouth; I would drink then pass it to him and he would put his mouth at the same place where I drank".[49] The Companions used to mix with non-Muslims and very often they used to eat and drink with each other. Jābir narrated that ʿĀmir al-Shaʿbī said: "There is no harm in the leftover of the person in the state of *janābah,* the woman in her menstruation, and the associator". [50]

[46] al-Bukhārī, *k. al-janā'iz, b. ghusl al-mayyit wa wuḍū'ihi;* Muslim, *k. al-janā'iz, b. ghusl al-mayyit.*

[47] al-Nasā'ī, *k. al-ṭahārah, b. dhikr al-ightisāl fī al-qaṣʿat allatī yuʿjanu fīhā.*

[48] *See:* al-Samarqandī, *Tuḥfat al-fuqahā' 30.*

[49] Muslim, *k. al-ḥayḍ, b. jawāz ghasl al-ḥā'iḍ ra'sa zawjihā.*

[50] Ibn Abī Shaybah, *al-Muṣannaf,* i. 39.

Similarly, water left over after a horse or any other allowable animal has drunk from is pure.[51] Such water is permissible for drinking or use in *wuḍū'*. Nāfiᶜ narrated that ᶜAbdullāh ibn ᶜUmar did not see any harm in the leftover of a horse.[52] The same has been narrated from al-Ḥasan al-Baṣrī and Ibn Sīrīn.[53] ᶜIkrimah said: "There is no harm in doing *wuḍū'* from the leftover of allowable animals".[54] Ibrāhīm al-Nakhaᶜī said: "There is no harm in the leftover of a cow, camel and goat".[55]

The leftover water of a cat is pure if there is no sign of impurity in its mouth. But *wuḍū'* or *ghusl* with this water is *makrūh tanzīhī*[56] as long as *muṭlaq* water is available. Kabshah bint Kaᶜb ibn Mālik who was married to the son of Abū Qatādah, reported that Abū Qatādah entered the house; then she poured water for his *wuḍū'*. A cat came and drank some of it and he tilted the vessel for it until it drank more. Kabshah said: "He saw me looking at him. He asked: 'Are you surprised, my niece?' I answered, 'Yes'. He said: 'The Messenger of Allāh ﷺ said: 'It is not impure, rather it is from those visiting you frequently'."[57] Another ḥadīth suggests that if a cat drinks from a container it should be washed once.[58]

Though the first ḥadīth is clear that the leftover water of a cat is pure, nevertheless the second ḥadīth implies that it is not wholly pure. Hence it is considered *makrūh tanzīhī*. Imām Muḥammad said: "There is no harm in doing *wuḍū'* from the leftover water of the cat, but any other water is preferable to us than that, and this is the opinion of Abū Ḥanīfah".[59]

The ruling about the leftover water of birds of prey and domesticated animals is similar. Yaḥyā ibn ᶜAbd al-Raḥmān ibn Ḥāṭib reported that

[51] *See:* al-Samarqandī, *Tuḥfat al-fuqahā' 30.*

[52] Ibn Abī Shaybah, *al-Muṣannaf*, i. 36.

[53] Ibid.

[54] Ibid.

[55] Ibid.

[56] *Makrūh* means disliked and has two categories*; makrūh taḥrīmī*, which means grossly disliked, and *makrūh tanzīhī* which means disliked.

[57] Abū Dāwūd, *k. al-ṭahārah, b. su'r al-hirrah;* al-Tirmidhī, *k. al-ṭahārah, b. mā jā'a fī su'r al-hirrah;* al-Nasā'ī, *k. ṭahārah, b. su'r al-hirrah;* Ibn Mājah, *k. al-ṭahārah, b. su'r al-hirrah wa al-rukhṣah fī dhālik.*

[58] al-Tirmidhī, *k. al-ṭahārah, b. mā jā'a fī su'r al-kalb.*

[59] Muḥammad, *al-Muwaṭṭa' i,* 348-353.

once ʿUmar was among a group that included ʿAmr ibn al-ʿĀṣ and, when they came upon a pond, ʿAmr said: "O owner of the pond, do the beasts of prey come to your pond?" ʿUmar said: "Do not inform us, because we drink after the wild beasts and the wild beasts after us".[60]

Ṭāhir

This class of water, though itself pure, cannot be used to purify oneself, i.e. *wuḍū'* and *ghusl* are not acceptable with such water. An example of this class of water is that which has already been used in *wuḍū'* or *ghusl* done with the intention of purification or reward. It is pure, not purifying; a subsequent *wuḍū'* or *ghusl* with the same water is not valid. However, this class of water can be used to wash off physical impurities from oneself or from one's clothes, etc.

Najis

Najis is still water of a small quantity (i.e. a little) mixed with an impurity (*najāsah*), whether or not there is a visible sign of impurity on its surface. If a sign of impurity appears on the water, it is considered impure even if the quantity of water is abundant.

'Abundant water' means water of a basin which is ten arms in length and width, and its depth is such that the ground cannot be seen if the water is taken from it with one's hand. What is less than this is called 'little water'. This is based on Imām Muḥammad's saying: "If the pond is big enough that if one side of it is stirred the other side does not stir, then it will not be dirty if any wild animal drinks from it or if any dirt falls in it as long as the smell and taste of the water are not affected by the dirt".[61]

[60] Mālik, *al-Muwaṭṭa'* 18; The leftover water of a mule or donkey is pure, but its qualification for *wuḍū'* and *ghusl* is doubtful. The donkey and mule are not allowed to be eaten, but they were used for riding and their sweat used to touch the body. This means that the sweat is pure. Saliva has the same ruling as sweat, but there is no evidence that either can purify. Ibrāhīm al-Nakhaʿī says: "There is no good in the leftover water of the mule and donkey, and no one should do *wuḍū'* with the leftover water of a mule and donkey". Imām Muḥammad says: "It is the opinion of Abū Ḥanīfah and we adhere to it". (Abū Ḥanīfah, *K. al-āthār, p.* 8.)

[61] Muḥammad, *al-Muwaṭṭa', i.* 268-269.

The leftover water of a pig or dog is impure. Allāh says about the pig: "*It is filth*".[62] Its leftover is certainly foul and impure. As for the dog, Abū Hurayrah narrated that the Messenger of Allāh ﷺ said: "If a dog drinks from the container of any one among you, wash it seven times".[63] This means that the container has become foul and it must be cleaned, and the least of such cleaning is to wash it three times; the command of washing it seven times is recommended as a precautionary measure. The same ruling applies to wild animals.

[62] *al-Anʿām* 145.

[63] Muslim, *k. al-ṭahārah, b. ḥukm wulūgh al-kalb.*

Chapter 2: Najāsah
and Purification from It

The term *najāsah* is used to refer to whatever is unclean in a religious sense. It is obligatory for the person intending *ṣalāh* to clean his body, clothing and the place of *ṣalāh* from any *najāsah*. Allāh says at the end of the verse of *wuḍū'* that "*He wants to purify you*",[64] and as such has prohibited all things that are foul. There are particular types of *najāsah* that He has commanded believers to purify themselves of. Such states of being unclean include *janābah*: "*If you are in a state of janābah, purify yourselves,*"[65] and menstruation: "*And they question you concerning menstruation. Say: It is an illness, so let women alone at such times and do not have relations with them until they are cleansed*".[66]

Types of Najāsah

What necessitates wuḍū' or ghusl

What necessitates *wuḍū'* or *ghusl* is impure bodily excretion, like faeces, urine, vomit, blood, *manī*, *madhy* and *wady*.

The faeces (of human beings, and all animals, whether or not their meat is permissible) are impure. Khuzāmah ibn Thābit reported: The Prophet ﷺ was asked about cleansing after relieving oneself. He said: "One should cleanse oneself with three stones which should be free from dung".[67] ʿAbdullāh ibn Masʿūd related that the Messenger of Allāh ﷺ went to answer a call of nature. He asked ʿAbdullāh to bring three stones. ʿAbdullāh said: "I found two stones, and looked for the third but I could not get it. So I took animal dung and took it to him. He took the two stones and threw away the dung saying, 'It is dirt'."[68]

[64] *al-Mā'idah* 6.
[65] *al-Mā'idah* 6.
[66] *al-Baqarah* 222.
[67] Abū Dāwūd, *k. al-ṭahārah, b. al-istinjā' bi al-aḥjār.*
[68] al-Bukhārī, *k. al-wuḍū', b. lā yustanjā bi rawth.*

The urine of those animals which are not permissible is impure like their stools. The urine of those animals which are permissible for food, however, is lighter in impurity. If a person contracts a minor impurity on his body or clothing, then he still is permitted to perform *ṣalāh* as long as such impurity does not amount to a quarter of any part of his clothing.

The urine of an unweaned baby can be cleaned by light washing. Umm Qays bint Miḥṣan reported that she went to the Messenger of Allāh ﷺ with her little son who had not attained the age of eating. The Messenger of Allāh ﷺ seated him on his lap, and he urinated on his clothes. The Prophet ﷺ called for some water, which he sprayed over his clothes, and did not give them a complete washing.[69] ᶜAlī narrated that the Messenger of Allāh ﷺ said: "The urine of a baby girl is to be washed thoroughly and the urine of a baby boy should have water sprinkled upon it".[70] Imām Muḥammad confirmed the concession about the urine of a male baby not on solid food, and the command to wash the urine of a female baby. However, he also stated that the washing of both is preferred and that that is also the opinion of Abū Ḥanīfah.[71]

Vomit is impure. However, an insignificant amount of it is not considered impure as it does not break one's *wuḍū'*.

Blood that has come out and has flowed away from the body is impure, like menstrual blood, or blood dripping from an injury. The Qur'ān states: "*Say: I do not find in that which is revealed to me anything forbidden to be eaten by one who wishes to eat it, unless it be a dead animal, or blood poured forth, or swine flesh, for that surely is foul*".[72] Scholars affirm that this means blood that flows out. Conversely, blood that does not so flow, but instead remains on the surface of the body has no objections.[73]

[69] al-Bukhārī, *k. al-wuḍū', b. bawl al-ṣibyān;* Muslim, *k. al-ṭahārah, b. ḥukm bawl al-ṭifl al-raḍīᶜ wa kayfiyyat ghaslih.*

[70] Abū Dāwūd, *k. al-ṭahārah, b. bawl al-ṣabī yuṣību al-thawb;* al-Tirmidhī, *k. al-ṭahārah, b. mā jā'a fī naḍḥ bawl al-ghulām qabla an yaṭᶜam.*

[71] Muḥammad, *al-Muwaṭṭa', i,* 256-8.

[72] *al-Anᶜām* 145.

[73] Imām Muḥammad did not agree with this, and he regarded blood that does not flow as impure. *(Badā'iᶜ al-ṣanā'iᶜ, i.* 363-364.*)*

Manī means sperm and is impure. If it is moist, then it must be washed off; if it has dried on one's clothing, it is acceptable to scrape it off. ʿĀ'ishah said: "I used to scratch the sperm off the Messenger of Allāh's ﷺ clothes if it was dry, and wash it off if it was still wet".[74] Ṭalḥah ibn ʿAbdullāh narrated that Abū Hurayrah said about clothing tainted with sperm: "Wash it if you see it, otherwise wash the whole cloth".[75] Ibrāhīm al-Nakhaʿī said: "Wash the sperm from your cloth".[76]

Madhy is a white sticky fluid that flows from one's private part because of thoughts about desire, foreplay and so on. It too is impure and it is obligatory to wash it off if it contaminates one's clothing or body. ʿAlī said: "I used to excrete *madhy*, so I asked a man to ask the Messenger of Allāh ﷺ about it. I was shy to do so because of my position with respect to his daughter [ʿAlī was the Prophet's son-in-law]. The Prophet ﷺ affirmed: 'Do *wuḍū'* and wash your private parts'."[77]

Wady is white drops following urination. ʿAbdullāh ibn ʿAbbās affirmed that if someone has got *madhy* or *wady*, he must wash his private parts and do *wuḍū'*.[78] Mujāhid and ʿIkrimah said: "From *madhy* and *wady*, one has to wash his private parts, then do *wuḍū'*".[79]

Pigs

The pig, as has been narrated from Abū Ḥanīfah, is *najis al-ʿayn*, i.e. every part of it is unclean.[80] The Qur'ān states: "*Say: I do not find in that which is revealed to me anything forbidden to be eaten by one who wishes to eat it, unless it be a dead animal, or blood poured forth, or swine flesh, for that surely is foul*".[81] This means that every part of the pig is unclean.

Dogs

The dog is impure and hence any container that has been licked by a

[74] al-Ṭaḥāwī, *Sharḥ maʿānī al-āthār*, i. 49; al-Dāraquṭnī, *al-Sunan*, i. 131.
[75] al-Ṭaḥāwī, ibid., i. 52.
[76] Ibn Abī Shaybah, *al-Muṣannaf*, i. 83.
[77] Muslim, *k. al-ḥayḍ, b. al-madhy*.
[78] al-Ṭaḥāwī, *Sharḥ maʿānī al-āthār*, *i*. 47.
[79] Ibn Abī Shaybah, *al-Muṣannaf*, i. 88.
[80] *Tuḥfat al-fuqahā' 30.*
[81] *al-Anʿām* 145.

dog must be washed. It has been narrated by Abū Hurayrah that the Messenger of Allāh ﷺ said: "If a dog drinks from the container of any one among you, wash it seven times".[82] As mentioned earlier, the cleaning that can be achieved by washing three times is compulsory, though washing the container seven times is recommended, as mentioned in the ḥadīth. If a dog licks a pot that has dry food in it, what it touched and what surrounds it must be thrown away. The remainder may be kept, as it is still pure. Similarly, if someone's body or clothing has been touched by a dog then it is not impure, unless what touches the body is wet (for example the dog's saliva, mouth or wet fur, etc.)

Animal carcasses

Animals that have died without being slaughtered in the prescribed manner are described as 'dead'. They are impure as the Qur'ān states: "*Say: I do not find in that which is revealed to me anything forbidden to be eaten by one who wishes to eat it, unless it be a dead animal, or blood poured forth, or swine flesh, for that surely is foul*".[83] It also includes any body part cut off a live animal – this too is to be regarded as 'dead'. Abū Wāqid al-Laythī reported that the Prophet ﷺ said: "What is cut off of a live animal is regarded as dead",[84] i.e. considered as an animal that has not been properly slaughtered.

Dead fish and dead locusts are pure. ʿAbdullāh ibn ʿUmar reported that the Messenger of Allāh ﷺ said: "Two types of dead animals and two types of blood have been made lawful for us. The types of dead animals are fish and locusts. The two types of blood are the blood of the liver and the spleen".[85]

Similarly, creatures such as flies, scorpions, wasps, and so on, from which blood does not flow, are pure. Salmān al-Fārisī narrated that the Messenger of Allāh ﷺ said: "Death in the water of such creatures from which blood does not flow, does not alter the condition of the water".[86] Abū Saʿīd al-Khudrī narrated that the Messenger of Allāh ﷺ said: "If a fly falls into a vessel [containing food or drink] of any of you, then dip

[82] Muslim, *k. al-ṭahārah, b. ḥukm wulūgh al-kalb.*

[83] *al-Anʿām* 145.

[84] Abū Dāwūd, *k. al-ṣayd, b. fī ṣayd quṭiʿa minhu qiṭʿah.*

[85] Ibn Mājah, *k. al-aṭʿimah, b. al-kabid wa al-ṭiḥāl.*

[86] al-Dāraquṭnī, *al-Sunan, i.* 37.

the fly in it, and then take it out. [The reason for doing so is] because on one wing of the fly there is disease and on the other wing the cure, and the fly always puts the wing with disease in first".[87]

The hide, hair, bones, horns, wool, and feathers of dead animals are considered pure. ʿAbdullāh ibn ʿAbbās reported that a client of Maymūnah was given a sheep as charity, and it died. The Messenger of Allāh ﷺ passed by it and said: "Why did you not remove its skin, tan it, and then you would have benefited from it?" She said: "It is dead". He said to her: "Only eating it is forbidden".[88] It is reported from Ibn ʿAbbās that the Prophet ﷺ also said: "What is forbidden from the dead is its meat. As for its skin, hair, teeth, and wool, they are permissible".[89] Ḥammād said: "There is no harm in the feather of the dead bird". As regards the bones of dead animals such as elephant and the like, Imām al-Zuhrī said: "I have known some scholars of the early generations who used objects made of them for combs and pots for oil, and they did not see anything wrong in that". Ibn Sīrīn and Ibrāhīm al-Nakhaʿī said: "There is no harm in the trade of elephant tusks".[90]

Alcohol

Alcohol is impure. Allāh says in the Qur'ān: "*O you who believe, intoxicants, games of chance, idols and divining arrows are filth from the infamy of Satan's handiwork*".[91] Abū Thaʿlabah al-Khushanī asked the Messenger of Allāh ﷺ about what should be done if they come into contact with the people of the Book, while they were cooking swine in their pans and drinking wine from their pots. The Messenger of Allāh ﷺ said: "If you find any other pan and pot then eat and drink from it; but if you do not find other than their containers then wash [them], then eat and drink".[92] Al-Ḥasan al-Baṣrī said: "If a drop of wine or blood drops into a container,

[87] al-Bukhārī, *k. al-ṭibb, b. idhā waqaʿa al-dhubābu fī al-inā'.*

[88] Muslim, *k. al-ḥayḍ, b. ṭahārat julūd al-maytati bi al-dibāgh.*

[89] al-Dāraquṭnī, *al-Sunan, i.* 43.

[90] al-Bukhārī, *k. al-wuḍū', b. mā yaqaʿu min al-najāsat fī al-samn wa al-mā'.*

[91] *al-Mā'idah* 90.

[92] Abū Dāwūd, *k. al-aṭʿimah, b. al-akl fī āniyat ahl al-kitāb.*

it should be poured out".[93] Mujāhid said: "If wine drops over your cloth, wash it; it is more severe than blood".[94]

Najāsah that is forgiven

The rulings about *najāsah* that has fallen into water were explained earlier. As for the *najāsah* that gets onto one's clothing and body, a little of it is forgiven. The definition of 'little' depends on the nature of *najāsah,* which is divided into two types:

Najāsah ghalīẓah

This refers to gross impurity affirmed as such by a text, and not contradicted by any other text, such as faeces, urine and blood. It is impure and it is obligatory to remove it. Only if the quantity of the *najāsah* is very little is the person permitted to do *ṣalāh* – the 'very little' is defined as the size of a *dirham* (about the size of a British fifty pence piece) in surface area or less. Ibrāhīm al-Nakhaʿī said: "If blood, urine, etc., are the size of a *dirham* then re-do your *ṣalāh,* and if they are less than that then carry on in your *ṣalāh*".[95] This means that what is forgiven is less than a *dirham* in size, though the opinion in the Ḥanafī *madhhab* is that the size of a *dirham* and less is forgiven. Hence why Imām Muḥammad said after quoting Ibrāhīm al-Nakhaʿī's opinion: "His *ṣalāh* is valid until it is more than the *dirham* of a big weight, if it is like that (i.e. more than a *dirham*) then *ṣalāh* is not valid. This is the opinion of Abū Ḥanīfah".[96]

Najāsah khafīfah

This refers to light or lesser impurity, about which there are differing texts, like the urine of those animals whose meat is permissible. If a light impurity, i.e. the urine of a sheep or cow gets on to someone's clothing it is permitted to do *ṣalāh* in that clothing as long as no more than a quarter of the clothing is affected. Imām Muḥammad narrated from Abū Ḥanīfah saying: "If the urine of these animals falls in the container used in *wuḍū'* it will corrupt it, and if plenty of it gets on

[93] Ibn Abī Shaybah, *al-Muṣannaf,* i. 154.
[94] Ibid., i. 176.
[95] Abū Ḥanīfah, *K. al-āthār* 29.
[96] Ibid.

one's clothing and one prays in them, then one has to repeat the *ṣalāh*". Imām Muḥammad said: "I do not see any harm in it; it does not spoil any water or clothing".[97] However, Abū Ḥanīfah's opinion is preferred over that of Imām Muḥammad's.

HOW TO PURIFY NAJĀSAH

It is permitted to clean *najāsah* with pure water and anything else clean as long as it is possible to remove the impurity by such means, for example, by using vinegar or rose water.[98] Details about how to clean different types of impurity are given below.

PURIFYING THE BODY AND CLOTHING

Removing an impurity that must be washed off the body and clothing is of two kinds:

1. Visible impurity, like blood and faeces. If this kind of impurity gets on the body or clothing, then it must be washed so that the impure substance itself is removed. However, there is no harm if some stains remain after necessary washing. Abū Hurayrah reported that Khawlah bint Yasār came to the Prophet ﷺ and said: "O Messenger of Allāh ﷺ, I have only one garment and I menstruate in it, what should I do? He said: "When you are purified, wash it and pray in it". She asked: "If blood is not removed, then what? He said: "It is enough for you to wash the blood off, its stain will not do any harm to you".[99]

2. Invisible impurity, like urine. In this case, purification is effected by washing it off until one considers that, in all likelihood, it has been removed. In most cases this can be achieved by washing at least three times.

Machine washing and dry cleaning

Clothes and the like washed by machine can be used for praying in.

[97] Ibid., 14.

[98] Imām Muḥammad does not allow any means other than water for the removal of the impurity, (*See*: *Badā'iʿ al-ṣanā'iʿ*, i. 437-438).

[99] al-Bukhārī, *k. al-ḥayḍ, b. ghasl dam al-maḥīḍ;* Muslim, *k. al-ṭahārah, b. najāsat al-dam wa kayfiyyat ghaslihi.*

Similarly, dry cleaning (which uses a liquid other than water) is an accepted means of purification insofar as it removes all dirt. As explained earlier, *ḥadath* can be removed by *wuḍū'*, *ghusl* or *tayammum*, but purification from *najāsah* can be achieved by removing it whether this is done by water or any other pure liquid.[100]

Purifying the ground and what is laid on it

Impurity on the ground can be purified by pouring water over the affected surface. Anas ibn Mālik narrated that a Bedouin urinated in the *masjid*. The Prophet ﷺ said: "Pour a bucket of water over it".[101] If impurity on the earth dries in the sun and all trace of it disappears, then it is permitted to do *ṣalāh* on that spot although *tayammum* is not permitted from it. If the impurity is a solid, the ground will only become pure by its removal or the impurity rotting away.[102]

If there is an impurity on a carpet, mattress or a sheet, it can be purified by washing the affected area until the impure substance is removed if the impurity is visible, or by washing it three times if it is invisible.

Purifying smooth objects

Mirrors, glass, knives, painted pots and other smooth surfaces, i.e. surfaces that have no pores (for example, glazed wall and floor tiles, plastic chairs), are purified by washing if the impurity is wet. If the impurity is dried then scraping off the impurity followed by wiping the affected surface will purify them.[103]

Purifying solid matter

If an impurity falls into a liquid substance, the entire liquid becomes impure. However if an impurity falls into a solid matter, what is touched by it and what is around it must be thrown away. Ibn ʿAbbās related from Maymūnah that the Prophet ﷺ was asked about a mouse that fell into

[100] al-Marghinānī, *al-Hidāyah*, i. 34.

[101] Muslim, *k. al-ṭahārah, b. wujūb ghasl al-bawl wa ghayrihi min al-najāsāt idhā ḥaṣalat fī al-masjid wa anna al-arḍa taṭhuru bi al-mā' min ghayr ḥājah ilā ḥafrihā.*

[102] *See*: *Badā'iʿ al-ṣanā'iʿ*, i. 441.

[103] *See*: al-Samarqandī, *Tuḥfat al-fuqahā'*. 39.

some butter. He said: "Take the mouse and what is around it out, and throw it away. Then eat the rest of your butter".[104]

Purifying hide

ʿAbdullāh ibn ʿAbbās narrated that the Prophet ﷺ said: "If the animal's skin is tanned, it is purified".[105] Ibn ʿAbbās also reported that a client of Maymūnah was given a sheep as charity, and it died. The Messenger of Allāh ﷺ passed by it and said: "Why did you not remove its skin, tan it, and then you would have benefited from it?" She said: "It is dead". He said to her: "Only eating it is forbidden".[106]

Based on these reports, scholars agree that tanning purifies the hide and the fur of any dead animal. However, they differ on whether tanning can purify the hide of a pig. Abū Yūsuf holds that it can. Considering this view, boots, shoes, belts or anything else made of tanned pig's hide are allowed.[107]

Istinjā'

Istinjā' means the cleaning of oneself after urinating or defecating. It is a Sunnah. This is acceptable if done with paper, stone or anything that serves the same purpose of wiping until the private parts are clean. There is no fixed number of times prescribed for this to be done in the Sunnah. However, using water to complete the cleaning is preferable. Imām Muḥammad said: "Washing with water in *istinjā'* is more preferred to us. This is the opinion of Abū Ḥanīfah".[108] If the impurity has spread then only cleaning with water or some other pure liquid is acceptable.

One must not do *istinjā'* with bones, droppings, foodstuffs or with one's right hand. The Prophet ﷺ prohibited this. Ruwayfiʿ ibn Thābit reported: "The Messenger of Allāh ﷺ said: 'You may live for a long time after me, so tell people that if anyone ties his beard, or wears round his neck a string, or cleanses himself with animal dung or bone, Muḥammad has nothing to do with him'."[109] ʿAbdullāh ibn Masʿūd narrated: "The

[104] al-Bukhārī, *k. al-wuḍū', b. mā yaqaʿu min al-najāsat fī al-samn wa al-mā'.*

[105] Muslim, *k. al-ḥayḍ, b. ṭahārat julūd al-maytah bi al-dibāgh.*

[106] Ibid.

[107] *See*: al-Samarqandī, *Tuḥfat al-fuqahā'*. 39.

[108] Abū Ḥanīfah, *K. al-āthār* 16.

[109] Abū Dāwūd, *k. al-ṭahārah, b. mā yunhā ʿanhu an yustanjā bihi.*

Messenger of Allāh ﷺ said: 'Do not do *istinjā'* with droppings or bones for they are taken as provision by your brothers from amongst the *jinn*'."[110]

The Sunnahs of istinjā'

Certain manners and courtesies of *istinjā'* are mentioned in the Sunnah. These are as follows:

Sunnahs relating to the person

CARRYING ANYTHING WITH THE DIVINE NAME ON IT

It is not proper for one to carry something that has Allāh's name upon it. Anas related that the Messenger of Allāh ﷺ had a ring engraved with *Muḥammad Rasūl Allāh* (Muḥammad, the Messenger of Allāh ﷺ), which he removed when he went to fulfil his need. Ibrāhīm al-Nakhaʿī did not like carrying anything that had Qur'ānic writing on it unless it were kept in a pocket or hidden elsewhere. Imām Muḥammad said: "This is the opinion of Abū Ḥanīfah and we adhere to it".[111]

SUPPLICATION

One should remember Allāh's name and seek refuge in Him at the time of entering the toilet or before removing one's clothes to relieve oneself. Anas reported that when the Messenger of Allāh ﷺ entered the toilet, he used to say:

بِسْمِ اللهِ اَللّٰهُمَّ إِنِّي أَعُوذُ بِكَ مِنَ الْخُبُثِ وَالْخَبَائِثِ

"In the name of Allāh. O Allāh I seek refuge in You from male and female devils".[112]

One should enter the toilet with one's left foot, and exit with one's right foot. While exiting one should say: غُفْرَانَكَ اَللّٰهُمَّ 'O Allāh I seek your forgiveness'. ʿĀ'ishah related that when the Messenger of Allāh ﷺ left the toilet, he would say this supplication.[113] It is related from Anas ibn Mālik that the Prophet ﷺ used to say:

[110] al-Tirmidhī, *k. al-ṭahārah, b. mā jā'a fī karāhiyati mā yustanjā bihi.*

[111] Abū Ḥanīfah, *K. al-āthār* 15.

[112] al-Bukhārī, *k. al-wuḍū', b. mā yaqūlu ʿinda al-khala'.*

[113] Abū Dāwūd, *k. al-ṭahārah, b. mā yaqūlu al-rajul idhā kharaja min al-khala';* al-Tirmidhī, *k. al-ṭahārah, b. mā yaqūlu idhā kharaja min al-khala'.*

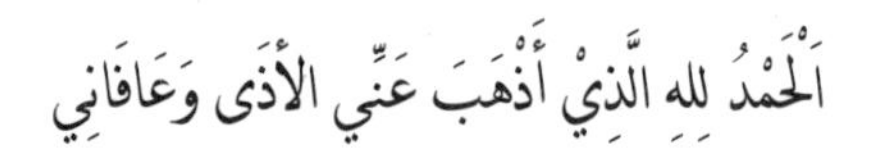

"Praise is due to Allāh Who made the filth leave me and Who has granted me well-being".[114]

TALKING

Abū Saʿīd reported that he heard the Messenger of Allāh ﷺ say: "When two persons go together for relieving themselves uncovering their private parts and talking to each other, Allāh, Exalted is He, becomes wrathful at this".[115] Al-Muhājir ibn Qunfudh related that he inadvertently went to the Prophet ﷺ while he was urinating, and greeted him. The Prophet ﷺ did not return his greeting, until he had done *wuḍū'*, then he apologised to him saying: "I did not like to mention Allāh's name without purity".[116]

URINATING WHILST STANDING

One should not urinate whilst standing. ʿĀ'ishah said: "If someone relates to you that the Messenger of Allāh ﷺ urinated while standing, do not believe him. He only urinated while sitting".[117] However, if the place is such that it is difficult or improper to sit, then one can urinate while standing. Ḥudhayfah reported that the Messenger of Allāh ﷺ went to a place where the people threw their waste and (for that reason) he did not sit but urinated while standing. Ḥudhayfah withdrew. When the Prophet ﷺ had finished he called him back and the Prophet ﷺ made *wuḍū'*.[118] Scholars affirm that it is desirable to urinate while sitting, but to do so standing is permissible if there is an excuse; in the Prophet's ﷺ case above, the place was dirty.

[114] Ibn Mājah, *k. al-ṭahārah wa sunanuhā, b. mā yaqūlu idhā kharaja min al-khala'.*
[115] Abū Dāwūd, *k. al-ṭahārah, b. karāhiyat al-kalām ʿinda al-ḥājah.*
[116] Abū Dāwūd, *k. al-ṭahārah, b. ayaruddu al-salāma wa huwa yabūlu.*
[117] al-Tirmidhī, *k. al-ṭahārah, b. mā jā'a fī al-nahy ʿan al-bawl qā'iman.*
[118] al-Bukhārī, *k. al-wuḍū', b. al-bawl qā'iman wa qaʿidan;* Muslim, *k. al-ṭahārah, b. al-masḥ ʿalā al-khuffayn.*

Sunnahs relating to place

PRIVACY

Abū Hurayrah narrated that the Prophet ﷺ said: "Whoever goes to the toilet, should hide".[119] Mughīrah ibn Shuʿbah narrated, "We were journeying with the Messenger of Allāh ﷺ. When he needed to relieve himself, he would go far away".[120]

AVOIDING THE DIRECTION OF THE QIBLAH

While urinating, one should neither face nor turn one's back towards the *qiblah*, whether the person is in a toilet or out in a field. Abū Ayyūb al-Anṣārī reported that the Messenger of Allāh ﷺ said: "When one of you relieves himself, he should neither face the *qiblah* nor turn his back to it".[121] Abū Hurayrah reported that the Messenger of Allāh ﷺ said: "I am like a father to you. When any of you goes to the privy, he should not face or turn his back towards the *qiblah*. He should not cleanse with his right hand." The Prophet ﷺ also commanded the use of three stones and forbade the use of dung or decayed bones.[122]

CHOOSING THE PLACE

In order to avoid any impurity reaching one's clothing one should locate a soft and low piece of ground. It is related from Abū Mūsā that the Messenger of Allāh ﷺ went to a low and soft part of the ground and urinated. He then said: "When one of you urinates, he should choose a proper place to do so".[123]

One should not urinate in bathing places or in still water. ʿAbdullāh ibn Mughaffal narrated that the Messenger of Allāh ﷺ said: "None of you should urinate in a bathing place and then make *ghusl* or *wuḍū'* there, for evil thoughts come from that".[124] Jābir and Abū Hurayrah said the Prophet ﷺ forbade urinating in still water.[125]

[119] Abū Dāwūd, *k. al-ṭahārah, b. al-istitār fī al-khala'*

[120] al-Tirmidhī, *k. al-ṭahārah, b. mā jā'a ann al-nabīyya ṣallallāhu ʿalayhi wa sallama kāna idhā arāda al-ḥājata abʿada fī al-madhhab.*

[121] al-Bukhārī, *k. al-wuḍū', b. lā tustaqbalu al-qiblah bi ghā'iṭ aw bawl.*

[122] Abū Dāwūd, *k. al-ṭahārah, b. karāhiyat al-istiqbāl ʿinda qaḍā' al-ḥājah.*

[123] Abū Dāwūd, *k. al-ṭahārah, b. al-rajul yatabawwa'u li bawlihi.*

[124] Abū Dāwūd, *k. al-ṭahārah, b. fī al-bawl fī al-mustaḥamm.*

[125] al-Bukhārī, *k. al-wuḍū', b. al-bawl fī al-mā' al-dā'im;* Muslim, *k. al-ṭahārah, b. al-nahy ʿan al-bawl fī al-mā' al-rākid.*

Shaded places where people go to rest, and those places where people walk and assemble should not be used for urinating. Abū Hurayrah reported that the Messenger of Allāh ﷺ said: "Be on your guard against two acts which provoke curse". They [his Companions] asked, "What are those acts?" He said: "Relieving yourself in people's walkways or in their shade".[126] Muʿādh ibn Jabal reported: The Messenger of Allāh ﷺ said: "Be on your guard against three things which provoke cursing: relieving oneself at watering places, on thoroughfares, and in the shade."[127]

A hole in the ground should not be used for urinating. ʿAbdullāh ibn Sirjis reported that the Prophet ﷺ forbade urinating into a hole. Qatādah (the narrator of this ḥadīth from ʿAbdullāh ibn Sirjis) was asked about the reason for such disapproval. He replied, "It is said that these holes are habitats of the *jinn*".[128]

Sunnahs relating to cleaning

It is preferable to clean oneself with tissue or stone, followed by water. If the impurity has spread then water or any other pure liquid must be used. ʿĀ'ishah reported that the Messenger of Allāh ﷺ said: "When one of you goes to relieve himself, he should take three stones to cleanse himself; for they will be enough for him".[129] Anas ibn Mālik reported: "The Messenger of Allāh ﷺ entered a park. He was accompanied by a boy who had a jug of water with him. He was the youngest of us. He placed it near the lote-tree. The Prophet ﷺ relieved himself. He came to us after he had cleansed himself with water".[130] Abū Hurayrah reported the Prophet ﷺ said: "The following verse was revealed in connection with the people of Qubā': '*In it are men who love to be purified*', (*al-Barā'ah* 108)." Abū Hurayrah said: "They used to cleanse themselves with water after relieving themselves. So the verse was revealed in connection with them".[131]

[126] Muslim, *k. al-ṭahārah, b. al-nahy ʿan al-takhallī fī al-ṭuruq wa al-ẓilāl.*

[127] Abū Dāwūd, *k. al-ṭahārah, b. al-mawāḍiʿ allatī nahā al-nabī ṣallallāhu ʿalayhi wa sallam ʿan al-bawl fīhā.*

[128] Abū Dāwūd, *k. al-ṭahārah, b. al-nahy ʿan al-bawl fī al-juḥr;* al-Nasā'ī, *k. al-ṭahārah, b. karāhiyat al-bawl fī al-juḥr.*

[129] Abū Dāwūd, *k. al-ṭahārah, b. al-istinjā' bi al-aḥjār.*

[130] Abū Dāwūd, *k. al-ṭahārah, b. fī al-istinjā' bi al-mā'.*

[131] Ibid.

The right hand should not be used for cleaning oneself. ʿAbd al-Raḥmān ibn Yazīd related that Salmān al-Fārisī was asked: "Your Prophet ﷺ has taught you everything, even how to relieve yourselves?" Salmān said: "Yes, he forbade us from facing the *qiblah* while relieving ourselves, from cleaning ourselves with our right hands, and from cleaning ourselves with less than three stones, and he forbade us to use a piece of dung or bone to clean ourselves".[132] Ḥafṣah, the wife of the Prophet ﷺ reported: "The Prophet ﷺ used his right hand for eating, drinking, and putting on his clothes. He used his left hand for other purposes".[133] ʿĀ'ishah reported: "The Prophet ﷺ used his right hand for *wuḍū'* and eating, and his left hand for *istinjā'* and anything repugnant".[134]

Any bad smell that may be on the hand after cleaning should be removed. Jarīr said: "Once I was with the Messenger of Allāh ﷺ. He relieved himself, then said: 'O Jarīr bring water'. I brought him water. He cleansed himself, then rubbed his hands against the soil".[135]

Sunan al-fiṭrah

There are certain Sunnahs, called *sunan al-fiṭrah* (actions that correspond to the proper form and nature of humankind), which Allāh preferred for His prophets, and which distinguish them and their followers from the rest of humankind. The Prophet ﷺ said: "Ten things constitute *fiṭrah*: trimming one's moustache, growing one's beard, using the tooth stick, gargling, cleaning one's nose with water, cutting one's nails, washing one's *barājim* (finger joints), plucking one's underarm hair, shaving one's pubic hair and circumcision".[136]

As regards trimming one's moustache, Ibn ʿUmar related that the Messenger of Allāh ﷺ said: "Be different from the polytheists: let your beard grow and cut your moustache".[137] Zayd ibn Arqam related that the Prophet ﷺ said: "Whoever does not cut his moustache is not one of

[132] Muslim, *k. al-ṭahārah, b. al-istiṭābah.*

[133] Abū Dāwūd, *k. al-ṭahārah, b. karāhiyat mass al-dhakar bi al-yamīn fī al-istibrā'.*

[134] Ibid.

[135] al-Nasā'ī, *k. al-ṭahārah, b. dalk al-yad bi al-arḍ baʿda al-istinjā'.*

[136] Abū Dāwūd, *k. al-ṭahārah, b. al-siwāk min al-fiṭrah;* Abū Dāwūd mentioned a few *aḥādīth* in this chapter which differ from each other in one or more things.

[137] Muslim, *k. al-ṭahārah, b. khiṣāl al-fiṭrah.*

us".[138] One should ensure that one's moustache is not so long that food particles, drink and dirt accumulate in it.

A beard is a sign of masculinity. In several *aḥādīth* the Prophet ﷺ advised Muslims to let their beards grow. All scholars agree that it is *Sunnah Mu'akkadah* (Emphatic or highly stressed Sunnah) to do so. No scholar has sanctioned shaving off one's beard or cutting it so short that it resembles shaving. However, beards should not be left so long that they become untidy. Whenever Ibn ᶜUmar performed Ḥajj or *ᶜumrah*, he would hold his beard in his fist and, whatever protruded beyond his fist, he would cut off.[139]

Abū Hurayrah reported that the Messenger of Allāh ﷺ said: "Five things form part of one's *fiṭrah*: circumcision, shaving one's pubic hair, trimming one's moustache, removing the hair from under one's arms and trimming one's nails".[140] It is Sunnah to pluck out underarm hair, but if someone shaves or trims this, it nonetheless suffices.[141]

Abū Hurayrah reported that the Messenger of Allāh ﷺ said: "Ibrāhīm circumcised himself when he was more than 80 years old".[142] This is a Sunnah, rather than being obligatory. Some scholars recommend it to be done on the seventh day, but there is nothing that explicitly states its time.

It is preferable to cut one's nails and trim one's moustache and so on, on a weekly basis. One is not allowed to leave them for more than forty days. Anas ibn Mālik reported, that the Messenger of Allāh ﷺ specified the period within which men should trim their moustaches, cut their nails, remove their underarm and pubic hair, as forty days.[143]

[138] al-Nasā'ī, *k. al-ṭahārah, b. qaṣṣ al-shārib.*

[139] al-Bukhārī, *k. al-libās, b. taqlīm al-aẓfār.*

[140] Muslim, *k. al-ṭahārah, b. khiṣāl al-fiṭrah.*

[141] *See* Muslim, *k. al-ṭahārah, b. khiṣāl al-fiṭrah.*

[142] al-Bukhārī, *k. aḥādīth al-anbiyā', b. qawl Allāh taᶜālā wattakhadha Allāhu Ibrāhīma khalīlan.*

[143] al-Nasā'ī, *k. al-ṭahārah, b. al-tawqīt fī dhālik.*

CHAPTER 3: *WUḌŪ'*

WUḌŪ' COMPRISES WASHING particular parts of the body with water. Allāh says in the Qur'ān: "*O you who believe, when you rise for ṣalāh, wash your faces and your hands up to the elbows and wipe your heads and wash your feet up to the ankles*".[144] Abū Hurayrah reported that the Messenger of Allāh ﷺ said: "Allāh does not accept the *ṣalāh* of one who has nullified his *wuḍū'* until he does it again".[145] There is a consensus among the Companions and all scholars that *ṣalāh* without *wuḍū'* is invalid.

THE VIRTUES OF WUḌŪ'

Numerous *aḥādīth* highlight the virtues of *wuḍū'*. Abū Hurayrah reported that the Messenger of Allāh ﷺ came to the graveyard and said: "Peace be upon you, O home of believing people. Allāh willing, we shall meet you soon, although I wish I could see my brothers". They asked: "Are we not your brothers, O Messenger of Allāh ﷺ?" He said: "You are my Companions. My brothers are those who have not come yet". They said: "How will you recognise the people of our nation who will come after you, O Messenger of Allāh ﷺ?" He said: "If a man has a group of horses with white forelocks amidst a group of horses with black forelocks, will he recognise his horses?" They said: "Certainly, O Messenger of Allāh ﷺ". He said: "They will come with white streaks from their *wuḍū'*, and I will receive them at my cistern. But there will be some who will be driven away from my cistern as a stray camel is driven away. I will call them to come. It will be said, 'They changed after you'. Then I will say: 'Be off, be off'."[146]

ʿAbdullāh ibn al-Ṣunābiḥī stated that the Messenger of Allāh ﷺ said: "When a slave of Allāh makes *wuḍū'* and rinses his mouth, his sins fall away from his mouth. As he rinses his nose, his sins fall away from it.

[144] *al-Mā'idah* 6.

[145] al-Bukhārī, *k. al-wuḍū', b. lā tuqbalu ṣalātun bighayri ṭuhūr.*

[146] Mālik, *al-Muwaṭṭa'* 21.

When he washes his face, his sins fall away from his face until they drop from beneath his eyelashes. When he washes his hands, his sins fall away from them until they drop from beneath his fingernails. When he wipes his head, his sins fall away from it until they drop from his ears. When he washes his feet, his sins fall away from them until they drop from beneath his toenails. Then his walking to the *masjid* and his *ṣalāh* earn him additional reward".[147]

Abū Hurayrah reported that the Messenger of Allāh ﷺ said: "Shall I inform you of that by which Allāh removes sins and raises degrees?" They said, "Certainly, O Messenger of Allāh ﷺ". He said: "Perfecting *wuḍū'* under difficult circumstances, making plenty of steps to the *masjid,* and waiting for one *ṣalāh* after another. This is *ribāṭ* (i.e. guarding the frontiers)".[148]

THE *FARḌS* OF *WUḌŪ'*

There are four *farḍs* in *wuḍū'*. These have been mentioned above in the verse quoted on *wuḍū'*.

Washing one's face

This means washing the whole face with water, from the top of the forehead to the bottom of the chin, and from one earlobe to the other.

Washing one's arms

The arms, including the elbows, must be washed, for the Prophet ﷺ always did so, and none of the Companions excluded their elbows from such washing. Jābir ibn ʿAbdullāh narrated that when the Messenger of Allāh ﷺ reached the elbows during the washing of his arms, he would pour water on them.[149]

Wiping one's head

It is *farḍ* to wipe a quarter of the head (i.e. the size of the forehead), because al-Mughīrah ibn Shuʿbah narrated that the Prophet ﷺ: "Went to the part of someone's yard reserved for rubbish, urinated, made

[147] Ibid., 21-22.

[148] Muslim, *k. al-ṭahārah, b. faḍl isbāgh al-wuḍū' ʿalā al-makārih.*

[149] al-Dāraquṭnī, *al-Sunan, i. 86.*

wuḍū' and wiped over his forehead and *khuffs* (leather socks)".[150] Sālim narrated that his father (ʿAbdullāh ibn ʿUmar) used to wipe his forehead when he did *wuḍū'*.[151]

Washing one's feet

The feet, including one's ankles must be washed, for the Prophet ﷺ and the Companions always did so. ʿAbdullāh ibn ʿAmr said: "The Prophet ﷺ lagged behind us during one of our travels. He caught up with us after we had delayed the *ʿAṣr Ṣalāh.* We started to do *wuḍū'* and were wiping over our feet, when the Prophet ﷺ said: 'Woe to the heels, save them from the hellfire', repeating it two or three times".[152] The practice of washing feet in *wuḍū'* has been narrated by many Companions and Followers, like ʿUmar, ʿAlī, ʿAbdullāh ibn ʿUmar, ʿAbdullāh ibn ʿAbbās, Anas, Rubayyiʿ ibn Muʿawwidh, ʿUrwah ibn Zubayr, Ibrāhīm al-Nakhaʿī, al-Ḥasan al-Baṣrī, Abū Mijlaz, ʿAṭā' and others.[153] Ḥakam said: "Washing the feet is a continuous Sunnah from the Prophet ﷺ through the generations of Muslims".[154] Al-Kāsānī said: "It is known by *tawātur* that the Prophet ﷺ washed his feet in *wuḍū'*; no Muslim can deny that".[155]

THE SUNNAHS OF *WUḌŪ'*

The Sunnah actions performed in *wuḍū'* are not considered obligatory, as the Prophet ﷺ did not stick to them rigorously, nor did he censure anyone for not doing them. However, if one does *wuḍū'* with all its *farḍs* and Sunnahs one's *wuḍū'* will be more perfected; on the Day of Judgement the light of those parts of the body purified by *wuḍū'* will increase. Abū Hurayrah reported that the Messenger of Allāh ﷺ said: "My nation will come with bright streaks of light from the traces of *wuḍū'*". Abū Hurayrah then said: "If one can lengthen one's streak of light, one should do so".[156]

[150] Muslim, *k. al-ṭahārah, b. al-masḥ ʿalā al-khuffayn.*

[151] al-Ṭaḥāwī, *Sharḥ maʿānī al-āthār, i. 32.*

[152] al-Bukhārī, *k. al-wuḍū', b. ghasl al-rijlayn wa lā yamsaḥu ʿalā al-qadamayn.*

[153] Ibn Abī Shaybah, *al-Muṣannaf*, i. 26-27.

[154] Ibid., i. 26.

[155] al-Kāsānī, *Badā'iʿ al-ṣanā'iʿ*, i. 121.

[156] al-Bukhārī, *k. al-ṭahārah, b. faḍl al-wuḍū', wa al-ghurr al-muḥajjalūna min āthār al-wuḍū'.*

SUNNAH ACTIONS WITHIN *WUḌŪ'* ARE AS FOLLOWS:

Sunnahs at the beginning of wuḍū'

Intention

Making intention is an inward wish to perform an action for the sake of Allāh. It is entirely a heartfelt action – verbal utterances are not necessary for intention. ʿUmar narrated that the Prophet ﷺ said: "Every action is based on intention, and everyone shall have what he intended".[157]

Mentioning Allāh's name

ʿAmrah said: "I asked ʿĀ'ishah how was the prayer of the Messenger of Allāh ﷺ? She said: 'When he did *wuḍū'* he would put his hand in the water, say Allāh's name, and then do *wuḍū'* perfectly'."[158] It is narrated from the Prophet ﷺ that: "There is no *wuḍū'* for the one who did not mention Allāh's name during his *wuḍū'*". After recording this ḥadīth, Imām al-Tirmidhī discusses its authenticity. He narrated that Aḥmad ibn Ḥanbal said: "I do not know any ḥadīth on this subject that has a good chain of narration; Imām al-Bukhārī said the best thing on this subject is the above-mentioned ḥadīth".[159] Ḥasan al-Baṣrī said: "One should mention Allāh's name when one does *wuḍū'*; if one does not, it is still valid."[160]

Washing one's hands

It is Sunnah to wash one's hands up to the wrists three times before putting them in a vessel containing the water used for *wuḍū'*. Abū Hurayrah reported that the Prophet ﷺ said: "When one of you rises from his sleep, he should not dip his hands into his pot until he has washed his hands three times, for he does not know where his hands

[157] al-Bukhārī, *k. bad' al-waḥy.*
[158] Ibn Abī Shaybah, *al-Muṣannaf,* i. 12.
[159] al-Tirmidhī, *k. al-ṭahārah, b. mā jā'a fī al-tasmiyati ʿinda al-wuḍū';* Ibn Abī Shaybah, *al-Muṣannaf, i.* 12.
[160] Ibn Abī Shaybah, ibid., i. 12.

have spent the night".[161] Aws ibn Abī Aws said: "I saw the Messenger of Allāh ﷺ do *wuḍū'*, and he washed his hands three times".[162]

Sunnahs during wuḍū'

Cleaning one's teeth

Cleaning the teeth with a tooth-stick or other means is a Sunnah in *wuḍū'* and other occasions. Abū Hurayrah reported that the Prophet ﷺ said: "Were it not to be a hardship on my community, I would have ordered them to clean their teeth for every *wuḍū'*".[163] ʿĀ'ishah reported that the Prophet ﷺ said: "Cleaning teeth is purification for the mouth and is pleasing to the Lord".[164] It is part of the Sunnah that one who has no teeth may use his fingers to clean his mouth. ʿĀ'ishah asked: "O Messenger of Allāh ﷺ, how should a toothless person cleanse his mouth?" He replied: "By putting his fingers into his mouth".[165]

Maḍmaḍah

Maḍmaḍah means gargling. It is a Sunnah of the Prophet ﷺ narrated by many Companions. The famous one occurred in ʿUthmān's description of the Prophet's *wuḍū'* when ʿUthmān mentioned that the Prophet ﷺ did *maḍmaḍah*.[166]

Istinshāq and istinthār

Istinshāq means sniffing water up into one's nostrils, and *istinthār* means blowing it out. Abū Hurayrah reported that the Prophet ﷺ said: "When one of you does *wuḍū'*, he should snuffle water up his nostrils and then blow it out".[167] The Sunnah is to pour water into the nostrils with one's

[161] al-Bukhārī, *k. al-wuḍū', b. al-istijmār witran;* Muslim, *k. al-ṭahārah, b. karāhat ghams al-mutawaḍḍī wa ghayrihi yadahu al-mashkūk fī najāsatihā fī al-inā'.*

[162] al-Nasā'ī, *k. al-ṭahārah, b. kam tughsalān.*

[163] al-Bukhārī, *k. al-jumuʿah, b. al-siwāk yawma al-jumuʿah;* Muslim, *k. al-ṭahārah, b. al-siwāk.*

[164] al-Nasā'ī, *k. al-ṭahārah, b. al-targhīb fī al-siwāk.*

[165] al-Ṭabarānī *as cited in Majmaʿ al-zawā'id, k. al-ṣalāh, b. al-siwāk liman laysat lahu asnān.*

[166] al-Bukhārī, *k. al-wuḍū', b. al-maḍmaḍah fī al-wuḍū'.*

[167] al-Bukhārī, *k. al-wuḍū', b. al-istinthār fī al-wuḍū';* Muslim, *k. al-ṭahārah, b. al-ītār fī al-istinthār wa al-istijmār.*

right hand and blow it out with the left. ʿAlī once called for water for *wuḍū'*, rinsed his mouth, snuffed water into his nostrils and blew it out with his left hand. He did this three times and then said: "That is how the Prophet ﷺ used to purify himself".[168]

Repeating the washing of each process three times

The Prophet ﷺ usually repeated each washing three times. ʿAmr ibn Shuʿayb, quoting his father on the authority of his grandfather, said: "A man came to the Prophet ﷺ and asked him: 'How is *wuḍū'*?' The Prophet ﷺ then called for water in a vessel and washed his hands up to the wrists three times, then washed his face three times, and washed his forearms three times. He then wiped his head and inserted his index fingers in his ear-holes; he wiped the back of his ears with his thumbs and the front of his ears with his index fingers. He then washed his feet three times. Then he said: 'This is the *wuḍū'*. Whoever does more or less than this has done wrong and transgressed'."[169] ʿUthmān and ʿAbdullāh ibn Zayd ibn ʿĀṣim al-Anṣārī reported that, "The Messenger of Allāh ﷺ would repeat each wash three times".[170]

It is also proven that sometimes the Prophet ﷺ performed each washing only once or twice. Abū Hurayrah reported that the Prophet ﷺ washed the limbs in *wuḍū'* twice.[171] ʿAṭā' ibn Yasār narrated that Ibn ʿAbbās said: "May I not tell you how the Messenger of Allāh ﷺ did *wuḍū'*?" He then did *wuḍū'* washing each limb once only.[172] Ḥammād ibn Abī Sulaymān said: "One washing, if it is comprehensive, is enough". Imām Muḥammad said: "This is the opinion of Abū Ḥanīfah and it is what we hold."[173]

Wiping one's whole head

It is Sunnah to wipe over the whole head once. ʿAbdullāh ibn Zayd reported: "The Prophet ﷺ wiped his entire head with his hands. He

[168] al-Nasā'ī, *k. al-ṭahārah, b. bi ayy al-yadayn yastanthir.*

[169] Abū Dāwūd, *k. al-ṭahārah, b. al-wuḍū' thalāthan thalāthan.*

[170] Muslim, *k. al-ṭahārah, b. faḍl al-wuḍū' wa al-ṣalāh ʿaqibahu,* and *b. fī wuḍū' al-nabī ṣallallāhu ʿalayhi wa sallam.*

[171] Abū Dāwūd, *k. al-ṭahārah, b. al-wuḍū' marratayn.*

[172] Abū Dāwūd, *k. al-ṭahārah, b. al-wuḍū' marratan marratan.*

[173] Abū Ḥanīfah, *K. al-āthār* 6.

started with the front of his head, then moved to the back, and then returned his hands to the front".[174] Imām Abū Dāwūd said: "All the sound *aḥādīth* recorded from ʿUthmān indicate that the head is to be wiped once, because they mentioned the washing of each part in *wuḍū'* three times. When it comes to wiping they said: 'He wiped his head'. In this case they did not mention any number as they did in other cases".[175]

Wiping one's ears

It is Sunnah to wipe the inner and outer parts of the ears with the water used to wipe the head. ʿAlī narrated: "The Messenger of Allāh ﷺ wiped his ears with the same water that he used to wipe his head".[176] Al-Miqdām ibn Maʿdīkarib reported: "The Prophet ﷺ wiped his head and his ears, the interior and exterior, while doing *wuḍū'*. He also put his finger inside his ear".[177] While describing the Prophet's *wuḍū'*, ʿAbdullāh ibn ʿAbbās and al-Rubayyiʿ bint Muʿawwidh narrated: "The Prophet ﷺ wiped his head and ears in a single movement". In one narration, it states: "He wiped the interior of his ears with his index finger, and the exteriors of his ears with his thumb".[178] Imām Muḥammad narrated from Abū Ḥanīfah saying: "It has come to our knowledge that the Messenger of Allāh ﷺ said: 'Both the ears are from the head'." Imām Muḥammad said: "It is liked by us that one wipes the ear, the front of it and the back of it, along with the head, and this is what we hold".[179]

Takhlīl of one's beard

Takhlīl of one's beard entails running one's fingers through it. It is a Sunnah in *wuḍū'*. Ḥassān ibn Bilāl narrated: "I saw ʿAmmār ibn Yāsir do *wuḍū'*. Then he ran his fingers through his beard. I asked: 'Do you run your fingers through your beard?' He said: 'Why should I not do so when I have seen the Messenger of Allāh ﷺ running his fingers through his beard'?"[180] Anas ibn Mālik said: "When the Messenger of Allāh ﷺ

[174] al-Bukhārī, *k. al-wuḍū', b. masḥ al-ra's marratan wāḥidah.*

[175] Abū Dāwūd, *k. al-ṭahārah, b. ṣifat wuḍu' al-nabī ṣallallāhu ʿalayhi wa sallam.*

[176] Ibid.

[177] Ibid.

[178] Ibid.

[179] Abū Ḥanīfah, *K. al-āthār* 6.

[180] al-Tirmidhī, *k. al-ṭahārah, b. mā jā'a fī takhlīl al-liḥyah.*

performed *wuḍū'*, he would take a handful of water and put it under his jaws and pass it through his beard. In the process he said: 'This is what my Lord, Allāh, ordered me to do'."[181] It has been narrated from ʿAbdullāh ibn ʿAbbās, ʿAbdullāh ibn ʿUmar, Anas ibn Mālik, Saʿīd ibn Jubayr, Abū Qilābah, Mujāhid, Ibn Sīrīn and others that when they did *wuḍū'* they would run their fingers through their beards.[182]

Takhlīl of one's fingers and toes

It is Sunnah to run one's fingers through the gaps of the other fingers and toes to ensure that they are properly washed. Laqīṭ ibn Ṣabirah narrated that the Prophet ﷺ said: "When you do *wuḍū'*, then run your fingers through your other fingers".[183] ʿAbdullāh ibn ʿAbbās said that the Messenger of Allāh ﷺ said: "When you do *wuḍū'*, then run the fingers through your fingers and toes".[184] If one has a ring on this should be moved to allow water to flow underneath. ʿAlī used to move his ring while doing *wuḍū'*.[185] The same practice has been narrated from ʿAbdullāh ibn ʿAmr, Ibn Sīrīn, Maymūn, ʿAmr ibn Dīnār, ʿUmar ibn ʿAbd al-ʿAzīz, al-Ḥasan al-Baṣrī and ʿUrwah ibn Zubayr.[186]

Rubbing one's limbs

One should also properly rub one's limbs while washing them in *wuḍū'*. ʿAbdullāh ibn Zayd related that the Messenger of Allāh ﷺ did *wuḍū'*, then rubbed (his limbs).[187]

Sequence of Action

One should follow the sequence of actions while doing *wuḍū'* as mentioned in the verse on *wuḍū'*. The Prophet ﷺ always followed the order in doing *wuḍū'*.[188]

[181] Abū Dāwūd, *k. al-ṭahārah, b. takhlīl al-liḥyah.*

[182] Ibn Abī Shaybah, *al-Muṣannaf*, i. 20-21.

[183] al-Tirmidhī, *k. al-ṭahārah, b. mā jā'a fī takhlīl al-aṣābiʿ*.

[184] Ibid.

[185] Ibn Abī Shaybah, *al-Muṣannaf*, i. 44.

[186] Ibid.

[187] Aḥmad, *al-Musnad* 16488.

[188] al-Kāsānī, *Badā'iʿ al-ṣanā'iʿ, i. 211.*

Starting with the right side

One should begin each action of *wuḍū'* with the right side, because the Prophet ﷺ always did so. It is a Sunnah in *wuḍū'* and in other actions. ʿĀ'ishah said: "The Messenger of Allāh ﷺ loved to begin with his right side when putting on his shoes, arranging his hair and cleaning or purifying himself and in all his acts".[189] Abū Hurayrah reported that the Prophet ﷺ said: "When you put on clothing or do *wuḍū'*, begin with your right side".[190]

Not interrupting wuḍū'

One should wash the parts of the body in the right order one after the other without interrupting the sequence. The actions of *wuḍū'* should not be separated by actions not related to *wuḍū'*. This is the practice of the Prophet ﷺ, which he always followed.

Avoiding any waste of water

ʿAbdullāh ibn ʿUmar narrated: "The Messenger of Allāh ﷺ passed by Saʿd while he was performing *wuḍū'* and said 'What is this extravagance Saʿd?'[191] He said: 'Is there extravagance in the use of water?' The Messenger of Allāh ﷺ said: 'Yes, even if you are at a flowing river'."[192] ʿAbdullāh ibn Mughaffal narrated that he heard the Prophet ﷺ say: "There will be people from my nation who will transgress in making supplications and in purifying themselves".[193] It has been narrated from many Companions and early scholars that they did not like excessive use of water in *wuḍū'*.[194]

[189] al-Bukhārī, *k. al-wuḍū', b. al-tayammun fī al-wuḍū' wa al-ghasl.*

[190] Abū Dāwūd, *k. al-libās, b. fī al-intiʿāl;* Ibn Mājah, *k. al-ṭahārah wa sunanihā, b. al-taymmun fī al-wuḍū'.*

[191] Extravagance means excess in spending, i.e. the use of water without any benefit, such as washing one's body more than three times.

[192] Ibn Mājah, *k. al-ṭahārah wa sunanihā, b. mā jā'a fī al-qaṣd fī al-wuḍū' wa karāhiyat al-taʿddī fīhi.*

[193] Abū Dāwūd, *k. al-ṭahārah, b. al-isrāf fī al-mā'.*

[194] *See*: Ibn Abī Shaybah, *al-Muṣannaf*, i. 67-8.

Sunnahs after wuḍū'

Supplications

There is nothing confirmed from the Prophet ﷺ regarding supplications during *wuḍū'*. As regards supplications after *wuḍū'* is completed there are several narrations: ʿUmar reported that the Prophet ﷺ said: "If one completes and perfects *wuḍū'* and then says:

أَشْهَدُ أَنْ لا إِلَهَ إِلاَّ اللهُ وَحْدَهُ لا شَرِيْكَ لَهُ وَأَشْهَدُ أَنَّ مُحَمَّدًا عَبْدُهُ وَرَسُوْلُهُ

'I testify that there is no god but Allāh, the One Who has no partner, and that Muḥammad is His slave and Messenger', the eight gates of Paradise will be opened for him and he may enter through any gate he wishes".[195] In another narration ʿUmar said that the Messenger of Allāh ﷺ said: "Whoever completes and perfects *wuḍū'* and then says:

أَشْهَدُ أَنْ لا إِلَهَ إِلاَّ اللهُ وَأَشْهَدُ أَنَّ مُحَمَّدًا عَبْدُهُ وَرَسُولُه اَللهُمَّ اجْعَلْنِي مِنَ التَّوَّابِيْنَ وَاجْعَلْنِي مِنَ الْمُتَطَهِّرِيْنَ

'I testify that there is no god but Allāh, the One Who has no partner, and that Muḥammad is His slave and Messenger, O Allāh, cause me to be from among the repentant, and cause me to be from among the pure', the eight gates of Paradise will be opened for him and he may enter any of them that he chooses'."[196]

Taḥiyyat al-wuḍū'

Taḥiyyat al-wuḍū' refers to *ṣalāh* after *wuḍū'*. Abū Hurayrah reported that the Messenger of Allāh ﷺ said to Bilāl: "O Bilāl, tell me what good deed you have done in Islam that I hear the sound of your shoes in Paradise?" Bilāl said: "Whenever I purify myself during the day or night, I pray with that purification as much as Allāh has destined for me".[197] ʿUqbah

[195] Muslim, *k. al-ṭahārah, b. al-dhikr al-mustaḥabb ʿaqiba al-wuḍū'*.

[196] al-Tirmidhī, *k. al-ṭahārah, b. fī mā yuqālu baʿda al-wuḍū'*.

[197] al-Bukhārī, *k. al-tahajjud, b. faḍl al-ṭuhūr bi al-layl wa al-nahār.*

ibn ʿĀmir related that the Messenger of Allāh ﷺ said: "If one performs and perfects one's *wuḍū'* and prays two *rakʿahs* with one's heart and face completely on *ṣalāh*, Paradise becomes this persons".[198] Ḥumrān, the client of ʿUthmān narrated at the end of his description of ʿUthmān's *wuḍū'* that ʿUthmān said: "I saw the Messenger of Allāh ﷺ do *wuḍū'* like this and then he said: 'Whoever does *wuḍū'* like this and then prays two *rakʿahs* without having any other concern on his mind, all his past sins will be forgiven".[199]

A description of wuḍū'

ʿAbd al-Raḥmān al-Taymī reported: "Ibn Abī Mulaykah was asked about *wuḍū'*. He said: 'I saw ʿUthmān ibn ʿAffān who was asked about *wuḍū'*. He called for water. A vessel was then brought to him. He poured water upon his right hand. Then he put his [right] hand in the water [to scoop up the water]; then he rinsed his mouth three times and cleansed his nose with water three times, and washed his face three times. He then put his hand in the water and took it out; then he wiped his head and ears, inside and outside only once. Then he washed his feet, and said: 'Where are those who asked about *wuḍū'*? I saw the Messenger of Allāh ﷺ doing *wuḍū'* like this'."[200]

ʿAbd Khayr said: "ʿAlī came upon us; he had already offered *ṣalāh*. He called for water. We said: 'What will he do with water when he has already offered *ṣalāh* – perhaps to teach us'. A utensil containing water and a washbasin were brought to him. He poured water from the utensil on his right hand and washed both his hands three times, rinsed the mouth, snuffed up water and cleansed the nose three times. He rinsed the mouth and snuffed up water with the same hand by which he took water. Then he washed his face three times, and washed his right hand three times and washed his left hand three times. Then he put his hand in water and wiped his head once. Then he washed his right foot three

[198] Muslim, *k. al-ṭahārah, b. al-dhikr al-mustaḥabb ʿaqiba al-wuḍū'*.

[199] Muslim, *k. al-ṭahārah, b. faḍl al-wuḍū' wa al-ṣalāh ʿaqibah.*

[200] Abū Dāwūd, *k. al-ṭahārah, b. ṣifat wuḍū' al-nabiyyi ṣallallāhu ʿalayhi wa sallam.*

times and left foot three times. Then he said: 'Whoever likes to know the *wuḍū'* of the Messenger of Allāh ﷺ this is how he did it'."[201]

When wuḍū' is farḍ

Wuḍū' is *farḍ* in any of the following situations:

Ṣalāh

Wuḍū' is obligatory before any *ṣalāh*, whether the *ṣalāh* is obligatory or voluntary. Allāh says: "*O you who believe, when you rise for ṣalāh, wash your faces and your hands up to the elbows and wipe your heads and wash your feet up to the ankles*".[202] Furthermore, the Messenger of Allāh ﷺ said: "Allāh does not accept a *ṣalāh* without purity, or a charity from misappropriated booty".[203]

The funeral *ṣalāh* is like any other *ṣalāh* in that it cannot be done without *wuḍū'*.

The sajdah of recitation

The *sajdah* of recitation is like *ṣalāh*. *Wuḍū'* is compulsory for the *sajdah* of recitation. Nāfiᶜ narrated from ᶜAbdullāh ibn ᶜUmar saying: "One should not do *sajdah* unless one is pure (has done *wuḍū'*)". Imām Zuhrī said: "One should not do *sajdah* unless one is pure". Al-Kāsānī affirms that the validity of *sajdah* has the same conditions as *ṣalāh*.[204]

Touching the Qur'ān

Allāh says: "*That (this) is indeed an honourable recital (the Noble Qur'ān). In a Book well-guarded (with Allāh in the heaven). Which none can touch but the purified*".[205] ᶜAbdullāh ibn Abī Bakr ibn Ḥazm reported that the letter the Prophet ﷺ wrote for ᶜAmr ibn Ḥazm stated: "No one is to touch the Qur'ān except one who is purified".[206] Because of the above verse and ḥadīth no one in a state of impurity is allowed to touch the Qur'ān. ᶜAbd

[201] Ibid.

[202] *al-Mā'idah* 6

[203] Muslim, *k. al-ṭahārah, b. wujūb al-ṭahārah li al-ṣalāh.*

[204] al-Kāsānī, *Badā'iᶜ al-ṣanā'iᶜ, i.* 742.

[205] *al-Wāqiᶜah* 79

[206] Mālik, *al-Muwaṭṭa'* 108.

al-Razzāq has narrated from ʿAṭā' ibn Abī Rabāḥ, al-Shaʿbī, Ṭāwūs, Qāsim ibn Muḥammad and others that they disliked the Qur'ān to be touched without *wuḍū'*.[207]

Nevertheless, one who does not have *wuḍū'* may recite it without touching it. Imām Muḥammad narrated from ʿAlī ibn Abī Ṭālib that he said on being asked about reading the Qur'ān without *wuḍū'*: "The Messenger of Allāh ﷺ used to recite the Qur'ān, and nothing other than *janābah* (major impurity) stopped him from doing so". Imām Muḥammad said: "We hold to it, we do not see any harm in one reading the Qur'ān in any condition except if one is in a state of *janābah*. This is the opinion of Abū Ḥanīfah".[208] It also has been narrated from ʿUmar, Ibn Masʿūd, Ibn ʿUmar, Ibn ʿAbbās, Abū Mūsā al-Ashʿarī, ʿĀ'ishah, Salmān al-Fārisī, Abū Hurayrah, Ibrāhīm al-Nakhaʿī and ʿAṭā' ibn Abī Rabāḥ that they allowed the reading of the Qur'ān without *wuḍū'*.[209]

When wuḍū' is wājib

There is only one condition when *wuḍū'* is *wājib* and that is for *ṭawāf*, i.e. circumambulation of the Kaʿbah. Ibn ʿAbbās reported that the Messenger of Allāh ﷺ said: "*Ṭawāf* is a *ṣalāh*, but Allāh has permitted speaking during it. Whoever speaks during it should only speak good".[210] Since *ṭawāf* is not *ṣalāh* in the full sense, if someone does *ṭawāf* without *wuḍū'*, he does not need to repeat the *ṭawāf*, but it is nevertheless deficient and must be completed – in this case by sacrificing an animal. In the same way, when a *wājib* act is omitted from the *ṣalāh*, the *ṣalāh* is deficient, and the deficiency is made up by doing the *sajdat al-sahw* (prostration of forgetting).

When wuḍū' is recommended

It is recommended that one be in a state of *wuḍū'* all the time. There are, however, certain situations when it has been specially recommended, such as:

[207] ʿAbd al-Razzāq, *al-Muṣannaf*, i. 342-5.

[208] Abū Ḥanīfah, *K. al-āthār* 70.

[209] ʿAbd al-Razzāq, *al-Muṣannaf*, i. 338-41.

[210] al-Tirmidhī, *abwāb al-ḥajj, b. mā jā'a fī al-kalām fī al-ṭawāf*.

When going to sleep

Al-Barā' ibn ʿĀzib reported that the Messenger of Allāh ﷺ said: "When you go to your bed, do *wuḍū'*, lie on your right side and then say:

اَللَّهُمَّ أَسْلَمْتُ وَجْهِيْ إِلَيْكَ وَفَوَّضْتُ أَمْرِيْ إِلَيْكَ وَأَلْجَأْتُ ظَهْرِي إِلَيْك رَغْبَةً وَرَهْبَةً إِلَيْك لا مَلْجَأَ وَلاَ مَنْجَى مِنْكَ إِلاَّ إِلَيْكَ اللَّهُمَّ آمَنْتُ بِكِتَابِكَ الَّذِيْ أَنْزَلْتَ وَبِنَبِيِّكَ الَّذِيْ أَرْسَلْتَ

'O Allāh, I submit my face to You. I entrust my affairs to You. I take refuge in You with hope and fear in You. There is no resort and no saviour but You. I believe in Your book which You sent down and in Your Prophet ﷺ You sent'." The Prophet ﷺ said further: "If you die during that night, you will be on the natural path. Make it your last word of the night".[211] Zuhrī reported that ʿUrwah ibn Zubayr preferred not to sleep without *wuḍū'*.[212]

When mentioning Allāh's name

Mentioning Allāh's name is permissible in any condition. ʿĀ'ishah said: "The Messenger of Allāh ﷺ used to remember Allāh at all times".[213] However, it is preferable to do *wuḍū'* before it. Al-Muhājir ibn Qunfudh related that he greeted the Prophet ﷺ but that the latter did not return his salutation until he had done *wuḍū'*; then the Prophet ﷺ said: "There is nothing that prevented me from responding to you except that I do not like to mention Allāh's name unless I am in a state of purity".[214]

For the one in a state of janābah

There is no harm for one in a state of *janābah* to eat, drink, sleep or have relations again. ʿĀ'ishah reported: 'The Messenger of Allāh ﷺ would sleep while he was in the state of *janābah* without touching water".[215] However it is recommended that such a person do *wuḍū'* before any of those actions. ʿĀ'ishah said: "When the Prophet ﷺ was in a state of

[211] al-Bukhārī, *k. al-ṭahārah, b. faḍl man bāta ʿalā al-wuḍū'.*

[212] Ibn Abī Shaybah, *al-Muṣannaf*, i. 111.

[213] Abū Dāwūd, *k. al-ṭahārah, b. fī al-rajul yadhkuru Allāha taʿālā ʿalā ghayr ṭuhr.*

[214] Abū Dāwūd, *k. al-ṭahārah, b. ayaruddu al-salāma wa huwa yabūl.*

[215] Abū Dāwūd, *k. al-ṭahārah, b. fī al-junub yu'akhkhiru al-ghusl.*

janābah and wanted to eat or sleep, he would do *wuḍū*'".[216] ʿAbdullāh ibn ʿUmar reported that the Prophet ﷺ said to someone who asked him what he should do if he found himself in a state of *janābah* at night: "You should wash your private parts and do *wuḍū'*, then sleep".[217] ʿAmmār ibn Yāsir reported that the Prophet ﷺ permitted a person in the state of *janābah* to eat, drink or sleep if he did *wuḍū'* first.[218] Abū Saʿīd reported that the Prophet ﷺ said: "If one has relations with one's wife and wants to repeat the act, one should do *wuḍū*'".[219]

Before doing ghusl

Doing *wuḍū'* before *ghusl* is also recommended. ʿĀ'ishah said: "When the Messenger of Allāh ﷺ did the *ghusl* of *janābah*, he would begin by washing his hands and then pour water from his right hand to his left and wash his private parts. He would then do *wuḍū'*, similar to his *wuḍū'* for *ṣalāh*".[220]

Nullification of wuḍū'

Excretions

Wuḍū' is nullified if anything comes out from either private parts. Allāh said: "*...or one of you comes after answering the call of nature*",[221] thus proving that such an act obligates a new purification. Similarly, releasing wind nullifies *wuḍū'*. Abū Hurayrah reported that the Messenger of Allāh ﷺ said: "Allāh does not accept the *ṣalāh* of a person who has released wind until he does a new *wuḍū'*." A person from Ḥaḍramawt asked Abū Hurayrah: "What does releasing wind mean?" He answered: "Wind with or without sound".[222]

[216] Muslim, *k. al-ḥayḍ, b. jawāz nawm al-junub.*
[217] al-Bukhārī, *k. al-ghusl, b. al-junub yatawaḍḍa'u thumma yanāmu.*
[218] Abū Dāwūd, *k. al-ṭahārah, b. man qāla yatawaḍḍa'u al-junub.*
[219] Muslim, *k. al-ḥayḍ, b. jawāz nawm al-junub.*
[220] al-Bukhārī, *k. al-ghusl, b. al-wuḍū' qabl al-ghusl.*
[221] *al-Nisā'* 43.
[222] al-Bukhārī, *k. al-wuḍū', b. man lam yara al-wuḍū' illā min al-makhrajayn min al-qubul wa al-dubur.*

As for *madhy* and *wady,* Ibn ʿAbbās said: "Wash your private parts and do *wuḍū*'".[223] ʿAlī said: "I used to excrete *madhy,* so I asked a man to ask the Messenger of Allāh ﷺ about it. I was shy to do so because of my position with respect to his daughter [ʿAlī was the Prophet's ﷺ son-in-law]. The Prophet ﷺ affirmed: 'Do *wuḍū'* and wash your private parts'."[224] ʿĀ'ishah said: "From *manī* there is *ghusl*; and from *madhy* and *wady,* one should do *wuḍū'*."[225]

Bleeding

Blood, pus, purulent matter, if excreted from the body and spread to a place that must be purified, necessitate *wuḍū'*. However, if the bleeding occurs inside the eye, *wuḍū'* will not be nullified, as washing inside the eye is not compulsory. The evidence of nullification of *wuḍū'* by bleeding is the ḥadīth of Tamīm al-Dārī whereby the Prophet ﷺ said: "*Wuḍū'* is required for every flowing blood".[226] This was reported from ʿUmar, ʿUthmān, ʿAlī, Ibn Masʿūd, Ibn ʿAbbās, Ibn ʿUmar, Thawbān, Abū al-Dardā', Zayd ibn Thābit and Abū Mūsā al-Ashʿarī – all being the juristic Companions.[227] ʿAṭā' ibn Abī Rabāḥ said: "If the blood flows, then one should do *wuḍū'*, and if it appears and does not flow, then there is no need for *wuḍū'*."[228] This is also the opinion of Ibrāhīm al-Nakhaʿī, Ḥasan al-Baṣrī, Qatādah and others.[229]

Vomit

If one vomits a mouthful of food or drink, then *wuḍū'* is nullified. Maʿdān ibn Abī Ṭalḥah said that Abū al-Dardā' narrated that the Prophet ﷺ vomited, then he did *wuḍū'*. Maʿdān said: "Later I met Thawbān in the *masjid* of Damascus and I mentioned it to him. Thawbān said: 'Abū al-Dardā' is right; I poured water for the *wuḍū'* of the Prophet ﷺ'."[230] In

[223] Ibn Abī Shaybah, *al-Muṣannaf, i.* 88.
[224] Muslim, *k. al-ḥayḍ, b. al-madhy.*
[225] Ibn Abī Shaybah, *al-Muṣannaf,* i. 88.
[226] al-Dāraquṭnī, *al-Sunan, i.* 163.
[227] al-Kāsānī, *Badā'iʿ al-ṣanā'iʿ, i. 228-9.*
[228] ʿAbd al-Razzāq, *al-Muṣannaf, i.* 143.
[229] Ibid., *i.* 143-147.
[230] al-Tirmidhī, *k. al-ṭahārah, b. al-wuḍū' min al-qay' wa al-ruʿāf.*

another ḥadīth the Prophet ﷺ said: "When anyone of you vomits in the *ṣalāh,* then he should return and perform *wuḍū*'".[231] Ibrāhīm al-Nakhaᶜī said: "When you vomit a mouthful [of food, etc] then repeat your *wuḍū*', and if it is less than [a mouthful] then do not repeat your *wuḍū*'". Imām Muḥammad said: "This is the opinion of Abū Ḥanīfah and we adhere to it".[232]

Sleep

Sleep in this respect means when a person is lying down, reclining or leaning on something such that they would fall if the support were removed. ᶜAlī ibn Abī Ṭālib narrated that the Prophet ﷺ said: "The eyes are the leather strap of the anus, so one who sleeps should do *wuḍū*'".[233] Ṣafwān ibn ᶜAssāl al-Murādī said: "The Prophet ﷺ used to command us while we were travelling not to take our leather socks off unless we were in a state of *janābah,* i.e. not for defecation, urination or sleep".[234]

If one falls asleep whilst standing, or in a state of *rukūᶜ* or *sajdah* or sitting, no new *wuḍū'* is necessary. Anas ibn Mālik said "The Companions of the Prophet ﷺ waited for the *ᶜIshā' Ṣalāh* until their heads began nodding up and down from drowsiness and sleep. They would then pray without doing *wuḍū*'".[235] Abū Hurayrah said: "There is no *wuḍū'* if someone sleeps in a state of sitting, standing, or prostration, unless he lies down, for when he lies down then he has to do *wuḍū*'".[236] Ibrāhīm al-Nakhaᶜī said: "If you sleep sitting, or standing, or in a posture of *rukūᶜ*, *sajdah,* or riding, then there is no *wuḍū'* [obligatory] upon you". Imām Muḥammad said: "We adhere to it. If one lies down and sleeps then there is *wuḍū*' [obligatory] upon him. And this is the opinion of Abū Ḥanīfah".[237]

[231] al-Dāraquṭnī, *al-Sunan, i.* 160.

[232] Abū Ḥanīfah, *K. al-āthār* 11.

[233] Abū Dāwūd, *k. al-ṭahārah, b. al-wuḍū' min al-nawm.*

[234] al-Tirmidhī, *k. al-ṭahārah, b. al-masḥ ᶜalā al-khuffayn li al-musāfir wa al-muqīm.*

[235] Muslim, *k. al-ḥayḍ, b. al-dalīl ᶜalā anna nawm al-jālis lā yanquḍu al-wuḍū';* Abū Dāwūd, *k. al-ṭahārah, b. al-wuḍū' min al-nawm.*

[236] al-Bayhaqī, *al-Sunan al-kubrā, k. al-ṭahārah, b. mā warada fī nawm al-sājid.*

[237] Abū Ḥanīfah, *K. al-āthār* 44.

Loss of consciousness or reason

One's *wuḍū'* is nullified if one loses self-awareness because of insanity or falling unconscious, or drunkenness, or the effect of some medicine. ʿĀ'ishah narrated, describing the illness of the Prophet ﷺ that the Prophet ﷺ asked if the people had prayed? "We said: 'No, O Messenger of Allāh ﷺ, they are waiting for you'. Then he said: 'Put water for me in the container'. We did that, then he had a bath. Then he went to stand up, but he fell unconscious; on recovering he asked: 'Have the people prayed?' We said 'No, they are waiting for you O Messenger of Allāh ﷺ'. Then he said: 'Put water for me in the container'. We did, then he had a bath".[238] Bathing after falling unconscious was preferred by the Prophet ﷺ and *wuḍū'* is sufficient. Ḥasan al-Baṣrī said about one who falls unconscious while sitting: "He has to do *wuḍū*'". [239] Ibrāhīm al-Nakhaʿī said: "When the affected person recovers he has to do *wuḍū*'".[240]

Bursting out in laughter during ṣalāh

This refers to laughing loudly during *ṣalāh* in which there is *rukūʿ* and *sajdah.* Abū al-ʿĀliyah narrated: "While the Prophet ﷺ was praying with the people, a person with a sight problem, walked into a covered well and fell. At this some people burst out laughing. The Prophet ﷺ commanded those who had laughed to repeat their *wuḍū'* and *ṣalāh*".[241] Imām Abū Ḥanīfah also narrated this ḥadīth from Ḥasan al-Baṣrī".[242] Ibrāhīm al-Nakhaʿī said about the person who laughs out loud during the *ṣalāh*: "He will repeat both the *wuḍū'* and the *ṣalāh,* and he has to ask forgiveness from his Lord, because it is one of the most severe of *ḥadath*". Imām Muḥammad said: "We adhere to it and it is the opinion of Abū Ḥanīfah".[243]

Since the ḥadīth refers to the daily ritual *ṣalāh,* the conditions mentioned are confined to it. *Wuḍū'* is not nullified, however, if someone laughs during the funeral *ṣalāh* for example.

[238] al-Bukhārī, *k. al-adhān, b. innamā juʿila al-imām li yu'tamma bihi;* Muslim, *k. al-ṣalāh, b. istikhlāf al-imām idhā ʿaraḍa lahu ʿudhr.*

[239] Ibn Abī Shaybah, *al-Muṣannaf, i.* 181.

[240] Ibid.

[241] al-Dāraquṭnī, *al-Sunan, i.* 169.

[242] Abū Ḥanīfah, *K. al-āthār* 43.

[243] Ibid.

Wiping over khuffs

Wiping over the *khuffs*, (leather socks) is a proven Sunnah, that has come through many chains of transmission. Ḥasan al-Baṣrī said: "Seventy people from among the Companions have narrated to me that they saw the Prophet ﷺ wiping over *khuffs*".[244] Abū Ḥanīfah said: "I did not accept the wiping until the evidence for it was clear to me like the light of the day". [245] Al-Karkhī said: "I fear [the danger of] unbelief for those who do not believe in [the Sunnah of] wiping over *khuffs*".[246] The strongest ḥadīth in this regard is the one related by Hammām ibn al-Ḥārith who said: "Jarīr ibn ᶜAbdullāh urinated, did *wuḍū'* and wiped over his leather socks. It was said to him: 'You do that and you have urinated?' He said: 'Yes, I saw the Messenger of Allāh ﷺ urinate and then he did *wuḍū'* and wiped over his leather socks'."[247] Ibrāhīm al-Nakhaᶜī said: "Jarīr ibn ᶜAbdullāh wiped over his *khuffs*, and it is more pleasing to me, because Jarīr had embraced Islam after Sūrah *al-Mā'idah* [a verse that mentions washing the feet in *wuḍū'*] was revealed".[248] Ibrāhīm al-Nakhaᶜī said that the Companions of the Prophet ﷺ wiped over *khuffs*, so whoever turns away from it, follows Satan.[249]

Conditions for wiping over khuffs

Wiping over *khuffs* is permitted in the case of any *ḥadath* which breaks *wuḍū'* provided one had put on the *khuffs* in a state of complete purity and then is affected by the *ḥadath*. Al-Mughīrah ibn Shuᶜbah said: "I was with the Messenger of Allāh ﷺ one night during an expedition. I poured water for him to do *wuḍū'*. He washed his face and arms and wiped his head. Then I went to remove his *khuffs* and he said: 'Leave them on, as I put them on while I was in a state of purity', and he just wiped over them".[250]

[244] al-Kāsānī, *Badā'iᶜ al-ṣanā'iᶜ*, *i.* 131.
[245] Ibid.
[246] Ibid.
[247] Muslim, *k. al-ṭahārah, b. al-masḥ ᶜalā al-khuffayn.*
[248] Ibn Abī Shaybah, *al-Muṣannaf*, *i.* 165-6.
[249] Ibid., *i.* 164.
[250] al-Bukhārī, *k. al-wuḍū', b. idhā adkhala rijlayhi wa humā ṭāhiratān.*

Wiping over *khuffs* is not permitted for someone on whom *ghusl* is obligatory. It is also not permitted to wipe over a *khuff* with a hole in it such that three toes are visible although less than this is permissible.

Whoever wears boots or galoshes over his *khuffs* may wipe over them.[251] Abū Ziyād said: "I saw Ibrāhīm al-Nakhaʿī wiping over galoshes".[252]

How the wiping is done

Wiping over the *khuffs* is done on the upper part of the foot by stroking with the fingers beginning with the tips of the toes to the base of the shin – the use of at least three fingers is obligatory. Al-Mughīrah said: "I saw the Messenger of Allāh ﷺ wipe over the top of his *khuffs*".[253] ʿAlī commented that if religion were based on opinion, the underside of the *khuff* would take preference in being wiped to the upper.[254] If someone reverses the order and wipes from the shin to the toe, it is allowed, but it is against the Sunnah.

Duration

If one is resident in a place, then one may wipe over the *khuff*s for a day and a night; if one is a traveller, then this can be done for three days and nights, beginning from the time of the nullification of the *wuḍū'* after putting on the *khuffs*. Ṣafwān ibn ʿAssāl al-Murādī said: "We were commanded by the Prophet ﷺ to wipe over our *khuffs* if we were in a state of purity when we put them on, for three days if we were travellers, and for one day and night if we were residents, and that we do not remove them unless we were in a state of *janābah*".[255] Shurayḥ ibn Hānī said: "I asked ʿĀ'ishah about wiping over *khuffs*; she said: 'Go to ʿAlī ibn Abī Ṭālib and ask him, because he used to travel with the Messenger of Allāh ﷺ'. We asked him; and he answered: 'For the traveller, three days and three nights; for the resident, one day and night'."[256]

[251] al-Kāsānī, *Badā'iʿ al-ṣanā'iʿ, i. 143.*

[252] Ibn Abī Shaybah, *al-Muṣannaf, i.* 173.

[253] Abū Dāwūd, *k. al-ṭahārah, b. kayfa al-masḥ.*

[254] Ibid.

[255] al-Tirmidhī, *k. al-ṭahārah, b. al-masḥ ʿalā al-khuffayn li al-musāfir wa al-muqīm.*

[256] Muslim, *k. al-ṭahārah, b. al-tawqīt fī al-masḥ ʿalā al-khuffayn.*

The above mentioned duration was reported from ʿUmar, ʿAlī, Ibn Masʿūd, Ibn ʿAbbās, Ibn ʿUmar, Saʿd ibn Abī Waqqāṣ, Jābir ibn Samurah, Abū Mūsā al-Ashʿarī and al-Mughīrah ibn Shuʿbah.[257] Imām Muḥammad narrated on the authority of Abū Ḥanīfah from ʿUmārah saying: "Wiping over the leather socks for the resident is one day and one night, and for the traveller, three days and nights, if one wears them and is pure". Imām Muḥammad said: "This is the opinion of Abū Ḥanīfah and we hold to it".[258]

Once the prescribed time elapses one should remove one's *khuffs*, wash one's feet and do the *ṣalāh*; one does not have to repeat the remaining elements of *wuḍū'*.

Whoever begins wiping while he is a resident, then goes on a journey before the full day and night elapses, should continue to do the wiping for a full three days and nights. Whoever begins the wiping and is a traveller then becomes resident and wiping was done for a day and a night or more, must remove his *khuffs* and wash his feet. If the wiping was for less than a day and a night, then he should wipe for a day and a night.

When the concession ends

Wiping the *khuffs* must be done on every occasion that *wuḍū'* is performed, except when it is impermissible to do so; namely, when the period allowed for wiping the *khuffs* has expired, when the *khuffs* have been removed, when the person falls into a state of *janābah* and whenever *ghusl* is compulsory.

Wiping over socks

Wiping over socks which are quite thick is allowed according to the opinions of Abū Yūsuf and Muḥammad; this was also the last opinion of Abū Ḥanīfah. It is not, however, permissible to wipe over thin socks.[259] Al-Kāsānī narrated that Abū Ḥanīfah wiped over his socks during an

[257] al-Kāsānī, *Badāʾiʿ al-ṣanāʾiʿ*, i. 133-4.

[258] Abū Ḥanīfah, *K. al-āthār* 9.

[259] al-Samarqandī, *Tuḥfat al-fuqahā'* 45.

illness, then he said to his visitors: "I did what I have been stopping people from".[260]

Wiping over casts and bandages

It is permitted to wipe over splints. It is not necessary for one to have been in a state of purity when the cast or bandages were applied. There is also no time limit for such wiping, for one can do so as long as the condition lasts. If a splint falls off before the wound has healed, the wiping is not invalidated, but if it falls off after the wound has healed, then the wiping is invalidated.[261] ᶜAlī narrated that the Prophet ﷺ said to him: "Wipe over bandages".[262]

Jābir said: "We set out on a journey. One of our people was hurt by a stone that injured his head. He then had a wet dream. He asked his companions: 'Do you find concession for me to do *tayammum*?' They said: 'We do not find any concession for you while you can use water'. He did *ghusl* and died because of it. When we came to the Prophet ﷺ the incident was reported to him. He said: 'They killed him, may Allāh kill them. Why did they not ask about what they do not know? The cure for ignorance is to ask. It would have been enough for him to do *tayammum* and wrap his wound then to wipe it and wash the rest of the body'."[263]

[260] al-Kāsānī, *Badā'iᶜ al-ṣanā'iᶜ*, *i.* 141.

[261] Ibid., *i.* 157-8.

[262] Ibn Mājah, *k. al-ṭahārah, b. al-masḥ ᶜalā al-jabā'ir.*

[263] Abū Dāwūd, *k. al-ṭahārah, b. al-majrūḥ yatayammamu.*

CHAPTER 4: *GHUSL*

TO PERFORM *GHUSL* means to wash the whole body with water. It is stated in the Qur'ān: "*If you are in a state of janābah, purify yourselves*".[264] "*They question you concerning menstruation. Say: It is an illness, so let women alone at such times and do not have relations with them until they are cleansed*".[265]

FARḌS OF *GHUSL*

The *farḍ* elements of *ghusl* are as follows: 1. rinsing one's mouth; 2. snuffling water up into the nostrils, and 3. washing the whole body once.

This is based on the above-cited verse whereby Allāh says: "*If you are in a state of janābah, purify yourselves*",[266] that is, do *ghusl*, and, "*And they question you concerning menstruation. Say: It is an illness, so let women alone at such times and do not have relations with them until they are cleansed*",[267] that is, until they do *ghusl*.

The proof that purifying means *ghusl* is the verse: "*O you who believe, approach not the ṣalāh when you are drunk until you know what you utter, nor when you are in a state of janābah, except when journeying upon the road, until you have bathed*". [268] This shows that *ghusl*, the washing of all parts of the body, is meant. It includes rinsing the mouth and snuffling water into one's nostrils, which was the regular practice of the Prophet ﷺ as his wives narrated when describing his *ghusl*. This practice is also narrated from ʿUmar, Ibn Sīrīn, Ibrāhīm al-Nakhaʿī, Ḥassān ibn Bilāl and Qatādah.[269]

[264] *al-Mā'idah* 6.
[265] *al-Baqarah* 222.
[266] *al-Mā'idah* 6.
[267] *al-Baqarah* 222.
[268] *al-Nisā'* 43.
[269] Ibn Abī Shaybah, *al-Muṣannaf*, i. 68.

Washing one's hair

It is compulsory for men to make sure that water reaches all the hair on the head and beard including the roots. ʿAlī ibn Abī Ṭālib reported: "The Messenger of Allāh ﷺ said: 'If anyone who is in the state of *janābah* leaves a spot equal to the breadth of a hair without washing, such and such an amount of hellfire will have to be suffered for it'." ʿAlī said: "On account of that I became an enemy of my head", meaning he shaved his head.[270]

Similarly, if a woman has short hair or not much hair, she must wash all her hair and its roots.[271] Abū Hurayrah reported: "The Messenger of Allāh ﷺ said: 'There is *janābah* under every hair, so wash it and cleanse the skin'."[272]

If the woman has plaited hair she does not have to undo it, provided that the water reaches the roots. Shurayḥ ibn ʿUbayd said: "Jubayr ibn Nufayr gave me a verdict about *ghusl* after a state of *janābah* that Thawbān reported to them that they asked the Prophet ﷺ about it. The Prophet ﷺ replied: 'As regards a man, he should undo the hair of his head and wash it until the water reaches the roots of the hair. But there is no harm if the woman does not undo it and pours three handfuls of water over her head'."[273]

Umm Salamah said: "O Messenger of Allāh ﷺ, I am a woman who keeps her hair closely plaited. Do I have to undo them for *ghusl* after *janābah*?" He said: "No, it is enough for you to throw three handfuls of water on your head and then pour water over all your body and you will be purified".[274] ʿUbayd ibn ʿUmayr narrated that ʿĀ'ishah came to know that ʿAbdullāh ibn ʿAmr was ordering the women to undo their plaits for *ghusl*. She observed: "It is amazing that Ibn ʿAmr orders the women to undo their hair plaits for *ghusl*. Why doesn't he order them to shave their heads? I and the Messenger of Allāh ﷺ used to bathe from one vessel, and all I did was pour three handfuls of water over my head".[275]

[270] Abū Dāwūd, *k. al-ṭahārah, b. fī al-ghusl min al-janābah.*

[271] al-Kāsānī, *Badāʾiʿ al-ṣanāʾiʿ*, *i.* 267-8.

[272] Abū Dāwūd, *k. al-ṭahārah, b. fī al-ghusl min al-janābah.*

[273] Abū Dāwūd, *k. al-ṭahārah, b. fī al-mar'ah hal tanquḍu shaʿrahā ʿinda al-ghusl.*

[274] Muslim, *k. al-ḥayḍ, b. ḥukm ḍafā'ir al-mughtasilah.*

[275] Ibid.

THE SUNNAHS OF GHUSL

Remembrance of Allāh

One should begin with the name of Allāh. The Prophet ﷺ said: "The curtain between the eyes of *jinn*s and the hidden parts of human beings when one of them takes off his clothes is to say 'In the name of Allāh'."[276]

Intention

One should have the intent to purify oneself. As mentioned earlier, intention belongs to the heart; one does not need to utter anything with the tongue.

Washing one's hands

One should wash one's hands up to the wrists. ʿĀ'ishah reported that when the Prophet ﷺ did his *ghusl* after *janābah*, he would wash his hands, then he would do *wuḍū'* like the *wuḍū'* before the *ṣalāh*.[277]

Cleaning

One should wash dirt from one's private parts, as Maymūnah, the wife of the Prophet ﷺ, related that the Prophet ﷺ washed his private parts while having his bath.[278]

Wuḍū'

One should do *wuḍū'* in the same way as the *wuḍū'* before the *ṣalāh*. The exception here is that if the place where one is bathing retains the used water, one should delay the washing of one's feet until the end so as to ensure the washed feet make no contact with unclean water. If, however, the place allows used water to drain away one may wash one's feet as well. This is mentioned by Maymūnah when she related that the Messenger of Allāh ﷺ did *wuḍū'* like the *wuḍū'* of the prayer, except washing the feet which he did after stepping away from the place he did his *ghusl*.[279]

[276] al-Ṭabarānī, *al-Muʿjam al-awsaṭ, iii.* 130.

[277] al-Bukhārī, *k. al-ghusl, b. al-wuḍū' qabl al-ghusl.*

[278] al-Bukhārī, ibid.; Muslim, *k. al-ḥayḍ, b. ṣifat ghusl al-janābah.*

[279] al-Bukhārī, ibid.

Rubbing

One should rub water through one's hair three times, letting the water penetrate down to the roots of the hair.

Pouring water

One should pour water over one's head and the rest of one's body three times. Jubayr ibn Muṭᶜim narrated that people mentioned the *ghusl* of *janābah* in the presence of the Messenger ﷺ. The Messenger of Allāh ﷺ said: "As for myself, I pour water on my head three times".[280]

Description of the ghusl

ᶜAbdullāh ibn ᶜAbbās narrated that Maymūnah the wife of the Prophet ﷺ said: "I put water out for the Messenger of Allāh ﷺ to do *ghusl.* He washed his hands two or three times, and then he poured water from his right hand to his left and washed his private parts, wiped his hands on the earth, rinsed his mouth and nose, washed his face and hands, washed his head three times, poured water over his body, and finally moved from his place and washed his feet. I brought him a towel, but he did not take it, for he shook the water off with his hands".[281]

ᶜĀ'ishah narrated: "When the Prophet ﷺ took his bath after *janābah,* he would begin by washing his hands. Then he would pour water from his right hand to his left and wash his private parts, do the *wuḍū'* for *ṣalāh,* take some water and put his fingers to the roots of his hair to the extent that he felt that the skin was wet, then pour water over his head three times and then over the rest of his body".[282] ᶜĀ'ishah also narrated: "When the Messenger of Allāh ﷺ intended to take a bath because of *janābah,* he would begin with his hands and wash them. Then he would wash the joints of his limbs and pour water upon them. When he cleansed both his hands, he would rub them on the wall. Then he would do *wuḍū'* and pour water over his head". [283]

[280] Abū Dāwūd, *k. al-ṭahārah, b. fī al-ghusl min al-janābah.*

[281] al-Bukhārī, *k. al-ghusl, b. al-wuḍū' qabla al-ghusl;* Muslim, *k. al-ḥayḍ, b. ṣifat ghusl al-janābah.*

[282] al-Bukhārī, ibid.; Muslim, ibid.

[283] Abū Dāwūd, *k. al-ṭahārah, b. fī al-ghusl min al-janābah.*

Jumayᶜ ibn ᶜUmayr (from the tribe of Banī Taymullāh ibn Thaᶜlabah) said: "Accompanied by my mother and aunt, I entered upon ᶜĀ'ishah. One of them asked her: 'How do you take a bath?' ᶜĀ'ishah replied: 'The Messenger of Allāh ﷺ did *wuḍū'* as he did for *ṣalāh.* Then he poured water upon his head three times. But we pour water upon our heads five times due to plaits". [284]

WHEN *GHUSL* IS *FARḌ*

There are three types of *ghusl*: *farḍ, wājib,* and Sunnah. *Wājib ghusl* is washing of the dead people. Sunnah *ghusl* are: for the Friday *Ṣalāh,* ᶜ*Īd Ṣalāhs, Iḥrām* and the Day of ᶜArafah. I will explain *wājib* and Sunnah *ghusls* in their respective places, if Allāh wills.

Ghusl becomes *farḍ* due to one of three things: *janābah* (major sexual impurity), *ḥayḍ* (menstruation) and *nifās* (post childbirth bleeding), which are explained below:

1. Janābah

Ghusl becomes compulsory for both a man and woman when there is an emission of fluid. Abū Saᶜīd reported that he heard the Messenger of Allāh ﷺ say: "*Ghusl* is needed after ejaculation of sperm".[285]

If seminal fluid comes out without desire, because of some medical condition, or carrying a heavy burden, or cold, *ghusl* is not obligatory. ᶜAlī reported that the Prophet ﷺ said to him: "If sperm is ejaculated, do *ghusl*".[286]

If one has a wet dream but does not find any traces of seminal fluid, then *ghusl* is not compulsory. Umm Sulaym said: "O Messenger of Allāh ﷺ, Allāh is not ashamed of the truth. Does a woman have to do *ghusl* if she has a wet dream?" He said: "Yes, if she sees the liquid".[287]

Ghusl is also obligatory if penetration takes place, even if there is no ejaculation. Abū Hurayrah reported that the Prophet ﷺ said: "When anyone exerts themselves during or before sexual acts, *ghusl* becomes

[284] Ibid.

[285] Muslim, *k. al-ḥayḍ, b. innamā al-mā' min al-mā'.*

[286] Abū Dāwūd, *k. al-ṭahārah, b. fī al-madhy.*

[287] al-Bukhārī, *k. al-ghusl, b. idhā iḥtalamat al-mar'ah;* Muslim, *k. al-ḥayḍ, b. wujūb al-ghusl ᶜalā al-mar'ah bi khurūj al-manī minhā.*

obligatory for both".[288] Saᶜīd ibn al-Musayyab reported that Abū Mūsā al-Ashᶜarī came to ᶜĀ'ishah, the wife of the Prophet ﷺ, and said to her: "It is hurting me that the Companions of the Prophet ﷺ have differed about a matter that I am embarrassed to ask you". She said: "What is that? Ask me whatever you can ask your mother". He asked about one having intercourse with his wife, but who does not ejaculate. She said: "When the private parts of each partner encountered the other, *ghusl* is obligatory". On hearing this, Abū Mūsā said: "I will never ask about this of anyone after you".[289]

2. Ḥayḍ

Ḥayḍ refers to the regular menstrual flow of blood, not to any other bleeding such as after childbirth. The red, yellow or muddy coloured liquid observed by a woman during her days of menstruation is counted as menstruation until she sees the pure white liquid. The women would send ᶜĀ'ishah small boxes with yellow-stained cotton, and she would say to them: "Do not be in haste until you see the pure white cotton".[290]

Ghusl is obligatory on a woman after her menstrual period. Allāh says in the Qur'ān: "*Do not approach them during menses until they are purified. When they have purified themselves, then go unto them as Allāh has ordained for you*".[291] The Messenger of Allāh ﷺ said to Fāṭimah bint Abī Ḥubaysh: "Do not pray during your period. After it has ended, do *ghusl* and pray".[292]

The duration of menstruation

The minimum period of menstruation is three days and nights; any less than this is not menstruation, but *istiḥāḍah,* i.e. extra-menstrual bleeding; its maximum is ten days, and any more than this is *istiḥāḍah.* Sufyān al-Thawrī said: "The least of menstruation is three days, and the most is ten days".[293] Anas ibn Mālik said: "The least of menstruation

[288] Muslim, *k. al-ḥayḍ, b. naskh al-mā' min al-mā' wa wujūb al-ghusl bi iltiqā' al-khitānayn.*

[289] Mālik, *al-Muwaṭṭa'* 29; Muslim, ibid.

[290] Mālik, ibid., 35.

[291] *al-Baqarah* 222.

[292] al-Bukhārī, *k. al-ḥayḍ, b. idhā ra'at al-mustaḥāḍah al-ṭuhr;* Muslim, *k. al-ḥayḍ, b. al-mustaḥāḍah wa ghusluhā wa ṣalātuhā.*

[293] al-Dāraquṭnī, *al-Sunan, i.* 217.

is three days".[294] Rabīʿ ibn Ṣabīḥ narrated from Ḥasan saying: "The maximum days of menstruation is ten days".[295] Rabīʿ ibn Ṣabīḥ also narrated from someone who heard Anas ibn Mālik saying: "What is beyond ten days is *istiḥāḍah*".[296]

If a woman has her own regular habit, she will follow this as long as it is not less than three days and not more than ten days. Umm Salamah asked the Prophet ﷺ about a woman with a prolonged flow of blood. He said: "She should look for the number of days and nights that she usually has her menses and the time of the month during which it occurs. Then she should leave the *ṣalāh* during those days, and then afterwards do *ghusl*, tie something around her private parts and pray".[297]

The minimum period between two menstruations cannot be less than fifteen days; of course, there is no maximum period of purity as the menstruation can be irregular.

3. Nifās

Nifās means the normal flow of blood from the womb after giving birth. *Ghusl* is also obligatory on a woman after *nifās* (post childbirth bleeding). There is no verse in the Qur'ān, and no report from the Prophet ﷺ concerning this point. The jurists affirm that this ruling is based on consensus.[298]

The blood observed by a pregnant woman and that while giving birth but before the child emerges is *istiḥāḍah*. There is no minimum period for *nifās*, while the maximum is forty days, and anything beyond this is *istiḥāḍah*. Therefore, if the bleeding continues beyond forty days after birth, the woman should reckon her number of days in accordance with her previous period of *nifās*. For a woman giving birth for the first time, her initial *nifās* is forty days. Umm Salamah said: "During the lifetime of the Prophet ﷺ, after childbirth a woman would be in confinement

[294] Ibid.

[295] ʿAbd al-Razzāq, *al-Muṣannaf*, *i*. 300.

[296] al-Dāraquṭnī, *al-Sunan*, *i*. 217.

[297] Abū Dāwūd, *k. al-ṭahārah, b. fī al-mar'ah tustaḥāḍu wa man qāla tadaʿu al-ṣalāta fī ʿiddat al-ayyām allatī kānat taḥīḍu*.

[298] al-Kāsānī, *Badā'iʿ al-ṣanā'iʿ*, *i*. 284-5.

for forty days".[299] Ḥasan al-Baṣrī said: "Once forty days are complete, she will do *ghusl* and *ṣalāh*".[300]

If she gives birth to more than one child in one pregnancy, then her *nifās* is reckoned as the bleeding which occurs after the birth of the first according to Abū Ḥanīfah and Abū Yūsuf, while Muḥammad and Zufar, say it is reckoned from after delivery of the second.

A woman doing *ghusl* after menstruation or post-childbirth bleeding should take some cotton dipped in perfume and use it to remove any lingering odour. ʿĀ'ishah reported: Asmā' bint Yazīd asked the Messenger of Allāh ﷺ about *ghusl* after menstruation has ended. He said: "She should use water mixed with the leaves of the lote-tree and cleanse herself. Then she should pour water over her head and severely rub it until water reaches the roots of her hair, after which she should pour water over it. Afterwards, she should take a piece of cotton dipped in musk and cleanse herself with it". Asmā' asked: "How should she cleanse herself with it?" He said: "Praise be to Allāh, she should cleanse herself with it". ʿĀ'ishah explained to her that she should apply it to the traces of blood.[301]

Istiḥāḍah

Istiḥāḍah refers to a prolonged flow of blood, observed by a woman for either less than the minimum period of *ḥayḍ* (three days), or for longer than the maximum period of *ḥayḍ* (ten days), or for longer than the maximum period of *nifās* (forty days). *Istiḥāḍah* is considered in the same category as a permanent nosebleed, which does not prevent the woman from performing the normal acts of worship.

[299] al-Tirmidhī, *k. al-ṭahārah, b. mā jā'a kam tamkuthu al-nufasā';* After recording the ḥadīth, al-Tirmidhī states that the knowledgeable Companions, the following generation and those that came later, agreed that a woman experiencing post-childbirth bleeding had to stop praying for forty days unless her blood stopped. If her bleeding stopped before that time, she was to do *ghusl* and start praying. If she saw blood after forty days, most scholars say that she is not to stop praying. That is the opinion of most jurists.

[300] ʿAbd al-Razzāq, *al-Muṣannaf, i.* 313.

[301] al-Bukhārī, *k. al-ḥayḍ, b. dalk al-mar'ah nafsahā idhā taṭahharat min al-maḥīḍ;* Muslim, *k. al-ḥayḍ, b. istiḥbāb istiʿmāl al-mughtasilah min al-ḥayḍ.*

Two kinds of *mustaḥāḍah* (women with *istiḥāḍah*) are distinguished:

1. The young woman who has just entered puberty and so does not have an established regular period for the duration of menstruation. In this case, her period of menstruation is reckoned as ten days in each month and anything more than that is regarded as *istiḥāḍah*.

2. The woman who does have an established, regular period for the duration of menstruation. If her regular period is less than ten days, and a menstruation continues for ten days, then she should, initially, regard the bleeding as *ḥayḍ*: this would mean her normal duties of worship are suspended. Now, if the bleeding continues even after the ten days, then this is *istiḥāḍah* and, moreover, the days that the bleeding continued after her regular period were also *istiḥāḍah* and she is under an obligation to make up any acts of worship missed during those days.[302]

Umm Salamah, the wife of the Prophet ﷺ reported that in the time of the Messenger of Allāh ﷺ, there was a woman who had an issue with bleeding. So Umm Salamah asked the Messenger of Allāh ﷺ to give a decision about her. He said: "She should consider the number of nights and days during which she used to menstruate each month before she was afflicted with this trouble and abandon *ṣalāh* during that period each month. When those days and nights are over, she should take a bath, tie a cloth over her private parts and do *ṣalāh*".[303]

Zaynab bint Umm Salamah narrated that Umm Ḥabībah bint Jaḥsh had a prolonged flow of blood. "The Prophet ﷺ commanded her to abandon *ṣalāh* for the period of her menses. She then should take a bath and offer *ṣalāh*".[304] Abū Dāwūd said: "Al-Ḥasan, Saᶜīd ibn al-Musayyab, ᶜAṭā, Makḥūl, Ibrāhīm, Sālim and al-Qāsim also hold that a woman suffering from a prolonged flow of blood should abandon *ṣalāh* during her menstrual period."[305]

What is not permitted for one who must perform ghusl

When *ghusl* becomes compulsory, one cannot do the *ṣalāh*, the *sajdah* of recitation, or circumambulate the *Kaᶜbah*, nor is one allowed to touch

[302] al-Samarqandī, *Tuḥfat al-fuqahā'* 21.

[303] Abū Dāwūd, *k. al-ṭahārah, b. fī al-mar'ah tustaḥāḍ*.

[304] Ibid.

[305] Ibid.

the Qur'ān. The Companions were all agreed that it is forbidden to touch the Qur'ān while one is in a state of impurity.

The person who must perform *ghusl* is also not allowed to recite any portion of the Qur'ān. ʿAbdullāh ibn ʿUmar reported that the Prophet ﷺ said: "The woman during her period and all those who are in the state of *janābah* will not read anything from the Qur'ān".[306] ʿAbīdah narrated from ʿUmar saying: "*Junubī* (one in a state of *janābah*) cannot read the Qur'ān".[307] ʿAlī ibn Abī Ṭālib stated that nothing kept the Messenger of Allāh ﷺ from reading the Qur'ān except being in a state of *janābah*.[308] He also related: "I saw the Messenger of Allāh ﷺ do *wuḍū'* and recite some of the Qur'ān, after which he said: 'This is for the one who is not in state of *janābah*. If one is in a state of *janābah*, he may not do so, not even one verse'."[309] Maʿmar said: "I asked al-Zuhrī about the woman during her period and the one who is in the state of *janābah*, can they read the Qur'ān? He said: 'No'."[310] That is also the opinion of Ḥasan al-Baṣrī, Qatādah, ʿAṭā' ibn Abī Rabāḥ and others.[311]

It is also forbidden for someone in a state of *janābah* to enter the *masjid*. ʿĀ'ishah said: "The Messenger of Allāh ﷺ saw that his Companions' houses were practically in the *masjid*. He said: 'Direct those houses away from the *masjid*'. He then entered the *masjid*, but the people did nothing, hoping that Allāh would reveal to the Messenger that what they were doing was permissible. After he came out, he said: 'Direct those houses away from the *masjid*, for it is not permitted for a menstruating woman or person in a state of *janābah* to be in the *masjid*'."[312] Umm Salamah related that the Prophet ﷺ came to the *masjid's* courtyard and said at the top of his voice: "The *masjid* is not allowed for *junubī* and menstruating women".[313] Manṣūr narrated from Ibrāhīm al-Nakhaʿī saying: "You can read the Qur'ān all the time as long you are not in a state of *janābah*, and

[306] al-Tirmidhī, *k. al-ṭahārah, b. mā jā'a fī al-junub wa al-ḥā'iḍ annahumā lā yaqra'ān al-qur'ān;* Ibn Mājah, *k. al-ṭahārah, b. mā jā'a fī qirā'at al-qur'ān ʿalā ghayr ṭahārah.*

[307] Ibn Abī Shaybah, *al-Muṣannaf*, i. 97.

[308] al-Tirmidhī, *k. al-ṭahārah, b. al-rajul yaqra'u al-qur'ān ʿalā kulli ḥāl mā lam yakun junuban.*

[309] Abū Yaʿlā, *al-Musnad* 365; *Majmaʿ al-zawā'id, k. al-ṭahārah, b. qirā'at al-junub.*

[310] ʿAbd al-Razzāq, *al-Muṣannaf, i.* 336.

[311] Ibid., *i.* 336-7.

[312] Abū Dāwūd, *k. al-ṭahārah, b. fī al-rajul yadkhulu al-masjid.*

[313] Ibn Mājah, *k. al-ṭahārah wa sunanihā, b. mā jā'a fī ijtināb al-ḥā'iḍ al-masjid.*

you can enter the *masjid* as long you are not in the state of *janābah*".[314] Ḥawshab said: "I heard ʿAṭā' saying: 'The *junubī* is not to enter the *masjid* except if in a forced situation'."[315] Sufyān al-Thawrī said: "The *junubī* is not allowed to pass through the *masjid*, except if he has no other way; in this case he will do *tayammum*, then can pass".[316]

The women in the state of *ḥayḍ* or *nifās* observe the same restrictions as mentioned above. They should observe two further points: *ḥayḍ* and *nifās* remove the obligation of *ṣalāh* and fasting – neither is permitted to a woman in this state. Although she must make up the days of missed fasts, she does not have to make up for missed *ṣalāh*. Muʿādhah said: "I asked ʿĀ'ishah: 'Why must we make up the fasts missed due to our menstruation, and not the *ṣalāhs*?' She said: 'That was what the Messenger of Allāh ﷺ told us to do. We were ordered to make up the fasts, and we were ordered not to make up the *ṣalāhs*'."[317]

A husband may not approach his wife for sexual relations. If the bleeding from menstruation stops before ten days, it is not permitted to have sexual relations with her until she has done *ghusl* or the time for a *ṣalāh* has passed, because it is compulsory upon her to do that prayer, which implies that the period of menstruation has ended. If the bleeding stops after ten days, it is permitted to have relations with her before she has done *ghusl*, because there is no menstruation after ten days.

Anas said: "When a Jewish woman was menstruating, her husband would not eat or sleep with her. The Companions asked the Prophet ﷺ about this, and Allāh revealed: '*And they question you concerning menstruation. Say: 'It is an illness, so let women alone at such times and do not go to them until they are cleansed. And when they have purified themselves, then go in to them as Allāh has enjoined upon you. Truly, Allāh loves those who turn to Him and loves those who have a care for cleanliness*'."[318] The Messenger of Allāh ﷺ allowed for a menstruating woman everything except intercourse.[319] All

[314] ʿAbd al-Razzāq, *al-Muṣannaf*, *i*. 413-4.

[315] Ibid., *i*. 413.

[316] Ibid.

[317] al-Bukhārī, *k. al-ḥayḍ, b. lā taqḍī al-ḥā'iḍ al-ṣalāh;* Muslim, *k. al-ḥayḍ, b. wujūb qaḍā' al-ṣawm ʿalā al-ḥā'iḍ dūna al-ṣalāh.*

[318] *al-Baqarah* 222

[319] *See:* Muslim, *k. al-ḥayḍ, b. mubāsharat al-ḥā'iḍ fawqa al-izār.*

scholars say that one may touch anything above the navel or below the knees. Maymūnah said: "The Prophet ﷺ would contact and embrace any of his wives while she was menstruating. She would wear the wrapper to half the thighs or cover her knees with it".[320] Abū Dāwūd narrated a similar ḥadīth from ʿĀ'ishah as well.[321]

Rulings for mustaḥāḍah and those like her

As for the *mustaḥāḍah* (women having *istiḥāḍah)* and anyone with urine incontinency, a permanent nosebleed and a wound which does not stop bleeding, they should do *wuḍū'* at the time of each *ṣalāh* and do any *farḍ* or voluntary *ṣalāh* they want with this *wuḍū'*, as long as they are not subject to any other *ḥadath*; if the time elapses, their *wuḍū'* becomes invalid and they must renew their *wuḍū'*. A *mustaḥāḍah* does not have to do *ghusl* for every *ṣalāh*, except for the one time when her period or blood flow has ended. She has to do *wuḍū'* for the time of every *ṣalāh*. The Prophet ﷺ said: "Do *wuḍū'* for every *ṣalāh*".[322]

ʿĀ'ishah said: "Fāṭimah bint Abī Ḥubaysh came to the Prophet ﷺ and spoke about what had happened to her. He said: 'Then take a bath and do *wuḍū'* for every *ṣalāh*, and do *ṣalāh*'." [323] Umm Salamah asked the Messenger of Allāh ﷺ about this condition. He said: "She should wait for the days and nights of her normal period and figure them out, and she should leave the *ṣalāh* during those days. Afterwards she should do *ghusl*, tighten something around her private parts and then pray."[324]

Since the *mustaḥāḍah* is pure and can do *ṣalāh*, she may fast, remain in the *masjid*, recite the Qur'ān, touch a copy of the Qur'ān, and so on. She may have relations with her husband even while the blood is flowing. Ibn ʿAbbās said: "Her husband can have relations with her if she can do *ṣalāh*, for *ṣalāh* is greater".[325] ʿIkrimah narrated that Umm Ḥabībah and Ḥamnah bint Jahsh had a prolonged flow of blood and that their husbands had relations with them.[326]

[320] Abū Dāwūd, *k. al-ṭahārah, b. fī al-rajul yuṣību minhā mā dūna al-jimāʿ*.

[321] Ibid.,

[322] al-Bukhārī, *k. al-ḥayḍ, b. ghasl al-dam;* Muslim, *k. al-ḥayḍ, b. al-mustaḥāḍah.*

[323] Abū Dāwūd, *k. al-ṭahārah, b. man qāla taghtasilu min ṭuhr ilā ṭuhr.*

[324] Mālik, *al-Muwaṭṭa'* 36.

[325] al-Bukhārī, *k. al-ḥayḍ, b. idhā ra'at al-mustaḥāḍah al-ṭuhr.*

[326] Abū Dāwūd, *k. al-ṭahārah, b. al-mustaḥāḍah yaghshāhā zawjuhā.*

CHAPTER 5: *TAYAMMUM*

THE LITERAL MEANING of *tayammum* is 'intending'. In the idiom of Islamic law, the word refers to intending or looking to find soil to wipe one's hands and face so as to be prepared for *ṣalāh*, and other acts requiring *wuḍū'* or *ghusl*.

The Qur'ān says: *"And if you are ill, or on a journey, or one of you comes from the privy, or you have been in contact with women, and you do not find water, then take for yourselves clean sand (or soil) and rub your face and hands therewith. Verily Allāh is Benign, Forgiving"*.[327] Abū Dharr reported that the Prophet ﷺ said: "The soil is a purifier for a Muslim, even if he does not find water for ten years".[328] Abū Umāmah related that the Messenger of Allāh ﷺ said: "All of the earth has been made for me and my people a place of *ṣalāh* and purifier. Wherever a person from my nation happens to be at the time of *ṣalāh*, he has his purifier".[329] There is a consensus on the legitimacy of *tayammum*.[330]

BLESSINGS FROM ALLĀH

Tayammum is a blessing from Allāh to the Muslims. Jābir related that the Prophet ﷺ said: "I have been given five things which were not given to anyone else before me: Allāh made me victorious by awe (by Him putting fright in my enemies) for a distance of one month's journey; the whole earth has been made pure and a place of *ṣalāh* for me, therefore anyone of my followers can pray wherever the time of a prayer is due; war booty has been made lawful for me, and this was not lawful for anyone before me; I have been given permission to intercede; and prophets

[327] *al-Nisā'*: 43.

[328] al-Tirmidhī, *k. al-ṭahārah, b. mā jā'a fī al-tayammum li al-junub idhā lam yajid al-mā'*.

[329] Aḥmad, *al-Musnad* 22190

[330] al-Kāsānī, *Badā'iʿ al-ṣanā'iʿ*, i. 308.

used to be raised for their own people only, but I have been raised for all of mankind".[331]

The cause

ʿĀ'ishah said: "We set out with the Messenger of Allāh ﷺ on one of his journeys until when we reached al-Bayḍā' or Dhāt al-Jaysh, a necklace of mine was broken and lost. Allāh's Messenger ﷺ stayed there to search for it, and so did the people along with him. There was no water at that place, so the people went to Abū Bakr al-Ṣiddīq and said: 'Don't you see what ʿĀ'ishah has done? She has made Allāh's Messenger and the people stay where there is no water and they have no water with them'. Abū Bakr came while Allāh's Messenger was sleeping with his head on my thigh; he said to me: 'You have detained Allāh's Messenger and the people where there is no water and they have no water with them.' So he admonished me and said what Allāh wished him to say and hit me on my flank with his hand. Nothing prevented me from moving, because of pain, but the position of Allāh's Messenger ﷺ on my thigh. Allāh's Messenger ﷺ got up when dawn broke and there was no water. So Allāh revealed the verses of *tayammum*. So they all did *tayammum*. Usayd ibn Ḥuḍayr said: 'O family of Abū Bakr, this is not the first blessing of yours'. Then the camel on which I was riding was caused to move from its place and the necklace was found beneath it".[332]

How to do tayammum

First, one must have a clear intention of doing *tayammum* – this is in contrast to *wuḍū'* when intention is a Sunnah but is obligatory (*farḍ*) in *tayammum*. Then, one strikes the ground with one's hands twice, wipes one's face after the first striking, and the hands up to the elbows after the second striking. These are the three *farḍ*s of *tayammum*.

There are six Sunnahs of *tayammum*: 1. to begin it saying the name of Allāh; 2. to follow the sequence; 3. continuation; 4. to move the hands to and fro in or on the soil or ground; 5. to shake one's hands after striking the ground, and 6. to have one's fingers apart when striking the ground or soil.

[331] al-Bukhārī, *k. al-tayammum*.

[332] al-Bukhārī, ibid., Muslim, *k. al-ḥayḍ, b. al-tayammum*.

ʿAbd al-Raḥmān ibn Abzā narrated: "A man came to ʿUmar ibn al-Khaṭṭāb and said: 'I became *junubī* but no water was available'. ʿAmmār ibn Yāsir said to ʿUmar: 'Do you remember that you and I became in a state of *janābah* while we were on a journey and you didn't pray but I rolled myself on the ground and prayed? I informed the Prophet ﷺ about it and he said: "It would have been sufficient for you to do like this". The Prophet ﷺ then stroked lightly the earth with his hands and then blew off the dust and passed his hands over his face and hands'."[333] In Abū Dāwūd's narration the words of the Prophet ﷺ are: "It would have been enough for you to strike the ground with your hands, blow into them, then wipe your face and hands up to the elbows".[334]

Abū Juhaym narrated: "The Messenger of Allāh ﷺ came from fulfilling his need, and I greeted him with *salām*, but he did not return the *salām*; he struck the wall with his hand once and wiped his face; then he struck it a second time and wiped his hands up to the elbows; then he responded to my *salām*".[335]

WHEN *TAYAMMUM* IS ALLOWED

Tayammum is allowed in the following two situations:

When one cannot find water

This concession is permissible for whoever does not find water while on a journey or about a mile or more outside of town. ʿImrān ibn Ḥuṣayn said: "We were with the Messenger of Allāh ﷺ during a journey. He led the people in *ṣalāh*. After he finished *ṣalāh*, he saw a man sitting aloof who had not prayed with the people. He asked: 'O so and so, what has prevented you from praying with us?' He replied; 'I am in the state of *janābah* and there is no water'. The Prophet ﷺ said, 'Do *tayammum* with clean earth and that is sufficient for you'."[336]

[333] al-Bukhārī, *k. al-tayammum, b. al-mutayammim hal yanfukhu fīhimā;* Muslim, *k. al-ḥayḍ, b. al-tayammum.*

[334] Abū Dāwūd, *k. al-ṭahārah, b. al-tayammum.*

[335] Abū Dāwūd, *k. al-ṭahārah, b. al-tayammum fī al-ḥaḍar*; al-Dāraquṭnī, *al-Sunan, i.* 185.

[336] al-Bukhārī, *k. al-tayammum.*

It is reported from Abū Dharr that he said: "I was away from the watering place and I had my family with me. I would be in the state of *janābah* and do *ṣalāh* without purification. I went to the Prophet ﷺ at noon. He was resting in the shade of the *masjid* along with a group of his Companions. I said: 'I am ruined, Messenger of Allāh ﷺ'. He said: 'What ruined you?' I said: 'I was away from the watering place and I had my family with me. I used to be in the state of *janābah* and do *ṣalāh* without purification'. He commanded someone to bring water for me. Then a black slave girl brought a vessel of water that was shaking as the vessel was not full. I concealed myself behind a camel, took a bath, and then came to the Prophet ﷺ. The Messenger of Allāh ﷺ said: 'Abū Dharr, clean earth is a purifier, even if you do not find water for ten years'."[337]

It is recommended that in the case of someone who does not find water at the beginning of a time of *ṣalāh* but who holds out hope of doing so by the end of that time, that he should delay the *ṣalāh* to the latest possible time. If he does find water, he should do *wuḍū'* and then pray; otherwise, he should do *tayammum.*

If a traveller forgets that he has water in his belongings and does *tayammum* and the *ṣalāh,* then remembers the water afterwards, he does not need to repeat the *ṣalāh* according to Abū Ḥanīfah and Muḥammad; however, according to Abū Yūsuf, he should repeat it.

A person considering doing *tayammum* does not have to search for water if he does not think in all likelihood that there is any in the vicinity. However, if he does think that in all likelihood water may be found in the vicinity, then he is not permitted to do *tayammum* until he has searched for it.

If a travelling companion has water, one should request it of him before doing *tayammum.* Only if one's request is refused, should one do *tayammum.*

When one is not able to use water

This concession is also permissible for whoever is not able to use water, even though he has access to water. This includes: a) one who lacks the

[337] Abū Dāwūd, *k. al-ṭahārah, b. al-junub yatayammam.*

proper means to get it, b) or between him and water there is a nearby enemy – beast or human, c) or one is a prisoner under harsh conditions, d) or the quantity of water one has is only enough to meet urgent necessities (for example, drinking, cooking or water for an animal), e) or one is ill and fears that using water will aggravate one's illness, f) or one is in a state of *janābah* and fears one may die from cold or become ill if one makes *ghusl* with water, provided one has no means to heat the water, or is unable to use public bathrooms.

Saʿīd ibn Jubayr narrated from Ibn ʿAbbās saying: "It is allowed for an ill person to do *tayammum* with the soil".[338] Jābir said: "We set out on a journey. One of our people was hurt by a stone, that injured his head. He then had a wet dream. He asked his companions: 'Do you find concession for me to do *tayammum*?' They said: 'We do not find any concession for you while you can use water'. He did *ghusl* and died because of it. When we went to the Prophet ﷺ the incident was reported to him. He said: 'They killed him, may Allāh kill them. Why did they not ask about what they do not know? The cure for ignorance is to ask. It would have been enough for him to do *tayammum* and wrap his wound then to wipe it and wash the rest of the body'."[339]

ʿAmr ibn al-ʿĀṣ said: "I had a wet dream on a cold night in the battle of Dhāt al-Salāsil. I was afraid if I did *ghusl* I would die. I therefore did *tayammum* and led the *Fajr Ṣalāh* with my companions. They mentioned this to the Messenger of Allāh ﷺ. He said: 'ʿAmr, you led your companions in *ṣalāh* while you were in a state of *janābah*?' I informed him of the cause which impeded me from *ghusl*. And I said: 'I heard Allāh say: *"Do not kill yourselves, verily Allāh is merciful to you"* (*al-Nisā'* 29). The Messenger of Allāh ﷺ just smiled and did not say anything'."[340]

Anyone who is in good health and resident in a town is permitted to do *tayammum* if they mean to attend a *Janāzah* (funeral) *Ṣalāh* and are not the *walī* (the guardian who is responsible for leading the *ṣalāh*) and fears that were he to occupy himself doing *wuḍū'* or *ghusl* he would miss the *ṣalāh*. In such a situation he should do *tayammum* and then join

[338] al-Dāraquṭnī, *al-Sunan, i.* 186.

[339] Abū Dāwūd, *k. al-ṭahārah, b. al-majrūḥ yatayammamu.*

[340] Abū Dāwūd, *k. al-ṭahārah, b. idhā khāfa al-junub al-barda ayatayammam.*

the *ṣalāh.* Similarly, if someone means to attend the *ᶜĪd Ṣalāh* and fears that if he were to occupy himself doing *wuḍū'* or *ghusl* he would miss the *ṣalāh,* then he should do *tayammum* and then do the *ṣalāh* with the congregation.

Whoever means to attend the *Jumuᶜah Ṣalāh* and fears that if he were to occupy himself with water purification he would miss the congregation *ṣalāh,* he should nevertheless do *wuḍū'* and not *tayammum.* Then, if he is in time for part of the *Jumuᶜah,* he should join in and complete it. If he is not in time, he should do the *ṣalāh* as for the *Ẓuhr Ṣalāh.*

If time is short, and one fears that by doing *wuḍū'* the time for the *ṣalāh* may pass, one should nevertheless do *wuḍū'* and not *tayammum,* and make up the *ṣalāh* after its due time.

The soil used for tayammum

One is only permitted to do *tayammum* with pure earth. Allāh says: "*Do tayammum with pure ṣaᶜīd (what is on the surface)*".[341] *Ṣa'īd* is understood as meaning whatever covers the earth's surface and is of the same genus as dust, sand, stone, etc. Abū Ḥanīfah and Muḥammad allow *tayammum* with dust (*turāb*), sand, pebbles, lime, kohl antimony, arsenic and stone. However, Abū Yūsuf said that it is only permitted with dust, earth and sand.

What is permissible?

After doing *tayammum,* one is pure and therefore in a position to do the acts that require prior purification, such as doing *ṣalāh, ṭawāf, sajdah* of recitation, touching and reading the Qur'ān. Indeed there is no limit as to how many *ṣalāhs* one is allowed to perform until the *tayammum* is nullified, just like normal *wuḍū'* and *ghusl.* Abū Dharr reported that the Prophet ﷺ said: "The soil is a purifier for a Muslim, even if he does not find water for ten years".[342]

What nullifies tayammum

What nullifies *tayammum* is divided into two types:

[341] *al-Mā'idah* 6.

[342] al-Tirmidhī, *k. al-ṭahārah, b. mā jā'a fī al-tayammum li al-junub idhā lam yajid al-mā'.*

1. General: everything that nullifies *wuḍū'* nullifies *tayammum*. The details of this were given earlier.

2. Specific: accessibility of water, with ability to use it, before beginning or while doing the *ṣalāh* nullifies *tayammum*; in this case, one must do *wuḍū'* with water and then do or resume the *ṣalāh*.

However, once a person with *tayammum* has finished praying, and then finds water, or then becomes able to use water, he is not required to repeat his *ṣalāh* even though there may be time available for him to do so. ᶜImrān ibn Ḥuṣayn said: "We were with the Messenger of Allāh ﷺ during a journey. He led the people in *ṣalāh*. After he finished *ṣalāh*, he saw a man sitting aloof who had not prayed with the people. He asked: 'O so and so, what has prevented you from praying with us?' He replied: 'I am in the state of *janābah* and there is no water'. The Prophet ﷺ said: 'Do *tayammum* with clean earth and that is sufficient for you'." ᶜImrān then mentioned that they later found water. The Prophet ﷺ gave the man water in a container and told him to do *ghusl*.[343] Abū Saᶜīd al-Khudrī said: "Two men went out on a journey. The time of *ṣalāh* came and, as they had no water, they did *tayammum* with pure earth matter, and did *ṣalāh*. Then they found some water during the time of the same *ṣalāh*. One of them repeated his *ṣalāh* with *wuḍū'* and the other did not. When they rejoined the Messenger of Allāh ﷺ, they mentioned this to him. He said to the one who did not repeat his *ṣalāh*: 'You have acted according to the Sunnah and your *ṣalāh* is sufficient for you'. He said to the other: 'You will get a double reward'."[344]

[343] al-Bukhārī, *k. al-tayammum, b. al-ṣaᶜīd al-ṭayyib wuḍū' al-muslim.*

[344] Abū Dāwūd, *k. al-ṭahārah, b. fī al-mutayammim yajid al-mā'a baᶜda mā yuṣallī fī al-waqt.*

كتاب الصلاة

THE BOOK OF *ṢALĀH*

CHAPTER 1: THE IMPORTANCE OF *ṢALĀH*

AFTER CLEANLINESS HAS BEEN ACHIEVED, one should be in a state of remembrance of one's Lord and pray to Him. *Ṣalāh* is the best form of worship that Allāh has provided as a gift to His slaves. In many of its verses, the Qur'ān emphasises the necessity, obligation and virtue of *ṣalāh*. For example: "*Verily ṣalāh is enjoined on the believers at fixed hours*".[345] "*Establish ṣalāh at the two ends of the day and in some hours of the night. Verily, good deeds remove the evil deeds. This is a reminder for the mindful.*"[346] "*Establish ṣalāh from the midday until the dark of the night, and the recital of the Qur'ān at dawn. Verily, the recital of the Qur'ān at dawn is ever witnessed.*"[347] "*Glorify the praises of your Lord before the rising of the sun, and before its setting, and during some hours of the night and at the sides of the day, that you may find acceptance.*"[348] "*Successful indeed are the believers, those who are fearful and humble in their ṣalāh, those who turn away from what is false, and those who pay zakāh. And those who guard their chastity, except from their wives or those that their right hands possess, for they are free from blame. But whoever seeks beyond that then those are the transgressors. Those*

[345] *al-Nisā'* 103
[346] *Hūd* 114
[347] *al-Isrā'* 78
[348] *Ṭā Hā* 130

who are faithfully true to their trusts and covenants. And those who strictly guard their ṣalāhs. These are indeed the inheritors, who shall inherit Paradise. They shall dwell therein forever."[349]

Abū Hurayrah narrated: "I heard the Messenger of Allāh ﷺ saying: 'If there was a river at the door of anyone of you and he took a bath in it five times a day would you notice any dirt on him?' They said: 'Not a trace of dirt would be left'. The Prophet ﷺ added: 'That is the example of the five prayers with which Allāh annuls evil deeds'."[350]

The Prophet ﷺ said: "The head of the matter is Islam; its pillar is the *ṣalāh*; and the top of its hump is *jihād* in the path of Allāh".[351] After death, *ṣalāh* is the first thing for which one is called to account. Abū Hurayrah related that the Messenger of Allāh ﷺ said: "The first act that a slave of Allāh will be accountable for on the Day of Judgement will be *ṣalāh*. If it is good, then the rest of his acts will be good. And if it is evil, then the rest of his acts will be evil".[352] It is one of the last things that the Prophet ﷺ commended his *ummah* to hold firmly to before he died, saying: "*ṣalāh*! *ṣalāh*! and your slaves".[353] *Ṣalāh* will be the last thing taken away from religion. When it perishes, Islam will perish. The Messenger of Allāh ﷺ said: "Islam will be stripped away, piece by piece; when one piece is broken, people will hold tight to the next one. The first thing taken will be judgement, and the last thing will be *ṣalāh*".[354]

The importance of *ṣalāh* is such that people are not allowed to miss it under any circumstances. Furthermore, one is ordered to do it even when travelling, and while in a state of fear: "*Be guardians of your ṣalāhs, especially the middle ṣalāh, and stand up with devotion to Allāh. And if you fear (an enemy), then pray standing or on horseback. When you are safe, remember Allāh, for He taught you that which heretofore you did not know*".[355]

[349] *al-Mu'minūn* 1-11

[350] al-Bukhārī, *k. mawāqīt al-ṣalāh, b. al-ṣalawāt al-khams kaffārah.*

[351] Aḥmad, *al-Musnad;* al-Ṭabarānī as cited in *Majmaᶜ al-zawā'id, k. al-jihād, b. faḍl al-jihād.*

[352] al-Nasā'ī, *k. al-ṣalāh, b. al-muḥāsabah ᶜalā al-ṣalāh.*

[353] al-Ṭabarānī as cited in *Majmaᶜ al-Zawa'id, k. al-ᶜitq, b. al-iḥsān ilā al-mawālī.*

[354] al-Ḥākim, *al-Mustadrak, iv.* 104.

[355] *al-Baqarah* 238-239.

HISTORY

Ṣalāh was the first act of worship to be made obligatory by Allāh. Its sanctioning as obligatory was revealed directly to the Prophet ﷺ during his ascension to heaven.

Abū Dharr narrated: "The Messenger of Allāh ﷺ said: 'While I was at Makkah the roof of my house was opened and Jibrīl descended, opened my chest, and washed it with Zamzam water. Then he brought a golden tray full of wisdom and faith and having poured its contents into my chest, he closed it. Then he took my hand and ascended with me to the nearest heaven; when I reached the nearest heaven, Jibrīl said to the gatekeeper of the heaven: "Open the gate". The gatekeeper asked: "Who is it?" Jibrīl answered: "Jibrīl". He asked: "Is there anyone with you?" Jibrīl replied: "Yes, Muḥammad is with me". He asked: "Has he been called?" Jibrīl said: "Yes". So the gate was opened and we went over the nearest heaven and there we saw a man sitting with some people on his right and some on his left. When he looked towards his right, he laughed and when he looked toward his left he wept. Then he said: "Welcome, O righteous Prophet ﷺ and righteous son". I asked Jibrīl: "Who is he?" He replied: "He is Ādam and the people on his right and left are the souls of his offspring. Those on his right are the people of Paradise and those on his left are the people of Hell and when he looks towards his right he laughs and when he looks towards his left he weeps". Then he ascended with me until he reached the second heaven and he said to its gatekeeper: "Open the gate". The gatekeeper said to him the same as the gatekeeper of the first heaven had said and he opened the gate'." Anas said: "Abū Dharr added that the Prophet ﷺ met Ādam, Idrīs, Mūsā, ʿĪsā and Ibrāhīm. Abū Dharr did not mention on which heaven they were but he mentioned that the Prophet ﷺ met Ādam on the nearest heaven and Ibrāhīm on the sixth heaven". Anas also said: "When Jibrīl along with the Prophet ﷺ passed by Idrīs, the latter said, 'Welcome, O righteous Prophet ﷺ and righteous brother'. The Prophet ﷺ asked, 'Who is he?' Jibrīl replied: 'He is Idrīs'. The Prophet ﷺ added: 'I passed by Mūsā and he said: "Welcome, O righteous Prophet ﷺ and righteous brother". I asked Jibrīl: "Who is he?" Jibrīl replied: "He is Mūsā". Then I passed by ʿĪsā and he said: "Welcome, O righteous brother and righteous Prophet ﷺ". I asked: "Who is he?" Jibrīl replied: "He is ʿĪsā". Then I passed by Ibrāhīm and he said: "Welcome, O righteous

Prophet ﷺ and righteous son". I asked Jibrīl: "Who is he?" Jibrīl replied: "He is Ibrāhīm".' The Prophet ﷺ added: 'Then Jibrīl ascended with me to a place where I heard the creaking of the pens. Then Allāh enjoined fifty prayers on my followers. When I returned with this order of Allāh, I passed by Mūsā who asked me: "What has Allāh enjoined on your followers?" I replied: "He has enjoined fifty prayers on them". Mūsā said: "Go back to your Lord, for your followers will not be able to bear it". So I went back to Allāh and requested a reduction, and He reduced it to half. When I passed by Mūsā again and informed him about it, he said: "Go back to your Lord as your followers will not be able to bear it". So I returned to Allāh and requested a further reduction and half of it was reduced. I again passed by Mūsā and he said to me: "Return to your Lord, for your followers will not be able to bear it". So I returned to Allāh and He said: "These are five prayers and they are all equal to fifty in reward, for My Word does not change". I returned to Mūsā and he told me to go back once again. I replied: "Now I feel shy of asking my Lord again". Then Jibrīl took me until we reached *Sidrat al-Muntahā* (lote-tree) which was shrouded in colours, indescribable. Then I was admitted into Paradise where I found small tents or walls made of pearls and its earth was of musk'."[356]

THOSE ON WHOM *ṢALĀH* IS *FARḌ*

Ṣalāh is obligatory upon Muslims who are sane and have reached puberty. ʿAlī ibn Abī Ṭālib related that the Messenger of Allāh ﷺ said: "The pen is raised for three," meaning that there is no obligation upon three, namely: "the one who is sleeping until he wakens, the child until he becomes an adult and one who is insane until he becomes sane".[357]

Children should be ordered to pray when they are seven, and they should be disciplined if they neglect the prayer after they reach the age of ten. ʿAmr ibn Shuʿayb related from his father on the authority of his grandfather that the Prophet ﷺ said: "Order your children to pray when they reach the age of seven. Punish them if they do not pray when they reach the age of ten. And have them sleep separately".[358]

[356] al-Bukhārī, *k. al-ṣalāh, b. kayfa furiḍat al-ṣalātu fī al-isrā'*.

[357] Abū Dāwūd, *k. al-ḥudūd, b. fī al-majnūn yasriq;* al-Tirmidhī, *k. al-ḥudūd, b. mā jā'a fī man lā yajibu ʿalayh al-ḥadd.*

[358] Abū Dāwūd, *k. al-ṣalāh, b. matā yu'maru al-ghulām bi al-ṣalāh.*

NEGLECTING *ṢALĀH*

If any Muslim denies that *ṣalāh* is obligatory then he becomes an unbeliever, and if, after being urged to repent, he does not do so, he will be executed for apostasy. Jābir reported that the Prophet ﷺ said: "Between a person and unbelief is discarding *ṣalāh*".[359] Buraydah reported that the Prophet ﷺ said: "The covenant between us and them is *ṣalāh*. Whoever abandons it is an unbeliever".[360] ʿAbdullāh ibn ʿAmr ibn al-ʿĀṣ reported that the Prophet ﷺ one day mentioned the *ṣalāh* and said: "Whoever guards his *ṣalāh*, it will be a light and a proof and a saviour for him on the Day of Resurrection. For whoever does not guard it, there will be no light, no proof and no saviour for him. On the Day of Resurrection, he will be with Qārūn, Firʿawn, Hāmān and Ubayy ibn Khalf".[361]

A group of Companions and later scholars believed that an intentional decision to skip one *ṣalāh* until its time was completely finished made one an unbeliever. ʿAbdullāh ibn Shaqīq said: "The Companions of Muḥammad ﷺ did not consider the abandonment of any act, with the exception of *ṣalāh*, as representing unbelief".[362] Those holding this opinion included ʿUmar ibn al-Khaṭṭāb, ʿAbdullāh ibn Masʿūd, Aḥmad ibn Ḥanbal, Isḥāq ibn Rāhwayh, ʿAbdullāh ibn al-Mubārak, Ibrāhīm al-Nakhaʿī and others.[363]

Some *aḥādīth* make it clear that one who wilfully abandons the obligation of *ṣalāh* may be killed. For example, Ibn ʿAbbās reported that the Prophet ﷺ said: "The ties of Islam and the foundations of the religion are three, and whoever leaves one of them becomes an unbeliever, and his blood becomes lawful: testifying that there is no god but Allāh, the obligatory *ṣalāhs*, and the fast of Ramaḍān".[364] This is a clear indication that such a person may be killed. Ibn ʿUmar related that the Messenger of Allāh ﷺ said: "I have been ordered to fight the people until they testify

[359] Muslim, *k. al-īmān, b. bayān iṭlāq al-kufr ʿalā man tarak al-ṣalāh;* Abū Dāwūd, *b. fī radd al-irjāʾ;* al-Tirmidhī, *k. īmān, b. mā jāʾa fī tark al-ṣalāh;* Ibn Mājah, *k. iqāmat al-ṣalāh, b. mā jāʾa fī tark al-ṣalāh.*

[360] al-Nasāʾī, *k. al-ṣalāh, al-ḥukm fī tārik al-ṣalāh.*

[361] Aḥmad, al-Ṭabarānī, Ibn Ḥibbān as cited in *Majmaʿ al-zawāʾid, k. al-ṣalāh, b. farḍ al-ṣalāh.*

[362] al-Tirmidhī, *k. īmān, b. mā jāʾa fī tark al-ṣalāh.*

[363] al-Baghawī, *Sharḥ al-sunnah, k. al-ṣalāh, b. waʿīd tark al-ṣalāh.*

[364] Abū Yaʿlā, *al-Musnad* 2349.

that there is no god but Allāh, and that Muḥammad is the Messenger of Allāh ﷺ, and establish *ṣalāh* and pay the *zakāh*. If they do this, their blood and wealth are protected from me except by the rights of Islam. Their reckoning will be with Allāh".[365]

On the basis of the above mentioned and similar *aḥādīth* some scholars held that such people become evildoers and must repent. If such a person does not repent, the *qāḍī* may sentence him to death – that being the prescribed punishment, according to Imāms Mālik, Ḥammād ibn Zayd and Shāfiʿī.[366]

Abū Ḥanīfah maintains that such people are not to be killed, but must be punished by confinement until they repent and their signs of repentance become evident. Al-Baghawī said: "That is the opinion of Zuhrī and the people of *ra'y*".[367] They say the ḥadīth that calls such people unbelievers refers to those who deny the obligation of *ṣalāh* and of fasting in *Ramaḍān,* etc. They say that any other interpretation is contradicted by other texts. For example, Allāh says: "*Verily, Allāh does not forgive one who associates partners with Him. He forgives whom He pleases in other than that*".[368] Abū Dharr narrated: "Allāh's Messenger ﷺ said: 'Someone came to me from my Lord and gave me the good tidings that if any of my *ummah* dies associating none along with Allāh, he will enter Paradise'. I asked: 'Even if he committed adultery and theft?' He replied: 'Even if he committed adultery and theft'."[369] Muʿādh ibn Jabal narrated that the Messenger of Allāh ﷺ said: "He whose last words are لَا إِلَٰهَ إِلَّا الله shall enter Paradise".[370] Abū Hurayrah related that the Prophet ﷺ said: "Every prophet has a special supplication that is answered. Every prophet hastened to make his supplication, but I reserved mine and will

[365] al-Bukhārī, *k. al-īmān, b. fa in tābū wa aqāmū al-ṣalāta wa ātaw al-zakāta fa khallū sabīlahum.*

[366] al-Baghawī, *Sharḥ al-sunnah, k. al-ṣalāh, b. waʿīd tark al-ṣalāh.*

[367] Ibid.

[368] *al-Nisā'* 116

[369] al-Bukhāri, *k. al-janā'iz, b. fī al-janā'iz wa man kāna ākhiru kalāmihi lā ilāha illā'llāh.*

[370] Abū Dāwūd, *k. al-janā'iz, b. fī al-talqīn.*

use it for my *ummah* on the Day of Resurrection. It will be granted, Allāh willing, to whoever dies without associating anything with Allāh".[371]

The number of farḍ ṣalāhs

The number of *farḍ ṣalāhs* is five. They are: *Fajr* (dawn), *Ẓuhr* (noon); *ᶜAṣr* (afternoon), *Maghrib* (sunset) and *ᶜIshā'* (night). The verses of the Qur'ān indicate this, and since the time of the Prophet ﷺ Muslims have been unanimous about it. A large number of *aḥādīth* emphasise that the number of *farḍ ṣalāhs* is five. I mention here just one of them whereby Ṭalḥah ibn ᶜUbaydullāh narrated: "A Bedouin with scattered hair came to the Messenger of Allāh ﷺ and said: 'O Messenger of Allāh ﷺ, inform me of what Allāh has made obligatory on me as regards *ṣalāhs*?' He replied: 'Five *ṣalāhs*, unless you do others voluntarily'. Then he said: 'Inform me what Allāh has made obligatory on me as regards fasting?' He replied: 'The fast of Ramaḍān, unless you do others voluntarily'. Then he said: 'Inform me what Allāh has made obligatory on me as regards *zakāh*?' Then the Messenger of Allāh ﷺ informed him of all the duties of Islam. The Bedouin then said: 'By the One Who has honoured you, I shall not add anything to it, nor shall I be deficient in what Allāh has made obligatory on me'. The Messenger of Allāh ﷺ then said: 'He will enter Paradise if he is true'."[372]

The number of rakᶜahs

The *farḍ* of *Fajr* comprises two *rakᶜahs*; *Ẓuhr*, four; *ᶜAṣr*, four; *Maghrib*, three and *ᶜIshā'*, four. These numbers are known from what the Prophet ﷺ himself did and have been transmitted to us in many *aḥādīth* by innumerable people in every generation. The Prophet ﷺ said: "Pray as you see me praying".[373]

[371] Muslim, *k. al-īmān, b. ikhtibā' al-nabī ṣallallāhu ᶜalayhi wa sallam daᶜwat al-shafāᶜah li ummatih.*

[372] al-Bukhārī, *k. īmān, b. al-zakāh min al-islām.*

[373] al-Bukhārī, *k. al-adhān, b. man qāla liyu'adhdhin fī al-safar mu'adhdhin wāḥid;* Muslim, *k. al-masājid, b. man aḥaqq bi al-imāmah.*

Chapter 2: The times of the *ṣalāhs*

The five daily *ṣalāh* must be performed at their specific appointed times. In the Qur'ān, Allāh says: "*Verily ṣalāh is enjoined on the believers at fixed hours*".[374] Allāh specifically says regarding the different times of prayer: "*Establish ṣalāh at the two ends of the day and in some hours of the night. Verily, good deeds remove the evil deeds. This is a reminder for the mindful*".[375] "*Establish ṣalāh from the midday till the dark of the night, and the recital of the Qur'ān at dawn. Verily, the recital of the Qur'ān at dawn is ever witnessed*".[376] "*Glorify the praises of your Lord before the rising of the sun, and before its setting, and during some hours of the night and at the sides of the day, that you may find acceptance*".[377]

Ibn Shihāb narrated: "Once ᶜUmar ibn ᶜAbd al-ᶜAzīz delayed *ṣalāh* and ᶜUrwah ibn al-Zubayr went to him and said: 'Once in Iraq, al-Mughīrah ibn Shuᶜbah delayed his *ṣalāh* and Abū Masᶜūd al-Anṣārī went to him and said: "O Mughīrah, what is this? Don't you know that once Jibrīl came and offered the *ṣalāh* (*Fajr Ṣalāh*) and Allāh's Messenger ﷺ prayed too, then he prayed again (*Ẓuhr Ṣalāh*) and so did Allāh's Messenger ﷺ and again he prayed (*ᶜAṣr Ṣalāh*) and Allāh's Messenger ﷺ did the same; again he prayed (*Maghrib Ṣalāh*) and so did Allāh's Messenger ﷺ and again prayed (*ᶜIshā' Ṣalāh*) and so did Allāh's Messenger ﷺ and Jibrīl said: 'I was ordered to do so (to demonstrate the *ṣalāhs* prescribed to you)'."' ᶜUmar ibn ᶜAbd al-ᶜAzīz) said to ᶜUrwah: 'Be sure of what you say. Did Jibrīl lead Allāh's Messenger ﷺ at the stated times of the *ṣalāhs*?' ᶜUrwah replied: 'Bashīr ibn Abī Masᶜūd narrated like this on the authority of his father'."[378]

[374] *al-Nisā'* 103

[375] *Hūd* 114

[376] *al-Isrā'* 78

[377] *Ṭā Hā* 130

[378] Mālik, *al-Muwaṭṭa'* 9; al-Bukhārī, *k. mawāqīt al-ṣalāh, b. mawāqīt al-ṣalāh wa faḍlihā;* Muslim, *k. al-masājid wa mawāḍiᶜ al-ṣalāh, b. awqāt al-ṣalawāt al-khams.*

ᶜAbdullāh ibn ᶜAbbās and Jābir ibn ᶜAbdullāh narrated: "The angel Jibrīl came to the Messenger of Allāh ﷺ and said to him: 'Stand and pray', and he prayed the *Ẓuhr Ṣalāh* when the sun had passed its meridian. He then came to him for the *ᶜAṣr Ṣalāh* and said: 'Stand and pray', and he prayed the *ᶜAṣr Ṣalāh* while the shadow of every thing was like their length. Then he came at sunset and said: 'Stand and pray', and he prayed the *Maghrib Ṣalāh* when the sun had just disappeared. Then he came at night and said, 'Stand and pray', and he prayed the *ᶜIshā' Ṣalāh* after the twilight had disappeared. He came again when dawn broke and he prayed the *Fajr Ṣalāh*. Then Jibrīl came on the next day at noon and said to the Messenger of Allāh ﷺ, 'Stand and pray', and he prayed the *Ẓuhr Ṣalāh* when the shadow of every thing was like their length. Then he came for the *ᶜAṣr Ṣalāh* and said, 'Stand and pray', and he prayed when the shadow of every thing was twice of their length. Then he came at the same time as the previous day for the *Maghrib Ṣalāh*, without any change. Then he came for the *ᶜIshā' Ṣalāh* after half of the night had passed, or one-third of the night, and he prayed *ᶜIshā' Ṣalāh*. Then he came when it became very bright in the early morning and said, 'Stand and pray', and he prayed the *Fajr Ṣalāh*. Then Jibrīl said, 'Between these two times is the time of the *ṣalāh*'."[379]

THE TIME OF THE *FAJR ṢALĀH*

The starting time for the *Fajr Ṣalāh* is when the true dawn breaks, that is, when whiteness marks the horizon; and lasts until sunrise. Anas narrated that: "A man came to the Prophet ﷺ and asked him about the time of the *Fajr Ṣalāh*. The Prophet ﷺ commanded that the *ṣalāh* be established when the dawn broke. Next day, when dawn became clear he commanded that the *ṣalāh* was established. Then he asked: 'Where is the person asking about the time of the *ṣalāh*? The time is between these two'."[380]

It is preferable to pray *Fajr Ṣalāh* when the morning light becomes clear. Rāfiᶜ ibn Khadīj related that the Prophet ﷺ said: "Make the *Fajr Ṣalāh* at the shining of the dawn, as your reward will be greater".[381] This

[379] al-Tirmidhī, *k. al-ṣalāh, b. mā jā'a fī mawāqīt al-ṣalāh.* Al-Bukhārī observed: "It is the most authentic report concerning the *ṣalāh* times".

[380] al-Nasā'ī, *k. al-mawāqīt, b. awwal waqt al-ṣubḥ.*

[381] al-Tirmidhī, *k. al-ṣalāh, b. mā jā'a fī al-isfār bi al-fajr.*

has also been narrated from ʿAlī ibn Abī Ṭālib, ʿAbdullāh ibn Masʿūd, Ḥusayn ibn ʿAlī, Abū al-Dardā', ʿUmar ibn ʿAbd al-ʿAzīz, Zayd ibn Aslam, Muḥammad ibn Sīrīn, ʿAlqamah, Ibrāhīm al-Nakhaʿī, Suwayd ibn Ghafalah, Saʿīd ibn Jubayr and others.[382] Ibrāhīm al-Nakhaʿī said: "The Companions of the Prophet ﷺ have not agreed on anything as they have agreed on praying *Fajr* when it is clear and shining".[383]

THE TIME OF THE *ẒUHR ṢALĀH*

The starting time for *Ẓuhr Ṣalāh* is after the sun has gone past its zenith; its last time, according to Abū Ḥanīfah, is when the shadow of anything becomes twice its length, excluding the amount of shadow when it first begins to lengthen, i.e. when the sun is just past its zenith. Abū Yūsuf and Muḥammad hold that it is when the shadow of anything is equal to its own length.[384] Their evidence is the ḥadīth of Jibrīl cited earlier. What supports Imām Abū Ḥanīfah's opinion is that everybody agrees that the time of *ʿAṣr Ṣalāh* starts when the time of *Ẓuhr Ṣalāh* ends. *ʿAṣr* is the later afternoon prayer according to the verse of the Qur'ān quoted above. When the shadow of a thing is equal only to its own length, it cannot be the later afternoon. In this respect ʿAbdullāh ibn Masʿūd used to delay *ʿAṣr Ṣalāh.*[385] Ḥasan al-Baṣrī, Muḥammad ibn Sīrīn and Abū Qilābah used to pray *ʿAṣr* in the late afternoon or early evening (*masā'*).[386]

Sālim ibn ʿAbdullāh narrated: "My father said: 'I heard Allāh's Messenger saying, "The period of your stay as compared to the previous nations is like the period equal to the time between the *ʿAṣr* Prayer and sunset. The people of the Tawrāh were given the Tawrāh and they acted upon it till midday then they were exhausted and were given one *qīrāṭ*

[382] Ibn Abī Shaybah, *al-Muṣannaf, i.* 283-285.

[383] Ibid. Imām ash-Shāfiʿī and others prefered to pray it during its early time. ʿĀ'ishah narrated: "Believing women would pray the *Fajr Ṣalāh* with the Prophet ﷺ, being enveloped in their clothing. They would return to their homes after the *ṣalāh* and no one could recognise them due to the darkness of the dawn", (Al-Bukhārī, *k. mawāqīt al-ṣalāh, b. waqt al-fajr*).

[384] This is the opinion of most jurists.

[385] ʿAbd al-Razzāq, *al-Muṣannaf,* i. 551.

[386] Ibid.

of gold each. And then the people of the Injīl were given the Injīl and they acted upon it till the *ʿAṣr Ṣalāh* then they were exhausted and were given one *qīrāṭ* each. And then we were given the Qur'ān and we acted upon it till sunset and we were given two *qīrāṭ*s each. On that the people of both the scriptures said, 'O our Lord, You have given them two *qīrāṭs* and given us one *qīrāṭ*, though we have worked more than they'. Allāh said: 'Have I usurped some of your right?' They said: 'No'. Allāh said: 'That is my blessing I bestow upon whomsoever I wish'."'"[387] This ḥadīth indicates that the time between *ʿAṣr* and *Maghrib* is less than the time between *Ẓuhr* and *ʿAṣr.* That is only possible if we take Abū Hanīfah's opinion about the end of the time for *Ẓuhr* into consideration.[388]

If it is hot, it is preferable to delay the *ṣalāh* until it is cooler, so as to retain the humility and awe of the prayer. Otherwise, *Ẓuhr* should be prayed early in its time. Abū Hurayrah narrated: "The Prophet ﷺ said: 'In very hot weather delay the *Ẓuhr* Prayer till it becomes cooler because the severity of the heat is from the raging of Hell-fire'."[389] Zayd ibn Wahb said: "I heard Abū Dharr saying: 'We were with the Prophet ﷺ on a journey. The *mu'adhdhin* stood up to give the *adhān*, the Prophet ﷺ said: "Let it cool down". Then, after a while, the *mu'adhdhin* stood up again to give the *adhān*, the Prophet ﷺ said: "Let it cool down". This happened two or three times, until we saw the shadows of the hills. Then the Prophet ﷺ said: "The extreme heat is from the raging of Hell-fire. If the heat becomes extreme, delay the *ṣalāh* until it becomes cool".'"[390] Imām Muḥammad said: "Delay *Ẓuhr* in the summer until it is cooled, and pray in the winter when the sun declines; this is the opinion of Abū Ḥanīfah".[391]

THE TIME OF THE *ʿAṢR ṢALĀH*

The time of *ʿAṣr* begins when the time of *Ẓuhr* has elapsed, i.e. when the shadow is equal to its own length according to Abū Yūsuf and Muḥammad, or twice its length according to Abū Ḥanīfah; and it lasts

[387] al-Bukhārī, *k. mawāqīt al-ṣalāh, b. man adraka rakʿatan min al-ʿaṣr qabla al-ghurūb.*

[388] Muḥammad, *al-Muwaṭṭa'* (with its commentary *al-Taʿlīq al-mumajjad*), *iii.* 540-4.

[389] al-Bukhārī, *k. mawāqīt al-ṣalāh, b. al-ibrād bi al-ẓuhr fī al-safar.*

[390] Ibid.

[391] Abū Ḥanīfah, *K. al-āthār* 22.

until the sun sets. Abū Hurayrah reported that the Prophet ﷺ said: "Whoever gets one *rakᶜah* of the *ᶜAṣr Ṣalāh* before the sun sets he has got the *ᶜAṣr Ṣalāh*".[392]

The preferred time to pray the *ᶜAṣr Ṣalāh* ends when the sun becomes yellowish on the horizon. To delay the *ṣalāh* until the sun becomes yellowish, although it is permissible, is much disliked, unless there is some need to do so. ᶜAlā' ibn ᶜAbd al-Raḥmān said: "We came to Anas ibn Mālik after *Ẓuhr Ṣalāh*. He stood up for the *ᶜAṣr Ṣalāh*. When he finished his *ṣalāh*, we mentioned to him about doing the *ṣalāh* in its early time, or he himself mentioned it. He said: 'I heard the Prophet ﷺ say: "It is the *ṣalāh* of the hypocrite: he waits until the sun is between the two horns of *Satan*, then he gets up and prays four quick *rakᶜah*s, and he does not remember Allāh therein except a little bit".'"[393]

On a cloudy day, *ᶜAṣr* should be prayed earlier in its time frame. Buraydah al-Aslamī reported: "We were with the Messenger of Allāh ﷺ during a battle and he said: 'Hasten in praying on a cloudy day, for one who misses the *ṣalāh* has destroyed all of his deeds'."[394]

THE TIME OF THE *MAGHRIB ṢALĀH*

The time of the *Maghrib Ṣalāh* begins after the sun has set, and lasts as long as the *shafaq* (i.e. twilight) has not disappeared. Salamah ibn al-Akwaᶜ said: "The Prophet ﷺ used to do the *Maghrib Ṣalāh* immediately after the sun had set when its upper side would disappear".[395] ᶜAbdullāh ibn ᶜAmr reported that the Prophet ﷺ said: "The time for *Maghrib Ṣalāh* is when the sun has disappeared until the *shafaq* has not gone".[396] *Shafaq* is the whiteness that follows the redness on the horizon according to Abū Ḥanīfah, while for Abū Yūsuf and Muḥammad, *shafaq* is the redness. Abū Hurayrah said: "Pray *ᶜIshā'* when the whiteness has disappeared

[392] al-Bukhārī, *k. mawāqīt al-ṣalāh, b. man adraka rakᶜatan min al-ᶜaṣr qabla al-ghurūb;* Muslim, *k. al-masājid, man adraka rakᶜatan min al-ṣalāh faqad adraka tilka al-ṣalāh.*

[393] Muslim, *k. al-masājid wa mawāḍiᶜ al-ṣalāh, b. istiḥbāb al-tabkīr bi al-ᶜaṣr;* Abū Dāwūd, *k. al-ṣalāh, b. fī waqt ṣalāt al-ᶜaṣr.*

[394] Ibn Mājah, *k. al-ṣalāh, b. mīqāt al-ṣalāh fī al-ghaym.*

[395] Abū Dāwūd, *k. al-ṣalāh, b. fī waqt al-maghrib.*

[396] Muslim, *k. al-masājid, b. awqāt al-ṣalawāt al-khams.*

from the horizon".[397] ʿUmar ibn ʿAbd al-ʿAzīz said: "Do not pray *ʿIshā'* until the whiteness has disappeared from the horizon".[398]

It is preferable to pray *Maghrib* early in its time duration. ʿAbbās ibn ʿAbd al-Muṭṭalib related that the Messenger of Allāh ﷺ said: "My nation will always be along the natural path as long as they do not delay the *Maghrib Ṣalāh* until the stars appear".[399] It is related from Rāfiʿ ibn Khadīj that: "We used to pray the *Maghrib Ṣalāh* with the Messenger of Allāh ﷺ, and one of us would leave afterwards and would still be able to see where he shot his arrow".[400] Imām Muḥammad said: "We do not like to delay *Maghrib* when the sun has set, and this is the opinion of Abū Ḥanīfah".[401]

THE TIME OF THE *ʿISHĀ' ṢALĀH*

The time for *ʿIshā' Ṣalāh* begins when the *shafaq* has disappeared and it lasts until the time of the *Fajr Ṣalāh*. ʿĀ'ishah reported: "One night the Prophet ﷺ prayed the *ʿIshā' Ṣalāh* after most of the night had gone and most of the people in the *masjid* had fallen asleep. Then he came out, prayed, and said: 'This would be the proper time if it were not a hardship on my nation'."[402] ʿAbdullāh ibn ʿAbbās said: "Between every two *ṣalāhs* there is time".[403] He also said: "No *ṣalāh* is missed until the *adhān* of the other *ṣalāh* is said".[404] Abū Hurayrah was asked what constitutes missing a *ṣalāh*. He said: "That you delay it until the time of the one after it enters".[405]

The preferred time of *ʿIshā'* is up to a third of the night. ʿĀ'ishah said: "They used to pray the *ʿIshā' Ṣalāh* between the disappearance of the *shafaq* and the final third of the night's beginning".[406] Abū Hurayrah

[397] Ibn Abī Shaybah, *al-Muṣannaf*, ii. 264.
[398] Ibid.
[399] Ibn Mājah, *k. al-ṣalāh, b. waqt ṣalāt al-maghrib.*
[400] Muslim, *k. al-masājid, b. bayān awwal waqt al-maghrib ʿinda ghurūb al-shams.*
[401] Abū Ḥanīfah, *K. al-āthār* 222.
[402] Muslim, *k. al-masājid wa mawāḍiʿ al-ṣalāh, b. waqt al-ʿishā' wa ta'khīrihā.*
[403] Ibn Abī Shaybah, *al-Muṣannaf, i.* 294.
[404] Ibid.
[405] Ibid.
[406] al-Bukhārī, *b. khurūj al-nisā' ilā al-masājid bi al-layl wa al-ghalas.*

reported that the Messenger of Allāh ﷺ said: "If it were not to be a hardship upon my *ummah*, I would order them to delay the *ʿIshā' Ṣalāh* until a third or a half of the night had passed".[407] Abū Naḍrah reported from Abū Saʿīd al-Khudrī saying: "Once, we waited for the Messenger of Allāh ﷺ to lead the *ʿIshā' Ṣalāh* until half the night had passed, at which time he came and prayed with us. He said: 'Stay in your places of sitting'. We stayed in our sitting positions, then he said: 'While the people have gone to their places of lying down for sleep, you are in *ṣalāh* and this for as long as you are waiting for the *ṣalāh*. If it were not for the weakness of the weak and the illness of the ill, I would have delayed the time of this *ṣalāh* to a half of the night'."[408]

SLEEPING BEFORE *ʿISHĀ'*

Sleeping before the *ʿIshā' Ṣalāh* is disapproved of, so also is talking after it. Abū Barzah al-Aslamī reported: "The Prophet ﷺ disliked sleeping before *ʿIshā'* and talking after it".[409] Ibn Masʿūd reported: "The Messenger of Allāh ﷺ ordered us not to talk after the *ʿIshā' Ṣalāh*".[410] Abū Ḥanīfah narrated from Ismāʿīl ibn ʿAbd al-Malik: "I asked Mujāhid about sleeping before the *ʿIshā' Ṣalāh*. He said: 'It is better to me to pray it alone than to sleep before it then pray in congregation'." Imām Muḥammad said: "We dislike the sleep before *ʿIshā' Ṣalāh* and this is the opinion of Abū Ḥanīfah".[411]

However, it is allowed to have useful conversation, if one is sure that one will not miss the morning *ṣalāh*. ʿAbdullāh ibn ʿAbbās reported: "I slept in the home of Maymūnah one night when the Prophet ﷺ was there. I watched to see how the Prophet ﷺ prayed during the night. He talked with his wife for a while and then slept".[412] ʿUmar said: "The Prophet ﷺ would discuss with Abū Bakr some of the affairs of the Muslims during the night, and I would be with them".[413]

[407] al-Tirmidhī, *k. al-ṣalāh, b. mā jā'a fī ta'khīr ṣalāt al-ʿishā' al-ākhirah.*

[408] Abū Dāwūd, *k. al-ṣalāh, b. waqt al-ʿishā' al-ākhirah.*

[409] al-Bukhārī, *k. mawāqīt al-ṣalāh, b. mā yukrahu min al-nawm qabla al-ʿishā'.*

[410] Ibn Mājah, *k. al-ṣalāh, b. al-nahy ʿan al-nawm qabla ṣalāt al-ʿishā' wa ʿan al-ḥadīth baʿdahā.*

[411] Abū Ḥanīfah, *K. al-āthār* 44.

[412] al-Bukhārī, *k. al-wuḍū', b. qirā'at al-qur'ān baʿda al-ḥadath wa ghayrihi;* Muslim, *k. ṣalāt al-musāfirīn wa qaṣrihā, b. al-duʿā' fī ṣalāt al-layl wa qiyāmihi.*

[413] al-Tirmidhī, *k. al-ṣalāh, b. mā jā'a fī al-rukhṣah fī al-samar baʿda al-ʿishā'.*

PROHIBITED TIMES

It is not permitted to do *ṣalāh* while the sun is rising, nor at midday, nor at sunset; nor should the Funeral *Ṣalāh* or *sajdah* for recitation be made at these times. The one exception is *ʿAṣr* of the same day, which may be made until the setting of the sun. ʿUqbah ibn ʿĀmir al-Juhanī said: "There are three times during which the Prophet ﷺ prohibited us from praying or burying our deceased: sunrise until the sun has risen, when the sun is at its meridian, and when the sun is setting until it has set".[414]

To do *nafl ṣalāh* after the *Fajr Ṣalāh* until the sun has risen, or after the *ʿAṣr Ṣalāh* until after the sun has set is disliked. There is no harm in making up missed *ṣalāhs* between these two times, making the *sajdah* for recitation and doing the *Janāzah Ṣalāh*, but one should not make the two *rakʿahs* of *ṭawāf*. To pray *nafl* after the dawn breaks, that is, more than the two Sunnah *rakʿahs* of *Fajr*, is also disliked.

Abū Saʿīd reported that the Prophet ﷺ said: "There is no *ṣalāh* after the *Fajr Ṣalāh* until the sun rises".[415] ʿAmr ibn ʿAbasah said: "I asked: 'O Prophet ﷺ of Allāh, inform me about the *ṣalāh*'. He said: 'Pray the *Fajr Ṣalāh* and then abstain from *ṣalāh* until sunrise and the sun has completely risen, for it rises between the two horns of *Satan*. That is when the unbelievers prostrate to it. Then pray, as your *ṣalāh* will be witnessed and attended to, until the shadow of a spear is confined to it. At that time stop praying, for at that time hell-fire is fed with fuel. When the shade comes, you may pray, for your *ṣalāh* will be witnessed and attended to by angels until you pray the *ʿAṣr ṣalāh*. Then abstain from praying until the sun sets, for it sets between the two horns of *Satan*, and that is when the unbelievers prostrate to it'."[416]

Abū Ḥanīfah narrated that ʿUmar ibn al-Khaṭṭāb used to strike people if they prayed after *ʿAṣr*. Imām Muḥammad said about this: "We adhere to it. We do not see that anyone prays *nafl* after *ʿAṣr* under any circumstances. This is the opinion of Abū Ḥanīfah".[417]

[414] Muslim, *k. ṣalāt al-musāfirīn wa qaṣrihā, b. al-awqāt allatī nuhiya ʿan al-ṣalāh fīhā.*
[415] al-Bukhārī, *k. mawāqīt al-ṣalāh, b. lā yataḥarrā al-ṣalāh qabla ghurūb al-shams.*
[416] Muslim, *k. ṣalāt al-musāfirīn wa qaṣrihā, b. islām ʿAmr ibn ʿAbasah.*
[417] Abū Ḥanīfah, *K. al-āthār* 41.

Ibrāhīm al-Nakhaʿī said: "To me the *ṣalāh* of a person when the sun becomes red is not worth two pence". Imām Muḥammad said after quoting Imām al-Nakhaʿī's opinion: "The *ṣalāh* is disliked at that time, except if the *ʿAṣr* of that day is missed by someone and then he should pray at that time. It is not appropriate for him to pray any *farḍ* or *nafl ṣalāh*. This is the opinion of Abū Ḥanīfah".[418]

DOING *QAḌĀ'* FOR MISSED *ṢALĀHS*

It is obligatory to make up any missed *ṣalāh*, whether it is missed knowingly or forgetfully or because of sleep. Missing a *ṣalāh* knowingly is a major sin and one should repent as soon as possible. Abū Qatādah narrated that the Prophet ﷺ said: "There is no negligence while one is asleep but negligence occurs when one is awake. If one of you forgets the *ṣalāh* or sleeps through its time, then he should do the *ṣalāh* when he recalls it".[419]

If one misses a certain *ṣalāh* unintentionally because of sleep or forgetfulness, one should pray it as soon as one wakes or remembers the *ṣalāh*. Anas ibn Mālik narrated that the Prophet ﷺ said: "Whoever forgets a *ṣalāh* should pray it when he remembers it, and there is no expiation for it other than that".[420]

Abū Hurayrah reported: "When the Messenger of Allāh ﷺ returned from the Battle of Khaybar, he travelled during the night. When we felt sleepy, he halted for rest. Addressing Bilāl he said: 'Keep vigilance at night for us'. But Bilāl, who was leaning against the saddle of his mount, was overcome by sleep. Neither the Prophet ﷺ nor Bilāl, nor any of his Companions could get up till the sunshine struck them. The Messenger of Allāh ﷺ got up first of all. The Messenger of Allāh ﷺ was frightened and said: 'O Bilāl!'. He replied: 'He who detained your soul, detained my soul, Messenger of Allāh ﷺ, my parents be sacrificed for you'. Then they drove their mounts to a little distance. The Prophet ﷺ did *wuḍū'* and commanded Bilāl who made the *adhān* for the *ṣalāh*. He led them in the *Fajr Ṣalāh*. When he finished the *ṣalāh*, he said: 'If anyone forgets

[418] Ibid.

[419] al-Tirmidhī, *k. al-ṣalāh, b. mā jā'a fī al-nawm ʿan al-ṣalāh.*

[420] al-Bukhārī, *k. mawāqīt al-ṣalāh, b. man nasiya ṣalātan falyuṣallihā idhā dhakarah.*

praying the *ṣalāh*, he should do it when he recalls it, for Allāh has said: "*Establish prayer for My remembrance*".'"[421]

One should also consider the order in making up missed *ṣalāhs* as long as the missed *ṣalāhs* are five or less. Ibrāhīm al-Nakhaʿī said about someone praying *ʿAṣr*, who then remembers while he is still in the *ṣalāh* that he has not prayed *Ẓuhr:* "This *ṣalāh* is invalid. He is to start *Ẓuhr*, then pray *ʿAṣr*". Imām Muḥammad said: "We adhere to this except in one thing, namely if he fears that he will miss *ʿAṣr* if he starts *Ẓuhr*. In that case, he should do *ʿAṣr*, then pray *Ẓuhr* when the sun has set. And this is the opinion of Abū Ḥanīfah".[422]

[421] Abū Dāwūd, *k. al-ṣalāh, b. man nāma ʿan ṣalāh aw nasiyahā*.

[422] Abū Ḥanīfah, *K. al-āthār* 43.

CHAPTER 3: THE *ADHĀN*

THE *ADHĀN* IS A CALL IN SPECIFIC WORDS to inform others that the time for a *farḍ ṣalāh* has begun. The *adhān* is a *mu'akkad* Sunnah, i.e. something on which particular emphasis is placed for the five *ṣalāhs* and the *Jumuᶜah*, but for no other *ṣalāh*.

THE HISTORY

The five daily prayers were made compulsory in Makkah, but there was no *adhān* at that time; the *adhān* was instituted during the first year after hijrah. Nāfiᶜ related that ᶜAbdullāh ibn ᶜUmar said: "When the Muslims arrived at Madīnah, they used to assemble for *ṣalāh*, and used to guess the time for it. During those days, the practice of *adhān* for the prayers had not yet been introduced. Once they discussed this problem regarding the call for prayer. Some people suggested the use of a bell like the Christians, others proposed a trumpet like the horn used by the Jews, but ᶜUmar was the first to suggest that a man should call for *ṣalāh*; so Allāh's Messenger ﷺ ordered Bilāl to get up and pronounce the *adhān* for *ṣalāhs*".[423]

ᶜAbdullāh ibn Zayd ibn ᶜAbd Rabbih reported: "When the Messenger of Allāh ﷺ ordered the use of a bell to gather people for *ṣalāh,* in my sleep a man came to me carrying a bell. I said to him: 'O slave of Allāh, will you sell me that bell?' He said: 'What would you do with it?' I replied: 'We shall use it to call the people to *ṣalāh*'. He said: 'Shall I not guide you to something better than that?' I said: 'Certainly'. He said: 'You should say:

اَللهُ أَكْبَر، اَللهُ أَكْبَر، اَللهُ أَكْبَر، اَللهُ أَكْبَر، أَشْهَدُ أَنْ لَا إِلَهَ إِلَّا الله، أَشْهَدُ أَنْ لَا إِلَهَ إِلَّا الله، أَشْهَدُ أَنَّ مُحَمَّدًا رَسُولُ الله، أَشْهَدُ أَنَّ مُحَمَّدًا رَسُولُ الله، حَيَّ عَلَى الصَّلَاة، حَيَّ عَلَى الصَّلَاة، حَيَّ عَلَى الْفَلَاح، حَيَّ عَلَى الْفَلَاح، اَللهُ أَكْبَرُ، اَللهُ أَكْبَرُ، لَا إِلَهَ إِلَّا الله.

[423] al-Bukhārī, *k. al-adhān, b. bad' al-adhān.*

"Allāh is Most Great, Allāh is Most Great, Allāh is Most Great, Allāh is Most Great. I bear witness that there is no god but Allāh, I bear witness that there is no god but Allāh. I bear witness that Muḥammad is the Messenger of Allāh ﷺ, I bear witness that Muḥammad is the Messenger of Allāh ﷺ. Come to *ṣalāh*, come to *ṣalāh*, come to success, come to success. Allāh is Most Great, Allāh is Most Great. There is no god but Allāh".'

"When the morning came, I went to the Messenger of Allāh ﷺ to tell him what I had seen. He said: 'Your dream is true, Allāh willing. Go to Bilāl, tell him what you have seen, and tell him to make the call to *ṣalāh*, for he has the best voice among you'. I went to Bilāl and told him what to do, and he made the call to *ṣalāh*. ᶜUmar was in his house when he heard it. He came out with his cloak, and said: 'By the One Who has raised you with the truth, I saw similar to what he saw'. The Prophet ﷺ said: 'Praise and thanks are due to Allāh'."[424]

IMPORTANCE

Shāh Walīullāh al-Dihlawī stated: "Allāh, in His Infinite Wisdom, wanted the *adhān* not to be a mere proclamation and warning but also to form a part of the fundamental practice of Islam and that its position in respect of the negligent should not only be that of an alarm or signal but also that it should be regarded as a symbol of loyalty and devotion. It was necessary that it should include the name of Allāh as well as the two affirmations and the call to *ṣalāh* so that the objects specified above may be served".[425]

VIRTUE

Calling the *adhān* has great virtue. According to some scholars, it is even better than leading the *ṣalāh*. There are a number of *aḥādīth* which describe the virtues of the *adhān* and the one who calls it. Among them are the following: Muᶜāwiyah reported that the Prophet ﷺ said: "The callers to *ṣalāh* will have the longest necks of all people on the Day of Resurrection".[426] Abū Hurayrah reported that the Prophet ﷺ said: "If the

[424] Abū Dāwūd, *k. al-ṣalāh, b. kayfa al-adhān.*

[425] Walīullāh Dihlawī, *Ḥujjatullāh al-bālighah, i.* 593.

[426] Muslim, *k. al-ṣalāh, b. faḍl al-adhān wa harab al-shaytan ᶜinda samᶜih.*

people knew the reward for pronouncing the *adhān* and for standing in the first row of the *ṣalāh*, and found no other way to get that except by drawing lots, they would draw lots. If they knew the reward for praying the *Ẓuhr Ṣalāh* early in its time, they would race to it. And if they knew the reward for the ʿ*Ishā'* and the *Fajr Ṣalāhs* in congregation, they would come to them even if they had to crawl".[427]

Abū Hurayrah reported that the Prophet ﷺ said: "The *mu'adhdhin* is forgiven for as far as his voice reaches and whoever hears him will confirm what he said".[428] Ibn Abī Shaybah narrated that ʿAbdullāh ibn ʿUmar said about someone who said the *adhān*: "How good is your work; everything that hears you, will bear witness for you".[429]

DESCRIPTION

How to say the *adhān* has been described in the above mentioned ḥadīth of ʿAbdullāh ibn Zayd. That is to say four *takbirs* at the beginning of the *adhān* and to say each of the other phrases twice, except for the final utterance of لا إله إلا الله, which is said only once; and there is no repetition of the first bearing witness *tarjī*ʿ. In this way, the *adhān* is made up of fifteen phrases.

After حَيَّ عَلَى الْفَلَاحِ, the phrase اَلصَّلَاةُ خَيْرٌ مِنَ النَّوْمِ, '*ṣalāh* is better than sleep' is added twice in the *adhān* before *Fajr*. It is not, however, to be said in any other *adhān*. Abū Maḥdhūrah asked the Prophet ﷺ to teach him the *adhān*, and he told him: "If it is the *Fajr adhān*, say: اَلصَّلَاةُ خَيْرٌ مِنَ النَّوْمِ اَلصَّلَاةُ خَيْرٌ مِنَ النَّوْمِ '*ṣalāh* is better than sleep'."[430] Zayd ibn Aslam reported that Bilāl came to the Prophet ﷺ informing him of *ṣalāh*. On finding him asleep, Bilāl said: اَلصَّلَاةُ خَيْرٌ مِنَ النَّوْمِ، اَلصَّلَاةُ خَيْرٌ مِنَ النَّوْمِ. The Prophet ﷺ said: "How good this is, make it a part of your *adhān*".[431] ʿAbd al-Raḥmān ibn Abī Laylā narrated from Bilāl saying that the Messenger of Allāh ﷺ said to him to say that in the *Fajr adhān* only.[432] Nāfiʿ narrated that ʿAbdullāh ibn ʿUmar used to say: حَيَّ عَلَى الْفَلَاحِ, then اَلصَّلَاةُ خَيْرٌ مِنَ النَّوْمِ، اَلصَّلَاةُ خَيْرٌ مِنَ النَّوْمِ.[433]

[427] al-Nasā'ī, *k. al-adhān, al-istihām ʿalā al-ta'dhīn.*

[428] Abū Dāwūd, *k. al-ṣalāh, b. rafʿ al-ṣawt bi al-adhān.*

[429] Ibn Abī Shaybah, *al-Muṣannaf*, i. 205.

[430] Abū Dāwūd, *k. al-ṣalāh, b. kayfa al-adhān.*

[431] al-Ṭabarānī, *al-Muʿjam al-kabīr* 1081.

[432] al-Tirmidhī, *abwāb al-ṣalāh, b. mā jā'a fī al-tathwīb fī al-fajr.*

[433] ʿAbd al-Razzāq, *al-Muṣannaf*, i. 473.

THE *IQĀMAH*

The *iqāmah* is like the *adhān* except one adds after حَيَّ عَلَى الْفَلَاحِ the phrase قَدْ قَامَتِ الصَّلَاة (*ṣalāh* is established) saying it twice. In this way, the *iqāmah* is made up of seventeen phrases. ʿAbdullāh ibn Zayd and Abū Maḥdhūrah both narrated this from the Prophet ﷺ.[434]

SUNNAHS OF THE *ADHĀN*

The Sunnahs of the *adhān* are of two types: those related to the *adhān*, and those related to the *mu'adhdhin*. Both types of Sunnahs are mentioned below:

Sunnahs related to the adhān

Raising one's voice

The *mu'adhdhin* should make his voice loud for the *adhān*, because the purpose of the *adhān* is attained by that. It was earlier stated in the ḥadīth of ʿAbdullāh ibn Zayd that the Prophet ﷺ said to him: "Go to Bilāl, tell him what you have seen, and tell him to make the call to *ṣalāh*, for he has the best voice among you".[435] ʿAbdullāh ibn ʿAbd al-Raḥmān related from his father that Abū Saʿīd al-Khudrī said to him: "I see that you love the sheep and the desert. If you are with your sheep or in the desert, then raise your voice while making the call to *ṣalāh*, for any *jinn*, human or thing that hears the voice of the *mu'adhdhin* will be a witness for him on the Day of Resurrection. I heard the Messenger of Allāh ﷺ say this".[436]

To sing the *adhān* or to mispronounce its words is disliked. ʿUmar ibn ʿAbd al-ʿAzīz heard someone singing in his *adhān*, so he said to him: "Say it in the normal way, otherwise leave us".[437] Yaḥyā al-Bakkā' reported: "I saw Ibn ʿUmar say to a man, 'I hate you for the sake of Allāh, because you beautify your voice to get money'."[438]

[434] al-Tirmidhī, *k. al-ṣalāh, b. mā jā'a anna al-iqāmata mathnā mathnā.*

[435] Abū Dāwūd, *k. al-ṣalāh, b. kayfa al-adhān.*

[436] al-Bukhārī, *k. al-adhān, b. rafʿ al-ṣawt bi al-nidā'.*

[437] Ibn Abī Shaybah, *al-Muṣannaf, i.* 207.

[438] Ibid.

Pausing between the phrases

The caller should pause between each of the phrases while calling the *adhān,* however he should be quicker while saying the *iqāmah.* The Prophet ﷺ said to Bilāl: "When you say the *adhān* then pause, and when you say the *iqāmah* then be quick".[439] Abū al-Zubayr, the *mu'adhdhin* of Bayt al-Maqdis, said: "ʿUmar ibn al-Khaṭṭāb came to us and said, 'When you say the *adhān* then pause, and when you say the *iqāmah* then be quick'."[440] Ibrāhīm al-Nakhaʿī said: "In the *adhān* one should pause, and in the *iqāmah* each phrase should be followed by the next without pause".[441]

Facing the qiblah

It is Sunnah to stand and face the *qiblah* in both the *adhān* and *iqāmah.* If one turns away from the *qiblah,* one's *adhān* will be valid, but the action is disliked. Ibn Sīrīn said: "When the *mu'adhdhin* says the *adhān* he should face the *qiblah*".[442] Ḥasan al-Baṣrī said: "The *mu'adhdhin* will face the *qiblah*".[443] Ibrāhīm al-Nakhaʿī said: "The *mu'adhdhin* should face the *qiblah* in the *adhān* and the *iqāmah*."[444] The same has been narrated from ʿAṭā' ibn Abī Rabāḥ and Ibn Sīrīn.[445]

If there is sufficient reason for it, then one may say the *adhān* without facing the *qiblah,* for example if one is travelling on a plane or train, or the like.[446] Ḥasan al-Baṣrī narrated that: "While travelling, the Prophet ﷺ asked Bilāl to do the *adhān,* and he did so while riding his camel".[447] ʿAbdullāh ibn ʿUmar used to say the *adhān* while riding his camel.[448] ʿAṭā' ibn Abī Rabāḥ said: "It is not liked if the *adhān* is said whilst sitting, except if there is a reason".[449]

[439] al-Tirmidhī, *k. al-ṣalāh, b. mā ja'a fī al-adhān.*

[440] Ibn Abī Shaybah, *al-Muṣannaf, i.* 195.

[441] Ibid.

[442] Ibid., *i.* 190.

[443] Ibid.

[444] Ibid.

[445] ʿAbd al-Razzāq, *al-Muṣannaf, i. 466-7.*

[446] *See:* al-Samarqandī, *Tuḥfat al-fuqahā'* 58.

[447] al-Bayhaqī, *al-Sunan al-kubrā, k. al-ṣalāh, b. al-adhān rākiban wa jālisan.*

[448] Ibn Abī Shaybah, *al-Muṣannaf, i.* 193.

[449] Ibid.

Turning right and left
The *mu'adhdhin* faces the *qiblah*, but on saying حَيَّ عَلَى الصَّلاَة he turns his face to the right, and on saying حَيَّ عَلَى الْفَلاَح he turns his face to the left, without moving his feet from the direction of the *qiblah*. Abū Juḥayfah narrated: "Bilāl said the *adhān*, and I saw the movement of his head from this side to that side upon saying حَيَّ عَلَى الصَّلاَة and حَيَّ عَلَى الْفَلاَح".[450] Ḥasan al-Baṣrī and Ibrāhīm al-Nakhaᶜī said: "The *mu'adhdhin* should not move his feet".[451] Ibn Sīrīn said: "The *mu'adhdhin* will turn upon saying حَيَّ عَلَى الصَّلاَة and then he will face the *qiblah* upon saying: اَللّٰهُ أَكْبَرُ، اَللّٰهُ أَكْبَرُ، لاَ إِلٰهَ إِلاَّ اللّٰهُ.[452]

Sunnahs related to the mu'adhdhin
The person designated to call people to the *ṣalāh* is the *mu'adhdhin* (muezzin). If someone other than the *mu'adhdhin* wants to make the *adhān*, he should get the latter's permission. If the *mu'adhdhin* is late and people fear that they will miss the time of the *adhān*, someone else should make the *adhān*.

Mu'adhdhin should be male
The *mu'adhdhin* should be male. All scholars agree that it is disliked for women to make the *adhān* or the *iqāmah* whether they are praying in congregation or individually.[453] ᶜAlī ibn Abī Ṭālib said: "The woman will say neither the *adhān* nor the *iqāmah*".[454] ᶜAṭā' ibn Abī Rabāḥ, Saᶜīd ibn al-Musayyab, Ḥasan al-Baṣrī, Muḥammad ibn Sīrīn, Jābir ibn Zayd, Zuhrī and others also hold the view that there is no obligation on women regarding the *adhān* and *iqāmah*.[455] Ibrāhīm al-Nakhaᶜī said: "There is no *adhān* or *iqāmah for* women". Imām Muḥammad said: "This is the opinion of Abū Ḥanīfah and we adhere to it".[456]

[450] al-Bukhārī, *k. al-adhān, b. hal yatatabbaᶜu al-mu'adhdhin fāhu hāhunā hāhunā;* Abū Dāwūd, *k. al-ṣalāh, b. fī al-mu'adhdhin yastadīru fī adhānih.*
[451] Ibn Abī Shaybah, *al-Muṣannaf, i.* 190.
[452] ᶜAbd al-Razzāq, *al-Muṣannaf, i. 467.*
[453] al-Kāsānī, *Badā'iᶜ al-ṣanā'iᶜ*, *i.* 645.
[454] Ibn Abī Shaybah, *al-Muṣannaf, i.* 202.
[455] Ibid.
[456] Abū Ḥanīfah, *K. al-āthār* 21.

Placing one's fingers in one's ears

Describing Bilāl's *adhān,* Abū Juḥayfah said: "He put his index fingers into his ears". Al-Tirmidhī said: "Scholars prefer callers to put their index fingers into their ears while saying the *adhān*".[457] Suwayd ibn Ghafalah said: "Bilāl and Abū Maḥdhūrah put their fingers in their ears during the *adhān*".[458] Ibn Sīrīn said: "When the *mu'adhdhin* says the *adhān* he should face the *qiblah* and put his fingers in his ears".[459] The reason for putting the index fingers in the ears is that blocking the ears in this way makes it easier for the caller to make his voice louder.

Purification

It is recommended that one says the *adhān* with *wuḍū'*. Al-Muhājir ibn Qunfudh reported that the Prophet ﷺ said to him: "Nothing prevented me from returning your salutations except that I dislike mentioning the name of Allāh when I am not clean".[460] Abū Hurayrah narrated that the Prophet ﷺ said: "The *adhān* should only be said by someone who has *wuḍū'*".[461] However, it is permissible to say the *adhān* without *wuḍū'*, but it is disliked for the *adhān* to be called in a state of *janābah.* Ibrāhīm al-Nakhaʿī said: "There is no harm in saying the *adhān* without *wuḍū'*". Imām Muḥammad said: "This is what we adhere to, we do not see any harm in it, but we dislike saying the *adhān* in a state of *janābah,* and this is also the opinion of Abū Ḥanīfah".[462]

Time

The *adhān* is to be made at the time of the *ṣalāh*; if, in error, it is said before the time, it should be repeated.[463] Enough time should be left between the *adhān* and *iqāmah* for people to prepare themselves for the *ṣalāh* and get to the *masjid,* except for the *Maghrib Ṣalāh,* which should

[457] al-Tirmidhī, *k. al-ṣalāh, b. mā jā'a fī idkhāl al-iṣbuʿ fī al-udhun ʿinda al-adhān,*

[458] ʿAbd al-Razzāq, *al-Muṣannaf, i. 468.*

[459] Ibn Abī Shaybah, *al-Muṣannaf, i.* 191.

[460] Abū Dāwūd, *k. al-ṭahārah, b. ayaruddu al-salāma wa huwa yabūlu.*

[461] al-Tirmidhī, *k. al-ṣalāh, b. mā jā'a fī karāhiyat al-adhān bi ghayr wuḍū'.*

[462] Abū Ḥanīfah, *K. al-āthār* 20.

[463] al-Samarqandī, *Tuḥfat al-fuqahā'* 60.

be established immediately after the *adhān*. Jābir ibn Samurah said: "The Prophet's ﷺ *mu'adhdhin* would make the *adhān* and then leave some time, doing the *iqāmah* only when they saw the Prophet ﷺ coming to the place of *ṣalāh*".[464]

Whoever calls the adhān should call the iqāmah

Normally, whoever calls the *adhān* should call the *iqāmah,* because the one who calls to the *ṣalāh* takes precedence in announcing the *iqāmah.* Al-Tirmidhī said: "The practice of most scholars is that whoever says the *adhān* says the *iqāmah*".[465] It is disliked for someone else to say the *iqāmah,* if the *mu'adhdhin* is offended. However if the *mu'adhdhin* is not offended, then there is no harm if someone else says the *iqāmah.*[466]

The adhān should be for Allāh's pleasure

The *mu'adhdhin* should say the *adhān* for the pleasure of Allāh's only and should not take any wages.[467] It is reported that ᶜUthmān ibn Abī al-ᶜĀṣ said: "Among the last things that the Messenger of Allāh ﷺ said as a covenant to me, is that I should appoint a *mu'adhdhin* who does not accept wages for his *adhān*".[468] However if the people realise that the *mu'adhdhin* is in need, and they give him something without any contract, then it is allowed.[469]

How to respond to the adhān

Those listening to the *adhān* should repeat it, except for the phrases حَيَّ عَلَى الصَّلَاة and حَيَّ عَلَى الْفَلَاح after which the listener should say لَا حَوْلَ وَلَا قُوَّةَ إِلَّا بِاللهِ there is no power or might save by Allāh, and after the phrases اَلصَّلَاةُ خَيْرٌ مِنَ النَّوم in the *Fajr adhān* the listener should say صَدَقْتَ وَبَرِرْتَ, "you have spoken the truth and your effort is accepted".[470] Abū Saᶜīd al-Khudrī

[464] Muslim, *k. al-masājid wa mawāḍiᶜ al-ṣalāh, b. matā yaqūmu al-nās li al-ṣalāh.*

[465] al-Tirmidhī, *abwāb al-ṣalāh, b. mā jā'a anna man adhdhana fahuwa yuqīm.*

[466] al-Kāsānī, *Badā'iᶜ al-ṣanā'iᶜ, i.* 648.

[467] Ibid., *i.* 650.

[468] al-Tirmidhī, *k. al-ṣalāh, b. mā jā'a fī karāhiyat an ya'khudha al-mu'adhdhin ᶜalā al-adhān ajran.* Al-Tirmidhī said that scholars agree with this whereby they dislike to see the caller receive wages for the *adhān.*

[469] al-Kāsānī, *Badā'iᶜ al-ṣanā'iᶜ, i.* 650.

[470] Ibid., *i.* 660.

reported the Messenger of Allāh ﷺ as saying: "When you listen to the *adhān*, you should repeat the same words as the caller pronounces".[471] Abū Rāfiᶜ narrated: "When the Messenger of Allāh ﷺ heard the *adhān*, he would repeat it; and when the *mu'adhdhin* said حَيَّ عَلَى الصَّلاة and حَيَّ عَلَى الْفَلاح he would say "لَا حَوْلَ وَلَا قُوَّةَ إِلَّا بِالله".[472]

After hearing the *adhān* one should pray for the Prophet ﷺ and ask Allāh to give him the place of *wasīlah*. ᶜAbdullāh ibn ᶜAmr related that the Messenger of Allāh ﷺ said: "If you hear the call to *ṣalāh*, repeat after it. Then supplicate for me, for whoever makes one supplication for me, Allāh makes ten for him. Then ask Allāh to grant me the place of *wasīlah*. It is a place in Paradise reserved for a slave from among Allāh's slaves. I hope to be him, and whoever asks Allāh to grant me the place of *wasīlah*, my intercession becomes permissible for him".[473] Jābir ibn ᶜAbdullāh reported that the Prophet ﷺ said: "Whoever says after hearing the call to *ṣalāh*:

اَللَّهُمَّ رَبَّ هَذِهِ الدَّعْوَةِ التَّامَّةِ وَالصَّلاةِ الْقَائِمَةِ، آتِ مُحَمَّداً الْوَسِيلَةَ وَالْفَضِيلَةَ، وَابْعَثْهُ مَقامًا مَحْمُودًا الَّذِي وَعَدْتَّهُ

'O Allāh, Lord of this perfect call and of the regular *ṣalāh* which is going to be established, grant Muḥammad the right of intercession and superiority and send him (on the Day of Judgement) to the best and the highest place in Paradise which You promised him', then my intercession will be permitted for him on the Day of Resurrection".[474]

As the interval between the *adhān* and the *iqāmah* is one of those times when supplications are more likely to be accepted, one should turn to Allāh and petition Him. Abū Iyās narrated from Anas ibn Mālik

[471] al-Bukhārī, *k. al-adhān, b. al-duᶜā' ᶜinda al-nidā'*; Abū Dāwūd, *k. al-ṣalāh, b. mā jā'a fī al-duᶜā' ᶜinda al-adhān*; al-Tirmidhī, *abwāb al-ṣalāh, b. mā ja'a mā yaqūlu al-rajul idhā adhdhana al-mu'adhdhin min al-duᶜā'*.

[472] al-Ṭaḥāwī, *Sharḥ maᶜānī al-āthār*, i, 144.

[473] Muslim, *k. al-ṣalāh, b. istiḥbāb al-qawl mithla qawl al-mu'adhdhin liman samiᶜahu thumma yuṣallī ᶜalā al-nabī ṣallallāhu ᶜalayhi wa sallam, thumma yas'alullāh lahu al-wasīlah*.

[474] al-Bukhārī, *k. al-adhān, b. al-duᶜā' ᶜinda al-nidā'*.

as saying: "The Prophet ﷺ said: 'The supplication made between the *adhān* and the *iqāmah* is not rejected'."[475] Abū ʿAbd al-Raḥmān al-Jubullī narrated from ʿAbdullāh ibn ʿAmr saying: "A man said: 'O Messenger of Allāh ﷺ, the callers to *ṣalāh* get more virtues than us'. He said: 'Say what they say and when you finish, ask and you shall be given'."[476]

Umm Salamah said: "The Prophet ﷺ taught me to say after the *Maghrib* call to *ṣalāh*:

اَللّٰهُمَّ إِنَّ هٰذَا إِقْبَالُ لَيْلِكَ وَإِدْبَارُ نَهَارِكَ، وَأَصْوَاتُ دُعَاتِكَ، فَاغْفِرْ لِي

'O Allāh, this is (the time of) the beginning of Your night, the end of Your day, and (this is the time) the sounds of supplication are made to You, so forgive me'."[477]

Now one should head towards the *masjid* to attend the congregation and make oneself busy with preparing for the *ṣalāh*. Leaving the *masjid* after the *adhān* has been called is disapproved of, unless there is some excuse or one intends to return for the *ṣalāh*. Abū Hurayrah related that the Prophet ﷺ said: "If one of you is in the *masjid* and the *adhān* is made, he should not leave the *masjid* until he prays".[478] Abū al-Shaʿthā' said: "We were with Abū Hurayrah in the *masjid*, and a man left the *masjid* after the *adhān* had been made and he said: 'That man disobeyed Abū al-Qāsim [meaning the Prophet] ﷺ'."[479]

How to respond to the iqāmah

It is recommended that one who hears the *iqāmah* repeat the words. This is so except when قَدْ قَامَتِ الصَّلاة is said, when the listener should say أَقَامَهَا اللهُ وَأَدَامَهَا, "may Allāh establish it and make it everlasting". Abū Umāmah and some of the Companions reported that: "When Bilāl said قَدْ قَامَتِ الصَّلاة the Prophet ﷺ would say "أَقَامَهَا اللهُ وَأَدَامَهَا".[480]

[475] Abū Dāwūd, *k. al-ṣalāh, b. mā jā'a fī al-duʿā' bayna al-adhān wa al-iqāmah.*
[476] Abū Dāwūd, *k. al-ṣalāh, b. mā yaqūlu idhā samiʿa al-mu'adhdhin.*
[477] Abū Dāwūd, *k. al-ṣalāh, b. mā yaqūlu ʿinda adhān al-maghrib.*
[478] Aḥmad, *al-Musnad* 10946.
[479] Abū Dāwūd, *k. al-ṣalāh, b. al-khurūj min al-masjid baʿda al-adhān.*
[480] Abū Dāwūd, *k. al-ṣalāh, b. mā yaqūlu idhā samiʿa al-iqāmah.*

When people stand for the ṣalāh
ʿUmar ibn ʿAbd al-ʿAzīz said: "When the *mu'adhdhin* says قَدْ قَامَتِ الصَّلاة then stand; now the *ṣalāh* has been established".[481] Imām Mālik stated: "I have not heard anything concerning the specific moment [in the *iqāmah* when it is best] to stand for *ṣalāh*. My view is that this depends on the ability of the people, because some people are quick and some are slower".[482] Ibn Jurayj asked ʿAṭā' if it was correct that it had been said that when the *mu'adhdhin* says: قَدْ قَامَتِ الصَّلاة then the people should stand. ʿAṭā' said: "Yes".[483] Imām Muḥammad narrated from Ibrāhīm al-Nakhaʿī: "When the *mu'adhdhin* says حَيَّ عَلَى الْفَلاح then the people should stand and make lines. When the *mu'adhdhin* says قَدْ قَامَتِ الصَّلاة then the imām should say the *takbīr*". He adds: "This is the opinion of Abū Ḥanīfah and we adhere to it; and if the imām waits until the *mu'adhdhin* finishes the *iqāmah*, and then says the *takbīr*, there is no harm in it either. All this is fine".[484]

The adhān for ṣalāh at home and missed ṣalāh
Someone praying alone at home does not need to say the *adhān* and the *iqāmah*, but if praying in congregation with others, it is preferable to say the *adhān* and *iqāmah*. ʿAbdullāh ibn Masʿūd prayed with his companions at his home without the *adhān* and *iqāmah*, and said: "The *iqāmah* of the imām is sufficient". Imām Muḥammad said: "We adhere to this if someone prays alone, but if they pray in congregation then it is preferable to say the *adhān* and the *iqāmah*, and if they say the *iqāmah* and leave out the *adhān*, then there is no harm".[485]

One who sleeps through the time of a *ṣalāh* or who forgets a *ṣalāh* can do the *adhān* and *iqāmah* when he intends to pray. In the incident reported earlier, when the Prophet ﷺ and his Companions slept through the time of the *Fajr Ṣalāh*, he ordered Bilāl to do the *adhān* and *iqāmah* for that *ṣalāh*.[486]

[481] Ibn Abī Shaybah, *al-Muṣannaf, i.* 356.
[482] Mālik, *al-Muwaṭṭa'* 41.
[483] ʿAbd al-Razzāq, *al-Muṣannaf, i.* 505.
[484] Abū Ḥanīfah, *K. al-āthār* 21.
[485] Ibid.
[486] Mālik, *al-Muwaṭṭa'* 14; Muslim, *k. al-masājid wa mawāḍiʿ al-ṣalāh, b. qaḍā' al-ṣalāt al-fā'itah wa istiḥbāb taʿjīl qaḍā'ihā.*

If one has missed many *ṣalāhs*, it is preferable to do one *adhān* at the beginning followed by an *iqāmah* for each missed *ṣalāh*. ʿAbdullāh ibn Masʿūd narrated: "The associators kept the Prophet ﷺ busy during four of his *ṣalāhs* at the battle of the *aḥzāb*. When part of the night had passed, he ordered Bilāl to do the *adhān* and the *iqāmah* and they prayed the *ʿAṣr, Maghrib* and *ʿIshā' Ṣalāhs* in succession, each time preceded by the *iqāmah*".[487]

[487] al-Bayhaqī, *al-Sunan al-kubrā, k. al-ṣalāh, b. al-adhān wa al-iqāmah li al-jamʿ bayna ṣalawāt fā'itāt.*

Chapter 4: Conditions of the *Ṣalāh*

There are two types of *farḍ*: those required before the *ṣalāh*, which are called *shurūṭ* (conditions), and those inside the *ṣalāh*, which are called *arkān* (pillars). There are six conditions of the *ṣalāh*:

1. TIME

The *ṣalāh* is not valid before its time. The times of the *ṣalāhs* have been given earlier in detail.

2. PURITY

The person doing the *ṣalāh* must purify himself from all types of *ḥadath* and impurity as mentioned earlier. As for *ḥadath*, Allāh says in the Qur'ān: "*O you who believe, when you rise for ṣalāh, wash your faces and your hands up to the elbows and wipe your heads and wash your feet up to the ankles*".[488] Ibn ᶜUmar reported that the Prophet ﷺ said: "Allāh does not accept any *ṣalāh* without purity, nor does he accept charity from what has been stolen from booty".[489]

One's clothing should be clean of all impurities. Allāh says: "*And purify your garments*".[490] Jābir ibn Samurah reported that he heard a man ask the Prophet ﷺ: "May I pray in the same clothes that I had on during relations with my wife?" He said: "Yes, but if you see some marks on it, you must wash it."[491] Muᶜāwiyah reported: "I asked Umm Ḥabībah: 'Did the Prophet ﷺ pray in the same clothes that he wore when he had relations?' She said: 'Yes, if there were no mark on it'."[492] Abū Naḍrah narrated from Abū Saᶜīd al-Khudrī saying: "While the Messenger of

[488] *al-Mā'idah* 6.

[489] Muslim, *k. al-ṭahārah, b. wujūb al-ṭahārah li al-ṣalāh.*

[490] *al-Muddaththir* 4

[491] Ibn Mājah, *k. al-ṭahārah wa sunanihā, b. al-ṣalāh fī al-thawb alladhī yujāmiᶜu fīh.*

[492] Abū Dāwūd, *k. al-ṭahārah, b. al-ṣalāh fī al-thawb alladhī yuṣību ahlahu fīh.*

Allāh ﷺ was leading his Companions in *ṣalāh,* he took off his shoes and the people behind him did likewise. When the Prophet ﷺ finished the *ṣalāh,* he asked: 'Why did you remove your shoes?' They said: 'We saw you remove yours'. He said: 'Jibrīl came to me and informed me that there was some filth on them. Therefore, when one of you comes to the *masjid,* he should notice if there is any dirt on his shoes, and if so he should wipe it off and pray in them'."[493]

Once it is established that the purity of clothing is a condition for the *ṣalāh,* then it obvious that the body must also be pure. Anas related that the Prophet ﷺ said: "Stay clean of urine, as the majority of punishments in the grave are due to it".[494] ʿAlī reported: "I used to have a great deal of prostatic fluid flowing, so I asked a man to ask the Prophet ﷺ about it as I was shy to ask him, due to my relationship with him through his daughter. He asked him and the Prophet ﷺ said: 'Do *wuḍū'* and wash your private parts'."[495] ʿĀ'ishah related that the Messenger of Allāh ﷺ said to women with a prolonged flow of blood: "Wash the blood from yourself and pray".[496]

Similarly, the purity of the place where one is praying is a condition for the validity of the *ṣalāh.* Allāh says: "*Purify My House for those who are circumambulating it, those staying in it, those bowing and those prostrating*".[497] Abū Hurayrah said: "A Bedouin stood and urinated in the *masjid.* The people got up to stop him. The Prophet ﷺ said: 'Leave him and pour a container of water over his urine. You have been raised to be easy on the people, not to be hard on them'."[498]

3. COVERING OF THE ʿ*AWRAH*

The ʿ*awrah* refers to those parts of the male or female body which must be covered. Allāh says in the Qur'ān: "*O Children of Adam, take your adornment for every masjid*".[499] Adornment here refers to what covers the

[493] Abū Dāwūd, *k. al-ṣalāh, b. al-ṣalāh fī al-naʿl.*

[494] al-Dāraquṭnī, *al-Sunan, i.* 136.

[495] al-Bukhārī, *k. al-ghusl, b. ghasl al-madhy wa al-wuḍū' minhu.*

[496] Muslim, *k. al-ḥayḍ, b. al-mustaḥāḍah wa ghusliha wa ṣalātiha.*

[497] *al-Baqarah* 125.

[498] al-Bukhārī, *k. al-wuḍū', b. ṣabb al-mā' ʿalā al-bawl fī al-masjid.*

[499] *al-Aʿraf* 31.

ᶜ*awrah,* and *masjid* means *ṣalāh.* Therefore, it means cover your ᶜ*awrah* for every *ṣalāh.* ᶜĀ'ishah reported that the Prophet ﷺ said: "Allāh does not accept the *ṣalāh* of an adult woman unless she is wearing a head covering (*khimār*)".[500] Salamah ibn al-Akwaᶜ said to the Prophet ﷺ: "O Messenger of Allāh ﷺ, may I pray in a single cloth?" He said: "Yes, but button it, even with just a thorn".[501] There is a consensus among scholars that the *ṣalāh* is not valid without the covering of ᶜ*awrah.*[502]

Women's ᶜawrah

The body of a woman is all ᶜ*awrah* except her face, palms and feet.[503] Allāh says in the Qur'ān: "*And do not show off their adornment except only that which is apparent*".[504] According to some scholars, '*that which is apparent*' refers to face, hands and feet. It has been related from ᶜĀ'ishah that the Prophet ﷺ said: "Allāh does not accept the *ṣalāh* of an adult woman unless she is wearing a head covering (*khimār*)".[505] It is related from Umm Salamah that she asked the Prophet ﷺ: "Can a woman pray in a long shirt and head covering without a loincloth?" He said: "If the shirt is long and flowing and covers the top of her feet".[506]

Men's ᶜawrah

A man's ᶜ*awrah* is from below the navel up to and including the knee – the thighs and so on are part of the ᶜ*awrah.* Muḥammad ibn Jaḥsh reported: "The Messenger of Allāh ﷺ passed by Maᶜmar while his thighs were exposed. He said to him: 'O Maᶜmar, cover your thighs, for they are part of the ᶜ*awrah*'."[507] Jarhad reported: "The Messenger of Allāh ﷺ passed by me when the cloak I was wearing did not cover my thigh. He said: 'Cover your thigh, for it is part of the ᶜ*awrah*'."[508]

[500] Abū Dāwūd, *k. al-ṣalāh, b. al-mar'ah tuṣallī bighayr khimār.*

[501] Abū Dāwūd, *k. al-ṣalāh, b. fī al-rajul yuṣallī fī qamīṣ wāḥid.*

[502] al-Kāsānī, *Badā'iᶜ al-ṣanā'iᶜ, i.* 544.

[503] al-Marghinānī, *al-Hidāyah, i.* 47.

[504] *al-Nūr* 31.

[505] Abū Dāwūd, *k. al-ṣalāh, b. al-mar'ah tuṣallī bighayr khimār.*

[506] Abū Dāwūd, *k. al-ṣalāh, b. fī kam tuṣallī al-mar'ah.*

[507] al-Bukhārī, *k. al-ṣalāh, b. mā yudhkaru fī al-fakhidh.* Imām al-Bukhārī mentioned it as *muᶜallaq;* Ḥāfiẓ Ibn Ḥajar mentioned the *isnād* from different sources. (*See: Fatḥ al-Bārī* in commentary on this ḥadīth.)

[508] al-Bukhārī, ibid.

Clothes must cover the *ᶜawrah,* and they should not be tight enough to highlight the features. If the clothes are so thin that one's skin colour can be seen, they are also not suitable for *ṣalāh.*

It is preferable for a man to wear at least two garments, but he can wear just one if that is all he has. ᶜAbdullāh ibn ᶜUmar reported that the Prophet ﷺ said: "If one of you is going to pray, one should wear two garments, for Allāh has the most right that you should look good for Him. If one does not have two garments, one should cover oneself with a cloak when praying, but not in the manner of the Jews."[509]

Covering the head for men

It is not a requirement of prayer that men cover their head with a cap or something similar. Ṣafwān ibn ᶜAmr said: "I have seen ᶜAbdullāh ibn Busr (a Companion) more than fifty times, and never saw on his head any cap or turban, neither in the winter, nor in the summer".[510] ᶜUmar took off his cap and prayed beside it.[511] According to many *aḥādīth* of the Prophet ﷺ and narrations from Companions and scholars of the early generations, prayer in a single cloth is valid and not disapproved of.[512] Masᶜūd ibn Ḥirāsh said: "ᶜUmar led the *ṣalāh* in a single cloth; nothing was on him other than that cloth".[513] ᶜUbaydullāh ibn Miqsam said: "I saw Jābir ibn ᶜAbdullāh praying in a single cloth. I asked him: 'Do you pray in a single cloth while your other clothes are put beside you?' Jābir said: 'Yes, because of someone stupid like you'."[514] This is also the opinion of Abū Ḥanīfah, Abū Yūsuf and Muḥammad.[515] There is no evidence in the Sunnah or books of Imām Muḥammad, al-Sarakhsī, al-Samarqandī, al-Kāsānī, al-Marghinānī and other experts of Ḥanafī *Fiqh* to suggest that it is required that men cover their heads while praying. Indeed, it is preferable to pray with the head bare provided that this is being done out of humility.[516]

[509] Abū Dāwūd, *k. al-ṣalāh, b. idhā kāna al-thawb ḍayyiqan yattaziru bihi.*
[510] Abū Zurᶜah, *al-Tārīkh, i.* 214.
[511] ᶜAbd al-Razzāq, *al-Muṣannaf,* ii. 15.
[512] *See:* Ibn Abī Shaybah, *al-Muṣannaf,* i. 275-278.
[513] Ibid., i. 276.
[514] ᶜAbd al-Razzāq, *al-Muṣannaf, i.* 354.
[515] al-Ṭaḥāwī, *Sharḥ maᶜānī al-āthār, i.* 383.
[516] *See: al-Fatāwā al-hindiyyah,* i. 106.

4- FACING THE *QIBLAH*

One must face the *qiblah* during every *ṣalāh*, and the *qiblah* is the Kaᶜbah. Allāh says in the Qur'ān: "*Direct your face to the Masjid al-Ḥarām. Wherever you may be, turn your faces to it*".[517] Al-Barā' reported: "We prayed with the Messenger of Allāh ﷺ for about sixteen or seventeen months towards Jerusalem, after which time he turned towards the Kaᶜbah".[518]

Wisdom

Shāh Walīullāh al-Dihlawī in explaining the wisdom behind facing the Kaᶜbah in *ṣalāh* said: "Since the Kaᶜbah is among the symbols of Allāh, it is incumbent on us to hold it in reverence, and the greatest token of reverence is that the face should be turned towards it in our best and most elevated state. To stand facing a particular direction is also among the signs of Allāh. Its object is that the attributes of fear, repentance and concentration may develop in the worshipper and he may feel that he is standing with his head bowed like a lowly slave in the presence of the Lord. That is why, it has been made an essential part of the *ṣalāh*". He goes on to say: "To turn in *ṣalāh* with reverence and a feeling of nearness to Allāh, towards a place marked out exclusively for Him is very efficacious in the cultivation of evenness of mind, fear, humility and concentration. In it the same attitude is manifest as that of standing before a king". And further: "As the attentiveness of the heart was a hidden condition, the turning of the face towards the Kaᶜbah has been prescribed as a sign and evidence of it and made an obligatory condition like *wuḍū'*, purity and covering the *ᶜawrah*. And as reverence is a state of feeling and an inner sensation, the physical acts and movements which are generally carried out in the presence of a king and regarded as a part of courtly behaviour have been enjoined as its outward proof and expression".[519]

Rulings

Those who are in Makkah must face the Kaᶜbah itself. Those who are not present there should face its direction.[520] Abū Hurayrah reported

[517] *al-Baqarah* 144.

[518] Muslim, *k. al-masājid wa mawāḍiᶜ al-ṣalāh, b. taḥwīl al-qiblah min al-quds ilā al-kaᶜbah.*

[519] Shāh Walīullāh, *Ḥujjatullāh al-bālighah, i.* 611-3.

[520] al-Marghinānī, *al-Hidāyah, i.* 48.

that the Prophet ﷺ said: "The *qiblah* is between the East and the West".[521] This ḥadīth refers to the people of Madīnah and whoever is in a position similar to them. If someone is in a position higher than the Kaᶜbah (for instance, when travelling on a plane) he must still face the direction, because the Kaᶜbah is not just the physical building, but also includes the whole space above it as far as the heavens. If the building were moved somewhere else, it would not be permitted to face the building. All scholars agree that if someone is praying on Abū Qubays (the mountain next to the Kaᶜbah) his *ṣalāh* is valid, this even though the person is not facing the Kaᶜbah building, but rather the location of the Kaᶜbah.[522]

If the direction of the *qiblah* is not clear, and there is no one to ask, one should do one's best to determine it. If one discovers after one has done the *ṣalāh* that one has made a mistake, one does not need to repeat it. If one realises while one is praying that one is facing the wrong direction, one must turn to the proper direction.[523] Ibn ᶜUmar reported: "The people were praying the *Fajr Ṣalāh* in the *Qubā' Masjid* when a person came to them and said: 'Allāh has revealed some of the Qur'ān to the Prophet ﷺ in which we have been ordered to face the Kaᶜbah, so face it'. They immediately turned their faces from Syria to the Kaᶜbah".[524] Imām Muḥammad said: "We adhere to this in respect of someone who erred about the *qiblah* and prayed one or two *rakᶜah*s. Then if he came to know that he was praying in a direction different from the *qiblah,* he should turn towards the *qiblah,* and what he has prayed will be counted. This is the opinion of Abū Ḥanīfah".[525]

If one is performing voluntary *ṣalāh* while travelling (on any vehicle – train, bus or on an animal), one should, to the extent possible, start the *ṣalāh* in the direction of the *qiblah*; and for the rest of the *ṣalāh* one does not then need to face the *qiblah.* ᶜAmr ibn Rabīᶜah narrated: "I saw the Messenger of Allāh ﷺ pray while riding, and he faced the direction

[521] al-Tirmidhī, *k. al-ṣalāh, b. mā jā'a anna mā bayna al-mashriq wa al-maghrib qiblah;* Ibn Mājah, *k. iqāmat al-ṣalāh wa al-sunnah fīhā, b. al-qiblah.*

[522] *See:* al-Kāsānī, *Badā'iᶜ al-ṣanā'iᶜ, i.* 555.

[523] al-Marghīnānī, *al-Hidāyah, i.* 48-49.

[524] Muslim, *k. al-masājid wa mawāḍiᶜ al-ṣalāh, b. taḥwīl al-qiblah min al-quds ilā al-kaᶜbah.*

[525] Muḥammad, *al-Muwaṭṭa', ii.* 47-48.

in which he was going".[526] If someone is doing the obligatory *ṣalāh*, then he must face the *qiblah*, and if he feels that during the *ṣalāh* the vehicle is changing direction, he should change as well. The Prophet ﷺ would pray on his mount while travelling facing wherever it headed.[527] Ibrāhīm al-Nakhaʿī said: "They would pray on their mounts and animals in the direction in which they were facing". Imām Muḥammad said: "There is no harm for the traveller to pray *nafl* while riding, in whatever direction he is heading; he will do the *sajdah* lower than the *rukūʿ*".[528]

In forced conditions, like illness, fear, or inability, it is permissible to pray even obligatory *ṣalāhs*, without facing the *qiblah*.[529] Allāh says: "*If you fear, then pray on foot or riding*".[530] ʿAbdullāh ibn ʿUmar said: "Facing the *qiblah* or not facing it".[531]

5. INTENTION

Allāh says: "*And they were not commanded, but to worship Allāh, making the religion sincerely for Him*".[532] The Prophet ﷺ said: "Every action is based upon intention. For everyone is that which he intended. Whoever made the migration to Allāh and His Prophet ﷺ, then his migration is to Allāh and His Prophet ﷺ. Whoever's migration was for something of this world or for the purpose of marriage, then his migration is to what he migrated to".[533]

As a result of this verse and the ḥadīth quoted, all scholars agree that an act of worship cannot be valid without intention. In the *nafl ṣalāh* it is enough to intend *ṣalāh* in general. In the *farḍ ṣalāh* one must make the intention of the *ṣalāh* about to be performed, for example for *Ẓuhr Ṣalāh* one must intend *Ẓuhr*, etc, and if one is in the congregation one must intend to follow the imām. Ibrāhīm al-Nakhaʿī said: "When you enter into the *ṣalāh* of the people and you do not intend their *ṣalāh*, then your *ṣalāh* is not valid. If the imām intends a *ṣalāh*, and the people behind

[526] al-Bukhārī, *abwāb taqṣīr al-ṣalāh, b. yanzilu li al-maktūbah.*

[527] al-Tirmidhī, *k. al-ṣalāh, b. mā jā'a fī al-ṣalāh ʿalā al-rāḥilah.*

[528] Muḥammad, *al-Muwaṭṭa', i.* 579.

[529] *See:* al-Kāsānī, *Badāʾiʿ al-ṣanāʾiʿ, i.* 549.

[530] *al-Baqarah* 239.

[531] al-Bukhārī, *k. al-tafsīr, b. fa in khiftum farijālan.*

[532] *al-Bayyinah* 5.

[533] al-Bukhārī, *k. bad' al-waḥy*

him intend another *ṣalāh*, the imām's *ṣalāh* is valid but not the followers". Imām Muḥammad said after quoting Imām al-Nakhaʿī's opinion: "We adhere to it. This is the opinion of Abū Ḥanīfah".[534] Intention, as mentioned earlier, is a condition of the heart, it does not stem from the tongue. For that reason, the Prophet ﷺ, his Companions, and scholars among the generation after them never uttered their intentions.

6. *TAKBĪR TAḤRĪMAH*

The *takbīr taḥrīmah* refers to the *takbīr* (اَللّٰهُ أَكْبَرُ) [535] said at the beginning of the *ṣalāh*. The Prophet ﷺ said: "No one's *ṣalāh* is complete unless he does *wuḍū'* properly and says the *takbīr*".[536] ʿAlī reported that the Prophet ﷺ said: "The key to *ṣalāh* is purity. Its *taḥrīm* [what makes one enter into the sanctity of *ṣalāh*] is the *takbīr*, and its *taḥlīl* [what marks its end] is the *taslīm*".[537] Ibrāhīm al-Nakhaʿī said: "The person who did not say the *takbīr* [*taḥrīm*] when starting the *ṣalāh*, is not in the *ṣalāh*". Imām Muḥammad said: "We adhere to it, except if someone says the *takbīr* of the *rukūʿ* while standing with the intention of [also] entering into the *ṣalāh*, then this will suffice for him, and this is the opinion of Abū Ḥanīfah".[538]

Importance

Shaykh Abū al-Ḥasan ʿAlī Nadwī stated, highlighting the importance of *takbīr taḥrīmah*: "It is that clear, eloquent and forceful affirmation which is capable of evoking a ready response among all peoples and at all times. Before it, the magic-spell of the mightiest of rulers and the most powerful of men, as well as of man-made deities, idols and images is broken and they are reduced to a heap of ashes provided, of course, that it is uttered with conviction". And, further: "When a person believes with a sincere heart in this affirmation ...and this conviction

[534] Abū Ḥanīfah, *K. al-āthār* 41.

[535] According to Abū Ḥanīfah and Muḥammad it is *farḍ* to start the *ṣalāh* with any word that is exlusively for the greatness of Allāh, and saying *Allāhu Akbar* is *wājib.*

[536] al-Ṭabarānī, *al-Muʿjam al-kabīr* 4522

[537] al-Tirmidhī, *k. al-ṣalāh, b. mā jā'a fī taḥrīm al-ṣalāh wa taḥlīlihā*.

[538] Abū Ḥanīfah, *K. al-āthār* 23.

sinks into the innermost depths of his heart and begins to pervade his entire existence, the might and splendour of worldly kings, political leaders and overlords loses its significance in his eyes and they evoke no fear or wonder in him".[539]

[539] Abū al-Ḥasan ʿAlī Nadwī, *The Four Pillars of Islam* pp. 26-7.

Chapter 5: The *Farḍs*, *Wājibs* and Sunnahs of *Ṣalāh*

Farḍs (Arkān)

The *arkān* of *ṣalāh* are those acts within prayer that are obligatory. There are five such *arkān* as follows:

1. Standing

While performing the *ṣalāh* one must stand. Allāh says: "*And stand before Allāh with devout obedience*".[540] ʿImrān ibn Ḥuṣayn reported: "I had some physical problem, so I asked the Prophet ﷺ about the *ṣalāh*, and he said: 'Pray standing. If you are not able to, pray sitting. If you are not able [to do that], pray while lying on your side'."[541]

Standing is compulsory in the *farḍ* and *wājib ṣalāhs*. In voluntary *ṣalāhs*, one may pray sitting even though one may be able to stand; however one who prays sitting receives less reward than one who prays standing. ʿAbdullāh ibn ʿAmr related that the Prophet ﷺ said: "The *ṣalāh* of one who sits is half of the *ṣalāh*".[542]

Someone unable to stand in the *farḍ* and *wājib ṣalāhs* because of incapacity or some other necessity such as travelling in a moving vehicle should pray according to what he is capable of doing, as Allāh does not burden a soul beyond its capacity. Therefore the person will receive the full reward for their *ṣalāh*. Abū Mūsā reported that the Prophet ﷺ said: "If a slave of Allāh is sick or is travelling, he will receive a reward for those acts [of worship] similar to what he would get if he was healthy and at home".[543]

[540] *al-Baqarah* 238.

[541] al-Bukhārī, *k. taqṣīr al-ṣalāh, b. idhā lam yuṭiq qāʿidan ṣallā ʿalā janb.*

[542] Muslim, *k. ṣalāt al-musāfirīn wa qaṣrihā, b. jawāz al-nāfilah qā'iman wa qāʿidan.*

[543] al-Bukhārī, *k. al-jihād, b. yuktabu li al-musāfir mithla mā kāna yaʿmalu fī al-iqāmah.*

2. Reciting the Qur'ān

Allāh says: "*Then recite what is easy of the Qur'ān*".[544] The imperative form of the verb is an indication that it is compulsory. Since reciting the Qur'ān is not compulsory outside of the *ṣalāh,* it is clear that this verse belongs with the *ṣalāh.* Abū ᶜUthmān al-Nahdī narrated that Abū Hurayrah said to him: "The Messenger of Allāh ﷺ said to me: 'Go and announce in Madīnah that there is no *ṣalāh* without reciting the Qur'ān, even if it is by reciting *al-Fātiḥah,* then what is more than that, even if it is by reciting *al-Fātiḥah,* then what is more than that'."[545]

Reciting *al-Fātiḥah* is not a *farḍ* of the *ṣalāh.* The *farḍ* of recitation is done by reading any verse of the Qur'ān. Abū Hurayrah narrated: "The Messenger of Allāh ﷺ entered the *masjid,* and at the same time another person entered who did his *ṣalāh,* then came to the Prophet ﷺ and said *salām*; the Prophet ﷺ replied to him and said: 'Go and pray because you have not prayed'. He went back and prayed again, then came and said *salām* to the Prophet ﷺ; he replied and said: 'Go and pray, because you have not prayed'. This happened three times. Then the person said: 'By the One Who sent you with the truth, I do not know what to do, so teach me'. The Prophet ﷺ said: 'When you stand for the *ṣalāh,* say *Allāhu Akbar,* then read what is for you to read of the Qur'ān, then do *rukūᶜ*'."[546]

Recitation behind the imām

If someone is praying behind an imām then the imām's recitation is his recitation, and he should not recite anything else of the Qur'ān. Jābir ibn ᶜAbdullāh narrated that the Prophet ﷺ said: "Every *ṣalāh* in which *al-Fātiḥah* is not recited is incomplete, except if it is behind the imām".[547] Abū Hurayrah narrated that the Messenger of Allāh ﷺ said: "The imām has been made to be followed, when he says *takbīr* say *takbīr,* and when he recites be quiet".[548] Jābir narrated from the Prophet ﷺ: "Whoever prays behind the imām, then the imām's recitation is his recitation".[549] Allāh says in the Qur'ān: "*When the Qur'ān is recited, then listen to it and be*

[544] *al-Muzzammil* 20.

[545] Abū Dāwūd, *k. al-ṣalāh, b. man taraka al-qirā'at fī ṣalātihi bi fātiḥat al-kitāb.*

[546] al-Bukhārī, *k. al-adhān, b. wujūb al-qirā'ah li al-imām wa al-ma'mūm fī al-ṣalawāt kullihā.*

[547] al-Dāraquṭnī, *al-Sunan, i.* 323.

[548] Ibid.

[549] Ibid 321.

silent, so the mercy will come to you."[550] Imām Aḥmad said: "The people see this command referring to the *ṣalāh*". Saᶜīd ibn al-Musayyab, Ḥasan al-Baṣrī, Ibrāhīm al-Nakhaᶜī, Muḥammad ibn Kaᶜb and Zuhrī said: "This verse was revealed about the *ṣalāh*". Zayd ibn Aslam and Abū al-ᶜĀliyah said: "The people used to recite behind the imām; then this verse was revealed". It has been narrated that ᶜAlī said: "Whoever reads behind the imām, he is not in his right nature". [551] Abū Wā'il narrated from Ibn Masᶜūd saying: "Be silent when the Qur'ān is read, and the imām will suffice you". [552] ᶜUbaydullāh ibn Miqsam narrated that he asked ᶜAbdullāh ibn ᶜUmar, Zayd ibn Thābit and Jābir ibn ᶜAbdullāh about reading behind the imām. All of them said: "Do not read behind the imām in any *ṣalāh*". [553] Imām Muḥammad narrated from Ibrāhīm al-Nakhaᶜī saying: "ᶜAlqamah never read behind the imām in the loud *ṣalāhs* or quiet *ṣalāhs*, nor in the last two *rakᶜahs* or during *al-Fātiḥah* or anything else. Imām Muḥammad said: "This is what we adhere to. We do not see (i.e. we do not recognise) reciting behind the imām in any loud or quiet *ṣalāh*".[554]

One who does not know any part of the Qur'ān

If one is not familiar with some part of the Qur'ān, then it must be learnt as soon as possible. Meanwhile, during the *ṣalāh*, one should say, the *tasbīḥ* سُبْحَانَ الله (glory be to Allāh), the *taḥmīd* اَلْحَمْدُ لله (all praise is due to Allāh), and *tahlīl* لَا إِلَٰهَ إِلَّا الله (there is no God except Allāh). It is related that the Prophet ﷺ said: "The best phrases are four: *Subhan Allāh, al-ḥamdu lillāh, Lā ilāha illa'llāh* and *Allāhu akbar*".[555] This is further supported by Rifāᶜah ibn Rāfiᶜ, who narrated that the Prophet ﷺ said: "If you have something from the Qur'ān, recite it. If not, then say *al-ḥamdulillāh, Allāhu akbar* and *lā ilāha illa'llāh* and then bow".[556]

[550] *al-Aᶜraf* 204.
[551] al-Ṭaḥāwī, *Sharḥ maᶜānī al-āthār, i.* 219.
[552] Ibid.
[553] Ibid.
[554] Abū Ḥanīfah, *K. al-āthār* 25.
[555] al-Bukhārī, *k. al-aymān wa al-nudhūr, b. idhā qāla wallāhi lā atakallamu al-yawma*; Ibn Mājah, *k. al-adab, b. faḍl al-tasbīḥ.*
[556] Abū Dāwūd, *k. al-ṣalāh, b. ṣalāti man lā yuqīmu ṣulbahu fī al-rukūᶜ wa al-sujūd.*

3. Rukūʿ

Allāh says: *"O you who believe, bow down and prostrate yourselves"*.[557] The *farḍ* elements in *rukūʿ* are accomplished by bending forward at the hip.

It is Sunnah in *rukūʿ* that one should rest one's hands over the knees with the fingers spread out, and hold the head level with the hips. One should neither raise his head, nor bend it lower than his back. ʿUqbah ibn ʿĀmir would bow with his arms separated, his hands on his knees, and his fingers opened beyond his knees. He said: "This is how I saw the Messenger of Allāh ﷺ pray".[558] Wā'il ibn Ḥujr reported: "When the Prophet ﷺ bowed he would have his fingers apart".[559] Abū Ḥumayd reported: "When the Prophet ﷺ bowed, he would be straight, his head neither high nor low with respect to his hips, and he would place his hands on his knees as if he was holding them".[560] ʿĀ'ishah reported: "When the Prophet ﷺ bowed, his head would be neither raised nor lowered, but rather between those two positions".[561] ʿAlī said: "If you put a cup of water on the back of the Prophet ﷺ while he was bowing, its contents would not spill".[562]

4. Sajdah

Allāh says: "*O you who believe, bow down and prostrate yourselves*".[563] The main *farḍ* in *sajdah* is achieved by putting the forehead on the ground.

The Sunnah of *sajdah* is attained by placing one's forehead, nose, palms, knees and feet on the ground. ʿAbbās ibn ʿAbd al-Muṭṭalib reported that he heard the Prophet ﷺ say: "When a slave of Allāh prostrates, seven bodily parts prostrate with him: his face, his hands, his knees and his feet".[564] ʿAbdullāh ibn ʿAbbās said: "The Prophet ﷺ ordered us to prostrate on seven bodily parts and not to push back one's hair or clothing [if it falls forward]: the forehead, the hands, the

[557] *al-Ḥajj* 77.
[558] al-Nasā'ī, *k. al-taṭbīq, b. mawḍiʿ aṣābiʿ al-yadayn fī al-rukūʿ*.
[559] al-Ḥākim, *al-Mustadrak*, i. 346.
[560] al-Nasā'ī, *k. al-taṭbīq, b. al-iʿtidāl fī al-rukūʿ*.
[561] Muslim, *k. al-ṣalāh, b. mā yajmaʿu ṣifat al-ṣalāh*.
[562] Aḥmad, *al-Musnad* 997.
[563] *al-Ḥajj* 77.
[564] Muslim, *k. al-ṣalāh, b. adā' al-sujūd wa al-nahy ʿan kaff al-shaʿr wa al-thawb wa ʿaqṣ al-ra's fī al-ṣalāh*.

knees and the feet". In another wording, the Prophet ﷺ said: "I have been ordered to prostrate on seven bodily parts: the forehead (and he pointed to his nose), the hands, the knees and the ends of the feet".[565] Abū Ḥumayd reported: "When the Prophet ﷺ prostrated, he placed his nose and forehead firmly on the ground, separated his hands from his sides and put his palms opposite to his shoulders".[566]

If one prostrates on just the forehead without the nose touching the ground, this is still sufficient. Imām al-Tirmidhī said: "If one prostrates on one's forehead without the nose, it is sufficient according to a group of scholars".[567]

While doing *sajdah,* one places one's knees on the floor before one's hands, and when one stands up from the *sajdah* after the first or third *rakᶜah* one should raise the hands from the ground before the knees. Wā'il ibn Ḥujr said: "I saw the Messenger of Allāh ﷺ while prostrating, placing his knees on the floor before his hands. Upon getting up, he would raise his hands before his knees".[568]

One should place one's nose, forehead and hands upon the floor, and the arms should be held apart from the sides of the body. Abū Ḥumayd reported: "When the Prophet ﷺ prostrated, he would place his nose and forehead upon the floor, keep his arms away from his sides, and place his hands parallel to his shoulders".[569]

For the *sajdah,* one should have one's fingers together. Wā'il ibn Ḥujr reported: "When the Prophet ﷺ prostrated he would keep his fingers together".[570]

Furthermore, the fingers should point in the direction of the *qiblah.* Al-Barā' ibn ᶜĀzib reported: "When the Prophet ﷺ prostrated, he would put his hands on the ground, and he would face the *qiblah* with his palms and his fingers".[571]

[565] Ibid.

[566] al-Tirmidhī, *k. al-ṣalāh, b. mā jā'a fī al-sujūd ᶜalā al-jabhah wa al-anf.*

[567] Ibid.

[568] Abū Dāwūd, *k. al-ṣalāh, b. kayfa yaḍaᶜu rukbatayhi qabla yadayhi;* al-Nasā'ī, *k. al-taṭbīq, b. rafᶜ al-yadayn ᶜan al-arḍ qabl al-rukbatayn.*

[569] al-Tirmidhī, *k. al-ṣalāh, b. mā jā'a fī al-sujūd ᶜalā al-jabhah wa al-anf.*

[570] al-Ḥākim, *al-Mustadrak, i. 350.*

[571] al-Bayhaqī, *al-Sunan al-kubrā, k. al-ṣalāh, b. yaḍummu aṣābiᶜa yadayhi fī al-sujūd wa yastaqbilu bihā al-qiblah.*

During *sajdah*, one should position the feet and toes in the direction of the *qiblah*, as was reported from Abū Ḥumayd in his description of the Prophet's ﷺ *sajdah*.[572]

The hips should be raised during *sajdah*, as al-Barā' ibn ʿĀzib narrated in his description of the Prophet's ﷺ *ṣalāh*.[573]

One should do *sajdah* on both palms, placing one's face between them. Al-Barā' ibn ʿĀzib was asked where the Prophet ﷺ placed his face while doing *sajdah*. He said: "Between his palms".[574]

The elbows should be raised off the ground. The Prophet ﷺ said: "When you do *sajdah* put your palms down [flat on the ground] and raise your elbows".[575] In another ḥadīth he said: "Be straight in the *sajdah*; no one should rest his forearms on the ground as dogs do".[576]

There is no harm if one prostrates upon one's clothing or headdress. Ibn ʿAbbās reported: "The Messenger of Allāh ﷺ prayed in one garment and covered his face with a portion of it to avoid the heat or coldness of the ground".[577]

Women's sajdah

The *sajdah* of women is a little different. They should do it with the body drawn together with the front of the thighs touching the stomach and the back placed on the calves, the shins placed flat on the ground and their buttocks should touch the heels of their feet. ʿAlī ibn Abī Ṭālib said: "When a woman does *sajdah* she should hold herself and join her thighs".[578] Ibn ʿAbbās was asked about the *ṣalāh* of woman. He answered: "She should gather and join herself".[579] Ibrāhīm al-Nakhaʿī said: "When the woman does *sajdah* she should [draw and] join her thighs, and her

[572] al-Bukhārī, *k. al-adhān, b. yastaqbil bi aṭrāf rijlayhi al-qiblah,* and *b. sunnat al-julūs fī al-tashahhud.*

[573] al-Nasā'ī, *k. al-taṭbīq, b. ṣifat al-sujūd.*

[574] al-Tirmidhī, *k. al-ṣalāh, b. mā jā'a ayna yaḍaʿu al-rajul wajhahu idhā sajada;* al-Ḥākim, *al-Mustadrak, i.* 227.

[575] Muslim, *k. al-ṣalāh, b. al-iʿtidāl fī al-sujūd.*

[576] Ibid.

[577] Aḥmad, *al-Musnad* 2320.

[578] Ibn Abī Shaybah, *al-Muṣannaf, i.* 242.

[579] Ibid.

stomach should touch her thighs".[580] Mujāhid disliked a man putting his stomach on his thighs in *sajdah* like a woman.[581] Ḥasan al-Baṣrī said: "The woman will gather herself in *sajdah*".[582] Ibrāhīm al-Nakhaᶜī said: "When the woman does *sajdah* she should rest her stomach on her thighs, not raise her buttocks, and leave no space [between her buttocks and the heels] as men do".[583]

5. The final sitting

The sitting for as long as one can read the *tashahhud* is *farḍ* at the end of the *ṣalāh*. The Prophet ﷺ said while teaching the Bedouin how to pray: "When you raise your head from the last *sajdah* and sit for the *tashahhud*, you have completed your *ṣalāh*".[584] ᶜAbdullāh ibn ᶜAmr ibn al-ᶜĀṣ has reported from the Prophet ﷺ saying: "When the imām raises his head from the last *sajdah* and sits some time for *tashahhud*, then (even) if his *wuḍū'* is nullified, his *ṣalāh* is complete".[585]

The Sunnah in sitting is that one should put the left foot down flat and sit upon it while keeping the right foot upright with the toes bent pointing toward the *qiblah*. ᶜĀ'ishah said: "The Prophet ﷺ would lay out [flat on the ground] his left foot and keep his right foot upright".[586] Ibn ᶜUmar reported: "It is Sunnah to keep the right foot upright, with one's toes pointing toward the *qiblah*, and to sit upon the left foot".[587] In Abū Ḥumayd's ḥadīth, in which he described the Prophet's *ṣalāh*, he stated: "Then he would sit down on his left foot and sit upon it until all of his bones were in place, and then he would go to make the *sajdah* again".[588]

[580] Ibid.
[581] Ibid.
[582] Ibid.
[583] Ibid.
[584] al-Bukhārī, *k. al-isti'dhān, b. man radda faqāla ᶜalayka al-salāmu;* Muslim, *k. al-ṣalāh, b. wujūb qirā'at al-fātiḥah.*
[585] Abū Dāwūd, *k. al-ṣalāh, b. matā yu'maru al-ghulām bi al-ṣalāh;* al-Tirmidhī, *k. al-ṣalāh, b. mā jā'a fī al-rajul yuḥdithu fī al-tashahhud.*
[586] Muslim, *k. al-ṣalāh, b. mā yajmaᶜu ṣifat al-ṣalāh.*
[587] al-Bukhārī, *k. al-adhān, b. sunnat al-julūs fī al-tashahhud;* Abū Dāwūd, *k. al-ṣalāh, b. kayfa al-julūs fī al-tashahhud.*
[588] Abū Dāwūd, *k. al-ṣalāh, b. iftitāḥ al-ṣalāh.*

While sitting, it is recommended that one place one's right hand on one's right thigh and the left hand on the left thigh, with the fingers stretched out in the direction of the *qiblah.* The fingers should be slightly separated and should not extend beyond the knees. When one says the *shahādah* one should raise the index during the denial part of the statement (there is no god) and putting it down again during the affirmation part (but Allāh). (al-Shāmī, *Radd al-muḥtār,* iii. 360)

How women should sit

How should a woman sit in the *ṣalāh*? Ibn Jurayj said: "I asked ʿAṭā': 'Should the woman sit on her left side?' He answered: 'Yes'. I asked: 'Is it better in your view than (that she sit on) the right side?' He said: 'Yes, and she should gather herself in sitting as much she can'. I asked: 'Should she sit like a man, or take out her left foot from under her thigh?' He answered: 'It does not harm her [prayers] to sit in any way so long as she gathers herself'."[589] Ibrāhīm al-Nakhaʿī said: "The woman [when sitting] will put her weight on one side in the *ṣalāh*".[590] Imām Muḥammad narrated from Ibrāhīm al-Nakhaʿī saying: "She sits as she likes". Imām Muḥammad also said: "It is better in our view that the woman gather both legs to one side, and that she does not raise her feet as the man does".[591]

WĀJIBS OF ṢALĀH

The following acts are *wājib* in *ṣalāh.* These are compulsory actions proven by the Sunnah. If someone misses any of these actions his *ṣalāh* is incomplete and he has to do *sajdah* of forgetting. If someone leaves aside any of these actions intentionally, then it is *wājib* on him to repeat the *ṣalāh,* otherwise he will be a sinner.

1. Reciting al-Fātiḥah

Reciting *al-Fātiḥah* in the first two *rakʿahs* of the *farḍ* and every *rakʿah* of the *Witr* and *nafl ṣalāhs* is *wājib.* ʿUbādah ibn al-Ṣāmit related that the

[589] Ibn Abī Shaybah, *al-Muṣannaf, i.* 242.

[590] Ibid.

[591] Abū Ḥanīfah, *K. al-āthār* 57.

Prophet ﷺ said: "There is no *ṣalāh* for one who does not recite *al-Fātiḥah*".[592] Abū Hurayrah reported that the Prophet ﷺ said: "Whoever prays a *ṣalāh* and does not recite *al-Fātiḥah*, then his *ṣalāh* is incomplete".[593]

2. Additional recitation

It is *wājib* to add a short sūrah or three verses after *al-Fātiḥah* in the first two *rakᶜahs* of the *farḍ*, and all the *rakᶜahs* of the *Witr* and *nafl*. Abū Qatādah reported: "The Prophet ﷺ would recite *al-Fātiḥah* and a sūrah in each of the first two *rakᶜahs* of the *Ẓuhr Ṣalāh*; he would make the first *rakᶜah* longer, and the second one shorter; and he would recite a verse aloud sometimes. This was how it was done in the *ᶜAṣr* and *Fajr Ṣalāhs*."[594] Abū Saᶜīd said: "We were ordered to recite *al-Fātiḥah* and whatever else was easy for us".[595]

ᶜĀmir al-Shaᶜbī narrated that ᶜUmar wrote to Shurayḥ asking him to read *al-Fātiḥah* and another sūrah in the first two *rakᶜahs*, and *al-Fātiḥah* alone in the last two *rakᶜahs*.[596] Ibrāhīm al-Nakhaᶜī said: "Do not add anything to *al-Fātiḥah* in the last two *rakᶜahs*". Imām Muḥammad said: "This is the opinion of Abū Ḥanīfah and we adhere to it".[597]

3. Reciting aloud or subdued

It is *wājib* to recite aloud in congregational *ṣalāh* in the two *rakᶜahs* of *Fajr*, in the first two *rakᶜahs* of the *Maghrib* and the *ᶜIshā' Ṣalāh*, in the Friday *Ṣalāh*, and in the two *ᶜĪd Ṣalāhs*. The recital should be subdued during all of the *Ẓuhr* and the *ᶜAṣr Ṣalāhs*, during the last *rakᶜah* of the *Maghrib Ṣalāh*, and during the last two *rakᶜahs* of the *ᶜIshā' Ṣalāh*.

Individual *farḍ*, and all voluntary *ṣalāhs*, made during the daytime should be subdued, while those made during the night can be either loud or subdued. ᶜAṭā' ibn Abī Rabāḥ narrated that Abū Hurayrah said: "In every *rakᶜah* there will be recitation; whatever the Prophet ﷺ read to

[592] al-Bukhārī, *k. al-adhān, b. wujūb al-qirā'ah li al-imām wa al-ma'mūm fī al-ṣalawāt kullihā;* Muslim, *k. al-ṣalāh, b. wujūb qirā'at al-fātiḥah.*

[593] Muslim, *k. al-ṣalāh, b. wujūb qirā'at al-fātiḥah.*

[594] al-Bukhārī, *k. al-adhān, b. al-qirā'ah fī al-ẓuhr.*

[595] Abū Dāwūd, *k. al-ṣalāh, b. man taraka al-qirā'ah fī ṣalātihi bi fātiḥat al-kitāb.*

[596] Ibn Abī Shaybah, *al-Muṣannaf*, i. 325.

[597] Abū Ḥanīfah, *K. al-āthār* 26.

us aloud we read it to you aloud, and whatever he read to us subdued we read it to you subdued".[598]

4. Completion of the rukūᶜ and sajdah

It is *wājib* to do *rukūᶜ* and *sajdah* properly, to separate them by proper standing in between, and to separate the two *sajdahs* with sitting in between. Abū Masᶜūd al-Badrī narrated from the Prophet ﷺ saying: "The *ṣalāh* of a person will not suffice unless he straightens his back in the *rukūᶜ* and *sajdah*".[599] Abū Ḥumayd reported: "The Prophet ﷺ would raise his head from *rukūᶜ*, then stand straight until all of his backbones returned to their places".[600] ᶜĀ'ishah related: "When the Prophet ﷺ raised his head from *rukūᶜ*, he would not prostrate until his back was straight".[601]

5. First sitting

In a ḥadīth from Rifāᶜah ibn Rāfiᶜ it is stated: "When you sit in the middle of your *ṣalāh*, sit properly".[602] ᶜAbdullāh ibn Buḥaynah narrated: "The Prophet ﷺ prayed two *rakᶜahs* in one of the *ṣalāhs*, then he stood up and did not sit, the people also stood up with him when he ended his *ṣalāh*, we waited for his *salām*; rather he said *takbīr* and did two *sajdahs* while sitting before *salām*; then he said *salām*".[603] In this ḥadīth it is clear that the first sitting is not *farḍ*; rather it is *wājib*.

6. Recital of the tashahhud

It is *wājib* to read the *tashahhud* in both sittings. ᶜAbdullāh ibn Masᶜūd said: "When we would sit with the Prophet ﷺ in the *ṣalāh*, we would say, 'Peace be upon Allāh before His slaves, peace be upon so and so'. The Prophet ﷺ said: 'Do not say peace be upon Allāh, for Allāh is peace. When one of you sits, he should say:

[598] Abū Dāwūd, *k. al-ṣalāh, b. mā jā'a fī al-qirā'ah fī al-ẓuhr.*

[599] Abū Dāwūd, *k. al-ṣalāh, b. ṣalāt man lā yuqīmu ṣulbahu fī al-rukūᶜ wa al-sujūd.*

[600] al-Bukhārī, *k. al-adhān, b. al-ṭu'manīnah ḥīna yarfaᶜu ra'sahu min al-rukūᶜ;* Abū Dāwūd, *k. al-ṣalāh, b. iftitāḥ al-ṣalāh.*

[601] Muslim, *k. al-ṣalāh, b. mā yajmaᶜu ṣifat al-ṣalāh.*

[602] al-Ṭabarānī, *al-Muᶜjam al-kabīr, vii,* 250.

[603] al-Bukhārī, *k. al-adhān, b. man lam yara al-tashahhud al-awwal wājiban.*

اَلتَّحِيَّاتُ للهِ وَالصَّلَوَاتُ وَالطَّيِّبَاتُ، اَلسَّلَامُ عَلَيْكَ أَيُّهَا النَّبِيُّ وَرَحْمَةُ اللهِ وَبَرَكَاتُه، اَلسَّلَامُ عَلَيْنَا وَعَلَى عِبَادِ اللهِ الصَّالِحِيْنَ، أَشْهَدُ أَنْ لَا إِلَهَ إِلاَّ اللهُ، وَأَشْهَدُ أَنَّ مُحَمَّدًا عَبْدُهُ وَرَسُوْلُه.

"The adorations of the tongue are due to Allāh, and acts of worship, and all good things. Peace be upon you, O Prophet ﷺ, and Allāh's mercy and His blessings. Peace be upon us and upon Allāh's upright slaves. I bear witness that there is no god except Allāh. I bear witness that Muḥammad is His slave and Messenger". Then you may choose whatever supplication you desire'."[604] Muslim said: "The people are in agreement over the *tashahhud* of Ibn Masᶜūd, and the Companions do not differ over it". Al-Tirmidhī, affirms that Ibn Masᶜūd's ḥadīth is the most authentic on this subject.[605] Imām Muḥammad said: "Abdullāh ibn Masᶜūd did not like to increase or decrease any letter from this *tashahhud*".[606]

Samurah said: "The Prophet ﷺ commanded that when we are in the middle of the *ṣalāh* or at the end of the *ṣalāh* we should say the *tashahhud*".[607] Ibn Masᶜūd narrated that the Prophet ﷺ said: "When you sit in the two *rakᶜah*s say the *tashahhud*".[608]

7. Sequence

Doing all the *farḍ* and *wājib* acts of the *ṣalāh* in their proper order and sequence is *wājib.* The Prophet ﷺ always prayed in a particular order, and when he forgot he did the *sajdah* of forgetting.

8. The salām

The saying of *salām* at the end of the *ṣalāh* is *wājib.* It is related by ᶜAlī that the Prophet ﷺ said: "The key to *ṣalāh* is purity; its opening is the *takbīr* and its closing is the *salām*".[609] ᶜAbdullāh ibn Masᶜūd said:

[604] al-Bukhārī, *k. al-adhān, b. al-tashahhud fī al-ākhirah;* Muslim, *k. al-ṣalāh, b. al-tashahhud fī al-ṣalāh.*

[605] al-Tirmidhī, *k. al-ṣalāh, b. mā jā'a fī al-tashahhud*

[606] Muḥammad, *al-Muwaṭṭa', i.* 476.

[607] al-Ṭabarānī, *al-Muᶜjam al-kabīr, vii,* 250.

[608] Ibn Ḥibbān, *al-Ṣaḥīḥ, v.* 1951.

[609] al-Tirmidhī, *k. al-ṭahārah, b. mā jā'a anna miftāḥ al-ṣalāt al-ṭuhūr;* al-Tirmidhī said that this is the most authentic report on this subject and also the best.

"The Prophet ﷺ used to say the *salām* on his right side and on his left side until the whiteness of his cheeks could be seen".[610] ᶜAlqamah ibn Wā'il narrated from his father saying: "I prayed with the Messenger of Allāh ﷺ. He would make the *salām* on his right side by saying: اَلسَّلَامُ عَلَيْكُمْ وَرَحْمَةُ الله 'Peace be upon you and the mercy of Allāh', and on his left side by saying: اَلسَّلَامُ عَلَيْكُمْ وَرَحْمَةُ الله 'Peace be upon you and the mercy of Allāh'."[611]

9. Calmness

Doing every action of the *ṣalāh* properly and with calmness is *wājib*. Abū Hurayrah narrated that the Prophet ﷺ said to a Bedouin while teaching him the *ṣalāh*: "When you stand up for the *ṣalāh*, say the *takbīr*, then read whatever is easy from the Qur'ān, then do *rukūᶜ* until you come to calmness in the *rukūᶜ*, then raise your head until you come to calmness in standing, then do *sajdah* until you come to calmness in *sajdah*, then raise your head until you come to calmness in sitting, then do *sajdah* until you come to calmness in *sajdah*, then do it in all of your *ṣalāh*".[612]

SUNNAH ACTS OF *ṢALĀH*

There are certain actions, though they are neither *farḍ*, nor *wājib*, they are highly recommended in order to merit the full reward of the *ṣalāh*. These actions are categorised as Sunnahs in the *ṣalāh*.

Raising one's hands at the taḥrīmah

It is Sunnah to raise both hands placing one's fingers to the level of one's ears at the time of the *taḥrīmah*. Wā'il ibn Ḥujr reported that he saw the Prophet ﷺ when he stood for the *ṣalāh* and that he raised both of his hands until they were in front of his shoulders, and he placed his thumbs next to his ears.[613] Al-Barā' reported: "The Messenger of Allāh ﷺ whenever he started the *ṣalāh* would raise his hands close to his ears. He would not raise his hands after that".[614] ᶜAlī used to raise his hands at

[610] Abū Dāwūd, *k. al-ṣalāh, b. fī al-salām.*

[611] Ibid.

[612] al-Bukhārī, *k. al-adhān, b. wujūb al-qirā'ah li al-imām wa al-ma'mūm;* Muslim, *k. al-ṣalāh, b. wujūb qirā'at al-fātiḥah fī kulli rakᶜah.*

[613] Abū Dāwūd, *k. al-ṣalāh, b. rafᶜ al-yadayn fī al-ṣalāh.*

[614] Abū Dāwūd, *k. al-ṣalāh, b. man lam yadhkur al-rafᶜa ᶜinda al-rukūᶜ.*

the opening *takbīr*, then he would not raise them again.[615] Al-Tirmidhī narrated: "ᶜAbdullāh ibn Masᶜūd remarked: 'Should I not pray for you as the Messenger of Allāh ﷺ prayed?' Then he prayed and did not raise his hands other than the first time".[616] Abū Isḥāq narrated that the students of ᶜAbdullāh ibn Masᶜūd and ᶜAlī did not raise their hands except at the opening *takbīr*.[617] Ibrāhīm al-Nakhaᶜī said: "Do not raise your hands in any aspect of your *ṣalāh* after the first time". Imām Muḥammad said: "This is the opinion of Abū Ḥanīfah and we adhere to it".[618]

How women should raise their hands

Women should not raise their hands higher than their shoulders. The great *tābiᶜiyyah* scholar Umm al-Dardā' used to raise her hands up to the level of her shoulders when she started the *ṣalāh*.[619] ᶜAṭā' ibn Abī Rabāḥ was asked how a woman should raise her hands in the *ṣalāh*. He said: "Opposite to her breasts".[620] Imām Zuhrī said that a woman should raise her hands up to her shoulders.[621] Ibn Jurayj said: "I asked ᶜAṭā': 'Does the woman raise her hands in the *takbīr* in the same way as the man?' He answered: 'She should not do as the man'. Then he raised his hands and lowered them considerably, and brought them very close to himself and said: 'The woman's condition is not like the man's, and there is no harm if she leaves it'."[622] ᶜĀṣim al-Aḥwal narrated: "I saw Ḥafṣah bint Sīrīn; she said the *takbīr* and raised her hands to the level of her breasts".[623]

Spreading one's fingers

While raising the hands one should also spread one's fingers. Abū Hurayrah reported that whenever the Prophet ﷺ said the *takbīr*, he would spread his fingers".[624]

[615] Ibn Abī Shaybah, *al-Muṣannaf*, i. 213.

[616] al-Tirmidhī, *k. al-ṣalāh, b. mā jā'a anna al-nabīyya sallallāhu ᶜalayhi wa sallam lam yarfaᶜ illā fī awwal marrah.*

[617] Ibn Abī Shaybah, *al-Muṣannaf*, i. 214.

[618] Abū Ḥanīfah, *K. al-āthār* 23.

[619] Ibn Abī Shaybah, *al-Muṣannaf*, *i.* 216.

[620] Ibid.

[621] Ibid.

[622] Ibid.

[623] Ibid.

[624] al-Tirmidhī, *k. al-ṣalāh, b. mā jā'a fī nashr al-aṣābiᶜ ᶜinda al-takbīr.*

Facing the palms towards the Kaᶜbah

While raising the hands one should face the palms towards the Kaᶜbah. ᶜAbdullāh ibn ᶜUmar said: "The Prophet ﷺ said: 'When one of you starts the *ṣalāh* you should raise your hands and your palms should face the *qiblah*, because Allāh, glorified is He, is in front of him'."[625]

Where to place one's hands

Abū Ḥāzim narrated that Sahl ibn Saᶜd said: "The people were ordered to place their right hand on their left forearm during *ṣalāhs*". Abū Hāzim said: "I believe that he linked it [the ḥadīth] to the Prophet ﷺ".[626] ᶜAbdullāh ibn Masᶜūd said: "The Prophet ﷺ saw him praying with his left hand over his right, and the Prophet ﷺ put his (ᶜAbdullāh ibn Masᶜūd's) right hand over his left".[627] Ḥajjāj ibn Ḥassān said: "I asked Abū Mijlaz where one should place one's hands? He said: 'One should place one's right palm over the back of the left, and place both of them under the navel".[628] Abū Maᶜshar said: "Ibrāhīm al-Nakhaᶜī used to place his right hand over his left hand under the navel". Imām Muḥammad said: "This is the opinion of Abū Ḥanīfah and we adhere to it".[629]

Where a woman should place her hands

A woman, however, will place her hands over her chest, because this provides more covering for her.[630]

The opening supplication

It is Sunnah to begin the *ṣalāh* with a supplication that was used by the Prophet ﷺ at the beginning of his *ṣalāhs*. This supplication is made after the opening *takbīr* and before the recitation of *al-Fātiḥah*. ᶜUmar used to say, after the beginning *takbīr*:

سُبْحَانَكَ اللَّهُمَّ وَبِحَمْدِكَ وَتَبَارَكَ اسْمُكَ وَتَعَالَى جَدُّكَ وَلَا إِلَهَ غَيْرُكَ

[625] al-Ṭabarānī, *al-Muᶜjam al-awsaṭ, ii.* 194.

[626] al-Bukhārī, *k. al-adhān, b. waḍᶜ al-yumnā ᶜalā al-yusrā.*

[627] Abū Dāwūd, *k. al-ṣalāh, b. waḍᶜ al-yumnā ᶜalā al-yusrā fī al-ṣalāh.*

[628] Ibn Abī Shaybah, *al-Muṣannaf;* Abū Dāwūd, *k. al-ṣalāh, b. waḍᶜ al-yumnā ᶜalā al-yusrā.*

[629] Abū Ḥanīfah, *K. al-āthār* 34.

[630] al-Mawṣilī, *al-ikhtiyār li taᶜlīl al-mukhtār, i.* 67.

"Glory be to You, O Allāh, and to You is the praise. Blessed is Your name and exalted is Your honour. There is no god besides You".[631]

ᶜUmar would recite it aloud and teach it to others. This fact is, thus, considered to have its source with the Prophet ﷺ. Hence Imām Muḥammad said: "We say this in the opening of the *ṣalāh*. But we do not say that the imām or follower should say it loudly; ᶜUmar said it loudly in order to teach others what they had asked him".[632]

Saying taᶜawwudh quietly

It is Sunnah for one praying alone and for the imām (but not one following the imām) to say the *taᶜawwudh* (أَعُوذُ بِاللهِ مِنَ الشَّيْطَانِ الرَّجِيْم) quietly before beginning any Qur'ānic recitation. Allāh says: "*When you recite the Qur'ān, seek refuge in Allāh from the outcast Satan*".[633] Jubayr ibn Muṭᶜim has narrated that the Prophet ﷺ said: "O Allāh, I seek refuge in You from Satan, the outcast".[634] The seeking of refuge is to be done in the first *rakᶜah* only. Abū Hurayrah reported: "When the Prophet ﷺ would get up for the second *rakᶜah*, he would begin with *al-Fātiḥah* without any period of silence".[635]

Saying the bismillāh quietly

It is Sunnah for one praying alone and for the imām (but not one following the imām) to recite بِسْمِ اللهِ الرَّحْمَنِ الرَّحِيْم quietly before *al-Fātiḥah.* Anas said: "I prayed behind the Messenger of Allāh ﷺ, Abū Bakr, ᶜUmar and ᶜUthmān, and I did not hear them reciting the *bismillāh* aloud".[636] Ibrāhīm al-Nakhaᶜī said: "Four things should be said quietly by the imām: *subḥānak Allāhumma, taᶜawwudh,* the *bismillāh*, and *āmīn*".[637]

Saying āmīn

It is Sunnah for those in *ṣalāh* to say '*āmīn*' quietly at the end of the recitation of *al-Fātiḥah.* The word *āmīn* is a supplication and not part of

[631] Muslim, *k. al-ṣalāh, b. ḥujjat man qāla lā yujharu bi al-basmalah.*

[632] Abū Ḥanīfah, *K. al-āthār* 23.

[633] *al-Naḥl* 98

[634] Abū Dāwūd, *k. al-ṣalāh, b. mā yustaftaḥu bihi al-ṣalātu min al-duᶜā'.*

[635] Muslim, *k. al-masājid, b. mā yuqālu bayna takbīrāt al-iḥrām wa al-qirā'ah.*

[636] al-Nasā'ī. *K. al-iftitāḥ, b. tark al-jahr bi bismillāh al-raḥmān al-raḥīm.*

[637] Abū Ḥanīfah, *K. al-āthār* 25.

al-Fātiḥah. *Āmīn* is said as a supplication to mean, "O Allāh, respond to or answer what we have said". Abū Hurayrah reported that the Prophet ﷺ said: "When the imām recites, غَيْرِ الْمَغْضُوبِ عَلَيْهِمْ وَلَا الضَّالِّينَ (*not of those with whom You are angered nor of those who have gone astray*), you should say '*āmīn*'. If this corresponds to when the angels say it, one will have all of one's previous sins forgiven".[638] He also reported that the Prophet ﷺ said: "When the imām recites, غَيْرِ الْمَغْضُوبِ عَلَيْهِمْ وَلَا الضَّالِّينَ (*not of those with whom You are angered nor of those who have gone astray*), then say '*āmīn*' along with the imām, for the angels say '*āmīn*' and the imām says '*āmīn*'. If one's *āmīn* corresponds to the *āmīn* of the angels, one will have one's previous sins forgiven".[639]

Wā'il ibn Ḥujr reported: "The Prophet ﷺ led the *ṣalāh*. When he recited غَيْرِ الْمَغْضُوبِ عَلَيْهِمْ وَلَا الضَّالِّينَ (*not of those with whom You are angered nor of those who have gone astray*), he said '*āmīn*' and lowered his voice".[640]

Recitation

Recitation in the *ṣalāh* is of three types: *farḍ*, *wājib* and Sunnah. The first two types have been mentioned earlier. What follows refers to the Sunnah recitation only. When the Prophet ﷺ finished *al-Fātiḥah*, he would sometimes make a lengthy recitation, and sometimes a short one, if he was travelling or similarly engaged. Most of the time, however, he made a recitation of intermediate length.

The Prophet ﷺ would read from 60-100 verses during the *Fajr Ṣalāh*.[641] Sometimes he would read Sūrah *Qāf* in the *Fajr*.[642] On Fridays he would read the whole of *Alif Lām Mīm Tanzīl al-Sajdah* or *al-Dahr*. He would recite *Qāf*, *al-Qamar*, *al-Aᶜlā* and *al-Ghāshiyah* on Fridays, *ᶜĪd* days and so on. Once Abū Bakr read *al-Baqarah* in the *Fajr Ṣalāh* until the sun was about to rise. The Companions said after the *ṣalāh*: "O successor of the Messenger of Allāh ﷺ, the sun was about to rise". He said: "Had it risen,

[638] al-Bukhārī, *k. al-adhān, b. faḍl al-ta'mīn.*

[639] al-Nasā'ī, *k. al-iftitāḥ, b. jahr al-imām bi āmīn.*

[640] al-Tirmidhī, *k. al-ṣalāh, b. mā jā'a fī al-ta'mīn.*

[641] al-Bukhārī, *k. ṣifat al-ṣalāh, b. al-qirā'ah fī al-fajr;* Muslim, *k. al-ṣalāh, b. al-qirā'ah fī al-ṣubḥ.*

[642] Muslim, *k. al- ṣalāh, b. al-qira'ah fi al-subh,* ibid.

it would not have found us negligent".[643] ᶜUmar would recite *Yūsuf, al-Naḥl, Hūd, al-Isrā'* and similar sūrahs. Jābir ibn Samurah narrated: "The Messenger of Allāh ﷺ recited *Qāf* in the *Fajr Ṣalāh*, and his subsequent *ṣalāhs*, i.e. recitations, during that day would be shorter".[644]

The imām should make the first *rakᶜah* of the *Fajr Ṣalāh* longer than the second to give people more time to join the congregation.[645] All scholars agree on this point.[646] The Prophet ﷺ would make the first *rakᶜah* of the *Fajr Ṣalāh* longer than the second[647]

For *Ẓuhr*, the Prophet's recitation used to be shorter than for *Fajr*. Al-Barā' narrated that: "We would hear behind the Prophet ﷺ one or more verses from *Luqmān* and *al-Dhāriyāt*". Abū Saᶜīd once said: "While he (the Prophet ﷺ) was standing in the *Ẓuhr Ṣalāh*, one could go to al-Baqīᶜ and take care of some matter, return to one's family, make *wuḍū'*, return, and still find the Prophet ﷺ in the first *rakᶜah* due to the length of his recital".[648] Jābir ibn Samurah narrated that: "I prayed the *Ẓuhr* behind the Prophet ﷺ and he recited the whole of *al-Aᶜlā*".[649]

In *ᶜAṣr*, the Prophet's recitation would be similar in length to that of the *Ẓuhr Ṣalāh's* recitation or shorter if that was a long one. Jābir ibn Samurah narrated that the Prophet ﷺ would read in *Ẓuhr* and *ᶜAṣr*: *Wa al-samā' dhāt al-burūj* and *Wa al-samā' wa al-ṭāriq*.[650] In another narration from him he reported that the Prophet ﷺ would read in *Ẓuhr: Wa al-layl idhā yaghshā*, and in *ᶜAṣr* similarly.[651]

The Prophet ﷺ would recite both short and long sūrahs in the *Maghrib Ṣalāh*. Sometimes he would recite *al-Aᶜrāf* in the two *rakᶜahs* and sometimes *al-Ṭūr* or *al-Mursalāt*. It is related that the Prophet ﷺ recited the following sūrahs in *Maghrib Ṣalāh*: *al-Aᶜrāf*, *al-Ṣāffāt, Ḥā Mīm Dukhān, al-Aᶜlā, al-Tīn* or the last two sūrahs of *al-Mufaṣṣal* (chapters of the Qur'ān from Sūrah *al-Ḥujurāt* to the end). Marwān ibn al-Ḥakam used to recite short

[643] Mālik, *al-Muwaṭṭa'*, 45; Ibn Abī Shaybah, *al-Muṣannaf*, *i*.310

[644] Muslim, *k. al-ṣalāh, b. al-qirā'ah fī al-ṣubḥ*.

[645] al-Marghinānī, *al-Hidāyah*, *i*. 59.

[646] al-Kāsānī, *Badā'iᶜ al-ṣanā'iᶜ*, *ii*. 42.

[647] Ibn Mājah: *k. iqāmat al-ṣalāh wa al-sunnah fīhā, b. al-qirā'ah fī ṣalāt al-fajr*.

[648] Muslim, *k. al-ṣalāh, b. al-qirā'ah fī al-ẓuhr wa al-ᶜaṣr*.

[649] Ibn Abī Shaybah, *al-Muṣannaf*, *i*.312

[650] Abū Dāwūd, *k. al-ṣalāh, b. qadr al-qirā'ah fī ṣalāt al-ẓuhr wa al-ᶜaṣr*; Ibn Abī Shaybah, *al-Muṣannaf*, *i*.312

[651] Abū Dāwūd, *k. al-ṣalāh, b. qadr al-qirā'ah fī ṣalāt al ẓuhr wa al-ᶜaṣr*.

sūrahs, but Zayd ibn Thābit objected to this, saying: "What is wrong with you that you always recite one of the short sūrahs from *al-Mufaṣṣal* during *Maghrib Ṣalāh*? I have seen the Prophet ﷺ reciting long sūrahs therein". Marwān asked: "And what is a long *sūrah*?" He answered: "*Al-Aʿrāf*".[652] ʿĀ'ishah said: "The Prophet ﷺ read *al-Aʿrāf* during the *Maghrib Ṣalāh* and he divided it between the two *rakʿahs*".[653] Imām Muḥammad said: "Most people hold that the recitation in the *Maghrib Ṣalāh* will be lightened; short sūrahs from *al-Mufaṣṣal* will be read in it; and we see that this, (i.e. reading the long sūrahs) was something that did happen, but then it was replaced, or the Prophet ﷺ read part of the sūrah then did *rukūʿ*".[654]

In the *ʿIshā' Ṣalāh*, the Prophet ﷺ would recite *al-Tīn* as has been narrated by al-Barā' ibn ʿĀzib.[655] The Prophet ﷺ taught Muʿādh to recite *al-Aʿlā*, *al-Layl*, and so on.[656] The Prophet ﷺ objected to Muʿādh reciting *al-Baqarah* at that time. After praying with the Prophet ﷺ Muʿādh went to the people of ʿAmr ibn ʿAwf, and when part of the night had passed, he led the *ṣalāh*, and recited *al-Baqarah*. On being informed of this, the Prophet ﷺ said to him: "Muʿādh, are you one who puts people to hardships?"[657]

Reciting a specific part

For the recitation after the *Fātiḥah*, specifying any part of the Qur'ān in any *ṣalāh* is disapproved because doing so implies neglect for other parts of the Qur'ān.[658] The Prophet ﷺ did not confine his recitation of the Qur'ān in *ṣalāhs* to specific parts. ʿAmr ibn Shuʿayb narrated from his father on the authority of his grandfather who said: "There is no sūrah from the sūrahs of *al-Mufaṣṣal*, large or small, but I heard the Prophet ﷺ recite them while leading the people in the obligatory *ṣalāhs*".[659] It is also narrated that the Prophet ﷺ sometimes recited the

[652] Abū Dāwūd, *k. al-ṣalāh, b. qadr al-qirā'ah fī al-maghrib.*

[653] al-Nasā'ī, *k. al-iftitāḥ, al-qirā'ah fī al-maghrib bi alif lām mīm ṣād.*

[654] Muḥammad, *al-Muwaṭṭa', i.* 643-645.

[655] Ibn Abī Shaybah, *al-Muṣannaf, i.* 315

[656] Abū Dāwūd, *k. al-ṣalāh, b. takhfīf al-ṣalāh.*

[657] Ibid.

[658] al-Marghīnānī, *al-Hidāyah, i.* 59.

[659] Abū Dāwūd, *k. al-ṣalāh, b. man ra'ā al-takhfīfa fīhā.*

same sūrah in both *rakᶜahs*. A man from the tribe of Juhaynah heard the Prophet ﷺ recite Sūrah *al-Zilzāl* in both *rakᶜahs* of *Fajr Ṣalāh*. The man commented, "I do not know if he did this out of forgetting or if he recited it twice intentionally".[660]

Saying the takbīr to mark the stages of the ṣalāh

It is Sunnah to say الله أكبر with every change of posture, except on straightening up after the *rukūᶜ* when one says سَمِعَ اللهُ لِمَنْ حَمِدَه . ᶜAbdullāh ibn Masᶜūd narrated: "I saw the Messenger of Allāh ﷺ make the *takbīr* upon every going down and coming up, and I saw Abū Bakr and ᶜUmar doing so".[661] Abū Hurayrah narrated: "When the Prophet ﷺ stood for *ṣalāh*, he would make the *takbīr* while standing. Then he made the *takbīr* while bowing. While coming up from *rukūᶜ*, he would say سَمِعَ اللهُ لِمَنْ حَمِدَه (Allāh hears him who praises Him), then, while standing, he would say, رَبَّنَا لَكَ الْحَمْد (Our Lord, to You is the praise). Then, he would say, اللهُ أكبر and go down for the *sajdah*, and again when he raised his head, and when he stood from his sitting after the two *sajdahs*. He did this in every *rakᶜah* until he finished the *ṣalāh*".[662]

The tasbīḥ of rukūᶜ

It is Sunnah to say in *rukūᶜ*, سُبْحَانَ رَبِّيَ الْعَظِيْم (Glory to my Lord, the Great), three times. ᶜUqbah ibn ᶜĀmir reported: "When '*Glorify the name of your Lord, the Great*', was revealed, the Prophet ﷺ told us, 'Do so in your *rukūᶜs*'."[663] ᶜAbdullāh ibn Masᶜūd reported the Messenger of Allāh ﷺ as saying: "When one of you bows, he should say three times سُبْحَانَ رَبِّيَ الْعَظِيْم (Glory to my Lord, the Great), and when he prostrates, he should say: سُبْحَانَ رَبِّيَ الأَعْلَى (Glory to my Lord, the Most High) three times. This is the minimum number".[664] Ḥudhayfah reported: "I prayed with the Messenger of Allāh ﷺ and while in the state of *rukūᶜ* he would say سُبْحَانَ رَبِّيَ الْعَظِيْم."[665]

[660] Abū Dāwūd, *k. al-ṣalāh, b. al-rajul yuᶜīdu sūratan wāḥidatan fī al-rakᶜatayn.*

[661] al-Nasā'ī, *k. al-taṭbīq, b. al-takbīr li al-sujūd.*

[662] al-Bukhārī, *k. al-adhān, b. al-takbīr idhā qāma min al-sujūd;* Muslim, *k. al-ṣalāh, b. ithbāt al-takbīr fī kull khafḍ wa rafᶜ fī al-ṣalāh.*

[663] Abū Dāwūd, *k. al-ṣalāh, b. mā yaqūlu al-rajul fī rukūᶜihi wa sujūdihi.*

[664] Abū Dāwūd, *k. al-ṣalāh, b. miqdār al-rukūᶜ.*

[665] al-Nasā'ī, *k. al-taṭbīq, b. al-dhikr fī al-rukūᶜ.*

Rising from rukūʿ

It is Sunnah for the one who is praying alone to say سَمِعَ اللهُ لِمَنْ حَمِدَه, (Allāh hears him who praises Him), upon rising up from *rukūʿ*. When he is standing straight, he should say, رَبَّنَا وَلَكَ الْحَمْد (Our Lord, and to You is the praise), or اللَّهُمَّ رَبَّنَا لَكَ الْحَمْد, (O Allāh, Our Lord, to You is the praise). If the *ṣalāh* is in congregation, the imām says the first phrase and then both the imām and followers say the second phrase. Abū Hurayrah reported: "When the Prophet ﷺ rose from *rukūʿ* he would say: 'Allāh listens to one who praises Him', and he would also say: 'O Allāh our Lord, and to You is the praise'."[666] In another ḥadīth Abū Hurayrah narrated from the Prophet ﷺ saying: "When the imām says, 'Allāh hears him who praises Him', you say, 'O Allāh, our Lord, and to You is the praise'. If one's utterance corresponds to that of the angels, all of one's previous sins will be forgiven'."[667]

The tasbīḥ of sajdah

It is Sunnah to say in *sajdah* سُبْحَانَ رَبِّيَ الأَعْلَى (Glory to my Lord, the Most High) three times. ʿUqbah ibn ʿĀmir related: "When *'Glorify the name of your Lord, the Most High'* was revealed, the Prophet ﷺ said: 'Do so in your *sajdahs*'."[668] Ḥudhayfah reported: "When the Prophet ﷺ prostrated, he would say سُبْحَانَ رَبِّيَ الأَعْلَى."[669] ʿAbdullāh ibn Masʿūd reported the Messenger of Allāh ﷺ as saying: "When one of you bows, he should say: سُبْحَانَ رَبِّيَ الْعَظِيم (Glory to my Lord, the Great) three times and when he prostrates, he should say: سُبْحَانَ رَبِّيَ الأَعْلَى (Glory to my Lord, the Most High) three times. This is the minimum number."[670]. Imām al-Tirmidhī, referring to this ḥadīth said: "The scholars prefer that in bowing or in prostration one should say the glorifications at least three times".[671]

[666] al-Bukhārī, *k. al-adhān, b. mā yaqūlu al-imām wa man khalfahu idhā rafaʿa ra'sahu min al-rukūʿ.*

[667] al-Bukhārī, *k. al-adhān, b. faḍl allāhumma rabbanā laka al-ḥamd;* Muslim, *k. al-ṣalāh, b. al-tasmīʿ wa al-ta'mīn.*

[668] Abū Dāwūd, *k. al-ṣalāh, b. mā yaqūlu al-rajul fī rukūʿihi wa sujūdihi.*

[669] Ibid.

[670] Abū Dāwūd, *k. al-ṣalāh, b. miqdār al-rukūʿ.*

[671] al-Tirmidhī, *k. al-ṣalāh, b. mā jā'a fī al-tasbīḥ fī al-rukūʿ wa al-sujūd.*

The tasbīḥ of sajdah in nafl ṣalāh

It is recommended in the *nafl ṣalāhs* that one should add some supplications to the glorifications. In a ḥadīth, it is recorded that the Prophet ﷺ said: "The closest one of you comes to his Lord is while he is prostrating, therefore make many supplications therein".[672] He also said: "I have prohibited you from reciting in the state of *rukūʿ* or *sajdah*. During the *rukūʿ*, glorify the Lord. During the *sajdahs*, strive your hardest in making supplications. Most likely, you will be listened to".[673]

Sitting between the two sajdahs

One should sit between the two *sajdahs* just as one does for the sitting of the *tashahhud*. The somewhat different manner of sitting for men and women has already been mentioned.

ʿAbdullāh ibn ʿAbbās narrated that between both *sajdahs*, the Prophet ﷺ would say: اللَّهُمَّ اغْفِرْ لِيْ وَارْحَمْنِيْ وَعَافِنِيْ وَاهْدِنِيْ وَارْزُقْنِيْ "O Allāh, forgive me, have mercy on me, grant me well-being, guide me and provide for me".[674]

Praying for the Prophet ﷺ

It is Sunnah to pray for the Prophet ﷺ in the last sitting after reciting the *tashahhud*. Faḍālah ibn ʿUbayd said: "The Messenger of Allāh ﷺ heard a man supplicating in his *ṣalāh* and he did not make the prayer for the Prophet ﷺ. The Prophet ﷺ said: 'He has hastened'. Then he called him and said: 'When one of you prays, begin with the praise and lauding of Allāh. Then make prayer for the Prophet ﷺ, and supplicate whatever you wish of Allāh'."[675]

Kaʿb ibn ʿUjrah reported how the Companions asked the Messenger of Allāh ﷺ to show them how to make salutations and prayers for him. He said: "Say:

اللَّهُمَّ صَلِّ عَلَى مُحَمَّدٍ وَعَلَى آلِ مُحَمَّدٍ كَمَا صَلَّيْتَ عَلَى آلِ إِبْرَاهِيمَ إِنَّكَ حَمِيدٌ مَجِيد ، اللَّهُمَّ
بَارِكْ عَلَى مُحَمَّدٍ وَعَلَى آلِ مُحَمَّدٍ كَمَا بَارَكْتَ عَلَى آلِ إِبْرَاهِيمَ إِنَّكَ حَمِيدٌ مَجِيد

[672] Muslim, *k. al-ṣalāh, b. mā yuqālu fī al-rukūʿ wa al-sujūd.*

[673] Muslim, *k. al-ṣalāh, b. al-nahy ʿan qirāʾat al-qurʾān fī al-rukūʿ wa al-sujūd.*

[674] Abū Dāwūd, *k. al-ṣalāh, b. al-duʿāʾ bayna al-sajdatayn.*

[675] Abū Dāwūd, *k. al-witr, b. al-duʿāʾ;* al-Tirmidhī, *k. al-daʿawāt.*

"O Allāh, bestow mercy upon Muḥammad and upon the family of Muḥammad as you have bestowed mercy upon the family of Ibrāhīm. You are the Praiseworthy, the Glorious. O Allāh, grant blessings to Muḥammad and the family of Muḥammad as you granted blessings to the family of Ibrāhīm. You are the Praiseworthy and Glorious".[676]

Supplications

It is Sunnah to supplicate after prayer for the Prophet ﷺ in the last sitting, for whatever one wishes of the good for oneself, one's parents and believing men and women. Ibn Masʿūd reported that the Prophet ﷺ taught him the *tashahhud* and then said: "Then choose whatever you wish to ask of Allāh".[677]

ʿAbdullāh ibn ʿAmr reported that Abū Bakr said to the Messenger of Allāh ﷺ: "Teach me a supplication that I may use in my *ṣalāhs*". He replied: "Say:

اَللَّهُمَّ إِنِّيْ ظَلَمْتُ نَفْسِيْ ظُلْمًا كَثِيْرًا وَلاَ يَغْفِرُ الذُّنُوْبَ إِلاَّ أَنْتَ فَاغْفِرْ لِيْ مَغْفِرَةً مِنْ عِنْدِكَ وَارْحَمْنِيْ إِنَّكَ أَنْتَ الْغَفُوْرُ الرَّحِيْم

'O Allāh, verily I have greatly wronged myself and no one forgives sins except You, so forgive me with a forgiveness from You, and have mercy on me. You are indeed the All-Forgiving, the All-Merciful'."[678]

ʿĀ'ishah reported that: "The Messenger of Allāh ﷺ would supplicate in his *ṣalāh* saying:

اَللَّهُمَّ إِنِّيْ أَعُوْذُ بِكَ مِنْ عَذَابِ الْقَبْرِ، وَمِنْ فِتْنَةِ الْمَسِيْحِ الدَّجَّالِ، وَمِنْ فِتْنَةِ الْمَحْيَا وَالْمَمَاتِ، اَللَّهُمَّ إِنِّيْ أَعُوْذُ بِكَ مِنَ الْمَأْثَمِ وَالْمَغْرَم

'O Allāh, I seek refuge in You from the torment of the grave, from the

[676] Muslim, *k. al-ṣalāh, b. al-ṣalāh ʿalā al-nabī ṣallallāhu ʿalayhi wa sallam baʿda al-tashahhud;* Abū Dāwūd, *k. al-ṣalāh, b. al-ṣalāh ʿalā al-nabī ṣallallāhu ʿalayhi wa sallam baʿda al-tashahhud.*

[677] Muslim, *k. al-ṣalāh, b. al-tashahhud fī al-ṣalāh.*

[678] Ibid.

trials of the anti-Christ the false, and from the trials of life and death. O Allāh, I seek refuge in You from sin and debt'." [679]

After the salām

Abū Hurayrah related that the Prophet ﷺ said: "Whoever says سُبْحَانَ الله after every *ṣalāh* 33 times, اَلْحَمْدُ لِله 33 times and اَللهُ أَكْبَر 33 times and then says: لاَ إِلَهَ إِلاَّ اللهُ وَحْدَهُ لاَ شَرِيْكَ لَهُ، لَهُ الْمُلْكُ وَلَهُ الْحَمْدُ وَهُوَ عَلَى كُلِّ شَيْءٍ قَدِيْرٌ "There is no god but Allāh, the One. There is no partner with Him. To Him belong the kingdom and the praise. He is All-powerful over all things". Such a person is forgiven, even if his sins are as abundant as the foam of the sea".[680]

One day, the Prophet ﷺ took Muʿādh ibn Jabal's hand and said to him: "O Muʿādh, I love you". Muʿādh responded: "May my father and mother be sacrificed for you, O Messenger of Allāh ﷺ, I love you". Then the Prophet ﷺ said: "I advise you, O Muʿādh, to say at the end of every *ṣalāh* اَللَّهُمَّ أَعِنِّي عَلَى ذِكْرِكَ وَشُكْرِكَ وَحُسْنِ عِبَادَتِكَ, 'O Allāh, help me in Your remembrance, Your thanks, and in nicely worshipping You'."[681]

Thawbān reported: "When the Prophet ﷺ finished his *ṣalāh*, he would seek Allāh's forgiveness three times and then say:

اَللَّهُمَّ أَنْتَ السَّلاَمُ وَمِنْكَ السَّلاَمُ، تَبَارَكْتَ يَا ذَا الْجَلاَلِ وَالإِكْرَام

'O Allāh, You are Peace and from You is peace. You are Blessed, O Sublime and Honourable One'." Walīd said: "I asked al-Awzāʿī how he sought Allāh's forgiveness? He said: 'By saying: أَسْتَغْفِرُ الله، أَسْتَغْفِرُ الله، أَسْتَغْفِرُ الله, "I seek Allāh's forgiveness, I seek Allāh's forgiveness, I seek Allāh's forgiveness"'."[682]

Al-Mughīrah ibn Shuʿbah reported: "The Prophet ﷺ would say at the end of every obligatory *ṣalāh:*

لاَ إِلَهَ إِلاَّ اللهُ وَحْدَهُ لاَ شَرِيْكَ لَهُ، لَهُ الْمُلْكُ وَلَهُ الْحَمْدُ وَهُوَ عَلَى كُلِّ شَيْءٍ قَدِيْرٌ، اَللَّهُمَّ لاَ مَانِعَ لِمَا أَعْطَيْتَ وَلاَ مُعْطِيَ لِمَا مَنَعْتَ وَلاَ يَنْفَعُ ذَا الْجَدِّ مِنْكَ الْجَدّ

[679] al-Bukhārī, *k. al-adhān, b. al-duʿā' qabla al-salām.*

[680] Muslim, *k. al-masājid wa mawāḍiʿ al-ṣalāh, b. istiḥbāb al-dhikr baʿda al-ṣalāh wa bayān ṣifatih.*

[681] al-Nasā'ī, *k. al-sahw, b. nawʿ ākhar min al-duʿā'.*

[682] Muslim, *k. al-masājid wa mawāḍiʿ al-ṣalāh, b. istiḥbāb al-dhikr baʿda al-ṣalāh wa bayān ṣifatih.*

'There is no god but Allāh, the One. There is no partner with Him. To Him belong the kingdom and the praise. He is All-powerful over all things. O Allāh, none can withhold what You have conferred, nor can anyone confer what You have withheld. A fortune does not benefit its owner against You'."[683]

Description of the ṣalāh

It is compulsory for all recitations and supplications in the *ṣalāh* to be said in Arabic. On commencing the *ṣalāh,* the believing man or woman says اَللّٰهُ أَكْبَر , and raises their hands with the *takbīr* – the man until his thumbs are level with the lobes of his ears, the woman to the level of her shoulders, and they do not raise them in any other *takbīr.* Then, the man places his right hand over his left, holding them thus below the navel; the woman places the palm of the right over the other hand, holding them on her chest; and then they say: سُبْحَانَكَ اللّٰهُمَّ وَبِحَمْدِكَ وَتَبَارَكَ اسْمُكَ وَتَعَالَى جَدُّكَ وَلَا إِلٰهَ غَيْرُكَ (Glory be to You, O Allāh, and to You is the praise. Blessed is Your name and exalted is Your honour. There is no god besides You). Then they say أَعُوْذُ بِاللّٰهِ مِنَ الشَّيْطَانِ الرَّجِيْم followed by بِسْمِ اللّٰهِ الرَّحْمٰنِ الرَّحِيْم both quietly (inaudible to others). Then, they recite *al-Fātiḥah* and a sūrah after it, or three consecutive verses from whichever sūrah they wish.

After the imām concludes the *Fātiḥah* with وَلَا الضَّالِّيْن he says آمِيْن. Those praying behind him also say *āmīn,* silently. Then on saying اَللّٰهُ أَكْبَر the imām bows for the *rukūʿ* (in the manner described above). During the *rukūʿ* he says سُبْحَانَ رَبِّيَ الْعَظِيْم at least three times, then raises his head and says سَمِعَ اللّٰهُ لِمَنْ حَمِدَه. Then both he and those following him say رَبَّنَا لَكَ الْحَمْد or رَبَّنَا وَلَكَ الْحَمْد or اَللّٰهُمَّ رَبَّنَا لَكَ الْحَمْد. As he straightens up, the imām says اَللّٰهُ أَكْبَر and then makes the *sajdah* in the manner described above; those following in the *ṣalāh* do likewise. (The posture in *sajdah* is slightly different for men and women; the details were given earlier.) In the *sajdah,* the imām says سُبْحَانَ رَبِّيَ الْأَعْلَى at least three times, then raises his head and says اَللّٰهُ أَكْبَر. After he has attained calmness in the sitting position, he says اَللّٰهُ أَكْبَر and makes the second *sajdah* in the same way as the first. Those following in the *ṣalāh* say اَللّٰهُ أَكْبَر and do the same. Then, the imām straightens up to a standing position and the followers behind him do likewise. One does not sit or rest on the ground after the second *sajdah* nor does one rest

[683] Ibid.

one's weight on one's hands when getting up to stand, unless there is an excuse or need to do so.

The second *rakʿah* begins directly with the *Fātiḥah* and then proceeds as the first *rakʿah*. After the second *sajdah* of the second *rakʿah*, the imām and those following him assume the sitting position for the *tashahhud*; there is some difference in the preferred manner of sitting between men and women, as described earlier. Unless this second *rakʿah* is the last of that particular *ṣalāh*, the imām says اللّٰهُ أَكْبَر and stands for the third, and then again for the fourth *rakʿah*. It is sufficient for the third and fourth *rakʿahs* of the *ṣalāh* to recite only the *Fātiḥah* during the *qiyām* (standing).

In the last *rakʿah*, the imām and those following him say the *tashahhud*, followed by the prayers for blessings on the Prophet ﷺ and then the supplication *(duʿā')* as described earlier. One should recite the *duʿā's* and not say them in a form resembling normal speech. The *ṣalāh* ends as the imām says اَلسَّلَامُ عَلَيْكُمْ وَرَحْمَةُ اللّٰه first to his right, then to his left, and the people following him do the same.

Excellence in the ṣalāh

The above description deals with the outward acts of the *ṣalāh*. However, if the person doing all this does not have sincerity, fear of Allāh and concentration, and if his worship does not help strengthen his faith and does not stop him from evil, then his *ṣalāh* is like a body without a soul. Allāh says in the Qur'ān: "*Successful indeed are the believers, those who are fearful and humble in their ṣalāh, those who turn away from what is false, and those who pay zakāh. And those who guard their chastity, except from their wives or those that their right hands possess, for they, they are free from blame. But whoever seeks beyond that then those are the transgressors. Those who are faithfully true to their trusts and covenants. And those who strictly guard their ṣalāhs. These are indeed the inheritors, who shall inherit Paradise. They shall dwell therein forever*".[684] In another place Allāh says: "*Recite what has been revealed to you of the Book, and establish ṣalāh. Verily, ṣalāh prevents from shameful acts and evil deeds*".[685]

To attain excellence, one should instead keep one's mind and heart attuned to the *ṣalāh* and one's Lord, and also keep one's thoughts on the

[684] *al-Mu'minūn* 1-11
[685] *al-ʿAnkabūt* 45

meaning of the Qur'ānic verses and on the significance of the different acts of the *ṣalāh*: a person has only that portion of the *ṣalāh* in which they maintain full awareness. ʿAmmār ibn Yāsir heard the Messenger of Allāh ﷺ say: "A man may complete the *ṣalāh* and only have recorded for himself one-tenth or one-ninth or one-eighth or one-seventh or one-fifth or one-fourth or one-third or one-half".[686]

Abū Hurayrah reported that the Messenger of Allāh ﷺ said: "Allāh, the Glorious, said: 'I have divided the *ṣalāh* (i.e., *al-Fātiḥah*) into two halves, between Me and My slave, and My slave shall receive what he asks for'. When the slave says, '*All praise and thanks are due to Allāh, the Lord of the Worlds*', Allāh, the Exalted, says, 'My slave has thanked Me'. When he says, '*The Compassionate, the Merciful*', Allāh, the Exalted, says, 'My slave has praised Me'. When he says, '*Master of the Day of Judgement*', Allāh, the Exalted says, 'My slave has glorified Me'. And when he says, '*You alone we worship and from You alone we seek help*', Allāh, the Exalted, says, 'This is between Me and My slave. And for My slave is what he asks'. And when he says '*Guide us to the straight path, the path of those whom You have favoured and not of those with whom You are angry nor of those who have gone astray*', Allāh says, 'That is for My slave and My slave shall get what he asks for'."[687]

Sayyid Abū al-Ḥasan ʿAlī Nadwī said: "*Ṣalāh* brings about a radical change in the moral and mental outlook of man and gives it a new orientation. It leads him from wicked to virtuous deeds and imbues his heart with the love of faith. It makes apostasy, defiance of Allāh and profligacy repugnant to him. But all this takes effect only when the *ṣalāh* is real and genuine and charged with life, warmth and vitality.

"When the Prophet Shuʿayb ﷺ gave the call to his people to follow the path of *tawḥīd*, piety and well-doing and warned them against the dreadful consequences of injustice, violation of the rights of others and cheating in weighing, they looked for the primary cause of the change that had come about in his life and came to the conclusion that it was the *ṣalāh* they had seen him offering up frequently which had done it. It was the only visible act he had latterly begun to perform which was totally non-existent in their lives. They, therefore, imagined that in it they had discovered the springhead of Shuʿayb's call and solved the

[686] Abū Dāwūd, *k. al-ṣalāh, b. mā jā'a fī nuqṣān al-ṣalāh.*

[687] Muslim, *k. al-ṣalāh, b. wujūb qirā'at al-fātiḥah fī kull rakʿah.*

riddle of his refutation of the hereditary religion of his community and its ancient way of life. Innocently, they enquired of him: '*O Shuʿayb, does your ṣalāh command you that we should forsake that which our fathers used to worship, or that we should leave off doing what we will with our property?*' (*Hūd:* 87)"[688]

[688] Abū al-Ḥasan ʿAlī Nadwī, *The Four Pillars of Islam* 42.

Chapter 6: *Masjids* and congregational *ṣalāhs*

MASJIDS

It is indeed a special blessing upon this *ummah* that Allāh has made the whole earth a *masjid* (a place for prayer). Abū Umāmah related that the Prophet ﷺ said: "All of the earth has been made for me and my *ummah*, pure and a place of *ṣalāh*".[689] Therefore, when the time for *ṣalāh* comes, a Muslim may pray wherever he may be.

However, it has always been part of the religion of Allāh, to build special places for His worship. These places are called *masjids*. Abū Dharr asked the Prophet ﷺ: "What was the first *masjid* on earth?" The Prophet ﷺ said: "*al-Masjid al-Ḥarām*". Abū Dharr asked: "Which is the next oldest *masjid?*" The Prophet ﷺ said: "*al-Aqṣā Masjid*". Abū Dharr then asked: "How much time was there between them". The Prophet ﷺ replied: "Forty years". Finally, the Prophet ﷺ said: "Wherever you may be at the time of *ṣalāh*, you may pray, for it (the earth) is all a *masjid*".[690]

The three distinguished masjids

Masjids are places for the worship of Allāh, and are equal in that regard. For only three *masjids*, is it permitted to travel to do the prayer in them; in order of excellence, they are: *al-Masjid al-Ḥarām* (the Inviolable *Masjid*) in Makkah, *al-Masjid al-Nabawī* (the *Masjid* of the Prophet ﷺ) in Madīnah and *al-Masjid al-Aqṣā* (the Further *Masjid*) in Jerusalem. The Prophet ﷺ said: "One should not undertake a journey, except for three *masjids*: *al-Masjid al-Ḥarām*, my *masjid*, and *al-Masjid al-Aqṣā*."[691] In another ḥadīth the Messenger of Allah ﷺ said: "Offering *ṣalāh* in my *masjid* is better than one thousand *ṣalāhs* elsewhere, except for those offered in *al-Masjid al-Ḥarām*. The *ṣalāh* in *al-Masjid al-Ḥarām* is better than one hundred thousand *ṣalāhs*".[692]

[689] Aḥmad, *al-Musnad* 22190

[690] Muslim, *k. al-masājid wa mawāḍiʿ al-ṣalāh.*

[691] al-Bukhārī, *k. faḍl al-ṣalāh fī masjid makkah wa al-madīnah, b. masjid bayt al-maqdis;* Muslim, *k. al-ḥajj, b. safar al-mar'ah maʿa maḥram ilā ḥajj wa ghayrih.*

[692] Aḥmad, *al-Musnad* 14735.

Building masjids

Since *masjids* are places built for the worship of Allāh alone, building a *masjid* and participating in its building are highly meritorious. ᶜUthmān reported that the Prophet ﷺ said: "Whoever builds for Allāh a *masjid*, seeking by it Allāh's pleasure, Allāh will build for him a house in Paradise".[693]

Maintaining the masjids

The *masjids* should be maintained well and kept clean. The Prophet ﷺ said: "These *masjids* are not meant for urine or filth but they are for the remembrance of Allāh and recital of the Qur'ān".[694] Abū Hurayrah and Abū Saᶜīd narrate that the Messenger of Allāh ﷺ said: "When one of you stands to pray, he should not spit in front of him as he is facing Allāh when he is in *ṣalāh*. And he should not spit to his right as there is an angel on his right. So, he should spit to his left or under his feet and he should bury it".[695]

Jābir reported that the Prophet ﷺ said: "Whoever eats garlic, onions, or leeks should not come close to our *masjid* for the angels are harmed by what harms the children of Ādam".[696]

Anas reported that the Prophet ﷺ said: "The rewards of my *ummah* were placed before me, even for removing a speck of dust from the *masjid*".[697] ᶜĀ'ishah reported that, "The Prophet ﷺ ordered that *masjids* built in the houses must be cleaned and perfumed".[698]

Maintaining the *masjid* and taking care of it is a great act of reward which is pleasing to Allāh; but it is disliked that money be wasted on embellishing the *masjid*.[699] The *masjid* connects one to the Hereafter and is not to be lavishly ornamented nor should one build a *masjid* in order to vie out of haughtiness. In this regard, Anas ibn Mālik reported that the Messenger of Allāh ﷺ said: "The Hour will not come

[693] al-Bukhārī, *k. al-ṣalāh, b. man banā masjidan.*

[694] Muslim, *k. al-ṭahārah, b. wujūb ghasl al-bawl wa ghayrihi min al-najāsāt.*

[695] al-Bukhārī, *k. al-ṣalāh, b. lā yabṣuq ᶜan yamīnhi fī al-ṣalāh.*

[696] Muslim, *k. al-masājid wa mawāḍiᶜ al-ṣalāh, b. nahy man akala thūman aw baṣalan.*

[697] Abū Dāwūd, *k. al-ṣalāh, b. fī kans al-masjid.*

[698] Abū Dāwūd, *k. al-ṣalāh, b. ittikhadh al-masājid fī al-dūr.*

[699] *See*: al-Marghinānī, *al-Hidāyah*, i. 70.

to pass until the people vie with each other in building the *masjids*".[700] Ibn ʿUmar reported that: "We were forbidden to pray in any high and lofty *masjids*".[701] Ibn ʿAbbās in his foresight mentioned that in time Muslims would forget and begin to adorn the *masjids* inappropriately; he said: "You will certainly embellish them as the Jews and Christians embellished (their places of worship)". [702] ʿUmar ordered *masjids* to be built and said: "Protect the people from the rain. Beware of colouring them with red and yellow for they distract people".[703]

The manner of going to the masjid

The *masjids* deserve special respect. It is Sunnah to make supplications while going to the *masjid*. ʿAbdullāh ibn ʿAbbās narrated that the Prophet ﷺ left for the *masjid* saying:

اَللَّهُمَّ اجْعَلْ فِيْ قَلْبِيْ نُوْرًا ، وَفِيْ بَصَرِيْ نُوْرًا ، وَفِيْ سَمْعِيْ نُوْرًا ، وَعَنْ يَمِيْنِيْ نُوْرًا ، وَخَلْفِيْ نُوْرًا ، وَفِيْ عَصَبِيْ نُوْرًا ، وَفِيْ لَحْمِيْ نُوْرًا ، وَفِيْ دَمِيْ نُوْرًا ، وَفِيْ شَعْرِيْ نُوْرًا ، وَفِيْ بَشَرِيْ نُوْرًا

"O Allāh, grant me light in my heart, light in my vision, light in my hearing, light on my right, light behind me, light in my nerves, light in my flesh, light in my blood, light in my hair and light in my skin".[704]

Anas reported that the Messenger of Allāh ﷺ said: "Whoever says upon leaving his house بِسْمِ الله تَوَكَّلْتُ عَلَى الله، وَلَا حَوْلَ وَلَا قُوَّةَ إِلَّا بِالله, 'In the name of Allāh, I put my trust in Allāh. There is no power or might except with Allāh', it will be said to him: 'That is sufficient for you; you are guided, defended, and protected and the devil will be driven away from you'."[705]

Umm Salamah reported: "When the Messenger of Allāh ﷺ left the house he would say:

[700] Abū Dāwūd, *k. al-ṣalāh, b. fī binā' al-masājid.*

[701] al-Ṭabarānī, *al-Muʿjam al-kabīr* 13499

[702] Abū Dāwūd, *k. al-ṣalāh, b. fī binā' al-masājid.*

[703] al-Bukhārī, *k. al-ṣalāh, b. bunyān al-masjid.*

[704] al-Bukhārī, *k. al-daʿawāt, b. al-duʿā' idhā intabaha min al-layl.*

[705] Abū Dāwūd, *k. al-adab, b. mā yaqūlu idhā kharaja min baytihi;* al-Tirmidhī, *k. al-daʿawāt, b. mā yaqūlu idhā kharaja min baytihi.*

بِسْمِ اللهِ تَوَكَّلْتُ عَلَى اللهِ، اَللَّهُمَّ إِنِّي أَعُوْذُ بِكَ أَنْ أَضِلَّ أَوْ أُضَلَّ، أَوْ أَزِلَّ أَوْ أُزَلَّ، أَوْ أَظْلِمَ أَوْ أُظْلَمَ، أَوْ أَجْهَلَ أَوْ يُجْهَلَ عَلَيَّ

'In the name of Allāh, I rely on Allāh. O Allāh, I seek refuge in You lest I stray or am led astray or slip or be made to slip, or wrong anyone or am wronged by someone or behave ignorantly to someone or am behaved ignorantly to by someone else."[706]

Abū Hurayrah reported that the Prophet ﷺ said: "Whoever goes to the *masjid* in the morning and evening, Allāh will prepare for him a feast in Paradise as often as he goes in the morning and evening".[707] Abū Hurayrah also narrated that the Messenger of Allāh ﷺ said: "If anyone purifies himself in his house, and then walks to one of the houses of Allāh to fulfil one of the obligations laid down by Allāh, then (each one) of his steps will erase one of his sins and the next will raise his degrees".[708] Abū Saʿīd reported that the Prophet ﷺ said: "If you see a man frequenting the *masjid*, then testify that he has faith. As Allāh says: '*The attendants of Allāh's masjid are those who believe in Allāh and the last day* (*al-Tawbah:* 18)'."[709]

It is a Sunnah for one who wants to enter the *masjid* to enter with his right foot first and say اَللَّهُمَّ افْتَحْ لِيْ أَبْوَابَ رَحْمَتِكَ, "O Allāh, open for me the doors of Your mercy". One who wants to leave the *masjid* should step out their left foot first and then say: اَللَّهُمَّ إِنِّيْ أَسْأَلُكَ مِنْ فَضْلِكَ, "O Allāh, I ask You of Your favour". Abū Ḥumayd reported: the Messenger of Allāh ﷺ said: "When one of you enters the *masjid* he should recite the prayer of peace for the Prophet ﷺ then he should say اَللَّهُمَّ افْتَحْ لِيْ أَبْوَابَ رَحْمَتِكَ, 'O Allāh, open for me the doors of Your mercy'. And when one leaves the *masjid* one should say اَللَّهُمَّ إِنِّيْ أَسْأَلُكَ مِنْ فَضْلِكَ, 'O Allāh, I ask You of Your favour'."[710]

[706] Abū Dāwūd, ibid., al-Tirmidhī, *k. al-daʿawāt, b. al-taʿawwudh min an tajhal;* al-Nasā'ī, *k. al-istiʿādhah, b. al-istiʿādhah min du'ā'in lā yustajāb;* Ibn Mājah, *k. al-duʿā', b. mā yadʿū bihi al-rajul idhā kharaja min baytihi.*

[707] al-Bukhārī, *k. al-adhān, b. faḍl man ghadā ilā al-masjid wa man rāḥa;* Muslim, *k. al-masājid, b. al-mashy ilā al-ṣalāh tumḥā bihi al-khaṭāyā wa turfaʿu bihi al-darajāt.*

[708] Muslim, ibid.

[709] Ibn Mājah, *k. al-masājid wa al-jamāʿat, b. luzūm al-masājid wa intiẓār al-ṣalāh.*

[710] Muslim, *k. ṣalāt al-musāfirīn wa qaṣrihā, b. mā yaqūlu idhā dakhala al-masjid*; Abū Dāwūd, *k. al-ṣalāh, b. mā yaqūluhu al-rajul ʿinda dukhūlihi al-masjid.*

Abū Hurayrah narrated that the Prophet ﷺ said: "When the *iqāmah* is said, then do not proceed to the *ṣalāh* running; rather proceed with calm and dignity. Pray what you can in congregation and complete what you miss".[711]

One special tribute while entering into the *masjids* is to offer *taḥiyyat al-masjid*. This means greeting the *masjid* upon entering into it; this is done by praying two *rakᶜahs*. Abū Qatādah reported that the Messenger of Allāh ﷺ said: "When one of you comes to the *masjid*, he should pray two *rakᶜahs* before he sits".[712]

What is prohibited in the masjids

Masjids are built for the remembrance of Allāh. One should busy oneself either with the *ṣalāh*, recitation of the Qur'ān, learning, teaching or any kind of remembrance of Allāh. One should not use them for worldly matters. Here are a few examples of the things that the Prophet ﷺ did not like in the *masjid*.

Abū Hurayrah related that the Prophet ﷺ said: "If you see someone buying or selling in the *masjid*, say to him: 'May Allāh not give you any profit in your trading'."[713] ᶜAbdullāh ibn ᶜAmr reported: "The Prophet ﷺ forbade buying and selling in the *masjid*, reciting poetry in it, or announcing lost property, and he especially prohibited making a circle before the Friday *Ṣalāh*".[714]

It is not liked to use the *masjid* for sleeping or eating and drinking except if there is a need. ᶜAbdullāh ibn al-Ḥārith said: "During the time of the Messenger of Allāh ﷺ, we would eat meat and bread in the *masjid*".[715] ᶜAbdullāh ibn ᶜUmar would sleep in the *masjid* while he was a young man and was not married.[716]

[711] al-Bukhārī, *k. al-jumuᶜah, b. lā yasᶜā ilā al-ṣalāh walya'ti bi al-sakīnah*; Ibn Mājah, *k. al-masājid, b. al-mashy ilā al-ṣalāh.*

[712] al-Bukhārī, *k. al-ṣalāh, b. idhā dakhala al-masjid falyarkaᶜ rakᶜatayn.*

[713] al-Tirmidhī, *k. al-buyūᶜ, b. al-nahy ᶜan al-bayᶜ fī al-masjid.*

[714] al-Nasā'ī, *k. al-masājid, b. al-nahy ᶜan al-bayᶜ wa al-shirā' fī al-masjid wa ᶜan al-taḥalluq qabla ṣalāt al-jumuᶜah.*

[715] Ibn Mājah, *k. al-aṭᶜimah, b. al-akl fī al-masjid.*

[716] al-Bukhārī, *k. al-ṣalāh, b. nawm al-rijāl fī al-masjid.*

Places where ṣalāh is not allowed

Ṣalāh is a great act of worship and obedience to Allāh; it should not be done in any improper place. Allāh says: "*Purify My House for those who are circumambulating it, those staying in it, those bowing and those prostrating*".[717] ᶜAbdullāh ibn ᶜUmar related: "The Prophet ﷺ prohibited *ṣalāh* in seven places: dunghills, slaughterhouses, graveyards, the middle of the road, bathhouses, watering places where camels drink and rest, and on the roof of the House of Allāh (i.e. the Kaᶜbah)".[718]

Dunghills, slaughterhouses, bathhouses and the resting places of camels are prohibited because of the presence of impurities there. Praying in the middle of the roads is prohibited because it can be a nuisance to those passing by. As for praying on the roof of the Kaᶜbah, it is not liked because it does not honour the Kaᶜbah. Praying in graveyards is prohibited, because it resembles the practice of some of the People of the Book.[719]

ᶜĀ'ishah reported that the Prophet ﷺ said: "Allāh cursed the Jews and Christians (because) they took the graves of their prophets as *masjids*".[720] Abū Marthad al-Ghanawī reported that the Prophet ﷺ said: "Do not pray facing graves and do not sit on them".[721] Jundub ibn ᶜAbdullāh al-Bajalī heard the Prophet ﷺ say, five days before he died: "The people before you took graves as *masjids*. I prohibit this to you".[722] ᶜUmar prohibited people from praying beside a grave.[723] Ibn Jurayj narrated that ᶜAṭā' disliked the prayer in a graveyard or in the direction of a grave.[724] Ṭāwūs severely disliked prayers in a graveyard.[725]

[717] *al-Baqarah* 125.

[718] Ibn Mājah, *k. al-masājid wa al-jamāᶜat, b. al-mawāḍiᶜ allatī tukrahu fīhā al-ṣalāh.*

[719] al-Kāsānī, *Badā'iᶜ al-ṣanā'iᶜ, i.* 539-40.

[720] Muslim, *k. al-masājid wa mawāḍiᶜ al-ṣalāh, b. al-nahy ᶜan binā' al-masājid ᶜalā al-qubūr.*

[721] Muslim, *k. al-janā'iz, b. al-nahy ᶜan al-julūs ᶜalā al-qabr wa al-ṣalāti ᶜalayh.*

[722] Muslim, *k. al-masājid wa mawāḍiᶜ al-ṣalāh, b. al-nahy ᶜan binā' al-masājid ᶜalā al-qubūr.*

[723] ᶜAbd al-Razzāq, *al-Muṣannaf, i.* 404.

[724] Ibid.

[725] Ibid.

Ṣalāh is also disliked in any place where there are pictures of living objects. ʿĀ'ishah reported that Umm Salamah mentioned to the Messenger of Allāh ﷺ the churches she saw in Abyssinia and the pictures they contained. The Prophet ﷺ said to her: "These are the people who, when a pious slave or pious man among them dies, build a *masjid* upon their graves and put pictures in it. They are the worst of all creation in Allāh's sight".[726] Abū Hurayrah reported that the Messenger of Allāh ﷺ said: "Jibrīl came to me and said: 'I came to you last night, and nothing stopped me from entering the house that you were in except that on the door of the house there was a picture of men, in the house there was a curtain on which there were pictures, and there was a dog in the house. So order the head of the picture that is at the door to be cut and made like a tree, and the curtain to be cut into two pieces and used as pillows, and the dog to be taken out'. Then the Prophet ﷺ did that".[727] Al-Kāsānī said: "There is no good in a place where angels do not enter".[728]

Ṣalāh in the Kaʿbah

Ṣalāh in the Kaʿbah is valid for both *farḍ ṣalāh* or *nafl ṣalāh*.[729] Nāfiʿ narrated that ʿAbdullāh ibn ʿUmar said: "The Messenger of Allāh ﷺ entered the house (the Kaʿbah) along with Usāmah ibn Zayd, Bilāl and ʿUthmān ibn Ṭalḥah al-Ḥajabī and closed the door and stayed there for some time. I asked Bilāl when he came out, 'What did the Prophet ﷺ do?' He replied: 'He offered prayer with one pillar to his left and one to his right and three behind'. In those days the Kaʿbah was supported by six pillars'." Mālik said: "There were two pillars on his (the Prophet's) right side".[730]

If the people pray in congregation inside the Kaʿbah, then the imām can stand facing any direction, and the best position for the followers is to stand behind him facing the same direction as the imām.[731]

[726] Muslim, *k. al-masājid wa mawāḍiʿ al-ṣalāh, b. al-nahy ʿan binā' al-masājid ʿalā al-qubūr.*

[727] Abū Dāwūd, *k. al-libās, b. al-ṣuwar;* al-Tirmidhī, *b. mā jā'a anna al-malā'ikah lā tadkhulu baytan fihi ṣūrah.*

[728] al-Kāsānī, *Badā'iʿ al-ṣanā'iʿ, i.* 542.

[729] al-Marghinānī, *al-Hidāyah, i.* 102.

[730] al-Bukhārī, *k. al-ṣalāh, b. al-ṣalāh bayna al-sawārī fī ghayr jamāʿah.*

[731] al-Kāsānī, *Badā'iʿ al-ṣanā'iʿ, i.* 557.

Congregational ṣalāh

Performing the *ṣalāhs* in congregation is a Sunnah *mu'akkadah* for men who are able to attend without undue hardship. Attending the congregation is not a Sunnah for women, children, travellers, the sick and the elderly, who cannot walk easily.[732]

Praying in congregation is a highly meritorious act. Abū Hurayrah reported that the Prophet ﷺ said: "The *ṣalāh* of a man in congregation is twenty-five times superior in reward to his *ṣalāh* in his home or the market place – and this is because he makes *wuḍū'* and perfects it and goes to the *masjid* with the sole purpose of performing the *ṣalāh*. He does not take a step without being raised a degree and having one of his sins erased. When he prays, as long as he does not lose his *wuḍū'*, the angels keep on praying for him: 'O Allāh, bless him. O Allāh, have mercy on him'. And he is considered to be in *ṣalāh* as long as he is waiting for the *ṣalāh*".[733]

ᶜAbdullāh ibn Masᶜūd said: "Whoever among you would like to meet Allāh tomorrow as a Muslim, he should persevere in observing these five *ṣalāhs* wherever the call for them is made, for Allāh has chosen for your Prophet ﷺ the way of right guidance. And they are part of this right guidance. If you were to pray them in your houses, as the man who stays behind in his house, you would be leaving the Sunnah of your Prophet ﷺ. If you leave the Sunnah of your Prophet ﷺ, you will go astray. I have seen a time when no one stayed away from congregational *ṣalāh* except for the hypocrites who were well known for their hypocrisy. A man would be brought, supported by two people (due to his weakness) until he was placed in a row".[734]

Two or more make a congregation

The least number that constitutes a congregation is two people, that is one person beside the imām, whether that other person is a man, or a woman, or a child.[735] Abū Mūsā al-Ashᶜarī narrated that the Messenger of Allāh ﷺ said: "Two people and above [that number] are congregation".[736]

[732] Ibid., *i*. 662-3.

[733] al-Bukhārī, *k. al-adhān, b. faḍl ṣalāt al-jamāᶜah.*

[734] Muslim, *k. al-masājid wa mawāḍiᶜ al-ṣalāh, b. ṣalāt al-jamāᶜah min sunan al-hudā.*

[735] al-Kāsānī, *Badā'iᶜ al-ṣanā'iᶜ*, *i*. 664-5.

[736] Ibn Mājah, *k. iqāmat al-ṣalāh wa al-sunnah fīhā, b. al-ithnāni jamāᶜah.*

Abū Saʿīd narrated: "A man entered the *masjid*, and the Prophet ﷺ and his Companions had already prayed. The Prophet ﷺ said: 'Who will give charity to him by praying with him?' So, a man from the people stood and prayed with him".[737]

When it is permissible not to attend congregation

Jābir said: "We went on a journey with the Prophet ﷺ and it rained upon us, so he said: 'Whoever wishes may pray in his stopping place'."[738] ʿAbdullāh ibn ʿUmar narrated that the Prophet ﷺ ordered the *mu'adhdhin* to say: "Pray in your places," on a cold, raining night.[739] Imām Muḥammad said: "This is good; and this is a concession; and the *ṣalāh* in congregation is better".[740]

What applies in cases of severe cold also applies in cases of extreme heat, darkness, or some other urgent circumstance. ʿĀ'ishah narrated that she heard the Prophet ﷺ say: "There is no *ṣalāh* when the meal is presented or when one needs to answer the call of nature".[741]

Women and congregational ṣalāhs

It is better for women to pray at home rather than to attend the congregational *ṣalāhs*. It is, however, allowed for women to go to the *masjid* for the congregational *ṣalāh* as long as they avoid using any attractive adornment, perfume, etc. ʿAbdullāh ibn ʿUmar reported that the Prophet ﷺ said: "Do not prevent the women from going to the *masjids*, although their homes are better for them".[742] Abū Hurayrah related that the Prophet ﷺ said: "Do not keep the female slaves of Allāh from the houses of Allāh. And they are to go out un-perfumed".[743] Abū Hurayrah also reported that the Prophet ﷺ said: "Any woman who uses some scent should not be present with us during the night *ṣalāh*".[744]

[737] Aḥmad, *al-Musnad* 11427.

[738] Muslim, *k. ṣalāt al-musāfirīn wa qaṣrihā, b. al-ṣalāh fī al-riḥāl fī al-maṭar.*

[739] al-Bukhārī, *k. al-adhān, b. al-rukhṣah fī al-maṭar wa al-ʿillah an yuṣallīya fī raḥlihi.*

[740] Muḥammad, *al-Muwaṭṭa', i.* 554-5.

[741] Muslim, *k. al-masājid wa mawāḍiʿ al-ṣalāh, b. karāhat al-ṣalāh bi ḥaḍrat al-ṭaʿām.*

[742] Abū Dāwūd, *k. al-ṣalāh, b. mā jā'a fī khurūj al-nisā' ilā al-masjid.*

[743] Ibid.

[744] Muslim, *k. al-ṣalāh, b. khurūj al-nisā' ilā al-masājid.*

Who should serve as imām?

The person with the most right to be the imām is the one who can best recite the Qur'ān and who has most knowledge of the Sunnah. If more than two people are equal in these skills, then righteousness, age or other factors can be taken into account.[745] Abū Saᶜīd narrated that the Prophet ﷺ said: "If you are three in number, then one of you should be the imām. And the one who has the most right to it is the one who is the most versed in the Qur'ān".[746]

Abū Masᶜūd al-Anṣārī reported that the Prophet ﷺ said: "The imām of a people should be the one who is the most versed in the Book of Allāh. If they are equal in their recital, then the one who is most knowledgeable of the Sunnah. If they are equal in the Sunnah, then the one who migrated first. If they are equal in that, then the eldest. And no man should be an imām for another man if the other holds authority".[747]

Abū Hurayrah reported that the Prophet ﷺ said: "It is not allowed for a man who believes in Allāh and the Last Day to be an imām for people, except with their permission, nor may he specifically make supplications for himself without including them. If he does so, he is disloyal to them".[748]

A person who must pray sitting because he has an excuse can be imām to those who are standing. In this respect the Prophet ﷺ led the *ṣalāh* in his last illness while he was sitting.[749]

The *imāmah* of a blind person to the seeing is allowed, as the Messenger of Allāh ﷺ appointed Ibn Umm Maktūm, a blind man, to lead the people in *ṣalāh*.[750]

A person praying *farḍ* can be imām for people who are praying *nafl*. Yazīd ibn al-Aswad reported the Messenger of Allāh ﷺ as saying: "If you

[745] al-Samarqandī, *Tuḥfat al-fuqahā'* 108.
[746] Muslim, *k. al-masājid wa mawāḍiᶜ al-ṣalāh, b. man aḥaqqu bi al-imāmah.*
[747] Ibid.
[748] Abū Dāwūd, *k. al-ṭahārah, b. ayuṣallī al-rajul wa huwa ḥāqin.*
[749] al-Bukhārī, *k. al-adhān, b. innamā juᶜila al-imām liyu'tamma bihi.*
[750] Abū Dāwūd, *k. al-ṣalāh, b. imāmat al-aᶜmā.*

have prayed at home and then come upon an imām [praying *farḍ*], pray with the imām and it will be supererogatory for you".[751]

A person who has done *wuḍū'* can be imām for people who have done *tayammum,* as can be one who has done *tayammum* for those who have done *wuḍū'*. ᶜAmr ibn al-ᶜĀṣ led others in *ṣalāh* when he had done *tayammum* only and the Prophet ﷺ approved of it.

It is not disallowed that a traveller acts as imām for residents, or a resident for travellers, or a less qualified person for people who are more qualified: the prayer does not become invalid thereby. The Prophet ﷺ after the Conquest of Makkah, led the people in *ṣalāh* by praying two *rakᶜahs* except for *Maghrib* and said: "O people of Makkah, stand and pray the last two *rakᶜahs* as we are travellers".[752]

If a traveller prays behind a resident, he must complete the four *rakᶜahs* even if he only prayed part of a *rakᶜah* behind the resident imām. Ibn ᶜAbbās was asked: "Why is the traveller to pray two *rakᶜah*s if he prays by himself and four if he prays behind a resident?" He answered: "That is the Sunnah". In another version, Mūsā ibn Salāmah asked him: "If we pray with you, we pray four *rakᶜah*s; otherwise we pray two?" He replied: "That is the Sunnah of Abū al-Qāsim (the Prophet ﷺ)."[753]

Those who should not be imāms

It is not permissible for someone who has a medical condition that does not allow him to remain in a state of purity to be an imām for others who do not have such a problem. One in a state of purity should not do *ṣalāh* behind someone who suffers from incontinency, nor women in a state of purity behind a woman in a state of *istiḥāḍah,* nor a reciter behind someone untutored in recitation, nor someone properly clothed behind one not clothed.

A person who is standing may do the *ṣalāh* behind one who is praying seated, but one who is capable of bowing and prostrating should not do the *ṣalāh* behind someone who, because of incapacity, only indicates the

[751] Abū Dāwūd, *k. al-ṣalāh, b. fī man sallā fī manzilihi thumma adraka al-jamāᶜah yuṣallī maᶜahum.*

[752] Abū Dāwūd, *k. al-ṣalāh, b. matā yutimmu al-musāfir.*

[753] Aḥmad, *al-Musnad* 1862.

movements. The person who is doing a *farḍ ṣalāh* should not do it behind someone doing a *nafl,* nor behind someone who is doing another *farḍ*, while the person doing a *nafl* may stand behind the one doing *farḍ*.

To pray behind an evildoer or innovator is not liked. Al-Sā'ib ibn Khallād narrated that a man was leading the people in *ṣalāh* and he spat in the direction of the *qiblah*. The Messenger of Allāh ﷺ saw this and said: "Do not let him lead you in *ṣalāh*". After this, the man wanted to lead the people in *ṣalāh* but they prevented him and told him what the Prophet ﷺ had said. The man went to the Prophet ﷺ to ask him about this, and the Prophet ﷺ replied: "Yes, (it is true) for you have offended Allāh and His Messenger".[754]

However, for anyone whose *ṣalāh* is valid on an individual basis, his being imām is also valid for others. ʿAbdullāh ibn ʿUmar narrated that the Prophet ﷺ, peace upon him, said: "Pray behind whoever says: There is no god but Allāh". [755] ʿAbdullāh ibn ʿUmar prayed behind al-Ḥajjāj.[756]

It is disliked for one to lead the *ṣalāh* if one is not liked by people because of one's religious conduct. ʿAbdullāh ibn ʿAbbās related that the Prophet ﷺ said: "Three people's *ṣalāhs* will not rise above their head the length of a hand's span: a man who leads a people in *ṣalāh* and they do not like him, a woman who has disobeyed her husband and he is displeased with her, and two brothers who are estranged".[757]

A woman's imāmah

There is a consensus among scholars that women do not lead the *ṣalāh,* except if the followers are only women. If women do the *ṣalāh* as a *jamaʿah,* the imām should stand in the middle of the other women. ʿĀ'ishah used to lead the women in *ṣalāh* and stand with the women in the middle of the first row, i.e. not stand separately in front of the others. Umm Salamah would also do so. After narrating the practice of ʿĀ'ishah, Imām Muḥammad said: "We do not like the woman to lead the

[754] Abū Dāwūd, *k. al-ṣalāh, b. fī karāhiyat al-buzāq fī al-masjid.*

[755] al-Dāraquṭnī, *al-Sunan, ii.* 43.

[756] al-Bukhārī, *k. al-ḥajj, b. al-tahjīr bi al-rawāḥ yawma ʿarafah.*

[757] Ibn Mājah, *k. iqāmat al-ṣalāh wa al-sunnah fīhā, b. man amma qawman wa hum lahu kārihūn.*

ṣalāh; if she does then she should stand in the middle of the row with the women, as ʿĀ'ishah did. This is the opinion of Abū Ḥanīfah".[758]

A man leading a group of women in ṣalāh

It is permissible for a man to lead a women only group in the prayer but only if they are in a public place. If they are in a private place, then it is only permissible if the imām is *maḥram* for all or some of the women – however, it is nevertheless disliked.[759]

How the imam should stand and his responsibility

It is preferable for the imām to stand in the centre of the rows and the people closest to him should be people of intellect and understanding. Abū Hurayrah reported that the Prophet ﷺ said: "Let the imām stand in the centre, and close the gaps in the rows".[760] ʿAbdullāh ibn Masʿūd reported that the Prophet ﷺ said: "Let those who are prudent and sedate be near me, then those who are next to them, then those who are next to them, and beware of the tumult of the marketplace".[761]

Abū Hurayrah reported that the Prophet ﷺ said: "If one of you leads the people in *ṣalāh*, he should be easy on them for among the people are the weak, sick, and elderly. If one prays alone, one may make it as long as one wishes".[762] Imām Muḥammad said: "We adhere to it and this is the opinion of Abū Ḥanīfah".[763] It is narrated from Anas that the Prophet ﷺ said: "Sometimes I enter *ṣalāh* and I intend to prolong it, but then I hear a child crying, I shorten my *ṣalāh* thinking of the distress of the child's mother".[764] Anas said: "I have not prayed behind anyone who prayed a lighter *ṣalāh* and a more complete *ṣalāh* than that of the Prophet ﷺ".[765]

[758] Abū Ḥanīfah, *K. al-āthār* 57.

[759] *al-Fatāwā al-hindiyyah, i.* 85.

[760] Abū Dāwūd, *k. al-ṣalāh, b. maqām al-imām min al-ṣaff.*

[761] Muslim, *k. al-ṣalāh, b. taswiyat al-ṣufūf wa iqāmatihā.*

[762] al-Bukhārī, *k. al-adhān, b. idhā ṣallā li nafsihi falyuṭawwil mā shā'a.*

[763] Muḥammad, *al-Muwaṭṭa', i.* 646.

[764] al-Bukhārī, *k. al-adhān, b. man akhaffa al-ṣalāta ʿinda bukā' ṣabī.*

[765] Ibid.

The responsibility of the followers and how they should stand

It is the responsibility of the followers that they must follow the imām. ʿĀ'ishah narrated from the Prophet ﷺ saying: "The imām has been made in order to be followed; so do not differ from the imām".[766] Abū Hurayrah reported that the Prophet ﷺ said: "Do you not fear that if you raise your head before the imām Allāh may change your head into that of a donkey?"[767]

If there is only one person beside the imām, he should stand to the right of the imām. Ibn ʿAbbās said: "I stayed with my aunt Maymūnah and the Prophet ﷺ got up to pray during the night. I got up to pray with him and stood on his left and the Prophet ﷺ took me by my hand and put me on his right side".[768] Jābir reported: "The Prophet ﷺ stood to pray and I came and stood on his left. He took me by my hand, and led me around him until I stood on his right. Then, Jābir ibn Ṣakhr came and stood on the left of the Messenger of Allāh ﷺ. He took both of us by our hands and made us stand behind him".[769]

If there are two others, the imām should stand in front of them. That is the practice of the Prophet ﷺ followed by the *ummah* in all generations. Anas ibn Mālik said that his grandmother Mulaykah invited the Messenger of Allāh ﷺ to take meals which she prepared for him. He took some of it and prayed. He said: "Get up; I shall lead you in prayer". Anas said: "I got up and took a mat which had become black on account of long use. I then washed it with water. The Messenger of Allāh ﷺ stood upon it. The orphan and I stood in a row behind him. The old woman stood behind us".[770]

If a woman is present within a group consisting only of men, then she is to stand in a row by herself behind the men; she is not to join the men in their rows. If a woman stands to the side of a man and they are taking

[766] al-Bukhārī, *k. al-adhān, b. innamā juʿila al-imām liyu'tamma bihi*; Muslim, *k. al-ṣalāh, b. i'timām al-ma'mūm bi al-imām.*

[767] al-Bukhārī, *k. al-adhān, b. ithm man rafaʿa ra'sahu qabla al-imām.*

[768] al-Bukhārī, *k. al-adhān, b. yaqūmu ʿan yamīn al-imām biḥidhā'ihi sawā' idhā kāna ithnayn*; Muslim, k. *ṣalāt al-musāfirīn, b. al-duʿā' fī ṣalāt al-layl.*

[769] Muslim, *k. al-zuhd, b. ḥadīth jābir al-ṭawīl.*

[770] al-Bukhārī, *k. al-masājid, b. jawāz al-jamāʿah fī al-nāfilah*; Abū Dāwūd, *k. al-ṣalāh, b. idhā kānū thalāthah.*

part in one *ṣalāh,* then his *ṣalāh* is invalidated while hers is not. This is mentioned in the earlier ḥadīth whereby Anas said: "An orphan and I prayed behind the Messenger of Allāh ﷺ in our house and my mother prayed behind us".[771] Imām Muḥammad said: "We adhere to all this; when one person prays with the imām he will stand on the imām's right, and if two people pray they will stand behind him; this is the opinion of Abū Ḥanīfah".[772]

Abū Mālik al-Ashʿarī narrated that the Messenger of Allāh ﷺ placed the men in rows, and then the young boys behind them.[773] Abū Hurayrah reported that the Messenger of Allāh ﷺ said: "The best rows for the men are the first rows and the worst rows for them are the last rows. The best rows for the women are the last rows and the worst for them are the front rows".[774]

If someone goes to a row and does not find sufficient space or a gap to stand therein, then he should pull someone back from the row so that they form a new one. ʿAṭā' ibn Abī Rabāḥ was asked about someone who enters the *masjid,* and finds that the row is complete. He said: "If he can enter into the row, then he should do so, but if he cannot enter, then he should take someone [by the arm] and draw him back to [make a row] with him, and he should not stand alone".[775]

As mentioned above, if there is a woman, and no other women with her, she will stand alone behind the row. ʿAṭā' ibn Abī Rabāḥ said: "The woman is a row on her own".[776] Jasrah bint Dajājah narrated that she prayed alone behind Abū Dharr, and there was no woman beside her.[777]

Improper positioning

If there is a barrier between the imām and the followers such that they are not aware of the imām's movements, for example, the followers are

[771] al-Bukhārī, *k. al-adhān, b. al-mar'ah waḥdahā takūnu ṣaffan.*

[772] Muḥammad, *al-Muwaṭṭa', i.* 535.

[773] Abū Dāwūd, *k. al-ṣalāh, b. maqām al-ṣibyān min al-ṣaff.*

[774] Muslim, *k. al-ṣalāh, b. taswiyat al-ṣufūf wa iqāmatihā.*

[775] Ibn Abī Shaybah, *al-Muṣannaf, ii.* 34.

[776] Ibid., ii. 153.

[777] Ibid.

in a different building outside the *masjid*, or there is a wide road between them and the rows of the congregation are not together, then the prayer is not valid.[778] But if the barrier is not such, then the prayer will be valid so long as they are aware of the imām's movements either by sight or hearing, and provided there is no confusion.[779] Abū Mijlaz said: "Follow the imām, even if between you and him there is a road or a wall, as long as you can hear the *takbīr*". [780] ᶜĀ'ishah narrated: "The people prayed behind the Prophet ﷺ while they were outside the room".[781]

It is not liked for an imām to pray on a place higher than the followers behind. Abū Masᶜūd al-Anṣārī said: "The Prophet ﷺ prohibited the imām from standing on something higher than the people behind him".[782] Mujāhid narrated that Salmān al-Fārisī saw Ḥudhayfah leading the *ṣalāh* from a high place. Salmān said to him: "Get off, you are one of the people, so do not raise yourself over them." Ḥudhayfah said: "You are right".[783] Similarly, it is not liked for a follower to pray on a higher place outside the *masjid*. However, if the rows are connected to that place, or one is praying in a higher place within the *masjid*, then it is permissible.[784] Abū Hurayrah narrated that he prayed on the roof of the *masjid* while following the imām.[785]

If a person does his opening *takbīr* behind a row and then he enters the row and does the *rukūᶜ* with the imām, his *ṣalāh* is valid, but it is not liked. Abū Bakrah reported that he went to the *ṣalāh* while the Prophet ﷺ was doing *rukūᶜ* and that he did the *rukūᶜ* before he entered the row. He mentioned this to the Prophet ﷺ and he said: "May Allāh increase your love for goodness, but do not repeat such an act".[786]

If a person prays behind the rows by himself, his *ṣalāh* is valid but again it is not liked. As mentioned above, Abū Bakrah said that he did

[778] *al-Fatāwā al-hindiyyah, i.* 87.

[779] Ibn ᶜĀbidīn, *al-Durr al-mukhtār, iii.* 619.

[780] al-Bukhārī, *k. al-adhān, b. idhā kāna bayna al-imām wa bayna al-qawm ḥā'iṭun aw sutratun.*

[781] Ibid.

[782] al-Dāraquṭnī, *al-Sunan,* ii. 74.

[783] ᶜAbd al-Razzāq, *al-Muṣannaf,* ii.413.

[784] *al-Fatāwā al-hindiyyah, i.* 88.

[785] al-Bukhārī, *k. al-ṣalāh, b. al-ṣalāh fī al-suṭūḥ.*

[786] al-Bukhārī, *k. al-adhān, b. idhā rakaᶜa dūna al-ṣaff.*

part of the *ṣalāh* behind the row, and the Prophet ﷺ did not order him to repeat his *ṣalāh*. Wābiṣah related: "The Messenger of Allāh ﷺ saw a man praying behind the rows by himself and the Prophet ﷺ ordered him to repeat his *ṣalāh*".[787] This ḥadīth from Wābiṣah refers to what is preferred and, as such, it is in harmony with that of Abū Bakrah's ḥadīth. It is clear, then, that it is not necessary to repeat the *ṣalāh* because such an act was not always ordered. Imām Mālik narrated that Zayd ibn Thābit entered the mosque, and he found the people in a state of *rukūʿ*, so he did *rukūʿ*, then he crept forward until he reached the row. Imām Muḥammad said after narrating this ḥadīth from Mālik: "This is sufficient; it is better in our view that one does not do *rukūʿ* until one reaches the row. This is also the opinion of Abū Ḥanīfah".[788]

Straightening the rows

When the people stand for prayer, they should join together, fill in any gaps, and align shoulder to shoulder in straight rows, and there is no harm if the imām instructs the followers to do so.[789] Anas ibn Mālik narrated: "The Prophet ﷺ would turn his face to us before he began the *ṣalāh* and he would say: 'Be close together and straighten your rows'."[790] He also reported that the Prophet ﷺ would say: "Make your rows straight for the straightening of the rows is part of the completion of the *ṣalāh*".[791] Jābir ibn Samurah said: "The Prophet ﷺ came to us and said: 'Why don't you make the rows like the angels make their rows in the presence of their Lord?' We asked: 'O Messenger of Allāh ﷺ, how do the angels make their rows in the presence of their Lord?' He replied: 'They complete the first row and stand closely together, side by side, in the row'."[792]

Abū Umāmah narrated: "The Prophet ﷺ said: 'Allāh and the angels send down blessings upon the first row'. The people inquired: 'O Messenger of Allāh ﷺ, and upon the second row?' The Prophet ﷺ again said: 'Allāh and the angels send down blessings upon the first row'. The

[787] Abū Dāwūd, *k. al-ṣalāh, b. al-rajul yuṣallī waḥdahu khalfa al-ṣaff.*

[788] Muḥammad, *al-Muwaṭṭa', ii.* 52-53.

[789] *al-Fatāwā al-hindiyyah, i.* 89.

[790] al-Bukhārī, *k. al-adhān, b. iqbāl al-imām ʿalā al-nās wa taswiyat al-ṣufūf.*

[791] Muslim, *k. al-ṣalāh, b. taswiyat al-ṣufūf wa iqāmatihā.*

[792] Ibid.

people asked again: 'O Messenger of Allāh ﷺ, and upon the second row?' Finally he said: 'And upon the second row'."[793]

Abū Saʿīd al-Khudrī reported that the Prophet ﷺ noticed his Companions going to the back rows, and he said: "Come close and follow me and let those behind follow you. People will continue going to the back until Allāh will put them in the back".[794]

Joining the congregation

Whoever joins a congregation should say the opening *takbīr* while standing and then move directly to the point in the *ṣalāh* that the congregation are engaged in: for instance, if the congregation is prostrating, he should do the opening *takbīr* and then join with them in the *sajdah*. However, a person is not considered as having done the *rakʿah* unless he joins the imām in the *rukūʿ*. The *rakʿah* will be completed even if one manages to bow and put one's hands on one's knees as the imām is finishing his *rukūʿ*. Abū Hurayrah reported that the Messenger of Allāh ﷺ said: "If you come to the *ṣalāh* and we are in *sajdah*, then do *sajdah* with us but do not count it (as a *rakʿah*). And whoever catches the *rukūʿ*, catches the *ṣalāh*".[795]

What the imām should do after the ṣalāh

It is recommended for the imām after finishing the *ṣalāh* to leave his place, or to change his position at least and not remain seated for longer than is needed to make those supplications mentioned in the Sunnah. When leaving his place, he may go to his right or left.[796]

Yazīd ibn al-Aswad narrated that, "I prayed behind the Messenger of Allāh ﷺ; when he finished the *ṣalāh* he would move from his place".[797] Qabīṣah ibn Hulb related that his father said: "The Prophet ﷺ would lead us in *ṣalāh* and then turn to both sides, to his right and to his left".[798]

[793] Aḥmad and al-Ṭabarānī as cited in *Majmaʿ al-zawā'id, k. al-ṣalāh, b. fī al-ṣaff al-awwal.*

[794] Muslim, *k. al-ṣalāh, b. taswiyat al-ṣufūf wa iqāmatihā.*

[795] Abū Dāwūd, *k. al-ṣalāh, b. fī al-rajul yudrik al-imām sājidan kayfa yaṣnaʿu.*

[796] *See:* al-Kāsānī, *Badā'iʿ al-ṣanā'iʿ*, i. 679-80.

[797] Abū Dāwūd, *k. al-ṣalāh, b. al-imām yanṣarifu baʿda al-taslīm.*

[798] Abū Dāwūd, *k. al-ṣalāh, b. kayfa al-inṣirāf min al-ṣalāh.*

ʿĀʾishah said: "After the Prophet ﷺ made the *taslīm*, he would only sit for the amount of time it takes to say اَللَّهُمَّ أَنْتَ السَّلَامُ وَمِنْكَ السَّلَامُ تَبَارَكْتَ ذَا الْجَلَالِ وَالْإِكْرَام 'O Allāh, You are the Peace, and from You is the Peace. Blessed are You, O Owner of Majesty and Honour'."[799]

Umm Salamah said: "Whenever the Messenger of Allāh ﷺ finished his *ṣalāhs* with the *taslīm*, the women would get up and he would stay in his place for a while before getting up. I think, and Allāh knows best, that he did this to allow the women to leave before the men".[800]

ʿAbdullāh ibn ʿAmr said that it is not liked for the imām to pray any *ṣalāh* in the same place where he has prayed *farḍ*. Something similar is narrated from ʿAlī ibn Abī Ṭālib, ʿAbdullāh ibn ʿUmar, Saʿīd ibn al-Musayyab, Ḥasan al-Baṣrī, Ibrāhīm al-Nakhaʿī and Ibn Abī Laylā.[801]

As for the followers, it is narrated from Imām Muḥammad, that it is recommended for them as well to break the rows and disperse.[802] Abū Hurayrah reported the Prophet ﷺ as saying: "Could you not, after finishing the *ṣalāh*, move forward or back?"[803]

Appointing another to lead the rest of the ṣalāh

If the imām loses his *wuḍū'* during *ṣalāh*, he should give up his place to someone among the followers who will lead the remainder of the *ṣalāh*. When indicating someone to take his place, he must not speak but only indicate by gesture. He should then leave the place of prayer and renew his *wuḍū'*.[804] ʿAmr ibn Maymūn said: "I was standing and there was no one between me and ʿUmar the morning he was killed, except ʿAbdullāh ibn ʿAbbās. He had barely pronounced the *takbīr* when he was stabbed and said: 'The dog has killed me or bitten me'. ʿUmar bade ʿAbd al-Raḥmān ibn ʿAwf lead the *ṣalāh* and he led them in a short *ṣalāh*".[805]

[799] Muslim, *k. al-masājid wa mawāḍiʿ al-ṣalāh, b. istiḥbāb al-dhikr baʿda al-ṣalāh wa bayān ṣifatih.*

[800] al-Bukhārī, *k. al-adhān, b. mukth al-imām fī musallāh baʿda al-salām.*

[801] Ibn Abī Shaybah, *al-Muṣannaf, ii.* 24.

[802] al-Kāsānī, *Badāʾiʿ al-ṣanāʾiʿ, i. 681.*

[803] Ibn Mājah, *k. iqāmat al-ṣalāh wa al-sunnah fīhā, b. mā jāʾa fī ṣalāt al-nāfilah ḥaythu tuṣallā al-maktūbah.*

[804] *al-Fatāwā al-hindiyyah, i.* 95.

[805] al-Bukhārī, *k. faḍāʾil aṣḥāb al-nabī ṣallallāhu ʿalayhi wa sallam, b. qiṣṣat al-bayʿah.*

Chapter 7: Actions that invalidate or are disliked in *Ṣalāh*

1. Actions that invalidate the *Ṣalāh*

Leaving out a sharṭ or rukn

If any of the conditions *(sharṭ)* for the correctness of the *ṣalāh* or any pillars (*rukn)* of the *ṣalāh* are missed, then the *ṣalāh* is invalid, and it becomes *farḍ* to repeat it. As quoted earlier, the Prophet ﷺ told a Bedouin who had not done his *ṣalāh* correctly: "Return and pray for you have not prayed".

Speaking

Speaking during the *ṣalāh* about something that is not part of the *ṣalāh*, whether done intentionally on unintentionally, invalidates it. Zayd ibn Arqam related: "We used to talk while we were in *ṣalāh* and a person would speak to the person next to him until the verse, '*And stand before Allāh in devout obedience*', was revealed and we were then commanded to observe silence during the *ṣalāh*".[806] ʿAbdullāh ibn Masʿūd reported: "We used to greet the Messenger of Allāh ﷺ while he was in *ṣalāh* and he would respond to our greeting. When we returned from Abyssinia, we greeted him during *ṣalāh* but he did not respond to our salutation. We said to him: 'O Messenger of Allāh ﷺ, we used to greet you while you were in *ṣalāh* and you used to respond to us'. He then said: '*Ṣalāh* requires one's complete attention'."[807] Imām Muḥammad said: "We adhere to this; it is

[806] Muslim, *k. al-masājid wa mawāḍiʿ al-ṣalāh, b. taḥrīm al-kalām fī al-ṣalāh;* Abū Dāwūd, *k. al-ṣalāh, b. al-nahy ʿan al-kalām fī al-ṣalāh.*

[807] al-Bukhārī, *k. al-ʿamal fī al-ṣalāh, b. mā yunhā min al-kalām fī al-ṣalāh;* Muslim, *k. al-masājid, b. taḥrīm al-kalām fī al-ṣalāh;* Abū Dāwūd, *k. al-ṣalāh, b. radd al-salām.*

not appropriate for the one in *ṣalāh* to answer *salām*; if he does then his *ṣalāh* is nullified; no one should be greeted when he is in *ṣalāh*. This is the opinion of Abū Ḥanīfah".[808]

Crying, moaning or groaning does not invalidate nor is it disliked in *ṣalāh* if it is due to a fear of Allāh. In sūrah Maryam (V:58) Allāh says: "*When the revelations of the Most Gracious were recited to them, they fell down prostrating and weeping*". ʿAbdullāh ibn al-Shikhkhīr related: "I saw the Messenger of Allāh ﷺ praying and his chest was 'buzzing', like the buzzing of a cooking pot, due to crying".[809] ʿAlī reported: "I saw that not one of us, at the Battle of Badr, was standing except the Messenger of Allāh ﷺ who was praying under a tree and crying until the dawn".[810]

The one in *ṣalāh* who is greeted or spoken to may reply by making some motion. ʿAbdullāh ibn ʿUmar narrated that Ṣuhayb said: "I passed by the Messenger of Allāh ﷺ while he was offering *ṣalāh*. I greeted him and he acknowledged by only gesturing".[811] ʿAbdullāh ibn ʿUmar said: "I asked Ṣuhayb: 'How did the Messenger of Allāh ﷺ respond to the people when they greeted him while he was praying?' He said: 'He would signal to them with his hand'."[812]

If the imām forgets during the *ṣalāh*, it is permissible for a follower to remind him of it. ʿAbdullāh ibn ʿUmar reported: "The Messenger of Allāh ﷺ prayed and had some confusion in his recitation. When he finished, he said to ʿUmar: 'Were you present with us during the *ṣalāh*?' He replied: 'Yes'. So, the Prophet ﷺ said to him: 'What prevented you from reminding me?'."[813]

It is allowed for men to say *subḥānallāh* and for women to clap if there is some need to do so. Sahl ibn Saʿd al-Sāʿdī related that the Prophet ﷺ said: "If something happens to someone during the *ṣalāh*, he should say *subḥānallāh*. Clapping is for the women and saying *subḥānallāh* is for the men".[814]

[808] Muḥammad, *al-Muwaṭṭa', i.* 531.

[809] Abū Dāwūd, *k. al-ṣalāh, b. al-bukā' fī al-ṣalāh.*

[810] Ibn Ḥibbān, *al-Ṣaḥīḥ* 2257.

[811] Abū Dāwūd, *k. al-ṣalāh, b. radd al-salām fī al-ṣalāh.*

[812] al-Nasā'ī, *k. al-sahw, b. radd al-salām bi al-ishārah fī al-ṣalāh.*

[813] Abū Dāwūd, *k. al-ṣalāh, b. al-fatḥ ʿalā al-imām fī al-ṣalāh.*

[814] Abū Dāwūd, *k. al-ṣalāh, b. al-taṣfīq fī al-ṣalāh.*

Eating or drinking

If one eats or drinks during *ṣalāh* intentionally or unintentionally, then the *ṣalāh* must be repeated. If one swallows some food stuck in the teeth, the amount of a chickpea or more, this too invalidates the *ṣalāh*; if it is less, then the *ṣalāh* is not invalid.

Excessive moving

If one makes some movement such that, if seen from a distance, one would be sure that the person was not engaged in *ṣalāh*, this is considered a major violation, and it invalidates the *ṣalāh*. Anything less than this is considered a minor action, and it does not invalidate the *ṣalāh*.

During *ṣalāh*, if creatures such as a snake, scorpion or other harmful animal approach one, killing them is allowed, provided this requires only a small action.[815] Abū Hurayrah reported that the Prophet ﷺ said: "Kill the snake and the scorpion during the *ṣalāh*".[816]

Similarly, taking a few steps for some necessity is allowed, provided such movement is in the direction of the *qiblah*.[817] ʿĀ'ishah said: "The Messenger of Allāh ﷺ was offering *ṣalāh* in the house and the door was closed. I came and knocked on the door and he walked over to open it for me and then returned to his place of *ṣalāh*. The door was in the direction of the *qiblah*".[818]

Carrying or holding a child during the *ṣalāh* is also allowed. Abū Qatādah reported: "The Prophet ﷺ was offering *ṣalāh* and he was carrying Umāmah the daughter of Zaynab, the daughter of Allāh's Apostle ﷺ, and she was the daughter of al-ʿĀṣ ibn Rabīʿ ibn ʿAbd Shams. When he prostrated, he put her down and when he stood, he carried her (on his shoulder)".[819]

Laughing during the ṣalāh

Laughing during the *ṣalāh* invalidates it. Jābir said: "If one laughs in the *ṣalāh* he will repeat the *ṣalāh*, and he will not repeat the *wuḍū'* ".[820]

[815] *al-Fatāwā al-hindiyyah, i.*103.
[816] Abū Dāwūd, *k. al-ṣalāh, b. al-ʿamal fī al-ṣalāh.*
[817] *al-Fatāwā al-hindiyyah, i.* 102-3.
[818] Abū Dāwūd, *k. al-ṣalāh, b. al-ʿamal fī al-ṣalāh.*
[819] al-Nasā'ī, *k. al-sahw, b. ḥaml al-ṣabāyā fī al-ṣalāh wa waḍʿihinna fī al-ṣalāh.*
[820] Ibn Abī Shaybah, *al-Muṣannaf*, i. 340.

Hishām ibn ʿUrwah said: "My brother laughed during the *ṣalāh*, then my father commanded him to repeat the *ṣalāh*; and he did not command him to repeat the *wuḍū'*."[821] Ibn Sīrīn said: "When we were children, if we laughed during the *ṣalāh*, they would command us to repeat the *ṣalāh*".[822] If the laughing is such that others can hear it, it invalidates *wuḍū'* as well as the *ṣalāh*. This ruling is based on the ḥadīth mentioned in the section on *ṭahārah* about the blind person falling down, and the Prophet ﷺ asking those who laughed in their *ṣalāh* to repeat the *wuḍū'* as well as the *ṣalāh*.

2. ACTIONS THAT ARE DISLIKED DURING THE *ṢALĀH*

There are certain actions that, though they do not make the *ṣalāh* invalid, are nonetheless disliked. Intentionally missing any Sunnah of the *ṣalāh* is one such action.

When one's mind is occupied

Anything that distracts a person in *ṣalāh* is disliked. ʿĀ'ishah reported that the Prophet ﷺ said: "If dinner is served and the *ṣalāh* is ready, start with the dinner (first)".[823] Nāfiʿ reported: "Food would be served for ʿAbdullāh ibn ʿUmar while the *iqāmah* was being called, but he would not come to the *ṣalāh* until he had finished his meal although he could hear the reciting of the imām".[824]

ʿĀ'ishah reported that she heard the Messenger of Allāh ﷺ say: "No one should pray when food is served or when one needs to answer a call of nature".[825]

ʿĀ'ishah also reported from the Messenger of Allāh ﷺ saying: "When one of you becomes drowsy in *ṣalāh*, he should lie down until he is refreshed; otherwise, he will not know if he is asking forgiveness or vilifying himself".[826] Abū Hurayrah reported that the Messenger of

[821] Ibid.

[822] Ibid.

[823] al-Bukhārī, *k. al-adhān, b. idhā ḥaḍara al-ṭaʿām wa uqīmat al-ṣalāh;* Muslim, *k. al-masājid wa mawāḍiʿ al-ṣalāh, b. karāhat al-ṣalāh bi ḥaḍrat al-ṭaʿām.*

[824] al-Bukhārī, ibid.

[825] Muslim, *k. al-masājid wa mawāḍiʿ al-ṣalāh, b. karāhat al-ṣalāh bi ḥaḍrat al-ṭaʿām.*

[826] Muslim, *k. ṣalāt al-musāfirīn, b. amr man naʿasa fī ṣalātihi.*

Allāh ﷺ said: "When one of you gets up at night for *ṣalāh* and his tongue falters in reciting the Qur'ān and he is not certain about what he is reciting, he should sleep".[827]

Looking aside or away

Looking at something which distracts one's attention is similarly disliked. ʿĀ'ishah reported: "The Messenger of Allāh ﷺ prayed in a cloak which had some designs on it. He said: 'These designs have distracted me. Take this cloak to Abū Jahm and bring me a plain cloak'."[828] Anas said: "ʿĀ'ishah had a curtain to cover the doorway of her house. The Prophet ﷺ said to her: 'Remove your curtain for its pictures always distract me during my *ṣalāhs*'."[829]

Raising one's gaze to the sky or upwards is equally disliked. Abū Hurayrah reported that the Messenger of Allāh ﷺ said: "Those who raise their gaze to the sky during the *ṣalāh* should stop doing so or their sight may be taken away".[830] Ibrāhīm al-Nakhaʿī did not like one to gaze beyond the place of *sajdah* during *ṣalāh.*[831]

Turning to look at something without any genuine need is also disliked. ʿĀ'ishah said: "I asked the Messenger of Allāh ﷺ about turning in *ṣalāh* and he said: 'This is the portion that Satan steals from the slave's *ṣalāh*'."[832] Abū al-Dardā' narrated from the Prophet ﷺ: "O people, be careful about turning for there is no *ṣalāh* for the one who turns. If you are overcome by it in the voluntary *ṣalāhs*, then you should not be so overcome in the obligatory *ṣalāhs*".[833]

Closing one's eyes during the *ṣalāh* is not liked. Ibn ʿAbbās reported that the Messenger of Allāh ﷺ said: "When one of you stands up in the

[827] Ibid.

[828] Muslim, *k. al-masājid wa mawāḍiʿ al-ṣalāh, b. karāhat al-ṣalāh fī thawb lahu aʿlām.*

[829] al-Bukhārī, *k. al-ṣalāh, b. in ṣallā fī thawb muṣallab aw taṣāwīr hal tafsudu ṣalātuhu wa mā yunhā ʿan dhālik.*

[830] al-Bukhārī, *k. al-adhān, b. rafʿ al-baṣar ilā al-samā' fī al-ṣalāh;* Muslim, *k. al-ṣalāh, b. al-nahy ʿan rafʿ al-baṣar ilā al-samā' fī al-ṣalāh.*

[831] Ibn Abī Shaybah, *al-Muṣannaf,* ii. 64..

[832] al-Bukhārī, *k. al-adhān, b. al-iltifāt fī al-ṣalāh.*

[833] Aḥmad, *al-Musnad* 27537.

ṣalāh he should not close his eyes".[834] Layth narrated that Mujāhid did not like eyes to be closed during *ṣalāh.*[835]

Turning to the side out of need is not disliked. ʿAbdullāh ibn ʿAbbās related: "The Messenger of Allāh ﷺ would turn to his right and left; he would not turn his head to see behind him".[836] Sahl ibn al-Ḥanẓaliyyah narrated: "Once the Prophet ﷺ prayed and he looked toward a valley that he had sent some horsemen to guard".[837] Anas ibn Sīrīn said: "I saw Anas ibn Mālik lift his eyes to something while he was praying".[838]

Fidgeting with one's clothing or body

Fidgeting with one's clothing or one's body, unless there is some need to do so, is also disliked. Abū Dharr reported that the Prophet ﷺ said: "When one of you stands for the *ṣalāh,* mercy is facing him. Therefore, he should not touch pebbles".[839] Umm Salamah reported: "There was a boy called Yasar who would blow air out during the *ṣalāh.* The Messenger of Allāh ﷺ said to him: 'May Allāh fill your face with dust'."[840]

Placing one's hands on one's hips is also disliked. Muḥammad ibn Sīrīn narrated from Abū Hurayrah saying: "The Messenger of Allāh ﷺ prohibited putting one's hands on one's hips during the *ṣalāh*".[841]

Not to gather one's garments around oneself in prayer and, instead, to leave them to hang loose or fall to the ground, is disapproved of. Abū Hurayrah said: "The Messenger of Allāh ﷺ prohibited *al-sadl* (letting one's clothes dangle) in the *ṣalāh*; and he prohibited a man from covering his mouth".[842] Abū Ḥanīfah narrated from ʿAlī ibn al-Aqmar that the Prophet ﷺ passed by a man who had let his clothing dangle in the *ṣalāh* and the Prophet ﷺ folded his clothing back over him. Imām Muḥammad said after this ḥadīth: "We adhere to it; letting the clothing

[834] al-Ṭabarānī, *al-Muʿjam al-kabīr, xi.* 29.

[835] Ibn Abī Shaybah, *al-Muṣannaf,* ii. 64..

[836] Aḥmad, *al-Musnad* 2485.

[837] Abū Dāwūd, *k. al-ṣalāh, b. al-rukhṣah fī dhālik.*

[838] Aḥmad, *al-Musnad* 4083.

[839] Abū Dāwūd, *k. al-ṣalāh, b. fī masḥ al-ḥaṣā fī al-ṣalāh.*

[840] Aḥmad, *al-Musnad* 26614.

[841] Muslim, *k. al-masājid wa mawāḍiʿ al-ṣalāh, b. karāhat al-ikhtiṣār fī al-ṣalāh;* Abū Dāwūd, *k. al-ṣalāh, b. al-rajul yuṣallī mukhtaṣiran.*

[842] Abū Dāwūd, *k. al-ṣalāh, b. mā jā'a fī al-sadl fī al-ṣalāh.*

dangle or any such action is disliked in the *ṣalāh*, because doing so is similar to the practice of the People of the Book. This is the opinion of Abū Ḥanīfah".[843]

Designating a place

To designate a place for oneself in the *masjid* is equally disapproved of. Even the imām's place is not reserved: he should sit with the rest of the people if he has arrived before the *ṣalāh*. ᶜAbd al-Raḥmān ibn Shibl said: "The Prophet ﷺ prohibited pecking like a crow, sitting like a beast, and a man picking a special place in the *masjid* to pray like a camel has its own place to sit".[844]

THE SUTRAH

A *sutrah* is a barrier or partition that is placed in front of the *ṣalāh*. It is recommended for the one who is praying outside to place a *sutrah* in front of himself; this is in order to prevent others from passing in front of him and also to avoid his sight and focus from drifting beyond the prayer space. Sahl ibn Abī Ḥathmah reported that the Prophet ﷺ said: "When one of you prays, he should pray toward his *sutrah* and he should be close to it".[845]

ᶜAbdullāh ibn ᶜUmar related that when the Prophet ﷺ went out to pray the *ṣalāh* of ᶜ*Īd*, he used to order that a *ḥarbah* (a short spear) be planted in front of him as a *sutrah* for his prayer, and then he used to pray facing it with the people behind him and used to do the same while on a journey. After the Prophet ﷺ, this practice was adopted by the Muslim rulers who followed his traditions.[846] Ibrāhīm al-Nakhaᶜī said that if they prayed in an open space, they preferred to place a *sutrah*.[847]

There is no harm in not placing a *sutrah* in front of oneself if one does not fear that someone may pass in front.[848] Al-Faḍl ibn ᶜAbbās reported: "The Prophet ﷺ prayed in an open area and there was nothing in front

[843] Abū Ḥanīfah, *K. al-āthār* 29.
[844] Aḥmad, *al-Musnad* 15571-73.
[845] Abū Dāwūd, *k. al-ṣalāh, b. al-dunuww min al-sutrah.*
[846] Muslim, *k. al-ṣalāh, b. sutrat al-muṣallī.*
[847] Ibn Abī Shaybah, *al-Muṣannaf*, i. 249.
[848] *al-Fatāwā al-hindiyyah,* i.104.

of him".[849] Ḥajjāj said: "I asked ʿAṭā' ibn Abī Rabāḥ about someone praying in an open space without a *sutrah*, and he said: 'There is no harm in it'."[850] Khālid ibn Abī Bakr said: "I saw al-Qāsim and Sālim praying in the open area without a *sutrah*".[851]

The requirement of a sutrah

The height of the *sutrah* should be the length of an arm, and its width at least that of a finger.[852] Sabrah ibn Maʿbad reported that the Messenger of Allāh ﷺ said: "When one of you prays, he should make a barrier for his *ṣalāh*, even if it is an arrow".[853] Ṭalḥah said: "We used to pray and the animals would pass in front of us. We mentioned this to the Prophet ﷺ and he said: 'If anything the size of a saddle is in front of you, nothing that passes beyond it will harm you'."[854] The size of a saddle has been interpreted by Nāfiʿ, ʿAṭā' and Sufyān al-Thawrī as the length of an arm.[855]

One should be close to the *sutrah* as mentioned in the ḥadīth of Sahl ibn Abī Ḥathmah where the Prophet ﷺ said: "When one of you prays, he should pray toward his *sutrah* and he should be close to it".[856]

If the people are praying in congregation, then the *sutrah* of the imām is sufficient for everyone praying behind him.[857] Abū Juḥayfah reported that the Messenger of Allāh ﷺ led the prayers of *Ẓuhr* and *ʿAṣr* in Baṭḥā', and stuck a spear in the ground in front of him.[858] ʿAbdullāh ibn ʿAbbās said: "Once I came riding a donkey when I had just attained the age of puberty. Allāh's Messenger was offering the *ṣalāh* at Minā with no wall in front of him and I passed in front of part of the row. There I dismounted and let my donkey loose to graze and entered the row and

[849] Abū Dāwūd, *k. al-ṣalāh, b. man qāla al-kalb lā yaqṭaʿ al-ṣalāh.*
[850] Ibn Abī Shaybah, *al-Muṣannaf*, i. 249.
[851] Ibid.
[852] Ibn ʿĀbidīn, *al-Durr al-mukhtār*, iv. 125-126.
[853] Aḥmad, Abū Yaʿlā and al-Ṭabarānī *as cited in Majmaʿ al-zawā'id, k. al-ṣalāh, b. sutrat al-muṣallī.*
[854] Muslim, *k. al-ṣalāh, b. sutrat al-muṣallī.*
[855] ʿAbd al-Razzāq, *al-Muṣannaf*, ii. 9.
[856] Abū Dāwūd, *k. al-ṣalāh, b. al-dunuww min al-sutrah.*
[857] al-Marghinānī, *al-Hidāyah, i.* 68.
[858] al-Bukhārī, *k. al-ṣalāh, b. al-ṣalāh ilā al-janāzah..*

nobody objected to me about it".[859] Nāfiᶜ narrated from ᶜAbdullāh ibn ᶜUmar saying: "The *sutrah* of the imām is the *sutrah* of those behind him". ᶜAbd al-Razzāq said after recording this report: "This is what I hold; and this is what people are on".[860]

The prohibition against passing

To cross between the one who is praying and his *sutrah* is a forbidden act. Busr ibn Saᶜīd said that Zayd ibn Khālid sent him to Abū Juhaym to ask him what he had heard from the Prophet ﷺ concerning passing in front of someone who is praying. He said that the Messenger of Allāh ﷺ said: "If the person who passes in front of another person in prayer knew the magnitude of his sin he would prefer to wait for forty (days, months or years) rather than to pass in front of him". Abū al-Naḍr (one of the narrators) said: "I do not remember exactly whether he said forty days, months or years".[861] Zayd ibn Khālid related that the Messenger of Allāh ﷺ said: "If the one who passes in front of the one who is praying knew what was upon him (of sin), it would be better for him to stand (and wait) for forty autumns (years) than to pass in front of him".[862]

If one passes in front of someone who does not have a *sutrah*, or he has a *sutrah*, and one is passing between him and the *sutrah*, then it is allowed for that person to stop you with a gesture or by saying *subḥānallāh*.[863] Abū Saᶜīd al-Khudrī said: "I heard the Prophet ﷺ say: 'If any of you prays and someone tries to pass in front of you, then turn him away. If he refuses, then fight him for he is a devil'."[864]

The *ṣalāh*, however, is not invalidated by anything passing in front of the person praying. Abū Saᶜīd al-Khudrī said: "The *ṣalāh* is not invalidated by anything passing in front".[865]

[859] al-Bukhārī, *k. al-ṣalāh, b. sutrat al-imām sutrah man khalfahu;* Muslim, *k. al-ṣalāh, b. sutrat al-muṣallī.*

[860] ᶜAbd al-Razzāq, *al-Muṣannaf*, ii. 18.

[861] al-Bukhārī, *k. al-ṣalāh, b. ithm al-mārr bayna yaday al-muṣallī.*

[862] al-Bazzār as cited in *Majmaᶜ al-zawā'id, k. al-ṣalāh b. fī man yamurru bayna yaday al-muṣallī.*

[863] al-Marghinānī, *al-Hidāyah*, i. 68.

[864] al-Bukhārī, *k. al-ṣalāh, b. yaruddu al-muṣallī mā marra bayna yadayh.*

[865] Abū Dāwūd, *k. al-ṣalāh, b. man qāla lā yaqṭaᶜ al-ṣalāta shay'.*

CHAPTER 8: THE *WITR* AND *NAFL ṢALĀHS*

WITR ṢALĀHS

THE *WITR ṢALĀH* is *wājib* according to Abū Ḥanīfah, and it is Sunnah according to Abū Yūsuf and Muḥammad. Abū Ḥanīfah refers to those *aḥādīth* which emphasise the importance of *Witr* more than any Sunnah *ṣalāh*. ᶜAbdullāh ibn ᶜAmr ibn al-ᶜĀṣ narrated that the Prophet ﷺ said: "Allāh has added a *ṣalāh* to your *ṣalāhs*; that is the *Witr*".[866] Buraydah al-Aslamī narrated that the Messenger of Allāh ﷺ said: "*Witr* is right; the one who does not perform *Witr* is not from us. *Witr* is right, the one who does not perform *Witr* is not from us; *Witr* is right, the one who does not perform *Witr* is not from us".[867] Abū Ayyūb said: "*Witr* is right or *wājib*".[868] Mujāhid said: "*Witr* is *wājib*, not *farḍ*".[869] Ṭāwūs said: "*Witr* is *wājib*".[870]

The number of rakᶜahs

The *Witr* is three *rakᶜahs* together, without them being interrupted by saying the *salām* after two *rakᶜahs*. ᶜAlī ibn Abī Ṭālib has narrated that the Prophet ﷺ used to pray three *rakᶜahs* of *Witr*.[871] ᶜĀ'ishah in her description of the Prophet's ﷺ night *ṣalāh* said: "He would pray four *rakᶜahs* and do not ask about their beauty and length, then he would pray four *rakᶜahs* and do not ask about their beauty and length, then he would pray three *rakᶜahs*".[872] In another ḥadīth, ᶜĀ'ishah said that he would pray *Witr* in three *rakᶜahs* and would not say *salām* except at the end.

Imām Muḥammad narrated from ᶜUmar ibn al-Khaṭṭāb saying: "I would not like to leave doing a *Witr* of three *rakᶜahs* even if I were to get

[866] Ibn Abī Shaybah, *al-Muṣannaf, ii.* 93.

[867] Abū Dāwūd, *k. al-ṣalāh, b. fī man lam yūtir.*

[868] Ibn Abī Shaybah, *al-Muṣannaf, ii.* 93.

[869] Ibid.

[870] ᶜAbd al-Razzāq, *al-Muṣannaf, iii.* 8.

[871] al-Tirmidhī, *k. al-witr, b. mā jā'a fī al-witr bi thalāth.*

[872] al-Ḥākim, *al-Mustadrak, i.* 304

red camels", i.e. the most valued camels. Imām Muḥammad also said: "This is what we adhere to: *Witr* is three *rakᶜahs,* not separated by *salām,* and this is the opinion of Abū Ḥanīfah".[873]

Imām al-Tirmidhī said that the ḥadīth of three *rakᶜahs* of *Witr* was narrated from ᶜImrān ibn Ḥuṣayn, ᶜĀ'ishah, Ibn ᶜAbbās, Abū Ayyūb, Ubayy ibn Kaᶜb and ᶜAbd al-Raḥmān ibn Abzā. Imām al-Tirmidhī also said that Sufyān al-Thawrī said: "I prefer to do *Witr* with three *rakᶜahs*". Al-Tirmidhī adds that this was the opinion of ᶜAbdullāh ibn al-Mubārak and the people of Kufah.[874] Ibn Abī Shaybah related the opinion of three *rakᶜahs* of *Witr* from ᶜUmar ibn al-Khaṭṭāb, ᶜAlī ibn Abī Ṭālib, Anas ibn Mālik, Abū Umāmah, Jābir ibn Zayd, ᶜAlqamah, Ḥasan al-Baṣrī, Saᶜīd ibn Jubayr, Makḥūl, Abū al-ᶜĀliyah and others".[875] It is narrated from Ḥasan al-Baṣrī saying: "Muslims are in agreement that *Witr* is three *rakᶜahs*, and there is no *salām* except in the last *rakᶜah*".[876]

The time of Witr

The time for the *Witr Ṣalāh* is same as the time of *ᶜIshā' Ṣalāh,* except that it is not prayed before *ᶜIshā'*. Abū Tamīm al-Jayshanī narrated that ᶜAmr ibn al-ᶜĀṣ said during Friday *Khutbah*: "Abū Basrah narrated to me that the Prophet ﷺ said: 'Allāh has added a *ṣalāh* for you, and it is the *Witr Ṣalāh.* Pray it between *ᶜIshā'* and *Fajr*'." Abū Tamīm said: "Abū Dharr took me by my hand to Abū Basrah. Abū Dharr asked him: 'Did you hear what ᶜAmr just said from the Messenger of Allāh ﷺ?' He answered: 'I heard it from the Messenger of Allah ﷺ'."[877] ᶜAbdullāh ibn Abī Qays related that he asked ᶜĀ'ishah about the *Witr Ṣalāh* of the Prophet ﷺ and she said: "Sometimes he would do the *Witr Ṣalāh* during the first part of the night and sometimes during the latter portion of the night".[878]

The preferred time

The preferred time of *Witr* is the end of the night.[879] Ibn Sīrīn said: "I have not seen anyone among those from whom the knowledge is

[873] Abū Ḥanīfah, *K. al-āthār* 34.
[874] al-Tirmidhī, *k. al-witr, b. mā jā'a fī al-witr bi thalāth.*
[875] Ibn Abī Shaybah, *al-Muṣannaf, ii.* 90-92.
[876] al-Kāsānī, *Badā'iᶜ al-ṣanā'iᶜ, ii.* 226.
[877] Aḥmad, and al-Ṭabarānī as cited in *Majmaᶜ al-zawā'id, k. al-ṣalāh, b. mā jā'a fī al-witr.*
[878] Abū Dāwūd, *k. al-ṣalāh, b. fī waqt al-witr.*
[879] al-Kāsānī, *Badā'iᶜ al-ṣanā'iᶜ, ii.* 228.

received but they had the view that *Witr* at end of the night is better for those who can".[880] Masrūq said: "I asked ʿĀ'ishah about the *Witr* of the Messenger ﷺ. She said: 'Out of the entire night, the Messenger of Allāh ﷺ would sometimes do *Witr Ṣalāh* during the early portion; sometimes he would do it during the middle portion; and sometimes in the latter portion of the night. At the end of his life he used to do *Witr* just before dawn".[881] Imām al-Tirmidhī said after narrating this ḥadīth: "Some people of knowledge prefer to do *Witr* at the end of night".[882]

If one suspects that one will not wake during the latter portion of the night, then it is preferable to pray the *Witr* early. Jābir reported that the Messenger of Allāh ﷺ said: "Whoever of you fears that he will not be able to wake during the latter portion of the night, he should do the *Witr Ṣalāh* during the early part of the night. And whoever of you believes that he will be able to wake during the latter portion of the night, he should do *Witr Ṣalāh* during that latter portion, as the *ṣalāhs* during the last portion of the night are attended by the angels".[883]

Jābir also narrated: "The Messenger of Allāh ﷺ said to Abū Bakr: 'When do you do the *Witr Ṣalāh*?' Abū Bakr replied: 'In the early portion of the night after the *ʿIshā' Ṣalāh*'. Then the Prophet ﷺ said: 'And you, O ʿUmar?' He answered: 'During the latter portion of the night'. The Prophet ﷺ said: 'As for you, O Abū Bakr, you have taken the reliable way; as for you, ʿUmar, you have taken the way of strength'."[884]

Only one Witr per night

Witr is the last *ṣalāh* of the night. Ibn ʿUmar reported the Prophet ﷺ saying: "Make *Witr* your last prayer at night".[885] However, if someone has performed the *Witr ṣalāh* and then wishes to do some more, he may do so but must not repeat the *Witr*. Ṭalq ibn ʿAlī narrated that he heard

[880] ʿAbd al-Razzāq, *al-Muṣannaf*, iii. 28.

[881] al-Bukhārī, *k. al-witr, b. sāʿat al-witr;* Muslim, *k. ṣalāt al-musāfirīn wa qaṣrihā, b. ṣalāt al-layl, wa ʿadad rakaʿāt al-nabī salallallāhu ʿalayhi wa sallam*; Ibn Majah, *k. iqāmat al-ṣalāh wa al-sunnah fīhā, b. mā jā'a fī al-witr fī akhir al-layl.*

[882] al-Tirmidhī, *k. al-witr, b. mā jā'a fī al-witr min awwal al-layl wa ākhirihi.*

[883] Muslim, *k. ṣalāt al-musāfirīn, b. man khāfa an lā yaqūma min ākhir al-layl falyūtir awwalahu.*

[884] Abū Dāwūd, *k. al-ṣalāh, b. fī al-witr qabl al-nawm.*

[885] Abū Dāwūd, *k. al-ṣalāh, b. fī waqt al-witr.*

the Messenger of Allāh ﷺ say: "There are not two *Witr Ṣalāhs* in one night."[886]

Recitation in the Witr

The reading of the Qur'ān is *farḍ* in every *rakᶜah* of the *Witr*; it is *wājib* to recite the *Fātiḥah* in every *rakᶜah* and then to add another sūrah. ᶜĀ'ishah narrated: "The Prophet ﷺ would recite *al-Aᶜlā* in the first *rakᶜah, al-Kāfirūn* in the second and the last three sūrahs in the third *rakᶜah*".[887] Ibn ᶜAbbās narrated that the Messenger of Allāh ﷺ read *al-Aᶜlā, al-Kāfirūn* and *qul huwa Allāhu aḥad* in the *rakᶜahs* of *Witr.*[888] Imām Muḥammad said: "Whatever one reads after *al-Fātiḥah* is fine. It has come to our knowledge that the Messenger of Allāh ﷺ read in the first *rakᶜah* of *Witr, al-Aᶜlā*, in the second *rakᶜah al-Kāfirūn* and in the third *rakᶜah, qul huwa Allāhu aḥad*".[889] Imām Muḥammad said: "If you read this it is good, and whatever you read in the *Witr* with the *Fātiḥah* is also good, as long as you read three or more verses with the *Fātiḥah.* This is the opinion of Abū Ḥanīfah".[890]

Qunūt

One recites the *Qunūt* in the third *rakᶜah* before the final *rukūᶜ*. After the completion of the *Fātiḥah* and any other sūrahs one says the *takbīr*, raises one's hands and then recites the *Qunūt.* It is not, however, recited in any other *ṣalāh.* Ubayy ibn Kaᶜb narrated that the Prophet ﷺ recited the *Qunūt* before the *rukūᶜ*.[891] ᶜAbdullāh ibn Masᶜūd used to recite the *Qunūt* before *rukūᶜ*. Imām Muḥammad said: "We adhere to it, and this is the opinion of Abū Ḥanīfah".[892] Ibrāhīm al-Nakhaᶜī said: "*Qunūt* before *rukūᶜ* is *wājib* in the *Witr* during the month of Ramaḍān and other months. When you want to say the *Qunūt* also say the *takbīr*, and when you want to do *rukūᶜ* say the *takbīr* again". Imām Muḥammad said:

[886] al-Nasā'ī, *k. qiyām al-layl wa taṭawwuᶜ al-nahār, b. nahy al-nabī ṣallallāhu ᶜalayhi wa sallam ᶜan al-witrayn fī laylah.*

[887] Abū Dāwūd, *k. al-ṣalāh, b. mā yuqra'u fī al-witr.*

[888] al-Tirmidhī, *k. al-witr, b. mā jā'a fī mā yuqra'u bihi fī al-witr.*

[889] al-Kāsānī, *Badā'iᶜ al-ṣanā'iᶜ, ii. 229.*

[890] Abū Ḥanīfah, *K. al-āthār* 34.

[891] Abū Dāwūd, *k. al-ṣalāh, b. al-qunūt fī al-witr.*

[892] Abū Ḥanīfah, *K. al-āthār* 55.

"We adhere to it, and one raises one's hands in the *takbīr* before the *Qunūt* just as one raises one's hands at the start of the *ṣalāh*, then one puts them down and reads the *Qunūt*; and this is the opinion of Abū Ḥanīfah".[893] Al-Aswad narrated that ʿAbdullāh ibn Masʿūd used to raise his hands for the *Qunūt* of *Witr.*[894] The *Qunūt* in *Witr Ṣalāh* is *wājib.* Ibrāhīm al-Nakhaʿī said: "There is no *Witr* without the *Qunūt*".[895]

Imām al-Tirmidhī said: "ʿAbdullāh ibn Masʿūd recited the *Qunūt* in *Witr* throughout the year before the *rukūʿ*; this is the opinion of some scholars and is also followed by Sufyān al-Thawrī, Ibn al-Mubārak, Isḥāq and the people of Kufah".[896] Recitation of the *Qunūt* before the *rukūʿ* is also the opinion of ʿAbdullāh ibn ʿUmar, al-Aswad, and Saʿīd ibn Jubayr and others.[897]

Abū ʿAbd al-Raḥmān said: "The *Qunūt* taught to us by ʿAbdullāh ibn Masʿūd reads:

اَللَّهُمَّ إِنَّا نَسْتَعِينُكَ وَنَسْتَغْفِرُكَ وَنُؤْمِنُ بِكَ وَنُثْنِي عَلَيْكَ الْخَيْرَ وَلاَ نَكْفُرُكَ وَنَخْلَعُ وَنَتْرُكُ مَنْ يَفْجُرُكَ اَللَّهُمَّ إِيَّاكَ نَعْبُدُ وَلَكَ نُصَلِّي وَنَسْجُدُ وَإِلَيْكَ نَسْعَى وَنَحْفِدُ وَنَرْجُوْ رَحْمَتَكَ وَنَخْشَى عَذَابَكَ إِنَّ عَذَابَكَ الْجِدَّ بِالْكُفَّارِ مُلْحِقٌ

"O Allāh we seek help from You. We seek Your forgiveness. We believe in You. We laud Your name. We do not turn from You in disbelief. We renounce and turn away from whoever disobeys You and breaks Your commandments. O Allāh we worship You. To You we pray and to You we kneel. To You we hasten to work for You and to serve You. We beg for Your mercy and fear Your punishment. Indeed Your severe punishment will overtake and strike the unbelievers".[898]

There is some minor variation in wordings of the *Qunūt* narrated by Ubayy ibn Kaʿb, ʿAlī ibn Abī Ṭālib, al-Ḥasan al-Baṣrī, Ṭāwūs and Ibrāhīm al-Nakhaʿī.[899]

[893] Ibid.

[894] Ibn Abī Shaybah, *al-Muṣannaf, ii.* 101.

[895] Ibid., *ii.* 102.

[896] al-Tirmidhī, *k. al-witr, b. mā jā'a fī al-qunūt fī al-witr.*

[897] Ibn Abī Shaybah, *al-Muṣannaf, ii.* 97-98.

[898] Ibid., *ii. 96.*

[899] ʿAbd al-Razzāq, *al-Muṣannaf, iii.* 112-23.

After the Witr

After finishing the *Witr,* it is recommended that one say aloud: سُبْحَانَ الْمَلِكِ الْقُدُّوس, 'Glory be to the King, the Holy,' three times, adding رَبُّ الْمَلَائِكَةِ وَالرُّوح 'Lord of the angels and the Spirit' after the third. Ubayy ibn Kaᶜb said: "The Prophet ﷺ would recite *al-Aᶜlā* and *al-Kāfirūn* in the *Witr Ṣalāh.* When he made the *taslīm,* he would say: 'Glory be to the King, the Holy', three times, prolonging the third repetition and saying it aloud".[900] ᶜAlī would say at the end of his *Witr:*

اَللَّهُمَّ إِنِّي أَعُوْذُ بِرِضَاكَ مِنْ سَخَطِكَ وَأَعُوْذُ بِمُعَافَاتِكَ مِنْ عُقُوْبَتِكَ وَأَعُوْذُ بِكَ مِنْكَ لَا أُحْصِي ثَنَاءً عَلَيْكَ أَنْتَ كَمَا أَثْنَيْتَ عَلَى نَفْسِك

"O Allāh, I seek refuge in Your pleasure from Your anger. And I seek refuge from Your punishment in Your granting well-being. And I seek refuge in You from You. I cannot count Your praise: You are as You have praised Yourself".[901]

Making up a missed Witr

It is *Wajib* to make up (*qaḍā'*) for a missed *Witr Ṣalāh.* Abū Hurayrah reported that the Prophet ﷺ said: "If the morning approaches, and you have yet to pray *Witr,* you should pray the *Witr Ṣalāh.*"[902] Abū Saᶜīd al-Khudrī narrated that the Prophet ﷺ said: "If one of you misses the *Witr ṣalāh* because of sleeping or forgets it, he should pray it when he remembers it."[903]

Imām Mālik narrated that ᶜUbādah ibn al-Ṣāmit used to lead the *ṣalāh.* One day he came for *Fajr Ṣalāh,* and the *mu'adhdhin* had started the *iqāmah.* ᶜUbādah ibn Ṣāmit asked him to stop. He prayed *Witr,* then led the *ṣalāh.* Imām Muḥammad said after narrating this ḥadīth from Mālik: "It is better in our view to pray *Witr* before *Fajr,* and one should not delay it until *Fajr* arises. If *Fajr* arises before one has prayed *Witr,*

[900] al-Nasā'ī, *k. qiyām al-layl wa taṭawwuᶜ al-nahār, b. al-tasbīḥ baᶜda al-farāgh min al-witr.*

[901] al-Nasā'ī, *k. qiyām al-layl wa taṭawwuᶜ al-nahār, b. al-duᶜā' fī al-witr.*

[902] al-Ḥākim, *al-Mustadrak, i.* 443.

[903] Abū Dāwūd, *k. al-witr, b. al-duᶜā' baᶜda al-witr;* al-Tirmidhī, *k. al-witr, b. mā jā'a fī al-rajul yanāmu ᶜan al-witr.*

then one should pray *Witr,* and one should not do this intentionally. This is the opinion of Abū Ḥanīfah".[904]

Qunūt al-nāzilah

Qunūt al-nāzilah means reading the *Qunūt* in times of calamity, or any hard situation for the community. When a calamity happens, it is allowed to read *Qunūt-al-nāzilah* in the *Fajr Ṣalāh,* or any of the five daily *ṣalāhs.* Al-Barā' ibn ᶜĀzib narrated that the Prophet ﷺ recited the *Qunūt* in *Maghrib* and *Fajr Ṣalāhs.*[905] Anas said: "The Prophet ﷺ recited the *Qunūt* for a month after the *rukūᶜ*, supplicating against some tribes, then he left it".[906] Abū Hurayrah recited the *Qunūt* in *Fajr, Ẓuhr* and *ᶜIshā' Ṣalāhs* after the *rukūᶜ*, in which he supplicated for believers, and cursed unbelievers.[907]

It is normally disliked to read the *Qunūt* in any prayer other than *Witr.* Ibrāhīm al-Nakhaᶜī said: "ᶜAbdullāh ibn Masᶜūd and his students never recited the *Qunūt* in *Fajr* for the whole of their lives".[908] Abū Mālik al-Ashjaᶜī said: "My father prayed behind the Prophet ﷺ when he was sixteen years old, and he prayed behind Abū Bakr, ᶜUmar, and ᶜUthmān. I asked him, 'Did they make the *Qunūt*'?' He said: 'No, son, it is something that has been innovated'."[909]

In times of calamities, the *Qunūt* is to be recited in *Fajr* or any other *ṣalāh* after the *rukūᶜ*. Ibn Sīrīn said: "Anas was asked: 'Did the Prophet ﷺ recite the *Qunūt* in the *Fajr Ṣalāh*?' He said: 'Yes'. Then he was asked: 'Did he recite the *Qunūt* before the *rukūᶜ*?' He replied: 'After it for a while'."[910] ᶜĀṣim narrated: "I asked Anas ibn Mālik about the *Qunūt.* Anas ibn Mālik answered: 'There was *Qunūt*'. I asked him: 'Before the *rukūᶜ* or after it?' He answered: 'Before the *rukūᶜ*'. I said: 'So-and-so has told me that you narrated it after the *rukūᶜ*'. Anas said: 'He lied. The

[904] Muḥammad, *al-Muwaṭṭa', ii.* 10-11.

[905] Ibn Ḥibbān, *al-ṣaḥīḥ, iii.* 171.

[906] Ibid., *iii.* 172.

[907] Ibid., *iii.* 171.

[908] Abū Ḥanīfah, *K. al-āthār* 55.

[909] al-Tirmidhī, *abwāb al-ṣalāh, b. mā jā'a fī tark al-qunūt;* al-Nasā'ī, *k. al-iftitāḥ, b. tark al-qunūt;* Ibn Mājah, *k. iqāmat al-ṣalāh, b. mā jā'a fī al-qunūt.*

[910] al-Bukhārī, *k. al-witr, b. al-qunūt qabl al-rukūᶜ wa baᶜdahu.*

Prophet ﷺ made the *Qunūt* after the *rukū*ᶜ for a month [i.e. for that particular occasion] only'. Then Anas explained that this *Qunūt* was the *Qunūt* during times of calamities".[911]

The supplication that is usually recited during *Qunūt al-nāzilah* is a narration by al-Ḥasan ibn ᶜAlī:

اَللَّهُمَّ اهْدِنِيْ فِيْمَنْ هَدَيْتَ وَعَافِنِيْ فِيْمَنْ عَافَيْتَ وَتَوَلَّنِيْ فِيْمَنْ تَوَلَّيْتَ وَبَارِكْ لِيْ فِيْمَا أَعْطَيْتَ وَقِنِيْ شَرَّ مَا قَضَيْتَ فَإِنَّكَ تَقْضِيْ وَلاَ يُقْضَى عَلَيْكَ وَإِنَّهُ لاَ يَذِلُّ مَنْ وَالَيْتَ وَلاَ يَعِزُّ مَنْ عَادَيْتَ تَبَارَكْتَ رَبَّنَا وَتَعَالَيْتَ وَصَلَّى اللهُ عَلَى النَّبِيِّ مُحَمَّدٍ

"O Allāh, guide me among those whom You have guided. Grant me well-being among those whom You have granted well-being. Take me into Your guardianship among those whom You have taken into Your guardianship. Bless me in what You have given me. Protect me from the evil that You have decreed, for You decree and nothing is decreed for You. And there is no humiliation for the one whom You take as a ward, and no honour for the one who You take as an enemy. Blessed and Exalted are You, our Lord. May Allāh bestow mercy upon the Prophet ﷺ Muḥammad".[912]

NAWĀFIL ṢALĀHS

Nawāfil is the plural of *nāfilah* (*nafl* and *taṭawwu*ᶜ are also used for the same meaning); it means supererogatory *ṣalāhs*, which are to raise one's position, to forgive one's sins, and to make up for any deficiencies in the performance of *farḍ ṣalāhs*. ᶜUbādah ibn al-Ṣāmit reported that he heard the Messenger of Allāh ﷺ saying: "No one does a *sajdah* for Allāh, but Allāh writes for him a good deed, forgives one sin, and raises him a degree, so do plenty of *sajdah*s (meaning *nafl ṣalāhs*)".[913]

[911] Ibid.

[912] Abū Dāwūd, *k. al-ṣalāh, b. al-qunūt fī al-witr;* al-Tirmidhī, *k. al-witr, b. mā jā'a fī al-qunūt fī al-witr,* al-Nasā'ī, *k. qiyām al-layl, b. al-du*ᶜ*ā' fī al-witr.*

[913] Muslim, *k. al-ṣalāh, b. faḍl al-sujūd wa al-ḥathth alayh;* Ibn Mājah, *k. iqāmat al-ṣalāh wa al-sunnah fīhā, b. mā jā'a fī kathrat al-sujūd.*

Abū Hurayrah reported that the Prophet ﷺ said: "The first thing that the people will be called to account out of their actions on the Day of Resurrection will be the *ṣalāhs.* Our Lord will say to the angels although He knows better: 'Look into the *ṣalāh* of My slave and see whether he has observed it perfectly or was negligent in it'. So if he observed it perfectly it will be recorded to his credit, but if he has been negligent in it in any way, Allāh will say: 'See if My slave has any supererogatory *ṣalāhs*'. Then if he has any supererogatory *ṣalāhs,* Allāh will say: 'Make up the deficiency in My slave's obligatory *ṣalāh* with his supererogatory *ṣalāhs*'. Thereafter, all his actions will be examined in like manner".[914]

Abū Umāmah narrated that the Prophet ﷺ said: "Allāh does not listen to anything from His slave as He does to the two *rakᶜah*s of *ṣalāh* that he offers. Mercy descends over the slave's head as long as he remains in *ṣalāh*."[915]

Al-Mughīrah ibn Shuᶜbah said: "The Prophet ﷺ would stand and pray until his feet swole. When he was asked about this, he said: 'Should I not be a thankful slave?'."[916]

When nafl becomes wājib

As one starts *nafl ṣalāh,* it becomes *wājib* (compulsory) to complete it. If one invalidates *nafl*, then it is compulsory to make it up later. Allāh says: "*And do not invalidate your deeds*".[917] This verse makes it compulsory to save deeds from being invalidated; which only can happen by completing them. If one invalidates them, then one is invalidating an act of worship which must be performed; so one has to make them up.

By starting a *nafl* prayer, only two *rakᶜah*s become compulsory, even if one intended four *rakᶜah*s.[918] If one intended to do four *rakᶜahs* but invalidates the last two, then one only needs to make up the remaining two.

[914] al-Tirmidhī, *k. al-ṣalāh, b. mā jā'a anna awwala mā yuḥāsabu bihi al-ᶜabdu yawm al-qiyāmati al-ṣalāh.*

[915] al-Tirmidhī, *k. faḍā'il al-qur'ān.*

[916] al-Bukhārī, *k. al-tafsīr, b. liyaghfira laka Allāhu mā taqaddama min dhanbika;* Muslim, *k. ṣifat al-munafiqīn wa aḥkāmihim, b. ikthār al-aᶜmāl wa al-ijtihād fī al-ᶜibādah.*

[917] Muḥammad 33.

[918] al-Kāsānī, *Badā'iᶜ al-ṣanā'iᶜ*, *ii.* 282-3.

Rakᶜahs of nafl

As for the *nafl ṣalāhs* during the day, one can do two *rakᶜahs* with one final *salām* or, if one wishes, four *rakᶜahs* with one final *salām*; to do more than four *rakᶜahs* in one *salām* is not liked. There is no narration from the Prophet ﷺ or from any Companion, that they did more than four *rakᶜahs* with one *salạm* during the day.[919] Furthermore, ᶜAbdullāh ibn ᶜUmar used to pray four *rakᶜahs* during the day.[920] Ibn ᶜAwn said: "I asked Nāfiᶜ about the *nafl ṣalāh* during the day; he said: 'As for myself I pray four *rakᶜah*'s."[921] Ibrāhīm al-Nakhaᶜī said: "The *nafl ṣalāhs* of the day are four *rakᶜahs*'."[922]

As for the *nafl* of the night, it has been narrated from the Prophet ﷺ and many Companions that they said night *ṣalāhs* constitute two *rakᶜahs.*[923] According to Imām Abū Ḥanīfah it is permitted to pray eight *rakᶜahs* with one final *salām.*[924] Abū Ḥanīfah said: "If you want you can pray a night *ṣalāh* with two *rakᶜahs*, or four, or six, or eight or more with one opening *takbīr*; though the best is four *rakᶜahs*".[925] However, Imām Muḥammad said: "The night *ṣalāh* in our view is two *rakᶜahs*". Abū Yūsuf also supports the view that one should not do more than two *rakᶜahs* at night before making the final *salām*. Therefore, to do the *nafl* of the night in units of two *rakᶜahs* is best since this is agreed upon by all.

Differences between nafl and farḍ ṣalāhs

It is allowed to do *nafl ṣalāhs* while sitting even though one has the ability to stand. It is also acceptable to do part of such *ṣalāhs* sitting and part of them standing even if all of this is in one *rakᶜah*, i.e. one sits for part of the first *rakᶜah* and then stands for the rest of it or vice versa.[926] Umm Salamah said: "By the One Who took the soul of the Prophet

[919] Ibn Abī Shaybah, *al-Muṣannaf, ii.* 18-19.

[920] Ibid., *ii.* 75.

[921] Ibid.

[922] Ibid.

[923] Ibid., *ii.* 74-75.

[924] al-Marghinānī, *al-Hidāyah, i.* 72.

[925] Muḥammad, *al-Muwaṭṭa', i.* 519-520.

[926] This is permitted according to Abū Ḥanīfah while Abū Yūsuf and Muḥammad held that it is only permitted with an excuse.

ﷺ, the Prophet ﷺ did not die until most of his *ṣalāhs* were done while sitting".[927] ʿAlqamah asked ʿĀ'ishah: "How did the Prophet ﷺ perform two *rakʿahs* while sitting?" She replied: "He would recite while sitting and then when he wished to make *rukūʿ*, he would stand and bow".[928] In another narration, ʿĀ'ishah said: "I never saw the Messenger of Allāh ﷺ ever sitting while reciting during the night *ṣalāh* until he became old, then he would sit until about thirty or forty verses were left of his recital and then he would stand, finish the recitation and do *rukūʿ*".[929]

Whoever is outside of a town may do *nafl ṣalāh* on his mount or any vehicle he is travelling in, facing the direction he finds himself in, and fulfilling the movements of the *ṣalāh* by gesture.[930]

Recitation of the Qur'ān is *farḍ* (obligatory) in all *rakʿahs* of *nafl;* it is *wājib* to recite *al-Fātiḥah* and another sūrah in every *rakʿah* of *nafl ṣalāh.*[931]

Congregation is not Sunnah in *nafl ṣalāh* except in *tarāwīḥ,* and it is better for *nafl ṣalāh* to be performed at home rather than *masjids.* ʿAbdullāh ibn Saʿd narrated that the Messenger of Allāh ﷺ said: "Don't you see how close my house is to the *masjid;* it is more beloved for me to pray in my house than the *masjid,* except for the *farḍ ṣalāh*".[932] Zayd ibn Thābit records that the Messenger of Allāh ﷺ said: "A person's *ṣalāh* in his home is better than his *ṣalāh* in my *masjid,* except for the *farḍ ṣalāh*".[933] Jābir narrated that the Messenger of Allāh ﷺ said: "If one of you offers his *ṣalāhs* in the *masjid* then he should also make a portion of his *ṣalāhs* in his home, as Allāh has made his *ṣalāhs* in his home a means of betterment for him".[934] Aʿmash narrated that he never saw Ibrāhīm

[927] al-Nasā'ī, k. *qiyām al-layl, b. ṣalāt al-qāʿid fī al-nāfilah;* Ibn Mājah, *k. iqāmat al-ṣalāh wa al-sunnah fīhā, b. fī ṣalāt al-nāfilah qāʿidan.*

[928] Muslim, *k. ṣalāt al-musāfirīn wa qaṣrihā, b. jawāz al-nāfilah qā'iman wa qāʿidan.*

[929] al-Bukhārī, *k. tafsīr al-ṣalāh, b. idhā ṣallā qāʿidan thumma ṣallā;* Muslim, *k. ṣalāt al-musāfirīn, b. jawāz al-nāfilah.*

[930] See: al-Kāsānī, *Badā'iʿ al-ṣanā'iʿ, ii.* 297.

[931] Ibid.

[932] al-Bukhārī, *k. al-adhān, b. ṣalāt al-layl;* Muslim, *k. ṣalāt al-musāfirīn, b. istiḥbāb ṣalāt al-nāfilah fī baytihi;* Ibn Mājah, *k. iqāmat al-ṣalāh wa al-sunnah fīhā, b. mā jā'a fī al-taṭawwuʿ fī al-bayt.*

[933] Abū Dāwūd, *k. al-ṣalāh, b. ṣalāt al-rajul al-taṭawwuʿ fī baytih.*

[934] Muslim, *k. ṣalāt al-musāfirīn, b. istiḥbāb ṣalāt al-nāfilah fī baytihi.*

al-Nakhaʿī praying any *nafl* (meaning any *ṣalāh* other than *farḍ*) in the *masjid*.[935]

Types of nawāfil

There are two types of *nawāfil:* general and specific *ṣalāhs.* The specific *nafl ṣalāhs* are referred to as *al-sunan al-rātibah,* or the Sunnah *ṣalāhs,* that have a specific order, number, and so on.

The Sunnah before *Fajr* is two *rakʿahs,* four before *Ẓuhr* and two *rakʿahs* after it, two *rakʿahs* after *Maghrib,* and two after *ʿIshā'.* Ibn ʿUmar said: "I preserved from the Prophet ﷺ ten *rakʿahs* (of Sunnah *ṣalāhs*): two before *Ẓuhr* and two after it, two after *Maghrib* in his house, two after *ʿIshā'* in his house and two *rakʿahs* before *Fajr*".[936] Although in this ḥadīth from Ibn ʿUmar the Sunnah before *Ẓuhr* is mentioned as two *rakʿahs,* Ḥanafīs prefer four *rakʿahs* because of the ḥadīth from ʿĀ'ishah and others given below. Taking four *rakʿahs* before *Ẓuhr* into account these Sunnah *ṣalāhs* add up to twelve *rakʿahs.* Umm Ḥabībah said: "I heard the Prophet ﷺ saying: 'Whoever prays twelve *rakʿahs* in a day and night as *nafl,* a house will be built for him in Paradise".[937]

The Sunnah of Fajr

ʿĀ'ishah related that the Prophet ﷺ said about the two *rakʿahs* before *Fajr*: "They are dearer to me than the whole world".[938] Abū Hurayrah reported that the Prophet ﷺ said: "Do not leave the two *rakʿahs* of *Fajr,* even if you are being attacked by cavalry".[939] ʿĀ'ishah said: "I have never seen him (the Prophet ﷺ) more in haste to do a good deed than he was to do the two *rakʿahs* before the *Fajr* (*ṣalāh*)".[940]

ʿĀ'ishah also narrated: "The Prophet ﷺ would pray the two *rakʿahs* before the dawn *ṣalāh* in my house so quickly that I wondered if he had recited the *Fātiḥah* in them or not".[941] She further reported that

[935] Ibn Abī Shaybah, *al-Muṣannaf, ii.* 52.

[936] al-Bukhārī, *k. al-tahajjud, b. al-rakʿatayn qabl al-ẓuhr.*

[937] Muslim, *k. ṣalāt al-musāfirīn wa qaṣrihā, b. faḍl al-sunan al-rātibah qabla al-farā'iḍ wa baʿdahunna wa bayān ʿadadihinn.*

[938] Muslim, *k. ṣalāt al-musāfirīn wa qaṣrihā, b. istiḥbāb rakʿatay sunnat al-fajr.*

[939] Abū Dāwūd, *k. al-ṣalāh, b. fī takhfīfihā.*

[940] Muslim, *k. ṣalāt al-musāfirīn wa qaṣrihā, b. istiḥbāb rakʿatay sunnat al-fajr.*

[941] al-Bukhārī, *k. al-tahajjud, b. mā yuqra'u fī rakʿatay al-fajr.*

the Prophet ﷺ after reading *al-Fātiḥah* would recite قُلْ يَا أَيُّهَا الْكَافِرُونَ, *'Say: O disbelievers'*, and قُلْ هُوَ اللهُ أَحَدٌ *'Say: He is Allāh, the One'*, silently in the two *rakʿahs* before *Fajr Ṣalāh*.[942]

The Sunnah of Ẓuhr

There are four *Sunnah rakʿahs* before *Ẓuhr*. ʿĀ'ishah said: "The Prophet ﷺ never left praying four *rakʿahs* before *Ẓuhr* and two *rakʿahs* before *Fajr* under any circumstances".[943] She also narrated that the Prophet ﷺ prayed four *rakʿahs* in his house before *Ẓuhr* and then went to the *masjid*.[944] ʿĀ'ishah further reported that if the Prophet ﷺ missed the four *rakʿahs* before *Ẓuhr*, he would pray them afterwards.[945] In another ḥadīth it is stated that if the Prophet ﷺ missed the four *rakʿahs* before *Ẓuhr*, he would pray them following the two *rakʿahs* after *Ẓuhr*.[946] ʿAmr ibn Maymūn narrated that the Companions of the Prophet ﷺ never missed four *rakʿahs* before *Ẓuhr* and two *rakʿahs* before *Fajr* under any circumstances.[947] ʿAbīdah al-Salmānī said: "The Companions of the Messenger of Allāh ﷺ never agreed on anything as they agreed on preserving four *rakʿahs* before *Ẓuhr*".[948] ʿAbdullāh ibn Masʿūd said: "Four *rakʿahs* before the *Ẓuhr* are with one *salām*".[949]

The Sunnah *ṣalāh* after *Ẓuhr* are two *rakʿahs* as has come down from Ibn ʿUmar's ḥadīth. Umm Salamah said: "The Prophet ﷺ prayed *Ẓuhr* and then he received some wealth and he sat to distribute it (and continued to do so) until the *mu'adhdhin* made the *adhān* for *ʿAṣr*. He prayed *ʿAṣr* and came to me, as it was my day, and he prayed two quick *rakʿahs*. I said: 'What are those two *rakʿahs*, O Messenger of Allāh ﷺ? Have you been ordered to perform them?' He said: 'No, they are the two *rakʿahs* that I perform after *Ẓuhr* but I was busy distributing this wealth until the

[942] Abū Dāwūd, *k. al-ṣalāh, b. fī takhfīfihā*.

[943] al-Bukhārī, *k. al-tahajjud, b. al-rakʿatayn qabla al-ẓuhr*.

[944] Abū Dāwūd, *k. al-ṣalāh, k. al-taṭawwuʿ*.

[945] al-Tirmidhī, *k. al-ṣalāh, b. minhu ākhar*.

[946] Ibn Mājah, *k. iqāmat al-ṣalāh wa al-sunnah fīhā, b. man fātathu al-arbaʿ qabla al-ẓuhr*.

[947] Ibn Abī Shaybah, *al-Muṣannaf, ii*. 16.

[948] al-Kāsānī, *Badā'iʿ al-ṣanā'iʿ, ii*. 265.

[949] Ibn Abī Shaybah, *al-Muṣannaf, ii*. 16.

adhān was made for ᶜ*Aṣr* and I did not like to miss them'."[950] ᶜAlī ibn Abī Ṭālib narrated that the Prophet ﷺ used to pray four *rak*ᶜ*ahs* before *Ẓuhr*, and two *rak*ᶜ*ahs* after *Ẓuhr*".[951]

The Sunnah of Maghrib

After *Maghrib* it is Sunnah to pray two *rak*ᶜ*ahs*. It is narrated by Ibn ᶜUmar that the Prophet ﷺ would not miss them. It is preferable to recite after *al-Fātiḥah* قُلْ يَا أَيُّهَا الْكَافِرُونَ *'Say: O Unbelievers'*, and قُلْ هُوَ اللهُ أَحَد *'Say: He is Allāh, the One'*. Ibn Masᶜūd said: "I cannot count how many times I heard the Messenger of Allāh ﷺ recite, in the two *rak*ᶜ*ah*s after *Maghrib* and in the two *rak*ᶜ*ah*s before *Fajr* '*Say: O disbelievers*', and '*Say: He is Allāh, the One*'."[952]

There is no Sunnah *ṣalāh* before *Maghrib*. Ṭāwūs narrated: "ᶜAbdullāh ibn ᶜUmar was asked about the two *rak*ᶜ*ah*s before *Maghrib*. He answered: 'I have not seen anyone in the time of the Prophet ﷺ praying them'."[953] Ḥammād ibn Abī Sulaymān said: "I asked Ibrāhīm about the *ṣalāh* before *Maghrib*, he forbade me from this and said: 'The Prophet ﷺ, Abū Bakr and ᶜUmar did not pray it'." Imām Muḥammad said: "We adhere to it. When the sun sets then there is no *ṣalāh* on *janāzah* or any other *ṣalāh* before the *ṣalāh* of *Maghrib*. And it is the opinion of Abū Ḥanīfah".[954]

The Sunnah of ᶜ*Ishā'*

The Sunnah after ᶜ*Ishā'* is two *rak*ᶜ*ahs* as is confirmed by the reports mentioned earlier. No Sunnah *ṣalāh* has been narrated from the Prophet ﷺ before ᶜ*Ishā'*. However, there is no harm in praying *taḥiyyat al-masjid* or *nafl* before ᶜ*Ishā'*. ᶜAlā' al-Dīn al-Samarqandī quoted from *Ẓāhir al-Riwāyah* that there is no *nafl* before ᶜ*Ishā'*, and if someone does, there is no harm. Al-Samarqandī prefers this, referring to the above mentioned

[950] al-Bukhārī, *k. mawāqīt al-ṣalāh, b. mā yuṣallā ba*ᶜ*da al-*ᶜ*aṣr min al-fawā'it wa naḥwihā;* Ibn Mājah, *k. iqāmat al-ṣalāh wa al-sunnah fīhā, b. fī man fātathu al-rak*ᶜ*atān ba*ᶜ*da al-ẓuhr.*

[951] al-Tirmidhī, *k. al-ṣalāh, b. mā jā'a fī al-arba*ᶜ*ah qabla al-ẓuhr.*

[952] al-Tirmidhī, *k. al-ṣalāh, b. mā jā'a fī al-rak*ᶜ*atayn ba*ᶜ*da al-maghrib wa al-qirā'ah fīhimā.*

[953] Abū Dāwūd, *k. al-ṣalāh, b. al-ṣalāh qabla al-maghrib.*

[954] Abū Ḥanīfah, *K. al-āthār* 39.

ḥadīth from Umm Ḥabībah which mentions two *rakᶜahs* after the *ᶜIshā'* and nothing before it.[955]

Sunnah before ᶜAṣr

Four *rakᶜahs* before *ᶜAṣr* are Sunnah *ghayr al-mu'akkadah* (Sunnahs that are not stressed). Ibn ᶜUmar reported that the Prophet ﷺ said: "May Allāh have mercy on a person who prays four *rakᶜahs* before *ᶜAṣr ṣalāh*".[956] ᶜAlī reported that the Prophet ﷺ prayed four *rakᶜahs* before *ᶜAṣr* while separating them with salutations to the angels close to Allāh, to the prophets, and to those who followed them, the believers and Muslims. Imām al-Tirmidhī said after recording this ḥadīth: "Isḥāq ibn Ibrāhīm prefers not to separate the four *rakᶜahs* before *ᶜAṣr*, and he brings this ḥadīth as evidence, and said that the meaning of 'separating them with salutations' is recitation of the *tashahhud*".[957]

Night Ṣalāhs

Night *ṣalāhs* or *qiyām al-layl* or *tahajjud* is Sunnah. The virtues of this *ṣalāh* and its importance is mentioned in many verses of the Qur'ān. Abū Umāmah related that the Prophet ﷺ said: "Observe the night *ṣalāh*, it was the practice of the righteous before you and it brings you closer to your Lord and it is penance for evil deeds and erases one's sins".[958]

When one wakes up for the night prayer, one should wipe one's face, use a tooth stick, and look to the sky and make the supplication which has been reported from the Prophet ﷺ:

لَا إِلَهَ إِلاَّ أَنْتَ سُبْحَانَكَ اَللَّهُمَّ وَبِحَمْدِكَ أَسْتَغْفِرُكَ لِذَنْبِي وَأَسْأَلُكَ رَحْمَتَكَ اَللَّهُمَّ زِدْنِي عِلْمًا وَلَا تُزِغْ قَلْبِي بَعْدَ إِذْ هَدَيْتَنِي وَهَبْ لِي مِنْ لَدُنْكَ رَحْمَةً إِنَّكَ أَنْتَ الْوَهَّاب

"There is no god but You, Glory be to You, and praise and thanks are due to You, I seek forgiveness from You for my sins, and I ask for Your

[955] al-Samarqandī, *Tuḥfat al-fuqahā'* 93.
[956] Abū Dāwūd, *k. al-ṣalāh, b. al-ṣalāh qabla al-ᶜaṣr.*
[957] al-Tirmidhī, *k. al-ṣalāh, b. mā jā'a fī al-arbaᶜah qabla al-ᶜaṣr.*
[958] al-Tirmidhī, *k. al-daᶜawāt, b. fī duᶜā' al-nabī ṣallallāhu ᶜalayhi wa sallam.*

mercy. O Allāh, increase my knowledge and let my heart not swerve after You have guided me, and bestow mercy upon me from Yourself. Indeed You are the Bestower".[959]

Then, one should recite the last ten *āyahs* of *Āli ʿImrān*. Then one should say:

اَللَّهُمَّ لَكَ الْحَمْدُ أَنْتَ قَيِّمُ السَّمَاوَاتِ وَالأَرْضِ وَمَنْ فِيهِنَّ وَلَكَ الْحَمْدُ أَنْتَ الْحَقُّ وَوَعْدُكَ الْحَقُّ وَلِقَاؤُكَ حَقٌّ وَقَوْلُكَ حَقٌّ وَالْجَنَّةُ حَقٌّ وَالنَّارُ حَقٌّ وَالنَّبِيُّوْنَ حَقٌّ وَمُحَمَّدٌ حَقٌّ وَالسَّاعَةُ حَقٌّ اَللَّهُمَّ لَكَ أَسْلَمْتُ وَبِكَ آمَنْتُ وَعَلَيْكَ تَوَكَّلْتُ وَإِلَيْكَ أَنَبْتُ وَبِكَ خَاصَمْتُ وَإِلَيْكَ حَاكَمْتُ فَاغْفِرْ لِي مَا قَدَّمْتُ وَمَا أَخَّرْتُ وَمَا أَسْرَرْتُ وَمَا أَعْلَنْتُ وَمَا أَنْتَ أَعْلَمُ بِهِ مِنِّي أَنْتَ الْمُقَدِّمُ وَأَنْتَ الْمُؤَخِّرُ لاَ إِلَهَ إِلاَّ أَنْتَ وَلاَ إِلَهَ غَيْرُكَ

"O Allāh, to You belong the praise and thanks. You are the Sustainer of the heavens and the earth and what is therein. And to You belong the praise and thanks. You are the Truth and Your promise is true. And the meeting with You is true, and Your word is true. Paradise is true, and the Fire is true. All the prophets are true, and Muḥammad is true. And the Hour is true. O Allāh, to You have I submitted. And in You have I believed. And on You have I relied. And to You have I turned. And by You I argue. And to You do I turn for judgement. Forgive me of my former and latter sins, and those done in secret and those done openly, and those which You know more than me. You are the One Who moves things forward and backward. There is no god besides You".[960]

Abū Hurayrah reported that the Prophet ﷺ said: "May Allāh bless the man who gets up during the night to pray and wakes up his wife and who, if she refuses to get up, sprinkles water on her face. And may Allāh bless the woman who gets up during the night to pray and wakes up her husband and who, if he refuses, sprinkles water on his face".[961] The Prophet ﷺ also said: "If a man wakes his wife during the night and he

[959] Abū Dāwūd, *k. al-adab, b. mā yaqūlu al-rajul idhā taʿārra min al-layl.*

[960] al-Bukhārī, *k. al-tahajjud, b. al-tahajjud bi al-layl;* Muslim, *k. ṣalāt al-musāfirīn, b. al-duʿāʾ fī ṣalāt al-layl.*

[961] Abū Dāwūd, *k. al-ṣalāh, b. qiyām al-layl.*

prays or they both pray two *rakᶜahs,* they will be recorded among those men and women who constantly remember Allāh".[962]

The timing of tahajjud

Tahajjud can be performed any time after *ᶜIshā'*; though it is preferred to pray it in the last part of the night. Abū Hurayrah reported that the Messenger of Allāh ﷺ said: "Our Lord descends to the lowest heaven during the last third of the night, inquiring: 'Who will call on Me so that I may respond to him? Who is asking something of Me so I may give it to him? Who is asking for My forgiveness so I may forgive him?'."[963] ᶜAmr ibn ᶜAbasah reported that he heard the Prophet ﷺ say: "The closest that a slave comes to his Lord is during the middle of the latter portion of the night. If you can be among those who remember Allāh, the Exalted One, at that time, then do so".[964]

The number of rakᶜahs

The minimum number of *rakᶜahs* in *tahajjud ṣalāh* are two, and the maximum *rakᶜahs* eight.[965] ᶜĀ'ishah said: "The Messenger of Allāh ﷺ never prayed in the night more than eleven *rakᶜahs,* during Ramaḍān or otherwise. He would pray four *rakᶜahs,* and don't ask about how excellent they were or how lengthy they were. Then, he would pray four *rakᶜahs,* and don't ask about how excellent they were or how lengthy they were. Then, he would pray three *rakᶜahs.* I asked: 'O Messenger of Allāh ﷺ, do you sleep before praying *Witr*?' He replied: 'O ᶜĀ'ishah, my eyes sleep but my heart does not sleep'."[966]

Tarāwīḥ

Tarāwīḥ is Sunnah for both men and women during the month of Ramaḍān and is to be performed after the *ᶜIshā' Ṣalāh* until dawn. Abū Hurayrah reported that the Prophet ﷺ said: "Whoever prays during the

[962] Ibid.

[963] al-Bukhārī, *k. al-tahajjud, b. al-duᶜā' wa al-ṣalāh min ākhir al-layl.*

[964] al-Tirmidhī, *k. al-daᶜawāt.*

[965] *al-Fatāwā al-hindiyyah,* i. 112.

[966] al-Bukhārī, *k. al-tahajjud, b. qiyām al-nabī ṣallallāhu ᶜalayhi wa sallam bi al-layl fī ramaḍān wa ghayrih.*

nights of Ramaḍān (*tarāwīḥ*) with a firm belief and hoping for reward, all of his previous sins will be forgiven".[967]

ʿĀ'ishah said: "The Prophet ﷺ offered *ṣalāh* in the *masjid* and many people prayed with him. The next day he did the same and more people prayed with him. Then the people gathered on the third night but the Prophet ﷺ did not come out to them. In the morning, he said to them: 'Surely I saw what you did, and nothing prevented me from coming out to you, save that I feared that (this *ṣalāh*) would be made obligatory upon you'. And this was during Ramaḍān".[968]

The number of rakʿahs

Tarāwīḥ consists of twenty *rakʿahs* with ten *salāms* and five *tarwīḥas* (resting). ʿAbdullāh ibn ʿAbbās narrated that the Prophet ﷺ prayed twenty *rakʿahs* during Ramaḍān.[969] At the time of ʿUmar, ʿUthmān and ʿAlī the people prayed twenty *rakʿahs*, and this is the opinion of the majority of jurists. Al-Tirmidhī said: "Most of the people of knowledge follow what was related from ʿUmar and ʿAlī and the other Companions, (i.e. that they prayed twenty *rakʿahs*). This is also the opinion of al-Thawrī, Ibn al-Mubārak and al-Shāfiʿī. Imām Shāfiʿī said: "I found the people of Makkah praying twenty *rakʿahs*".[970] Abū al-Hasnā' said: "ʿAlī commanded a man to lead the *tarāwīḥ ṣalāh* in Ramaḍān and to pray twenty *rakʿahs*".[971] Yaḥyā ibn Saʿīd said: "ʿUmar ibn al-Khaṭṭāb commanded a man to lead the *tarāwīḥ* with twenty *rakʿahs*".[972] ʿAbd al-ʿAzīz ibn Rufayʿ said: "Ubayy ibn Kaʿb prayed twenty *rakʿahs* with the people in Madīnah during the month of Ramaḍān and prayed three *rakʿahs* for *Witr*".[973] Nāfiʿ ibn ʿUmar said: "Ibn Abī Mulaykah would pray

[967] al-Bukhārī, *k. ṣalāt al-tarāwīḥ, b. faḍl man qāma ramaḍān;* Muslim, *k. ṣalāt al-musāfirīn wa qaṣrihā, b. al-rāghibīn fī qiyām ramaḍān wa huwa al-tarāwīḥ*

[968] al-Bukhārī, *k. al-tahajjud, b. taḥrīḍ al-nabī ṣallallāhu ʿalayhi wa sallam ʿalā ṣalāt al-layl;* Muslim, *k. ṣalāt al-musāfirīn wa qaṣrihā.*

[969] Ibn Abī Shaybah, *al-Muṣannaf, ii.* 166.

[970] al-Tirmidhī, *k. al-ṣawm, b. mā jā'a fī qiyām shahr ramaḍān.*

[971] Ibn Abī Shaybah, *al-Muṣannaf, ii.* 165.

[972] Ibid.

[973] Ibid.

with us in Ramaḍān twenty *rakᶜahs*".[974] ᶜAṭā' ibn Abī Rabāḥ said: "I have found people praying twenty-three *rakᶜahs* including *Witr*".[975]

Praying in congregation

It is Sunnah to perform *tarāwīḥ* in congregation in the *masjid*.[976] The Prophet ﷺ, as stated earlier, did so, but discontinued since he feared it would make it obligatory. ᶜUmar was the one who gathered the Muslims for *tarāwīḥ ṣalāhs* behind one imām. ᶜAbd al-Raḥmān ibn ᶜAbd al-Qārī reported: "One night during Ramaḍān, I went with ᶜUmar to the *masjid* and the people were praying in different groups. Some were praying by themselves and others were praying in small groups. ᶜUmar said: 'I think it would be better if I gathered them under one imām'. Then he did so and appointed Ubayy ibn Kaᶜb as the leader of the *ṣalāh*. I went out with him on another night and all the people were praying behind one imām and ᶜUmar said: 'What a good new way this is'."[977] *Tarāwīḥ* in congregation is also narrated from ᶜAlī ibn Abī Ṭālib, ᶜAbdullāh ibn Masᶜūd, their students and many others".[978]

The recitation of the Qur'ān in tarāwīḥ

It is preferable to read the whole Qur'ān at least once in the *tarāwīḥ*.[979] The imām should read what is easy for people, for example, one *juz'* and a quarter in a night. It is related from Saᶜīd ibn Jubayr that he recited twenty-five verses in each *rakᶜah* and ᶜUmar ibn ᶜAbd al-ᶜAzīz asked people to read ten verses in each *rakᶜah*.[980]

[974] Ibid.

[975] Ibid.

[976] al-Kāsānī, *Badā'iᶜ al-ṣanā'iᶜ, ii.* 275.

[977] al-Bukhārī, *k. ṣalāt al-tarāwīḥ, b. faḍl man qāma ramaḍān;* Ibn Abī Shaybah, *al-Muṣannaf, ii.* 167.

[978] Ibn Abī Shaybah, *al-Muṣannaf, ii.* 166-167.

[979] *al-Fatāwā al-hindiyyah, i.* 117.

[980] Ibn Abī Shaybah, *al-Muṣannaf, ii.* 164-165

CHAPTER 9: SPECIAL *SAJDAHS*

THE *SAJDAH* FOR FORGETTING

THE *ṢALĀH* OF SOMEONE who misses any *rukn* (*farḍ* parts) of the *ṣalāh*, whether intentionally or forgetfully, is invalid; it cannot be repaired by *sajdah*, and they must repeat the *ṣalāh*. If someone misses any *wājib* of the *ṣalāh* intentionally, then they have committed a sin, and it is *wājib* for them to repeat the *ṣalāh*, and it cannot be repaired by *sajdah*. If someone misses a *wājib* forgetfully then it is *wājib* on them to do *sajdah* for forgetting, and the *ṣalāh* will be repaired by that *sajdah*.

When these sajdahs are compulsory

It is incumbent on a person to do *sajdah* if he makes an addition to his *ṣalāh* action, which although a normal part of the *ṣalāh* was not at the moment when he did it, or if he omits a *wājib* action, such as the recitation of the *Fātiḥah* or *Qunūt*, or the *tashahhud*, or if the imām recites aloud where he should recite silently or silently where he should recite aloud.

ᶜAbdullāh ibn Masᶜūd narrated: "The Prophet ﷺ prayed five *rakᶜahs* and the people asked him: 'Has there been an addition to the *ṣalāh*?' He asked: 'Why do you say that?' They replied: 'You prayed five *rakᶜahs*'. Then he made two *sajdah* after doing the *taslīm*".[981]

Abū Hurayrah narrated: "The Prophet ﷺ prayed either *Ẓuhr* or *ᶜAṣr Ṣalāh* with us and he prayed only two *rakᶜahs* and made the *taslīm*. He got up and leaned against a piece of wood in the *masjid* as if he was angry. He put his right hand on his left and interlocked his fingers. Then, he placed his cheek on the back of his left hand. And some people left the *masjid* in a hurry. And they said: 'Has the *ṣalāh* been shortened?' Among the people were Abū Bakr and ᶜUmar, and they did not dare to speak to him. Among the people, there was someone called Dhū al-Yadayn who said: 'O Messenger of Allāh ﷺ have you forgotten or has the *ṣalāh* been shortened?' He answered: 'I have not forgotten and it has not been

[981] al-Bukhārī, *k. al-sahw, b. idhā ṣallā khamsan.*

shortened'. Then he asked: 'Is it as Dhū al-Yadayn has said?' The people answered: 'Yes'. At that, he led the people in what he had missed and made the *taslīm.* After which he made the *takbīr* and prostrated the way he usually prostrated or perhaps even longer. Next, he raised his head and made the *takbīr.* Then, he made the *takbīr* (again) and prostrated, like one of his customary *sajdah* or perhaps even longer, and finally, he raised his head".[982]

How to perform these sajdahs

The *sajdah* of forgetting should be done after the *salām* in the final sitting. ʿAbdullāh ibn Masʿūd reported that the Prophet ﷺ said: "If one of you has some doubts during his *ṣalāh* and he does not recall the number of *rakʿahs* he has prayed, three or four, then he should build upon what he was more certain of [the lesser amount] and then do two *sajdahs* after the *taslīm.*"[983]

Thawbān narrated that the Messenger of Allāh ﷺ said: "For every forgetting there are two *sajdahs* after the *salām*".[984]

When the person on whom the *sajdahs* of forgetting are compulsory has finished *tashahhud* in the last sitting, he says one *salām* to his right, then says the *takbīr* and does two *sajdahs* like the *sajdah* of *ṣalāh* then, remaining seated, he recites the *tashahhud*, the prayer of blessing on the Prophet ﷺ and supplication for himself, and then says the two *salāms* to conclude the *ṣalāh.*[985]

Some important points

Should the imām forget, this necessitates that the person following him also prostrate but if the imām does not prostrate, then the person following does not. Ibrāhīm al-Nakhaʿī said: "If the imām forgets and does the *sajdahs* of forgetting then do *sajdah* with him; but if he does

[982] al-Bukhārī, *k. al-adhān, b. hal ya'khudhu al-imām idhā shakka bi qawl al-nās;* Muslim, *k. al-masājid wa mawāḍiʿ al-ṣalāh, b. al-sahw fī al-ṣalāh wa al-sujūd lahu.*
[983] al-Nasā'ī, *k. al-ṣahw, b. at-taḥarrī.*
[984] Abū Dāwūd, *k. al-ṣalāh, b. man nasiya an yatashahhada;* Ibn Mājah, *k. iqāmat al-ṣalāh, b. mā jā'a fīman sajadahumā baʿda al-salām.*
[985] *See*: *al-Fatāwā al-hindiyyah,* i. 125.

not do *sajdah,* then it is not obligatory upon you to do *sajdah*". Imām Muḥammad said: "We adhere to it, and this is the opinion of Abū Ḥanīfah".[986]

If the person following the imām neglects something, neither the imām nor the person is required to do the *sajdah.*

Whoever forgets the first sitting, then remembers straight away should return to the sitting position and do the *tashahhud*; but if he is almost at the standing position, he does not return but does the *sajdah* of forgetting.

Whoever neglects to do the final sitting and stands up for a fifth *rakᶜah* must return to the sitting as long as he has not made a *sajdah* in the fifth and then make a *sajdah* of forgetting. If the fifth has been completed with a *sajdah,* he should add a sixth *rakᶜah* to it to complete the *ṣalāh.* In this case, his *farḍ ṣalāh* is invalid and his *ṣalāh* is reduced to a *nafl ṣalāh.*

If one sat in the fourth *rakᶜah* for the duration of the *tashahhud* and instead of doing the final *salām* got up for a fifth, as long as one has not prostrated for the fifth *rakᶜah,* one should return to the sitting position and do the final *salām* followed by the *sajdah* of forgetting. However, if one seals the fifth with a *sajdah,* then one should add another *rakᶜah* to it and do the *sajdah* of forgetting and so complete the *ṣalāh.* The additional two *rakᶜahs* will be counted as *nafl.*

Whoever is in doubt as to his *ṣalāh* and does not know whether he has made three or four *rakᶜahs* and it is the first time this has happened to him must recommence the *ṣalāh.* However, if this doubt frequently afflicts him, he should continue on the basis of what he thinks in all likelihood to be true, but if he has no thoughts on the matter, then he confirms on the basis of what he can be certain of. Imām Muḥammad narrated from Ibrāhīm al-Nakhaᶜī about someone who forgets and does not know whether he has prayed four *rakᶜahs* or three. Ibrāhīm al-Nakhaᶜī said: "If it is his first forgetting, he should repeat the *ṣalāh*; if it happens to him quite often then he has to exert himself to know what he has prayed. If he feels strongly that he has completed the *ṣalāh,* then he concludes the *ṣalāh* and does the two *sajdahs* of forgetting. But if he strongly feels that he has prayed three *rakᶜahs* then he must add to them one *rakᶜah* (to make up the four *rakᶜahs*) and do the *sajdahs* of

[986] Abū Ḥanīfah, *K. al-āthār* 47.

forgetting". Imām Muḥammad said: "We adhere to it and this is the opinion of Abū Ḥanīfah".[987]

The sajdah for recitation

Abū Hurayrah narrated that the Prophet ﷺ said: "If a son of Ādam recites an *āyah* of *sajdah* and prostrates, Satan departs from him and cries: 'O woe, he was ordered to prostrate and he did, so for him is Paradise. I was ordered to prostrate and I disobeyed, so for me is Hell'."[988]

The āyahs of sajdah

The 14 *āyahs* in the Qur'ān at which one must prostrate are as follows:.

1- إِنَّ الَّذِيْنَ عِنْدَ رَبِّكَ لاَ يَسْتَكْبِرُوْنَ عَنْ عِبَادَتِهِ وَيُسَبِّحُوْنَهُ وَلَهُ يَسْجُدُوْن

"*Surely, those who are with your Lord are not too proud to do acts of worship to Him, but they glorify His praise and prostrate to Him*".[989]

2- وَللهِ يَسْجُدُ مَنْ فِي السَّمَاوَاتِ وَالأَرْضِ طَوْعًا وَكَرْهًا وَظِلاَلُهُمْ بِالْغُدُوِّ وَالآصَال

"*And unto Allāh falls in sajdah whoever is in the heavens and the earth, willingly or unwillingly, and so do their shadows in the morning and the evening hours.*"[990]

3- وَللهِ يَسْجُدُ مَا فِي السَّمَاوَاتِ وَمَا فِي الأَرْضِ مِنْ دَابَّةٍ وَالْمَلاَئِكَةِ وَهُمْ لاَ يَسْتَكْبِرُوْن

"*And to Allāh prostrate whatever is in the heavens and whatever is in the earth of living creatures, and the angels and they are not proud.*"[991]

4- قُلْ آمِنُوْا أَوْ لاَ تُؤْمِنُوْا إِنَّ الَّذِيْنَ أُوْتُوا الْعِلْمَ مِنْ قَبْلِهِ إِذَا يُتْلَى عَلَيْهِمْ يَخِرُّوْنَ لِلأَذْقَانِ سُجَّدًا

"*Say: Believe therein or believe not. Verily those who were given knowledge before it, when it is read to them, they fall down on their faces in sajdah.*"[992]

[987] Ibid., 46.

[988] Muslim, *k. īmān, b. bayān iṭlāq ism al-kufr ʿalā man taraka al-ṣalāh.*

[989] *al-Aʿrāf* 206

[990] *al-Raʿd* 15

[991] *al-Naḥl* 49

[992] *al-Isrā'* 107

5– إِذَا تُتْلَى عَلَيْهِمْ آيَاتُ الرَّحْمَنِ خَرُّوْا سُجَّدًا وَبُكِيًّا

"*When the revelations of the Most Gracious were recited to them, they fell down prostrating and weeping.*"[993]

6– أَلَمْ تَرَ أَنَّ اللهَ يَسْجُدُ لَهُ مَنْ فِي السَّمَاوَاتِ وَمَنْ فِيْ الأَرْضِ وَالشَّمْسُ وَالْقَمَرُ وَالنُّجُوْمُ وَالْجِبَالُ وَالشَّجَرُ وَالدَّوَابُّ وَكَثِيْرٌ مِنَ النَّاسِ وَكَثِيْرٌ حَقَّ عَلَيْهِ الْعَذَابُ وَمَنْ يُهِنِ اللهُ فَمَا لَهُ مِنْ مُكْرِمٍ إِنَّ اللهَ يَفْعَلُ مَا يَشَاء

"*Have you not seen that whoever is in the heavens and whoever is in the earth, and the sun, and the moon, and the stars, and the mountains, and the trees, and the beasts, and many of mankind prostrate themselves to Allāh? But there are many on whom the doom is justly due. He whom Allāh disgraces, there is none to give him honour. Verily Allāh does what He wills.*"[994]

7– وَإِذَا قِيْلَ لَهُمُ اسْجُدُوْا لِلرَّحْمَنِ قَالُوْا وَمَا الرَّحْمَنُ أَنَسْجُدُ لِمَا تَأْمُرُنَا وَزَادَهُمْ نُفُوْرًا

"*And when it is said to them: 'Prostrate yourselves to the Most Gracious,' they say: 'And what is the Most Gracious? Shall we fall down in sajdah to whatever you command us?' And it increases in them only aversion.*"[995]

8– أَلَّا يَسْجُدُوْا للهِ الَّذِيْ يُخْرِجُ الْخَبْءَ فِيْ السَّمَاوَاتِ وَالأَرْضِ وَيَعْلَمُ مَا تُخْفُوْنَ وَمَا تُعْلِنُوْن

"*So they do not prostrate themselves before Allāh, Who brings to light what is hidden in the heavens and the earth, and knows what you conceal and what you reveal.*"[996]

[993] *Maryam* 58

[994] *al-Ḥajj* 18; and according to some scholars there is another *sajdah* in *Sūrah al-Ḥajj*, and that is verse 77: يا أيها الذين آمنوا اركعوا واسجدوا واعبدوا ربكم وافعلوا الخير لعلكم تفلحون "*O you who believe, bow down and prostrate yourselves, and worship your Lord and do good, that you may prosper*".

[995] *al-Furqān* 60

[996] *al-Naml* 25

9- إِنَّمَا يُؤْمِنُ بِآيَاتِنَا الَّذِيْنَ إِذَا ذُكِّرُوْا بِهَا خَرُّوْا سُجَّدًا وَسَبَّحُوْا بِحَمْدِ رَبِّهِمْ وَهُمْ لاَ يَسْتَكْبِرُوْن

"*Only those believe in Our verses who, when they are reminded of them, fall down prostrate and glorify the praise of their Lord, and they are not proud.*"[997]

10- وَظَنَّ دَاوُودُ أَنَّمَا فَتَنَّاهُ فَاسْتَغْفَرَ رَبَّهُ وَخَرَّ رَاكِعًا وَأَنَاب

"*And David guessed that We had tried him, and he sought the forgiveness of his Lord, and he fell down prostrate and turned in repentance.*"[998]

11- وَمِنْ آيَاتِهِ اللَّيْلُ وَالنَّهَارُ وَالشَّمْسُ وَالْقَمَرُ لاَ تَسْجُدُوْا لِلشَّمْسِ وَلاَ لِلْقَمَرِ وَاسْجُدُوْا للهِ إِنْ كُنْتُمْ إِيَّاهُ تَعْبُدُوْن

"*And of His signs are the night and the day and the sun and the moon. Prostrate yourselves not to the sun nor to the moon, but prostrate yourselves to Allāh Who created them, if you worship Him.*"[999]

12- فَاسْجُدُوْا للهِ وَاعْبُدُوْا

"*So fall down in sajdah to Allāh and worship Him.*"[1000]

13- وَإِذَا قُرِئَ عَلَيْهِمُ الْقُرْآنُ لاَ يَسْجُدُوْن

"*And when the Qur'ān is recited to them, they do not prostrate.*"[1001]

[997] *al-Sajdah* 15
[998] *Ṣād* 24
[999] *Ḥā Mīm* 37
[1000] *al-Najm* 62, Ibn Masʿūd reported that the Prophet ﷺ recited *al-Najm* and prostrated, and all of the people with him prostrated, save one old man from the Quraysh who simply lifted some pebbles or dirt to his forehead and said: "That is sufficient for me". Ibn Masʿūd said: "After (some time) I found that he was killed while still an unbeliever". (Al-Bukhārī, *k. sujūd al-qur'ān, b. sajdat al-najm;* Muslim, *k. al-masājid, b. sujūd al-tilāwah.*)
[1001] *al-Inshiqāq* 21

14– وَاسْجُدْ وَاقْتَرِبْ

"Fall prostrate and draw near [to Allāh]."[1002]

Those on whom the sajdah is compulsory

The *sajdah* of recitation is *wājib* both for the one who recites the *āyah* and for the one who hears it, whether he intended to hear it or not.[1003] Allāh says without making any distinction between the reader and the listener: "*Only those believe in Our Signs, who, when they are recited to them fall down in prostration and celebrate the praise of their Lord, and they are not proud*".[1004] "*And when the Qur'ān is recited to them, they do not prostrate.*"[1005]

These *sajdahs* are *wājib* on those on whom the *ṣalāh* is *farḍ*, even if they are in a state of minor or major impurity, but not on children or women in a state of *ḥayḍ* or *nifās.*[1006]

The *sajdah* is not *wājib* on listening to recitation of an *āyah* of *sajdah* from a radio, TV, tape or CD or similar means.[1007]

The conditions for sajdah

The same conditions and prerequisites for *ṣalāh* apply to the *sajdah* of recital, in terms of purity, facing the *qiblah* and covering the *ᶜawrah;* however, it does not require *takbīr taḥrīmah.* This *sajdah* is invalidated by anything that makes the *ṣalāh* invalid, like *ḥadath*, talking, or laughing loudly.[1008]

How to do sajdah

Whoever recites an *āyah* of *sajdah* or hears it should say the *takbīr* and prostrate, and then say the *takbīr* again and rise from *sajdah.* There is no *tashahjud* or *taslīm* with the *sajdah.* Ibn ᶜUmar said: "The Prophet ﷺ would recite the Qur'ān to us and when he came to an *āyah* of *sajdah,*

[1002] *al-ᶜAlaq* 19.
[1003] al-Marghinānī*, al-Hidāyah, i.* 85
[1004] *as-Sajdah* 15
[1005] *al-Inshiqāq* 21
[1006] *al-Fatāwā al-hindiyyah, i.* 132.
[1007] Ibid.
[1008] Ibid., *i.* 135.

he would say the *takbīr* and go into *sajdah* and so did we".[1009] ᶜĀ'ishah said: "When the Prophet ﷺ made the *sajdah* of the Qur'ānic recital in the night, he would say, سجد وجهي للذي خلقه وشق سمعه وبصره بحوله وقوته 'My face has prostrated to the One Who created it and brought forth its hearing and seeing by His might and power'."[1010]

Sajdah during the ṣalāhs

When one recites an *āyah* of *sajdah* during the *ṣalāh*, one should prostrate while in the *ṣalāh*. If the imām recites an *āyah* of *sajdah*, he will prostrate during the *ṣalāh* and all those who follow him, whether they heard the imām or not, and whether the recital is audible or inaudible. Abū Rāfiᶜ said: "I prayed *ᶜIshā' Ṣalāh* with Abū Hurayrah and he recited *'Idhā al-samā'u inshaqqat'* and he prostrated during the *ṣalāh*. I asked: 'O Abū Hurayrah, what *sajdah* is this?' He said: 'I made a *sajdah* when reciting this sūrah behind Abū al-Qāsim (the Prophet ﷺ), so I will never stop making a *sajdah* whenever I recite it until I meet him (on the Day of Judgement)'."[1011] ᶜAbdullāh ibn ᶜUmar said: "The Prophet ﷺ made a *sajdah* during the first *rakᶜah* of the *Ẓuhr Ṣalāh* and his Companions were of the opinion that he had recited Sūrah *al-Sajdah*".[1012]

Combining sajdahs

If one recites an *āyah* of *sajdah* a number of times, and one does not move from one's place, then one has to make only one *sajdah*. Similarly, if one hears it being recited a number of times, and one has not changed one's place, then one *sajdah* is sufficient. If either the reciter or the listener change their place, and they recite or hear the *āyah* of *sajdah* again, then they have to do *sajdah*s for all those places where they recited or heard the *āyah*.[1013]

[1009] Abū Dāwūd, *k. al-ṣalāh, b. fī al-rajul yasmaᶜu al-sajdah wa huwa rākib.*

[1010] Abū Dāwūd, *k. al-ṣalāh, b. mā yaqūlu idhā sajada;* al-Tirmidhī, *abwāb al-ṣalāh, b. mā yaqūlu fī sujūd al-qur'ān;* al-Nasā'ī, *k. al-taṭbīq.*

[1011] al-Bukhārī, *k. sujūd al-qur'ān, b. sajdah idhā al-samā' inshaqqat,* Abū Dāwūd, *k. al-ṣalāh, b. al-sujūd fī idhā al-samā' inshaqqat.*

[1012] Abū Dāwūd, *k. al-ṣalāh, b. qadr al-qirā'ah fī ṣalāt al-ẓuhr wa al-ᶜaṣr.*

[1013] *See*: al-Marghinānī, *al-Hidāyah,* i. 86.

Chapter 10: The *Ṣalāhs* of the traveller and disabled

THE *ṢALĀH* OF THE TRAVELLER

Allāh says in the Qur'ān: "*And when you go forth in the land, there is no sin upon you, if you shorten your ṣalāh when you fear the disbelievers may attack you*".[1014] Yaʿlā ibn Umayyah said: "I said to ʿUmar ibn al-Khaṭṭāb: 'Explain to me why the people shorten the *ṣalāh* when Allāh says, "*And when you go forth in the land, there is no sin upon you, if you shorten your ṣalāh when you fear the disbelievers may attack you*" – but those days are gone now.' ʿUmar said: 'I wondered about it too and I mentioned it to the Prophet ﷺ and he said: '"This is a charity that Allāh, the Exalted, has bestowed upon you, so accept His charity".'"[1015]

The pre-condition

The concessions regarding *ṣalāh* for a person travelling apply when he intends to go somewhere which is a distance of three days away by camel or on foot. Imām Muḥammad said: "If someone is travelling for less than three days and nights, then he must complete the *ṣalāh*; and if he is travelling for a distance of three days and nights or more then he will shorten the *ṣalāh*. This is the opinion of Abū Ḥanīfah".[1016] Such a distance in today's measurements is seventy-seven kilometres or forty-eight miles.

One has to shorten one's *ṣalāh* as soon as one leaves one's residence and is outside of the locality; this is a condition. Imām Muḥammad said: "The traveller who intends to travel for the prescribed distance will shorten the *ṣalāh* when he leaves the vicinity of his locality and has his home behind his back. This is the opinion of Abū Ḥanīfah".[1017] When the traveller returns to his own locality, then he does the *ṣalāh* in full, even if he is not intending a long stay.

[1014] *al-Nisā'* 101.

[1015] Muslim, *k. ṣalāt al-musāfirīn wa qaṣrihā, b. ṣalāt al-musāfirīn wa qaṣrihā.*

[1016] Abū Ḥanīfah, *K. al-āthār* 50.

[1017] Muḥammad, *al-Muwaṭṭa', i.* 561.

If one has changed locality and settles in a new place but travels back to the previous place of residence, one will still be considered a traveller and does not have to perform the *ṣalāh* in full as long as the condition for the minimum distance is met.

Whoever misses his *ṣalāh* while a resident makes it up in full while travelling (i.e. by doing four *rakᶜahs*), and whoever misses a *ṣalāh* while travelling makes it up when resident in the shortened form, i.e. in two *rakᶜahs.*

The concession

The *farḍ* obligation of the traveller for each *ṣalāh* of four *rakᶜahs* is two *rakᶜahs,* and it is not permitted to add to this. If he does four and he sits in the second for the length of the *tashahhud,* then the two *rakᶜahs* are accepted from him for his *farḍ* obligation and the last two are counted as *nafl*; if he does not sit for the length of the *tashahhud* in the first two *rakᶜah*s, his *ṣalāh* is invalidated. The Prophet ﷺ would pray only two *rakᶜah*s for those *ṣalāhs* which consisted of four whenever he travelled, and this until he returned to Madīnah. There is no confirmation that he ever prayed four *rakᶜahs* while travelling. ᶜImrān ibn Ḥuṣayn narrated: "Whenever the Prophet ﷺ travelled, he would pray two *rakᶜahs* except *Maghrib*".[1018] ᶜUmar said: "The *ṣalāh* of travelling is two *rakᶜahs* and this is from the tongue of the Prophet ﷺ".[1019] ᶜĀ'ishah said: "When the prayers were first enjoined they were of two *rakᶜahs* each. Later the prayer in a journey was kept to two *rakᶜahs* but the prayers for non-travellers were completed [to make four *rakᶜahs*]".[1020]

Sunnahs and nawāfil during travel

Sunnahs are like *nawāfil* during travelling; in other words, one is permitted to do them. The Prophet ﷺ made *ghusl* in the house of Umm Hānī on the day of the Conquest of Makkah and then he prayed eight *rakᶜahs.*[1021] Ibn ᶜUmar reported: "The Prophet ﷺ prayed *nafl ṣalāh* while

[1018] al-Ṭabarānī, as cited by al-Haythamī, *Majmaᶜ al-zawā'id, ii.* 158.

[1019] Ibn Abī Shaybah, *al-Muṣannaf, ii.* 205.

[1020] al-Bukhārī, *k. taqṣīr al-ṣalāh, b. yaqṣuru idhā kharaja min mawḍiᶜihi;* Muslim, *k. ṣalāt al-musāfirīn wa qaṣrihā, b. ṣalāt al-musāfirīn wa qaṣrihā.*

[1021] Muslim, *k. ṣalāt al-musāfirīn wa qaṣrihā, b. istiḥbāb ṣalāt al-ḍuḥā.*

riding in whatever direction he was facing and nodding his head (i.e. for the movements of the *ṣalāh*)".[1022]

Combining two ṣalāhs

During *Ḥajj,* one must combine the *Ẓuhr* and *ʿAṣr Ṣalāhs* at the time of the *Ẓuhr ṣalāh* at ʿArafah, and the *Maghrib* and *ʿIshāʾ Ṣalāhs* at the time of the *ʿIshāʾ* at Muzdalifah, following the example of the Prophet ﷺ. Imām Muḥammad said: "We do not combine two *ṣalāhs* at one time, except *Ẓuhr* and *ʿAṣr* in ʿArafah, and *Maghrib* and *ʿIshāʾ* in Muzdalifah; and this is the opinion of Abū Ḥanīfah." Imām Muḥammad further said: "It has come to our knowledge that ʿUmar ibn al-Khaṭṭāb wrote to the cities prohibiting them from combining two *ṣalāhs,* and told them that combining two *ṣalāhs* at one time is a major sin".[1023]

Apart from the above mentioned combination of ʿArafah and Muzdalifah, there is no combination of two *ṣalāhs* for any other circumstance. However, one can delay *Ẓuhr* until its last appointed time then pray it, wait a short while and as soon as the time of *ʿAṣr* enters, pray it in its earliest time. Similarly, one can delay the *Maghrib* and pray *ʿIshāʾ* at its earliest time. Abū Hurayrah narrated: "The Messenger of Allāh ﷺ used to combine *Ẓuhr* and *ʿAṣr* during his travels to Tabūk".[1024] Imām Muḥammad said after narrating this ḥadīth: "This is what we hold; and the combination is that the first *ṣalāh* is delayed and prayed at its last time and the second is hastened and prayed in its earliest time".[1025] Nāfiʿ and ʿAbdullāh ibn Wāqid narrated that the *muʾadhdhin* of Ibn ʿUmar said, "*al-ṣalāh*", Ibn ʿUmar said, "walk, walk". This continued until just before the disappearance of *shafaq,* then he came down and prayed *Maghrib.* Then he waited until the *shafaq* disappeared and he prayed *ʿIshāʾ.* Then he said that the Messenger of Allāh ﷺ did just as he had done when he hastened.[1026]

[1022] *al-Bukhārī, k. al-witr, b. al-witr fī al-safar;* Muslim, *k. ṣalāt al-musāfirīn wa qaṣrihā, b. jawāz ṣalāt al-nāfilah ʿalā al-dābbah fī al-safar ḥaythu tawajjahat*

[1023] Muḥammad, *al-Muwaṭṭaʾ, i.* 571-572.

[1024] Mālik, *al-Muwaṭṭaʾ* 78.

[1025] Muḥammad, *al-Muwaṭṭaʾ, i.* 569-570.

[1026] Abū Dāwūd, *k. al-ṣalāh, b. al-jamʿ bayn al-ṣalātayn.* Most scholars are of the opinion that it is permissible to combine *Ẓuhr* and *ʿAṣr* during the time of either one of them, and *Maghrib* and *ʿIshāʾ* during the time of either one of them while travelling. Muʿādh

The ṣalāh on a plane, train, bus or ship

Ṣalāh when one is on board a plane, ship, train, bus or other vehicle, is valid, and therefore one is not allowed to delay the *farḍ ṣalāh* because of being on the move. Ibn ʿUmar said: "I asked the Prophet ﷺ about *ṣalāh* on a ship and he said: 'Pray standing upon them unless you fear that you will be drowned'."[1027] ʿAṭā' said: "They should pray in the ship standing, except if they fear that they will be drowned, then they should pray sitting".[1028] Mughīrah narrated from Ibrāhīm al-Nakhaʿī saying: "Pray in the ship standing; if you cannot do so then sitting. You should turn to the *qiblah* when the ship turns".[1029]

When the concession is over

A traveller remains subject to the travel ruling until he makes the intention of residing in a place for fifteen days or more, in which case he must do the full number of *rakʿahs*. If he intends to reside for less than this, he does not need to perform the full number. Imām Muḥammad narrated from ʿAbdullāh ibn ʿUmar saying: "If you are a traveller and intended to stay fifteen days then complete the *ṣalāh*, and if you do not know then shorten the *ṣalāh*". Imām Muḥammad said: "We adhere to it, and this is the opinion of Abū Ḥanīfah".[1030] Mujāhid said: "When Ibn ʿUmar intended to stay fifteen days he would pray in full".[1031] The same has been narrated from Saʿīd ibn al-Musayyab, and Saʿīd ibn Jubayr.[1032]

If someone enters a town but does not intend to reside for fifteen days and says 'tomorrow I will leave, or after tomorrow', and remains in this state of indecision for years, then he still does two *rakʿahs*. If a soldier enters *dār al-ḥarb,* i.e. enemy territory, as opposed to *dār al-Islām,* and

---

ibn Jabal reported that the Prophet ﷺ combined the *Ẓuhr* and *ʿAṣr Ṣalāhs* and the *Maghrib* and *ʿIshā' Ṣalāhs* in the Expedition of Tabūk while journeying. (Muslim, *k. ṣalāt al-musāfirīn, b. al-jamʿ bayna al-ṣalātayni fī al-safar;* Ibn Mājah, *k. iqāmat al-ṣalāh wa al-sunnah fīhā, b. al-jamʿ bayn al-ṣalātayn fī al-safar*; Abū Dāwūd, *k. al-ṣalāh, b. al-jamʿ bayn al-ṣalātayn*).

[1027] al-Ḥākim, *al-Mustadrak, i.* 409.

[1028] ʿAbd al-Razzāq, *al-Muṣannaf,* ii. 581.

[1029] Ibid.

[1030] Abū Ḥanīfah, *K. al-āthār* 49.

[1031] Ibn Abī Shaybah, *al-Muṣannaf, ii.* 211.

[1032] Ibid.

intends to reside fifteen days, he does not make the *ṣalāh* in full. The Messenger of Allāh ﷺ stayed in Tabūk for twenty days and during that time he shortened his *ṣalāh*.[1033] ʿImrān ibn Ḥuṣayn said: "The Prophet ﷺ stayed in Makkah, after the conquest, for eighteen days and he prayed only two *rakʿahs*".[1034] Abū Jamrah Naṣr ibn ʿImrān said: "I said to Ibn ʿAbbās: 'We stay longer in Khurasan for *jihād*, so how should we do [the prayer]?' He answered: 'Pray two *rakʿahs* even if you stay ten years'."[1035] ʿAbd al-Raḥmān ibn Samurah stayed for two years in Kabul, and he shortened his *ṣalāh*.[1036]

A traveller praying behind a resident

If a traveller joins the *ṣalāh* of someone resident, then he does the *ṣalāh* in full. Imām Muḥammad narrated on the authority of Abū Ḥanīfah from Ibrāhīm al-Nakhaʿī: "'When the traveller enters into the *ṣalāh* of a resident then he prays in full'. We adhere to it; when the traveller is with the resident it is compulsory for him to pray four *rakʿahs* like the resident, and this is the opinion of Abū Ḥanīfah."[1037]

Residents praying behind the traveller

If residents pray behind the traveller, the traveller will pray two *rakʿah*s, then, after his *salām*, the residents complete their *ṣalāh*. It is recommended for the imām to say, 'complete your *ṣalāh* for we are travelling' when he makes the final *salām*. Imām Muḥammad narrated from Abū Ḥanīfah: "ʿUmar ibn al-Khaṭṭāb lead the *Ẓuhr* in Makkah consisting of two *rakʿahs*, then after the *salām* he said: 'O people of Makkah we are travellers, so whoever is resident should complete (the *ṣalāh*)'." The people of the town completed the *ṣalāh*. Imām Muḥammad also said: "We adhere to it, when the resident enters into the *ṣalāh* of a traveller, and the traveller finishes his *ṣalāh* then the resident will stand up and complete his *ṣalāh*. This is the opinion of Abū Ḥanīfah".[1038]

[1033] Ibid., *ii*. 210.
[1034] Ibid., *ii*. 209.
[1035] Ibid., *ii*. 210.
[1036] Ibid.
[1037] Abū Ḥanīfah, *K. al-āthār* 50.
[1038] Ibid.

THE *ṢALĀH* OF SOMEONE WHO IS ILL

If a sick person is unable to stand, then he should make the *ṣalāh* sitting, and bow and prostrate; if he cannot bow or prostrate, he should gesture in place of the movements making the *sajdah* lower than the *rukūʿ*, but need not raise anything to his face to prostrate on; if he cannot sit, he should lie on his back, placing his legs in the direction of the *qiblah* and gesture for the *rukūʿ* and *sajdah*; if he lies on his side with his face towards the *qiblah* and he gestures, this is permitted. This is understood on the basis of Allāh's words: "*...celebrate Allāh's praises, standing, sitting, and lying on your sides*".[1039] ʿImrān ibn Ḥuṣayn said: "I had piles, so I asked the Prophet ﷺ about the *ṣalāh* and he said: 'Offer the *ṣalāh* while standing and if you cannot do so, pray while sitting, and if you can't do that, then do *ṣalāh* while lying on your side'."[1040] Lying on one's side also includes lying on one's back.

ʿAlī stated that the Prophet ﷺ said: "The sick person is to pray standing if he is able. If he cannot do so, he should pray sitting. If he is not able to make the *sajdah*, he should nod with his head and make the nod of his *sajdah* lower than that of his *rukūʿ*. If he cannot pray in a sitting posture, he should pray while lying down on his right side facing the *qiblah*. If he cannot pray on his right side, he should pray while lying on his back with his legs stretched out toward the *qiblah*".[1041] Imām Muḥammad said: "It is not appropriate for an ill person to do *sajdah* on any wood or something raised to him. He should do his *sajdah* lower than his *rukūʿ*. This is the opinion of Abū Ḥanīfah".[1042]

If the ill person cannot even gesture with his head, then he should delay (until he is able) the *ṣalāh* – he does not gesture with his eyes, heart or eyebrows. This is because to gesture with one's heart is intention, and *ṣalāh* is other than intention.[1043]

If a healthy person does part of his *ṣalāh* standing and then is afflicted by an illness which prevents him from standing, then he can complete it sitting, bowing and prostrating: if he cannot sit then gesturing is

[1039] *al-Nisāʾ* 103.
[1040] al-Bukhārī, *k. taqṣīr al-ṣalāh, b. idhā lam yuṭiq qāʿidan ṣallā ʿalā janb.*
[1041] al-Dāraquṭnī, *al-Sunan, ii.* 31.
[1042] Muḥammad, *al-Muwaṭṭaʾ, ii.* 40-41.
[1043] al-Samarqandī, *Tuḥfat al-fuqahāʾ* 91.

permitted. Whoever does the *ṣalāh* sitting, bowing and prostrating on account of some incapacity, and then finds himself better should continue his *ṣalāh* standing. However, Imām Muḥammad holds that he must recommence his *ṣalāh*.[1044] If one does some of his *ṣalāh* with gestures and then finds he is able to bow and prostrate, then he should begin the *ṣalāh* again.[1045]

THE OBLIGATION OF ONE WHO FALLS UNCONSCIOUS

Whoever falls unconscious for a period of five *ṣalāhs* or less, must make up the missed *ṣalāhs* when he recovers. If the period of unconsciousness lasts longer than this, he does not need to make them up. On being asked about an ill person who falls unconscious and misses the *ṣalāhs*, Ibrāhīm al-Nakhaʿī said: "If it is one day then I prefer for him to do *qaḍā'*; if it is more than this then he has an excuse, if Allāh wills". Imām Muḥammad said: "If someone is unconscious for a day and night then he will do *qaḍā'*, and if it is more than that then there is no *qaḍā'* upon him. This is the opinion of Abū Ḥanīfah".[1046] Imām Mālik narrated from Nāfiʿ that Ibn ʿUmar fell unconscious. When he recovered he did not do the *qaḍā'* of the *ṣalāh*. After narrating this ḥadīth from Mālik, Imām Muḥammad said: "We hold that (opinion), if someone remains unconscious for more than a day and night, but if he is unconscious for only a day and night, then he is to do *qada*. It has come to our knowledge that ʿAmmār ibn Yāsir fell unconscious for four *ṣalāhs*, when he became conscious he did *qaḍā'* of those *ṣalāhs*".[1047]

[1044] al-Marghinānī, *al-Hidāyah, i. 84.*

[1045] Ibid.

[1046] Abū Ḥanīfah, *K. al-āthār* 45.

[1047] Muḥammad, *al-Muwaṭṭa', ii.* 39-40.

CHAPTER 11: *JUMUᶜAH ṢALĀH*

ABŪ HURAYRAH NARRATED: "I heard the Messenger of Allāh ﷺ saying: 'We (Muslims) are the last to come but will be the foremost on the Day of Resurrection though the former nations were given the Holy Scriptures before us. And this was their day (Friday) the celebration of which was made compulsory for them but they differed about it. So Allāh gave us the guidance for it (Friday) and all the other people are behind us in this respect: the Jews tomorrow, and the Christians after tomorrow'."[1048]

Abū Saᶜīd and Abū Hurayrah reported that the Messenger of Allāh ﷺ said: "On *Jumuᶜah* there is a time that if a believing slave asks Allāh during it for some good, (Allāh will surely) give it to him, and that time is after the *ᶜAṣr Ṣalāh*".[1049]

Abū Hurayrah reported that the Messenger of Allāh ﷺ said: "The best day on which the sun has risen is Friday. On that day Ādam was created and on that day he entered Paradise and on that day he was expelled from Paradise. And the Hour will come on Friday".[1050]

THAT WHICH IS PREFERABLE ON FRIDAY

It is Sunnah for those attending the Friday *Ṣalāh*, to do *ghusl* before the *ṣalāh*, though *wuḍū'* is sufficient. ᶜAbdullāh ibn ᶜUmar narrated: "Allāh's Messenger ﷺ said: 'Anyone of you attending the Friday *Ṣalāh* should take a bath'."[1051] Abū Hurayrah reported that the Prophet ﷺ said: "Whoever does *wuḍū'* on Friday, then it is good, and whoever bathes it is better".[1052] Abū Hurayrah also reported the Prophet ﷺ as saying:

[1048] al-Bukhārī, *k. al-jumuᶜah, b. farḍ al-jumuᶜah.*

[1049] Aḥmad, *al-Musnad* as cited in *Majmaᶜ al-zawā'id, k. al-ṣalāh, b. fī al-sāᶜah allatī fī yawm al-jumuᶜah.*

[1050] Muslim, *k. al-jumuᶜah, b. faḍl yawm al-jumuᶜah.*

[1051] al-Bukhārī, *k. al-jumuᶜah, b. faḍl al-ghusl yawm al-jumuᶜah.*

[1052] Abū Dāwūd, *k. al-ṭahārah, b. tark al-ghusl yawma al-jumuᶜah;* al-Tirmidhī, *k. al-jumuᶜah, b. al-wuḍū' yawma al- jumuᶜah.*

"Whoever does *wuḍū'* and does it nicely, then goes to Friday *Ṣalāh* and listens attentively, will have forgiveness during the period between the Friday and the next Friday, and an additional three days".[1053]

It is recommended for males attending the Friday *Ṣalāh* to wear their best clothes and apply perfume. Abū Saᶜīd narrated: "I testify that Allāh's Messenger ﷺ said: 'Taking a bath on Friday is compulsory for every male Muslim who has attained the age of puberty and also the cleaning of his teeth, and the use of perfume if it is available'."[1054] Abū Saᶜīd also reported that the Prophet ﷺ said: "Every Muslim should have a *ghusl* on Friday and wear his best clothing, and if he has perfume, he should use it".[1055] Salmān al-Fārisī reported that the Prophet ﷺ said: "A man who does *ghusl* on Friday, purifies himself as much as he can, then uses his hair oil, and perfumes himself with scent, then proceeds to the *masjid*, and does not separate between two people sitting together, then prays what Allāh has written for him, and then listens quietly while the imām speaks, all his sins between that Friday and the next Friday will be forgiven".[1056] ᶜIkrimah narrated from ᶜAbdullāh ibn ᶜAbbās saying: "The Sunnahs of *Jumuᶜah* are: *ghusl*, cleaning one's teeth, applying perfume, and that you wear your cleanest clothes". [1057]

It is preferable to recite Sūrah *al-Kahf* on *Jumuᶜah*. Abū Saᶜīd al-Khudrī reported that the Prophet ﷺ said: "Whoever recites Sūrah *al-Kahf* on *Jumuᶜah* will have illumination from one *Jumuᶜah* to the next".[1058] Abū al-Dardā' narrated that the Messenger of Allāh ﷺ said: "Whoever memorises ten verses from the beginning of Sūrah al-*Kahf* will be protected from the trials of the *Dajjāl* (Anti-Christ)".[1059]

It is also preferable to go early to the *Jumuᶜah Ṣalāh*. Abū Hurayrah reported that the Prophet ﷺ said: "Whoever makes *ghusl* on *Jumuᶜah* like the *ghusl* of *janābah*, and then goes to the *masjid*, it is as if he had offered a camel; and whoever goes in the second hour, it is as if he had offered

[1053] Muslim, *k. al-jumuᶜah, b. faḍl man istamaᶜa wa anṣata fī al-khuṭbah.*

[1054] al-Bukhārī, *k. al-jumuᶜah, b. al-ṭīb yawm al-jumuᶜah.*

[1055] Muslim, *k. al-jumuᶜah, b. wujūb ghusl al-jumuᶜah ᶜalā kulli bāligh min al-rijāl.*

[1056] al-Bukhārī, *k. al-jumuᶜah, b. al-duhn li al-jumuᶜah.*

[1057] ᶜAbd al-Razzāq, *al-Muṣannaf, iii.* 204.

[1058] al-Bayhaqī, *al-Daᶜawāt al-kabīr* as cited in *Mishkāt al-maṣabīḥ, i.* 398.

[1059] Muslim, *k. ṣalāt al-musāfirīn, b. faḍl sūratᶜ al-kahf*

a cow; and whoever goes in the third hour, it is as if he had offered a ram; and if one goes in the fourth hour, then it is as if he had offered a hen; and whoever goes in the fifth hour, then it is as if he had offered an egg. When the imām comes, the angels will be present to listen to the remembrance".[1060]

ᶜAlqamah said: "I went with ᶜAbdullāh ibn Masᶜūd to the *masjid* and we found that three people had arrived there before us. Ibn Masᶜūd said: 'The fourth of four, and the fourth of four is not far from Allāh, for I have heard the Messenger of Allāh ﷺ say: 'The people will be seated on the day of resurrection according to how they came to the *Ṣalāt al-Jumuᶜah*: the first, then the second, then the third, then the fourth, and the fourth of four is not far from Allāh'."[1061]

WHAT IS DISLIKED ON THIS DAY

Praying *Ẓuhr Ṣalāh* in a place where *Jumuᶜah Ṣalāh* is established is disliked. This is what has been narrated from ᶜAlī ibn Abī Ṭālib.[1062] It has also been a continuous tradition to close those *masjids* where *Jumuᶜah Ṣalāh* is not performed in the towns.

It is also disliked to engage in any kind of buying and selling or any other business once the *adhān* has been made. Allāh says: "*O you who believe, when the call for the Jumuᶜah Ṣalāh is proclaimed, hasten to the remembrance of Allāh, and leave off business. That is better for you if you did but know*".[1063]

It is also disliked to step over people who are already seated in the *masjid*. ᶜAbdullāh ibn Busr said: "A man came and he was stepping over the necks of the people while the Prophet ﷺ was delivering the *Jumuᶜah Khutbah*. The Prophet ﷺ said to him: 'Sit down! You have harmed the people'."[1064]

[1060] al-Bukhārī, *k. al-jumuᶜah, b. faḍl al-jumuᶜah;* Muslim, *k. al-jumuᶜah, b. wujūb ghusl al-jumuᶜah ᶜalā kull bāligh min al-rijāl.*

[1061] Ibn Mājah, *k. iqāmat al-ṣalāh wa al-sunnah fīhā, b. mā jā'a fī al-tahjīr ilā al-jumuᶜah.*

[1062] al-Kāsānī, *Badā'iᶜ al-ṣanā'iᶜ, ii.* 220.

[1063] *al-Jumuᶜah* 9.

[1064] Abū Dāwūd, *k. al-ṣalāh, b. takhaṭṭī riqāb al-nās yawm al-jumuᶜah.*

A *FARḌ ṢALĀH*

Jumuʿah Ṣalāh is *farḍ* and comprises two *rakʿahs*; it is not allowed to miss it, and rejection of its obligatory status is an act of unbelief.[1065] This is based on the Qur'ān, Sunnah and the consensus of Muslims throughout all generations. Allāh says in the Qur'ān: "*O you who believe, when the call for the Jumuʿah Ṣalāh is proclaimed, hasten to the remembrance of Allāh, and leave off business. That is better for you if you did but know*".[1066]

Jābir narrated that the Prophet ﷺ said: "Allāh has made *Jumuʿah Ṣalāh* obligatory upon you at this place, in this day, in this month, in this year. So whoever leaves it in my life or after my death, out of rejecting it or negligence, whether he has a just leader or unjust, then none of his *ṣalāh*, or *zakāh*, or Ḥajj, or fasting will be accepted, except if he repents. And whoever repents, Allāh accepts his repentance".[1067] ʿAbdullāh ibn ʿUmar reported that the Prophet ﷺ said: "Whoever misses three Friday *Ṣalāhs* out of negligence, Allāh will seal his heart".[1068]

ʿAbdullāh ibn Masʿūd reported that the Prophet ﷺ said to some people staying away from *al-Jumuʿah*: "I had decided to order someone to lead the people in *ṣalāh*, and then to go and burn the houses of those who stayed away from *al-Jumuʿah*".[1069] Abū Hurayrah and ʿAbdullāh ibn ʿUmar reported that they heard the Prophet ﷺ say: "Those who are not attending the Friday *Ṣalāh* should stop doing this; otherwise, Allāh will seal their hearts and they will be reckoned the heedless".[1070]

Upon whom it is farḍ

Jumuʿah Ṣalāh is *farḍ* upon every free, adult, sane, resident, male Muslim who has the ability to attend the *ṣalāh*; it is not *farḍ* upon a woman, child, traveller and an ill person who faces hardship in attending the *masjid*.[1071] Abū Ḥāzim reported that the Prophet ﷺ said: "*Jumuʿah* is a

[1065] al-Kāsānī, *Badāʾiʿ al-ṣanāʾiʿ, ii. 180.*

[1066] *al-Jumuʿah 9.*

[1067] Ibn Mājah, *k. iqāmat al-ṣalāh, b. fī farḍ al-jumuʿah.*

[1068] al-Nasāʾī, *k. al-jumuʿah, b. al-tashdīd fī al-takhalluf ʿan al-jumuʿah.*

[1069] Muslim, *k. al-masājid, b. faḍl ṣalāt al-jamāʿah wa bayān al-tashdīd fī al-takhallī ʿanhā.*

[1070] Muslim, *k. al-jumuʿah, b. al-taghlīẓ fī tark al-jumuʿah.*

[1071] See: al-Kāsānī, *Badāʾiʿ al-ṣanāʾiʿ*, *ii.* 186.

duty upon every adult, save a child, a slave, a woman, and a person who is ill".[1072] Jābir narrated from the Prophet ﷺ: "Whoever believes in Allāh and the Last Day, on them the *Jumuʿah* is a compulsory duty, except a traveller, a slave, a child, a woman, or someone who is ill".[1073]

All those people who are exempted from the obligation of *Jumuʿah Ṣalāh* are obliged to pray the *Ẓuhr*. Nevertheless, if they pray *Jumuʿah*, it will be valid for them and they are not obliged to pray *Ẓuhr*.[1074] Ḥasan al-Baṣrī narrated that the women during the time of the Prophet ﷺ used to pray *Jumuʿah Ṣalāh* with him.[1075] Abū Ḥanīfah narrated from Muḥammad ibn Kaʿb al-Quraẓī that the Prophet ﷺ said: "For four people, there is no *Jumuʿah*: the woman, the slave, the ill and the traveller". Imām Muḥammad said after narrating this: "This is the opinion of Abū Ḥanīfah, but if they pray *Jumuʿah* it is sufficient for them".[1076] ʿAbdullāh ibn Maʿdān narrated from his grandmother saying that ʿAbdullāh ibn Masʿūd said: "When you pray *Jumuʿah* with the imām then pray his *ṣalāh*, and when you pray in your homes, then pray four *rakʿahs*".[1077]

CONDITIONS

There are certain conditions for the validity of *Jumuʿah Ṣalāh*:

An independent town or city

Jumuʿah Ṣalāh can only be established in a town or city which has its own administrative body and judge. The *Jumuʿah* will not be valid in those villages or scattered populations which have no administrative identity. ʿAlī said: "There is no *Jumuʿah* and no *ʿĪd Ṣalāh* except in a large town or city".[1078] The same was narrated from ʿAṭā'.[1079] Ibrāhīm al-Nakhaʿī narrated from Ḥudhayfah saying: "There is no *Jumuʿah* on

[1072] Ibn Abī Shaybah, *al-Muṣannaf*, *i*. 446.

[1073] al-Dāraquṭnī, *al-Sunan*, ii. 3; al-Bayhaqī, *k. al-jumuʿah, b. man talzamuhu al-jumuʿah*.

[1074] *See*: al-Kāsānī, *Badāʾiʿ al-ṣanāʾiʿ*, ii. 187.

[1075] Ibid.

[1076] Abū Ḥanīfah, *K. al-āthār* 52.

[1077] Ibn Abī Shaybah, *al-Muṣannaf*, *i*. 446.

[1078] Ibid., *i*. 439.

[1079] Ibid.

the people of the villages".[1080] Ibrāhīm al-Nakhaʿī also said: "They did not do *Jumuʿah* in the army camps".[1081] The aim is to encourage larger gatherings for these occasions and to discourage small gatherings so that the community can come together, mix and meet.

The time

It is also a condition to pray the *Jumuʿah Ṣalāh* in the time of *Ẓuhr*; it is not allowed to pray it before the time of *Ẓuhr* or after. Anas ibn Mālik reported that the Prophet ﷺ would pray *Jumuʿah* when the sun had passed its meridian.[1082] Salamah ibn al-Akwaʿ said: "We would pray *Jumuʿah* with the Prophet ﷺ when the sun had passed the meridian, and when we returned, we would be following our shadow".[1083] The same has been narrated from a number of Companions and from scholars among the Followers.[1084]

The congregation

Congregation is a necessary condition for *al-Jumuʿah* to be valid. The Messenger of Allāh ﷺ never performed *Jumuʿah* without the congregation; there is a consensus on this, and this is what the name of *Jumuʿah* itself implies.[1085]

However, scholars differ on how many people are required for *Jumuʿah*. Abū Ḥanīfah's opinion is that *Jumuʿah* is valid if there are three people other than the imām, and Abū Yūsuf and Muḥammad hold the opinion that there should be at least two people other than the imām.[1086]

Khuṭbah

The *khuṭbah* is also an obligatory condition, and it is Sunnah that the imām gives two *khuṭbahs*, separating them by a short sitting. The Prophet ﷺ always gave two *khuṭbahs*. Allāh says: "*O you who believe, when the call for*

[1080] Ibid.

[1081] Ibid., *i.* 440.

[1082] al-Bukhārī, *k. al-jumuʿah, b. waqt al-jumuʿah idhā zālat al-shams.*

[1083] Muslim, *k. al-jumuʿah, b. ṣalāt al-jumuʿah ḥīna tazūl al-shams.*

[1084] Ibn Abī Shaybah, *al-Muṣannaf, i.* 445-446.

[1085] al-Kāsānī, *Badāʾiʿ al-ṣanāʾiʿ*, ii. 205-6.

[1086] al-Marghinānī: *al-Hidāyah*, i. 90.

the Jumuah Salah is proclaimed, hasten to the remembrance of Allah".[1087] This verse contains an order to hasten to the remembrance, which implies it is obligatory, and scholars interpret this remembrance of Allāh to include the *khuṭbah.*

ʿAbdullāh ibn ʿUmar said: "When the Prophet ﷺ delivered the *Jumuʿah Khuṭbah,* he did so standing, and then he would sit, and then he would stand (again, for the second *khuṭbah*) as you do now".[1088] Jābir ibn Samurah said: "The Prophet ﷺ would deliver the *khuṭbah* while standing, and then he would sit, and then he would stand and speak again. Whoever says that he gave the *khuṭbah* while sitting has lied. I prayed more than two thousand *ṣalāhs* (including the five daily *ṣalāhs* with him)".[1089] ʿAbdullāh ibn Masʿūd said *Jumuʿah Khuṭbah* is given standing. Imām Muḥammad said: "It is two *khuṭbahs*; in between [them] the imām sits for a little while. And this is the opinion of Abū Ḥanīfah".[1090]

It is recommended that the imām greets the people once he ascends the pulpit, then it is Sunnah to make the *adhān* as the imām sits on the pulpit. The imām should face the people during the *adhān.* Jābir reported that when the Prophet ﷺ mounted the pulpit, he would greet the people.[1091] ʿĀmir al-Shaʿbī reported: "When the Prophet ﷺ, walked to the top of the pulpit, he would turn to the people and say: اَلسَّلَامُ عَلَيْكُم, 'peace be upon you'." And this was the practice of Abū Bakr, ʿUmar, ʿUthmān and ʿUmar ibn ʿAbd al-ʿAzīz.[1092]

It is Sunnah that the *khuṭbah* includes praises of Allāh, prayers for the Prophet ﷺ, Qur'ānic recitations and a sermon. Jābir ibn Samurah said: "The Messenger of Allāh ﷺ would deliver his *khuṭbah* standing, would sit in between the two *khuṭbahs,* recite some verses, and would remind the people (about Allāh)".[1093] Jābir ibn Samurah also related that the

[1087] *al-Jumuʿah* 9

[1088] al-Bukhārī, *k. al-jumuʿah, b. al-khuṭbah qā'iman;* Muslim, *k. al-jumuʿah, b. dhikr al-khuṭbatayn qabla al-ṣalāh wa mā fīhimā min al-jalsah.*

[1089] Muslim, ibid.

[1090] Abū Ḥanīfah, *K. al-āthār* 52.

[1091] Ibn Mājah, *k. iqāmat al-ṣalāh wa al-sunnah fīhā, b. mā jā'a fī al-khuṭbah yawm al-jumuʿah.*

[1092] Ibn Abī Shaybah, *al-Muṣannaf, i. 449-50.*

[1093] Muslim, *k. al-jumuʿah, b. dhikr al-khuṭbatayn qabla al-ṣalāh wa mā fīhimā min al-jalsah.*

Prophet ﷺ would not make his admonitions on Friday too long, rather they were of few words.[1094]

It is obligatory upon the congregation to be silent during the *khuṭbah*, i.e. one must not indulge in conversation during the *khuṭbah*, not even if it is to do some good or to stop some wrong action, and this rule applies whether or not the person sitting in the *masjid* can actually hear the *khuṭbah* or not. ʿAbdullāh ibn ʿAbbās reported that the Prophet ﷺ said: "Whoever speaks in *Jumuʿah* while the imām is delivering the *khuṭbah* is like a donkey who is carrying books, and for those who tell him to be quiet, there is no (reward) for the *Jumuʿah*".[1095] Imām Muḥammad narrated from ʿAbdullāh ibn Saʿīd ibn Abī Hind who said: "I said to Saʿīd ibn al-Musayyab that so-and-so sneezed while the imām was delivering the *khuṭbah*, then someone answered him and said 'يرحمك الله.' Saʿīd said: 'Tell him not to do it again'." In this respect Imām Muḥammad said: "We adhere to it; the *khuṭbah* is like the *ṣalāh*. In it one who sneezes will not be answered, and a *salām* will not be replied to. This is the opinion of Abū Ḥanīfah".[1096]

The language of the khuṭbah

The *khuṭbah*, as mentioned earlier, consists of praising Allāh, praying for the Prophet ﷺ, his descendants and Companions, recitation from the Qur'ān and a sermon. Some scholars regard the *khuṭbah* as *ṣalāh* or part of the *ṣalāh* and, because of this, make it a condition that the *khuṭbah* be in Arabic. According to Abū Ḥanīfah, Arabic is not a condition for the *khuṭbah*; one is allowed to give it in any language.[1097]

[1094] Abū Dāwūd, *k. al-ṣalāh, b. iqṣār al-khuṭab.*

[1095] Aḥmad, al-Bazzār, and al-Ṭabarānī as cited in *Majmaʿ al-zawā'id, k. al-ṣalāh, b. al-inṣāt wa al-imām yakhṭubu.*

[1096] Abū Ḥanīfah, *K. al-āthār* 47-48.

[1097] al-Sarakhsī, *al-Muḥīṭ, al-faṣl al-khāmis wa al-ʿishrūn, baḥth al-nawʿ al-thānī;* al-Shāmī, *Radd al-muḥtār, i.* 543; al-Ṭaḥṭāwī, *Marāqī al-falāḥ; al-Fatāwā al-sirājiyyah, b. al-jumuʿah* 17; ʿAbd al-Ḥaqq al-Muḥaddith al-Dihlawī, *Sharḥ Sifr al-saʿādah* 267; ʿAbd al-Ḥayy al-Firangī Maḥallī, *Majmūʿat al-fatāwā.* (*See*: Khālid Sayfullāh Raḥmāni, *Jadīd fiqhī masā'il*, i. 164-167.)

By way of reconciling both opinions, many jurists of our time assert that in an Arab land and wherever people understand Arabic the whole *khuṭbah* should be delivered in Arabic. But in a non-Arab land where most people do not understand Arabic the sermon part of the *khuṭbah* should be done in the language of the people, because there is no use of a sermon if people do not understand it. The rest of it, however, should be said in Arabic".[1098]

Joining the Ṣalāh late

Ibrāhīm al-Nakhaʿī said of someone arriving at the *masjid* on the day of *Jumuʿah* while the imām is sitting for the end of the *ṣalāh*, that they should say the *takbīr*, and enter the *ṣalāh*. Then he will say another *takbīr*, sit with them and recite the *tashahhud*. When the imām says *salām*, he should stand and perform two *rakʿahs*. Imām Muḥammad said: "This is the opinion of Abū Ḥanīfah but we do not adhere to it. Whoever catches one *rakʿah* with the imām should add another *rakʿah* to it, and if he joins them at the time of the sitting he should pray four *rakʿahs*".[1099] Abū Wā'il narrated that ʿAbdullāh ibn Masʿūd said: "Whoever joins the *ṣalāh* when the imām is doing the *tashahhud* has performed the *ṣalāh* of *Jumuʿah* [and does not need to do *Ẓuhr*]".[1100] Shuʿbah said: "I asked Ḥakam and Ḥammād about a person who joins (the *ṣalāh* of) the imām before the *salām*. Both of them said he prays two *rakʿahs*".[1101] Ḍaḥḥāk said: "If one joins (the *ṣalāh* when) other people are in the sitting position one should pray two *rakʿahs*".[1102]

Sunnah ṣalāhs

It is Sunnah to offer supererogatory *ṣalāhs* before and after *Jumuʿah*. Al-Samarqandī stated that: "Sunnah before *Jumuʿah* is four *rakʿahs*".[1103] Ibn ʿUmar used to perform a long *ṣalāh* before *Jumuʿah* and then two *rakʿahs*

[1098] It is the opinion agreed upon by members of the Islamic Fiqh Academy in its seminar in Jeddah on 8-16th *Rabīʿ al-Thānī* 1402 AH.

[1099] Abū Ḥanīfah, *K. al-āthār* 36.

[1100] Ibn Abī Shaybah, *al-Muṣannaf, i.* 463.

[1101] Ibid.

[1102] Ibid.

[1103] al-Samarqandī, *Tuḥfat al-fuqahā'* 93.

after it, and he said that the Prophet ﷺ used to do so.[1104] Abū Hurayrah reported that the Prophet ﷺ said: "Whoever makes *ghusl* on the day of *Jumuʿah* and then goes to the *masjid* and prays what has been prescribed for him, and remains quiet while the imām delivers the *khuṭbah*, and then prays with the imām, Allāh will forgive for him what is between that *Jumuʿah* and the next and an additional three days".[1105]

It is Sunnah to pray four *rakʿahs* after *Jumuʿah* according to Abū Ḥanīfah, and six *rakʿahs* according to Abū Yūsuf and Muḥammad. Al-Samarqandī stated that Ibn Masʿūd came to Kufah and prayed four *rakʿahs* after *Jumuʿah*, then ʿAlī came and he would pray six *rakʿahs* after *Jumuʿah*. Abū Ḥanīfah followed the practice of Ibn Masʿūd whilst Abū Yūsuf and Muḥammad followed ʿAlī's practice. It is narrated from Abū Yūsuf that one should pray four *rakʿahs* first, then two more *rakʿahs*. This is so one does not pray after the *farḍ* a prayer similar to it [in the number of *rakʿahs*].[1106] Abū Hurayrah reported that the Prophet ﷺ said: "Whoever wants to pray after the *Jumuʿah* should pray four *rakʿahs*".[1107] It has been narrated from ʿAbdullāh ibn ʿUmar that he prayed two *rakʿah*s after *Jumuʿah*, then he prayed four *rakʿah*s.[1108]

Imām Muḥammad narrated from Ibrāhīm al-Nakhaʿī saying: "Four *rakʿahs* before the *Ẓuhr* and four *rakʿahs* after the *Jumuʿah* should not be separated by a *salām*". Imām Muḥammad said: "We adhere to this and it is also the opinion of Abū Ḥanīfah".[1109]

[1104] Abū Dāwūd, *k. al-ṣalāh, b. al-ṣalāh baʿda al-jumuʿah.*

[1105] Muslim, *k. al-jumuʿah, b. faḍl man istamaʿa wa anṣata fī al-khuṭbah.*

[1106] al-Samarqandī, *Tuḥfat al-fuqahā'* 93.

[1107] Muslim, *k. al-jumuʿah, b. al-ṣalāh baʿda al-jumuʿah.*

[1108] al-Ṭaḥāwī, *Sharḥ maʿānī al-āthār, i. 337.*

[1109] Abū Ḥanīfah, *K. al-āthār* 31.

Chapter 12: ʿĪd Ṣalāhs

Every community in the world has their festival days where they are involved in recreation and amusement. Muslims have two festival days: the first is after fasting during the month of Ramaḍān, and the second, at the time of Ḥajj. The celebration of these two *ʿĪds* and the *ṣalāhs* of *ʿĪd* was prescribed in the second year of Hijrah. Anas reported: "When the Prophet ﷺ came to Madīnah they had two days of sport and amusement. The Prophet ﷺ said: 'Allāh, has exchanged these days for two days better than them: the day of breaking the fast and the day of sacrifice'."[1110]

ʿĀ'ishah said: "The Abyssinians were performing in the *masjid* on the day of *ʿĪd*. I looked over the Prophet's shoulders and he lowered them a little so I could see them until I was satisfied and left".[1111] Nubayshah narrated that the Prophet ﷺ said: "The days of *tashrīq* (i.e. the days in which the second *ʿĪd* is celebrated) are days of eating and drinking and of remembering Allāh".[1112]

What is recommended on the day of ʿĪd

It is Sunnah to do *ghusl* for *ʿĪd Ṣalāhs.* Al-Fākih ibn Saʿd narrated that the Messenger of Allāh ﷺ took a bath on Fridays, the Day of ʿArafah and both *ʿĪds.*[1113] Muḥammad al-Bāqir narrated that ʿAlī used to take a bath on the day of *ʿĪd al-Fiṭr* and on the day of *ʿĪd al-Aḍḥā* before leaving for the *ṣalāh.*[1114] ʿAbdullāh ibn ʿUmar took a bath for *ʿĪd al-Fiṭr.*[1115] Abū Isḥāq narrated that ʿAlqamah used to take a bath before leaving for *ʿĪd al-Fiṭr.*[1116]

[1110] al-Nasā'ī, *k. al-ʿīdayn.*

[1111] al-Bukhārī, *k. al-ʿīdayn, b. al-ḥirāb wa al-daraq yawm al-ʿīd.*

[1112] Muslim, *k. ṣalāt al-ʿīdayn, b. al-rukhṣah fī al-laʿib alladhī lā maʿṣiyata fīhi fī ayyām al-ʿīd.*

[1113] Aḥmad, *al-Musnad* 16766.

[1114] ʿAbd al-Razzāq, *al-Muṣannaf, iii.* 309.

[1115] Mālik, *al-Muwaṭṭa'* 93.

[1116] ʿAbd al-Razzāq, *al-Muṣannaf, iii.* 308.

It is recommended that males put on their best clothing and use perfume before leaving for the ᶜ*Īd Ṣalāh.* Ḥasan ibn ᶜAlī ibn Abī Ṭālib said: "The Messenger of Allāh ﷺ ordered us to wear the best clothes we could find for the two ᶜ*Īds* and to apply the best perfume we could find and to sacrifice the best animal we could find".[1117] ᶜAlī ibn al-Ḥusayn ibn Abī Ṭālib narrated that the Prophet ﷺ would wear a cloak specially designed for him on every ᶜ*Īd.*[1118] Nāfiᶜ narrated that ᶜAbdullāh ibn ᶜUmar used to wear his best clothes on both ᶜ*Īds.* [1119]

It is recommended for ᶜ*Īd al-Fiṭr,* to eat something before going to prayer, while for ᶜ*Īd al-Aḍḥā* the eating should be delayed until one returns from the ᶜ*Īd Ṣalāh* and then one should eat from a sacrifice.[1120] Anas reported: "The Prophet ﷺ would not go out on the festival of breaking the fast until he had eaten an odd number of dates".[1121] Buraydah reported: "The Prophet ﷺ would not go out on the day of breaking the fast, ᶜ*Īd al-Fiṭr,* until he had eaten, and on the day of sacrifice *(*ᶜ*Īd al-Aḍḥā)* he would not eat until he had returned (from *ṣalāh*)".[1122] Saᶜīd ibn al-Musayyab said: "The people were ordered to eat before they went out on the day of breaking the fast".[1123] Imām Muḥammad narrated on the authority of Abū Ḥanīfah about Ibrāhīm al-Nakhaᶜī, that he used to eat on the day of ᶜ*Īd al-Fiṭr* before going for the *ṣalāh,* and did not eat on the day of ᶜ*Īd al-Aḍḥā* until he had returned from the *ṣalāh.* Imām Muḥammad said of this: "We adhere to it, and this is the opinion of Abū Ḥanīfah".[1124]

It is recommended that one take special care for the day of ᶜ*Īd al-Fiṭr* and the ten days of *Dhū al-Ḥijjah* by remembering Allāh and glorifying Him. ᶜAbdullāh ibn ᶜAbbās reported that the Prophet ﷺ said: "No good deeds done on other days are superior to those done on these days". The Companions asked: "O Messenger of Allāh ﷺ, not even *jihād* in the way of Allāh?" He said: "Not even *jihād,* save for the man who leaves with his life and wealth in the path of Allāh and returns with neither

[1117] al-Ḥākim, *al-Mustadrak, iv.* 256.

[1118] al-Bayhaqī, *al-Sunan al-kubrā, k. ṣalāt al-*ᶜ*īdayn, b. al-zīnah li al-*ᶜ*īd.*

[1119] Ibid.

[1120] al-Kāsānī, *Badā'i*ᶜ *al-ṣanā'i*ᶜ, *ii.* 249.

[1121] al-Bukhārī, *k. al-*ᶜ*īdayn, b. al-akl yawm al-fiṭr qabla al-khurūj.*

[1122] al-Tirmidhī, *k. al-jumu*ᶜ*ah, b. fī al-akl yawma al-fiṭr qabla al-khurūj.*

[1123] Mālik, *al-Muwaṭṭa'* 96.

[1124] Abū Ḥanīfah, *K. al-āthār* 54.

of them".[1125] ʿAbdullāh ibn ʿUmar narrated that the Messenger of Allāh ﷺ said: "There is no day more honourable in Allāh's sight and no acts more beloved therein to Allāh than those in these ten days. So say the *tahlīl* لَا إِلَهَ إِلَّا الله (there is no God but Allāh), the *takbīr,* الله أَكْبَر (Allāh is the Greatest), and *taḥmīd,* اَلْحَمْدُ لِلّٰه (all praise is due to Allāh) a lot".[1126]

On ʿ*Īd* days, it is Sunnah to pronounce the *takbīrs* on the way to and from the *muṣallā* (place where ʿ*Īd Ṣalāh* is performed). The most authentic form of *takbīr* is related from ʿUmar and ʿAbdullāh ibn Masʿūd and is as follows: "الله أَكْبَر الله أَكْبَر لَا إِلَهَ إِلَّا الله وَالله أَكْبَر الله أَكْبَر وَلِلّٰه الْحَمْد, Allāh is the Greatest, Allāh is the Greatest. There is no god but Allāh. Allāh is the Greatest, Allāh is the Greatest. All praise and thanks are due to Allāh". These *takbīrs* are *wājib* after every *farḍ ṣalāh* in congregation. The time for these *takbīr* is from the *Fajr* of the day of ʿArafah until the time of the ʿ*Aṣr* on the thirteenth day of Dhū al-Ḥijjah. Imām Muḥammad narrated from ʿAlī ibn Abī Ṭālib that he would make the *takbīr* from the *Fajr Ṣalāh* of the Day of ʿArafah to ʿ*Aṣr* on the last day of *tashrīq*. Imām Muḥammad also said: "This is what we adhere to, but Abū Ḥanīfah did not adhere to it; rather he followed the opinion of ʿAbdullāh ibn Masʿūd who used to say the *takbīr* from the *Fajr Ṣalāh* of the Day of ʿArafah until the ʿ*Aṣr Ṣalāh* of the Day of *Naḥr* (Day of Sacrifice) he would say the *takbīr* in ʿ*Aṣr* then he would stop".[1127]

It is preferable to go to *Ṣalāt al-*ʿ*Īd* by one route and then return home by another route. Jābir reported: "On the days of ʿ*Īd*, the Prophet ﷺ would take different routes".[1128] Abū Hurayrah said: "When the Prophet ﷺ went to *Ṣalāt al-*ʿ*Īdayn*, he would return by a different route".[1129]

People should congratulate each other on the days of ʿ*Īd*. Jubayr ibn Nufayr reported: "When the Companions of the Prophet ﷺ met each other on the day of ʿ*Īd*, they would say to each other, تَقَبَّلَ الله مِنَّا وَمِنْك, 'may Allāh accept it from us and you'." Ḥabīb ibn ʿUmar al-Anṣārī narrated from his father: "I met Wāthilah on the day of ʿ*Īd* and I said, تَقَبَّلَ الله مِنَّا وَمِنْك,

[1125] al-Bukhārī, *k. al-*ʿ*īdayn, b. faḍl al-*ʿ*amal fī ayyām al-tashrīq.*

[1126] Aḥmad, *al-Musnad* 5446.

[1127] Abū Ḥanīfah, *K. al-āthār* 54.

[1128] al-Bukhārī, *k. al-*ʿ*īdayn, b. man khālafa al-ṭarīq idhā rajaʿa yawm al-*ʿ*īd.*

[1129] al-Tirmidhī, *abwāb al-ṣalāh, b. mā jā'a fī khurūj al-nabī ṣallallāhu* ʿ*alayhi wa sallama ilā al-*ʿ*Īd.*

'may Allāh accept it from us and you'. Then he said: 'Yes, may Allāh accept it from us and you'."[1130]

ON WHOM IT IS *WĀJIB*

ᶜĪd Ṣalāh is *wājib* upon all those on whom *Jumuᶜah Ṣalāh* is *farḍ,* i.e. on every free, adult, sane, resident and male Muslim who has the ability to attend the *ṣalāh;* it is not *wājib* upon a woman, child, traveller and an ill person who face hardship in attending the *muṣallā.*

Women are allowed to attend *ᶜĪd Ṣalāh* if it is safe for them. Umm ᶜAṭiyyah reported: "We used to be ordered to come out on the day of *ᶜĪd* and even bring out virgin girls from their houses and menstruating women so that they might stand behind the men and say the *takbīr* along with them and invoke Allāh along with them and hope for the blessings of that day and for purification from sins".[1131] Ibn ᶜAbbās said that the Prophet ﷺ would take his wives and daughters to the two *ᶜĪds.*[1132] ᶜAbdullāh ibn ᶜAbbās further reported: "I went out with the Prophet ﷺ on the day of either *ᶜĪds,* and he prayed and gave a *khuṭbah,* and then he went to the women and admonished them, reminded them of Allāh, and ordered them to give charity".[1133]

However, if it is not safe, then women should not attend the *ᶜĪd Ṣalāh.* Imām Muḥammad said: "It is not pleasing for us that women go out for the two *ᶜĪds,* except old women, and this is the opinion of Abū Ḥanīfah".[1134]

THE TIME AND PLACE

The time for *ᶜĪd Ṣalāh* begins from the time the sun is the length of a spear above the horizon until the sun reaches its meridian.[1135] Yazīd ibn Khumayr al-Raḥabī said: "ᶜAbdullāh ibn Busr, the Companion of

[1130] al-Ṭabarānī as cited in *Majmaᶜ al-zawā'id, k. al-ṣalāh, b. al-tahni'ah bi al-ᶜīd.*

[1131] al-Bukhārī, *k. al-ᶜīdayn, b. khurūj al-nisā' wa al-ḥuyyaḍ ilā al-muṣallā.*

[1132] Ibn-Mājah, *k. iqāmat al-ṣalāh wa al-sunnah fīhā, b. mā jā'a fī khurūj al-nisā' fī al-ᶜīdayn.*

[1133] al-Bukhārī, *k. al-ᶜīdayn, b. khurūj al-ṣibyān ilā al-muṣallā.*

[1134] Abū Ḥanīfah, *K. al-āthār* 53.

[1135] al-Kāsānī, *Badā'iᶜ al-ṣanā'iᶜ, ii.* 242.

the Messenger of Allāh ﷺ, came out along with the people on the day of *ᶜĪd al-Fiṭr* or *ᶜĪd al-Aḍḥā*. He disliked the delay of the imām, and said we would finish at this moment, that is, at the time of forenoon".[1136] It is narrated that the Prophet ﷺ prayed the *ᶜĪd Ṣalāh* while the sun was one or two spears above the horizon.[1137] Nāfiᶜ said: "ᶜAbdullāh ibn ᶜUmar prayed *Fajr* in the *masjid* of the Prophet ﷺ; then he would go straight to the place of *ᶜĪd Ṣalāh*".[1138] Ibrāhīm al-Nakhaᶜī said: "They used to pray *Fajr Ṣalāh* in *ᶜĪd* clothes".[1139] Jābir narrated from Muḥammad ibn ᶜAlī, ᶜĀmir and ᶜAṭā' saying: "One should not leave for the *ᶜĪd Ṣalāh* until the sun rises".[1140]

If the people miss *ᶜĪd al-Fiṭr Ṣalāh* on the 1st of *Shawwal*, then they can pray the next day; but if they miss the second day as well, then they cannot pray after it, and there is no *qaḍā'*. If people miss the *ᶜĪd al-Aḍḥā Ṣalāh* on the 10th of *Dhū al-Hijjah*, then they can pray the next day; if they miss the second day, then they can pray the third day.[1141]

As for the place of *ᶜĪd Ṣalāh*, it can be prayed in the *masjid*, though it is preferable to do it in the *muṣallā*, i.e. a place outside specified for *ᶜĪd ṣalāhs* and other large gatherings, as long as there is no excuse or reason to do otherwise (for example rain). The Prophet ﷺ would pray the two *ᶜĪds* in the outskirts of Madīnah: he never prayed it in his *masjid*, except once and that because it was raining. Abū Hurayrah reported that it was raining on the day of *ᶜĪd*, so the Prophet ﷺ led them in *Ṣalāt al-ᶜĪd* in the *masjid*.[1142]

HOW TO PRAY *ᶜĪD ṢALĀHS*

The *ᶜĪd Ṣalāh* consists of two *rakᶜahs* during which it is *wājib* to pronounce six additional *takbirs*. Three *takbīrs* should be recited in the first *rakᶜah* after the *takbīr taḥrīmah* and the opening supplication but before the Qur'ānic recital. In the second *rakᶜah*, the remaining three *takbīrs*

[1136] Abū Dāwūd, *k. al-ṣalāh, b. waqt al-khurūj ilā al-ᶜīd.*

[1137] *See:* al-Kāsānī, *Badā'iᶜ al-ṣanā'iᶜ*, ii. 242.

[1138] Ibn Abī Shaybah, *al-Muṣannaf*, i. 486.

[1139] Ibid., i. 487.

[1140] Ibid.

[1141] al-Kāsānī, *Badā'iᶜ al-ṣanā'iᶜ, ii.* 242.

[1142] Abū Dāwūd, *k. al-ṣalāh, b. yuṣallā bi al-nās al-ᶜīd fī al-masjid idhā kāna yawm maṭar.*

should be said after recitation of the Qur'ān and before *rukūᶜ*. Imām Muḥammad, after narrating this from ᶜAbdullāh ibn Masᶜūd, said: "This is also the opinion of Abū Ḥanīfah".[1143] It is preferable to raise one's hands in these additional *takbīrs* as one raises one's hands in the opening *takbīr.* The Prophet ﷺ said: "Hands should not be raised except in seven places". Among those place, he mentioned the *takbīrs* of *ᶜĪd* as well. Imām Abū Ḥanīfah stated that there should be silence between each *takbīr* equivalent to the time it takes to say *subḥānallāh* three times.[1144]

There is no *adhān* or *iqāmah* in the *ᶜĪd Ṣalāh.* When the Messenger of Allāh ﷺ went to the *muṣallā,* he would perform the *ṣalāh* without any *adhān* or *iqāmah.* ᶜAbdullāh ibn ᶜAbbās and Jābir both reported that there was no *adhān* on the day of breaking the fast or on the day of sacrifice.[1145] Imām Muḥammad narrated from Ibrāhīm al-Nakhaᶜī: "*ᶜĪd Ṣalāhs* are alone without any *adhān* or *iqāmah*". [1146]

THE *KHUṬBAH*

The *khuṭbah* for the *ᶜĪd Ṣalāh* consists of two *khuṭbahs* with a lighter sitting in between, like the *Jumuᶜah Khuṭbah.* However, the *khuṭbah* of *ᶜĪd* is given after the prayer and it is a Sunnah and listening to it is *wājib.*[1147] ᶜAbdullāh ibn ᶜAbbās said: "I prayed behind the Messenger of Allāh ﷺ and behind Abū Bakr, ᶜUmar and ᶜUthmān – they would start the *ṣalāh* before the *khuṭbah*".[1148] Abū Saᶜīd al-Khudrī said: "On the *ᶜĪds,* the Prophet ﷺ would go to the *muṣallā* and begin with the *ṣalāh* and when he had finished, he would face the people while they were sitting in rows, and he would render a sermon".[1149]

[1143] Abū Ḥanīfah, *K. al-āthār* 53.

[1144] al-Kāsānī, *Badāʾiᶜ al-ṣanāʾiᶜ, ii.* 244.

[1145] al-Bukhārī, *k. al-ᶜīdayn, b. al-mashy wa al-rukūb ilā al-ᶜīd bighayr adhān wa lā iqāmah;* Muslim, *k. ṣalāt al-ᶜīdayn.*

[1146] Abū Ḥanīfah, *K. al-āthār* 53.

[1147] al-Kāsānī, *Badāʾiᶜ al-ṣanāʾiᶜ, ii.* 242.

[1148] al-Bukhārī, *k. al-ᶜīdayn, b. al-mashy ilā al-ᶜīd bighayr adhān wa lā iqāmah; Muslim, k. ṣalāt al-ᶜīdayn, b. ṣalāt al-ᶜīdayn.*

[1149] al-Bukhārī, *k. al-ᶜīdayn, b. al-khurūj ilā al-muṣallā bighayr minbar.*

NAFL BEFORE OR AFTER ᶜĪD

No *ṣalāh* should be offered before or after the *ᶜĪd Ṣalāhs* in the place where the *ᶜĪd* prayers are done. However, people are allowed to pray after the *ᶜĪd* prayer in a different place. The Prophet ﷺ did not perform any *ṣalāh* nor did the Companions upon arrival at the *muṣallā* nor after the *ᶜĪd Ṣalāh*. ᶜAbdullāh ibn ᶜAbbās reported: "The Messenger of Allāh ﷺ went out to the site of the *ᶜĪd Ṣalāh* and prayed two *rakᶜahs* (i.e. the *ᶜĪd Ṣalāh*) without praying anything before or after it".[1150] Nāfiᶜ reported that ᶜAbdullāh ibn ᶜUmar did the same and he stated that this was the practice of the Prophet ﷺ.[1151] Al-Bukhārī recorded that Ibn ᶜAbbās did not like anyone performing a *ṣalāh* before *Ṣalāt al-ᶜĪd*.[1152] Ibn Sīrīn said: "Ibn Masᶜūd and Ḥudhayfah used to stop people from praying before *ᶜĪd*".[1153] ᶜAlqamah said: "The Companions did not pray before the *ᶜĪd Ṣalāh*".[1154] Ismāᶜīl ibn Abī Khālid said: "I accompanied al-Shaᶜbī on the day of *ᶜĪd*; he prayed neither before nor after it'.[1155] Imām Muḥammad said: "There is no *ṣalāh* before the *ᶜĪd Ṣalāh*; after it, one can pray if one wants. This is the opinion of Abū Ḥanīfah".[1156]

[1150] al-Bukhārī, *k. al-ᶜīdayn, b. al-ṣalāh qabla al-ᶜīd wa baᶜdahā.*

[1151] Mālik, *al-Muwaṭṭa'* 97.

[1152] al-Bukhārī, *k. al-ᶜīdayn, b. al-ṣalāh qabla al-ᶜīd wa baᶜdahā.*

[1153] ᶜAbd al-Razzāq, *al-Muṣannaf, iii.* 273.

[1154] Ibid.

[1155] Ibid.

[1156] Muḥammad, *al-Muwaṭṭa', i.* 612-613.

CHAPTER 13: OCCASIONAL *ṢALĀHS*

ṢALĀT AL-KUSŪF

ṢALĀT AL-KUSŪF (the solar eclipse *ṣalāh*) is Sunnah, and it consists of two *rakᶜahs,* and should be done in congregation. As in any *ṣalāh,* in each *rakᶜah* there is one *rukūᶜ* and two *sajdahs*, and the imām prolongs the recitation in both of them. Furthermore, the imām recites silently,[1157] and then makes *duᶜās* until the sun reappears. This *ṣalāh* must be led by the people's imām who leads the *Jumuᶜah.* If he is not present, then the people cannot pray in congregation, and must pray individually. There is no *khuṭbah* for the sun's eclipse.[1158]

Al-Nuᶜmān ibn Bashīr said: "The Messenger of Allāh ﷺ prayed the *Ṣalāt al-kusūf* with us like one of your *ṣalāhs.* He went into *rukūᶜ* and performed *sajdah,* praying two *rakᶜahs* with two *rukūᶜs,* and supplicated to Allāh until the sun clearly reappeared". [1159] Ibrāhīm al-Nakhaᶜī said: "They (the Companions) used to say: 'When that happens then pray your *ṣalāh* until the sun is clear'."[1160] Samurah ibn Jundub said: "The Prophet ﷺ led the *ṣalāh* during the solar eclipse and did not recite aloud".[1161] Qabṣah al-Hilālī narrated that the Prophet ﷺ said: "If you see that (i.e. an eclipse), pray as you pray the obligatory *ṣalāh*".[1162]

Imām Muḥammad said: "We adhere to it. We hold that in every *rakᶜah* there will be one *rukūᶜ* and two *sajdahs* like the other *ṣalāhs.* We hold that the people will pray in congregation during the solar eclipse, which will be led by the imām who leads *Jumuᶜah Ṣalāh*". Furthermore,

[1157] This is the opinion of Abū Ḥanīfah; though Abū Yūsuf says that the recitation should be made aloud. Imām Muḥammad narrated both opinions. The *fatwā* is on the opinion of Abū Ḥanīfah. (al-Samaraqandī, *Tuḥfat al-fuqahā'* 88.)

[1158] al-Samarqandī, ibid.

[1159] Abū Dāwūd, *k. al-ṣalāh, b. man qāla yarkaᶜu rakᶜatayn;* al-Nasā'ī, *k. al-kusūf, b. nawᶜ ākhar.*

[1160] Ibn Abī Shaybah, *al-Muṣannaf, ii.* 220.

[1161] Ibid., *ii.* 222.

[1162] al-Nasā'ī, *k. al-kusūf, b. nawᶜ ākhar.*

Imām Muḥammad also said: "It has not come to our knowledge that the Prophet ﷺ read the Qur'ān aloud in it; though it has come to our knowledge that ʿAlī ibn Abī Ṭālib read the Qur'ān aloud in it at Kufah. We consider it preferable not to read the Qur'ān aloud. If the solar eclipse happens at a time when it is not the (permitted) time of *ṣalāh*: at the time of sunrise, midday, or after ʿ*Aṣr*, then there will be no *ṣalāh* at that time; there is rather a supplication until the eclipse passes or the *ṣalāh* becomes lawful then *ṣalāh* should be done if anything of the eclipse remains".[1163]

There is no *ṣalāh* in congregation for a lunar eclipse, earthquake or any other disaster,[1164] rather each person does the *ṣalāh* individually. Imām Muḥammad said: "As for a lunar eclipse, people pray individually, and not in congregation, neither with the imām, nor with anyone else. Similarly, in all upheavals of nature (catastrophes) there is no *ṣalāh* in congregation".[1165] ʿĀ'ishah narrated that the Messenger of Allāh ﷺ said: "The sun and the moon are two signs from among Allāh's Signs and there is no eclipse due to the life or death of anyone. If you see that [eclipses] supplicate to Allāh, glorify His greatness, give charity and pray".[1166]

ṢALĀT AL-ISTISQĀ'

Ṣalāt al-istisqā' refers to the *ṣalāh* for seeking rain. Abū Ḥanīfah holds that there is no specific *ṣalāh* prescribed as Sunnah which is done in congregation when petitioning Allāh for rain. If the people pray *Ṣalāt al-istisqā'* individually, it is permitted. The *ṣalāh* done as a petition for rain is a *duʿā'* and a seeking of forgiveness according to Abū Ḥanīfah.[1167] Allāh says on the tongue of Nūḥ ﷺ: "*I said to them: 'Ask forgiveness from your Lord, Verily, He is Oft-Forgiving; He will send rain to you in abundance; and give you increase in wealth and children, and bestow on you gardens and bestow on you rivers'.*"[1168] Anas ibn Mālik narrated: "A man came to the Prophet ﷺ and said: 'Livestock are destroyed and the roads are cut off'. So Allāh's

[1163] Abū Ḥanīfah, *K. al-āthār* 58.

[1164] al-Samarqandī, *Tuḥfat al-fuqahā'* 88.

[1165] Abū Ḥanīfah, *K. al-āthār* 58.

[1166] Muslim, *k. al-kusūf, b. ṣalāt al-kusūf.*

[1167] al-Samarqandī, *Tuḥfat al-fuqahā'* 89.

[1168] *Nūḥ* 10-12.

Messenger ﷺ invoked Allāh for rain and it rained from that Friday till the next Friday. The same person came again and said, 'Houses have collapsed, roads are cut off, and the livestock are destroyed. Please pray to Allāh to withhold the rain'. Allāh's Messenger ﷺ said, 'O Allāh, Let it rain on the plateaus, on the hills, in the valleys and over the places where trees grow'. So the clouds lifted off from Madīnah as clothes are lifted off".[1169]

Abū Yūsuf and Muḥammad hold in this context that the people are led in the *ṣalāh* in two *rakᶜahs* and the recitation is made aloud. Then there is a *khuṭbah*, and one faces the *qiblah* making *duᶜā'* and the imām reverses his cloak. The people, however, do not turn their cloaks around.[1170]

ᶜĀ'ishah said: "The people complained to the Messenger of Allāh ﷺ about lack of rain, so he gave orders for a pulpit, and when it was set up for him, he appointed a day for the people to gather. He came out on that day when the sun had just appeared and sat down on the pulpit. He extolled Allāh's Greatness and praised Him. Then he said: 'You have complained of drought in your areas and of delay in receiving rain at the beginning of its season. You have been ordered by Allāh to supplicate to Him and He has promised that He will answer your prayers'. Then he said: 'All praise is for Allāh, the Lord of the people, the Compassionate, the Merciful, the King of the Day of Judgement. There is no god but Allāh Who does what He wishes. O Allāh, there is no god but You. You are the Self-sufficient and we are the poor. Send down rain upon us and make it a source of strength and satisfaction for us'. He then raised his hands and kept raising them till the whiteness of his armpits could be seen. After this, he turned his back to the people and reversed his cloak, keeping his hands raised. Finally, he faced the people, descended from the pulpit, and prayed two *rakᶜahs.* At that time Allāh produced a cloud, thunder and lightning. And, by Allāh's permission, it rained and before he reached the *masjid* there was flooding. Then he saw how quickly the people were running for shelter, he smiled until his molar teeth could be seen. He said: 'I bear witness that Allāh has power over all things and I am Allāh's slave and Messenger'."[1171]

[1169] al-Bukhārī, *k. al-istisqā', b. al-istisqā' fī al-masjid al-jāmiᶜ;* Muslim, *k. ṣalāt al-istisqā', b. al-duᶜā' fī al-istisqā'.*

[1170] al-Samarqandī, *Tuḥfat al-fuqahā'* 89.

[1171] al-Ḥākim, *al-Mustadrak, i.* 476.

ṢALĀT AL-KHAWF

Ṣalāt al-khawf refers to *ṣalāh* in situations of fear. To do *ṣalāh* is a firm command of Allāh and is prescribed for the benefit of people. Their function as individuals and in society depends on the proper offering of *ṣalāh*. The benefit of *ṣalāh* is such that even in situations of fear, conflict or strife, people should offer it in order to deserve Allāh's help in that situation and generally. According to Sayyid Abū al-Ḥasan ʿAlī Nadwī: "*Ṣalāh* is a more secure, a more soothing, pleasing and comforting refuge for the believer than the lap of the mother is for a weak and orphaned child. Just as when the child feels hurt or is annoyed or seized with fear or afflicted with thirst or hunger, it clings to its mother or sits on her lap thinking that now it is safe. *Ṣalāh* is the greatest shelter and haven of peace for the believer. It is the rope, strong and unbreakable, which is stretched between him and his Lord and Creator. He can gain the assurance of safety by holding it whenever he wants. It is the sustenance for his soul, balm for his wound and panacea for his ills".[1172]

In times of war and fear Muslims are given concessions in their prayers. The Qur'ān says: "*When you (O Messenger) are with them, and lead them in ṣalāh, let one party of them stand up in ṣalāh with you, taking their arms with them; when they finish their sajdahs, let them take their positions in the rear and let the other party come up which have not yet prayed and let them pray with you, taking all the precautions, and bearing arms. Those who disbelieve wish, if you were negligent of your arms and your baggage, to attack you in a single rush, but there is no blame on you if you put away your arms because of the inconvenience of rain or because you are ill; but take every precaution for yourselves. Verily Allāh has prepared a humiliating torment for the disbelievers*".[1173]

How to perform this ṣalāh

If the people are travellers, then the imām will pray two *rakʿah*s with them. The imām separates the people into two groups, one group facing the enemy and one group behind him whom he leads in *ṣalāh*: he does one *rakʿah* and two *sajdah*s, and when he raises his head from the second *sajdah*, those praying go off to face the enemy, and the other group come and the imām does a *rakʿah* and two *sajdah*s with them.

[1172] Abū al-Ḥasan ʿAlī Nadwī, *The Four Pillars of Islam* 21.
[1173] *al-Nisā'* 101-102.

The imām then says the *tashahhud,* the final *salām* and they then go to face the enemy; the first group return and they do a *rakʿah* and two *sajdahs* individually without recitation, say the *tashahhud* and the final *salām,* and then go to face the enemy. Then the other group comes and they make a *rakʿah* and two *sajdahs* with a recitation, and then make the *tashahhud* and the final *salām.*

ʿAbdullāh ibn ʿUmar said: "The Messenger of Allāh ﷺ prayed one *rakʿah* with one group while the other group faced the enemy. At that point, those who had prayed took the place of their Companions facing the enemy and the second group came and prayed one *rakʿah* with the Prophet ﷺ and then he did the *taslīm.* Then each group completed their *ṣalāh* individually doing the remaining one *rakʿah*".[1174]

If the people are in their own locality, the imām leads the first group in two *rakʿahs* and then the second group in two *rakʿahs.*[1175]

At *Maghrib* the imām does two *rakʿahs* with the first group and one *rakʿah* with the second.[1176]

The condition is that those in the *ṣalāh,* do not fight while doing the *ṣalāh*; doing so invalidates the *ṣalāh.* If the danger is still more pressing, they do the *ṣalāh* individually, and on their mounts, making gestures in place of the *rukūʿ* and *sajdah* movements, in whatever direction is possible if they are unable to face the *qiblah.* ʿAbdullāh ibn ʿUmar narrated that the Prophet ﷺ said: "If the enemy are more in number, then the people should pray standing or riding".[1177]

[1174] al-Bukhārī, *k. al-khawf, b. ṣalāt al-khawf.*

[1175] al-Kāsānī, *Badāʾiʿ al-ṣanāʾiʿ*, ii. 150.

[1176] Ibid., *ii,* 153.

[1177] al-Bukhārī, *k. al-khawf, b. ṣalāt al-khawf rijālan wa rukbānan.*

كتاب الجنائز

THE BOOK OF FUNERAL *ṢALĀH*

CHAPTER 1: DEATH

DEATH IS ONLY THE COMPLETION of one phase of life and a bridge to the other in which servanthood in this earthly life is rewarded. It is not a subject to be avoided or hidden. Islam provides guidance for death, its preparation, dealing with it when it arrives and for its remembrance. Therefore, one should reflect often about death and prepare for it. Abū Hurayrah said that Allāh's Messenger ﷺ said: "You should remember the reality that brings an end to all worldly joys and pleasures, namely, death".[1178] ʿAbdullāh ibn ʿUmar reported: "I came to the Prophet ﷺ and I was the tenth in a group of ten. A man from among the Anṣār got up and said: 'O Prophet ﷺ of Allāh, who are the most wise and the most prudent among the people?' He replied: 'Those who most remember death and prepare for it. Those are the wise who were granted honour and nobility in this world and in the Hereafter'."[1179]

WHAT IS PREFERABLE AT THE TIME OF DEATH

Upon death, one should remember Allāh's mercy and have good thoughts about Him. Jābir ibn ʿAbdullāh reported: "I heard the Messenger of Allāh ﷺ saying, three nights before his death, 'Let none of you die

[1178] al-Tirmidhī, *k. al-zuhd, b. mā jā'a fī dhikr al-mawt;* al-Nasā'ī, *k. al-janā'iz, b. kathrat dhikr al-mawt;* Ibn Mājah, *k. al-zuhd, b. dhikr al-mawt wa al-istiʿdād lahu.*

[1179] Ibn Abī al-Dunyā, *k. al-mawt,* al-Ṭabarānī, *al-Muʿjam al-ṣaghīr* as cited in *al-Muntaqā min kitāb al-Targhīb wa al-tarhīb li al-Mundhirī, ii* 866

except with good thoughts about Allāh'."[1180] Jābir also reported that the Prophet ﷺ said: "Everyone will be raised on the Day of Resurrection in the condition in which he died".[1181] Anas narrated: "The Prophet ﷺ went to see a young man who was on his deathbed. The Prophet ﷺ asked him: 'How are you?' The young man said: 'I hope from Allāh and fear Him'. The Prophet ﷺ said: 'These two things never gather in the heart of a person at such a time, but Allāh will grant him what he hopes for and shelter him from what he fears'."[1182]

It is preferable to make the dying person lie on his right side facing the *qiblah* as one is laid in the grave.[1183] Abū Qatādah narrated: "Upon arrival in Madīnah, the Prophet ﷺ enquired about al-Barā' ibn Maᶜrūr. The people told the Prophet ﷺ that he had died, and had willed one-third of his property to the Prophet ﷺ and that his face be turned toward the Kaᶜbah at the time of his death. Hearing this, the Prophet ﷺ praised him".[1184] Fāṭimah, the daughter of the Prophet ﷺ, at the time of her death, turned towards the Kaᶜbah and lay on her right hand.[1185] Ibrāhīm al-Nakhaᶜī said: "They preferred to face the dying person towards the *qiblah*". [1186] The same is narrated from Ḥasan al-Baṣrī and ᶜAṭā' ibn Abī Rabāḥ.[1187]

It is Sunnah to do *talqīn*, i.e. persuading the dying person to say, لَا إِلَٰهَ إِلَّا الله "There is no god but Allāh". Abū Hurayrah and Abū Saᶜīd al-Khudrī reported that the Prophet ﷺ said: "Persuade your dying people to say لَا إِلَٰهَ إِلَّا الله".[1188] Abū Dharr narrated: "Allāh's Messenger ﷺ said: 'Someone came to me from my Lord and gave me the good tidings

[1180] Muslim, *k. al-jannah wa ṣifat naᶜīmihā wa ahlihā, b. al-amr bi ḥusn al-ẓann billāh taᶜalā ᶜinda al-mawt.*

[1181] Muslim, *k. al-jannah, b. al-amr bi ḥusn al-ẓann billāh taᶜalā ᶜinda al-mawt.*

[1182] al-Tirmidhī, *k. al-janā'iz, b. mā jā'a anna al-mu'min yamūtu bi ᶜarq al-jabīn;* Ibn Mājah, *k. al-zuhd, b. dhikr al-mawt wa al-istiᶜdād lahu.*

[1183] al-Kāsānī, *Badā'iᶜ al-ṣanā'iᶜ*, *ii.* 302.

[1184] al-Ḥākim, *al-Mustadrak, i.* 505; al-Ḥākim observed: "I know of no ḥadīth, other than this one, with regard to turning the face of a dying person towards the Kaᶜbah".

[1185] Aḥmad, *al-Musnad* 27656.

[1186] Ibn Abī Shaybah, *al-Muṣannaf, ii.* 447.

[1187] Ibid.

[1188] Muslim, *k. al-janā'iz, b. talqīn al-mawtā lā ilāha illā Allāh.*

that if any of my *ummah* dies associating none along with Allāh, he will enter Paradise'. I asked: 'Even if he committed adultery and theft?' He replied: 'Even if he committed adultery and theft'."[1189] Muʿādh ibn Jabal narrated that the Messenger of Allāh ﷺ said: "He whose last words are لَا إِلَهَ إِلَّا اللهُ shall enter Paradise".[1190] ʿUmar said: "Be near your dying people, persuade them to recite لَا إِلَهَ إِلَّا اللهُ, close their eyes and read the Qur'ān next to them".[1191] Ibrāhīm al-Nakhaʿī narrated that ʿAlqamah instructed in his will that al-Aswad should prompt him to say لَا إِلَهَ إِلَّا اللهُ.[1192]

It is recommended that one recites Sūrah *Yāsīn* next to the dying person. Maʿqil ibn Yasār narrated that the Prophet ﷺ said: "Recite in the presence of your men departing from this world", i.e. recite *Yāsīn.*[1193] In another narration, the Prophet ﷺ said: "*Yāsīn* is the heart of the Qur'ān. None recites it seeking the pleasure of Allāh and the Hereafter, but will be forgiven. So recite it to your dead".[1194]

As soon as someone dies, it is recommended that their eyes be closed, because if they are left otherwise, it will have a bad effect on people.[1195] The Prophet ﷺ visited Abū Salamah after his death, closed his eyes and said: "When a soul is seized, the eyesight follows it".[1196] Yaḥyā ibn Abī Rāshid al-Baṣrī narrated that ʿUmar said to his son at the time of his death: "When I die, then close my eyes."[1197] Bakr said: "When you close the eyes of the dead person, then say بِسْمِ اللهِ وَعَلَى مِلَّةِ رَسُولِ اللهِ"[1198]

WHAT IS RECOMMENDED FOR THE BEREAVED

Allāh says in the Qur'ān: "*O you who believe, seek help in patience and ṣalāh. Truly, Allāh is with the patient. And say not of those who are killed in the path of Allāh, 'They are dead'. Nay, they are living, but you perceive it not. And certainly, We shall test you with something of fear, hunger, loss of wealth, lives*

[1189] al-Bukhāri, *k. al-janā'iz, b. fī al-janā'iz wa man kāna ākhiru kalāmihi lā ilāha illā allāh.*

[1190] Abū Dāwūd, *k. al-janā'iz, b. fī al-talqīn.*

[1191] ʿAbd al-Razzāq, *al-Muṣannaf, iii.* 386.

[1192] Ibn Abī Shaybah, *al-Muṣannaf, ii.* 446.

[1193] Ibn Mājah, *k. al-janā'iz, b. mā jā'a fīmā yuqālu ʿind al-marīḍ idhā ḥuḍira.*

[1194] Abū Dāwūd, *k. al-janā'iz, b. al-qirā'ah ʿinda al-mayyit.*

[1195] al-Kāsānī, *Badā'iʿ al-ṣanā'iʿ*, ii. 304-5.

[1196] Muslim, *k. al-janā'iz, b. ighmād al-mayyit wa al-duʿā' lahu idhā ḥuḍira.*

[1197] Ibn Abī Shaybah, *al-Muṣannaf, ii.* 448.

[1198] Ibid.

and fruits, but give glad tidings to the patient, who, when afflicted with calamity, says: 'Truly, to Allāh we belong and truly to Him we shall return'. They are those on whom are blessings from their Lord, and mercy, and it is they who are the guided ones".[1199]

On the basis of the above verses, it is recommended that when someone loses any of his family members or friends they should be patient, and realise that everyone has to return to Allāh. No one is going to live here forever. Anas ibn Mālik narrated that the Prophet ﷺ passed by a woman crying next to a grave. He said to her: "Fear Allāh and be patient". [1200] In another version it is reported that the Prophet ﷺ said: "Patience is to be shown at the first shock".[1201] It is recommended that on hearing of the death of a Muslim, one should invoke Allāh. Umm Salamah said: "I heard the Prophet ﷺ saying: 'If a slave of Allāh is afflicted with a trouble and says:

إِنَّا لله وَإِنَّا إِلَيْهِ رَاجِعُوْنَ اَللَّهُمَّ آجِرْنِيْ فِيْ مُصِيْبَتِيْ وَأَخْلِفْ لِيْ خَيْرًا مِنْهَا

"Truly, to Allāh we belong and truly to Him we shall return. O Allāh, Reward me in this trouble and replace it with something better", Allāh will accept his prayer, grant him reward for his trouble, and replace it with something better'." She said: "When Abū Salamah [my husband] died, I invoked Allāh in the words taught to me by the Prophet ﷺ and Allāh did grant me someone better than him, i.e. He gave me the Messenger of Allāh ﷺ as a husband".[1202]

Wailing loudly over the dead is disliked. Abū Mālik al-Ashᶜarī narrated that the Prophet ﷺ said: "Wailing over the dead is a practice of the [time of] ignorance; a professional wailer, unless she repents before her death, will be raised on the Day of Judgement wearing a garment of tar and an armour of blistering pus".[1203] Jarīr, a client of Muᶜāwiyah, narrated that Muᶜāwiyah delivered a sermon in Hims and mentioned in his sermon that Allāh's Messenger prohibited bewailing over the dead.[1204] Umm

[1199] *al-Baqarah* 153-7.

[1200] al-Bukhāri, *k. al-janā'iz, b. qawl al-rajul li al-ma'rah ᶜinda al-qabr iṣbirī.*

[1201] Ibn Mājah, *k. al-janā'iz, b. mā jā'a fī al-ṣabr ᶜalā al-muṣībah.*

[1202] Muslim, *k. al-janā'iz, b. mā yuqāl ᶜinda al-muṣībah.*

[1203] Muslim, *k. al-janā'iz, b. al-tashdīd fī al-niyāḥah.*

[1204] Ibn Majah, *k. al-janā'iz, b. al-nahy ᶜan al-niyāḥah.*

ᶜAṭiyyah reported: "The Messenger of Allāh ﷺ made us pledge that we would not wail over the dead".[1205]

However, weeping over the dead is permissible, as long as there is no crying aloud and wailing. ᶜAbdullāh ibn ᶜUmar reported that the Prophet ﷺ said: "Allāh does not punish a person for shedding tears or feeling pain in his heart. But He does punish, though He may show mercy, because of what he utters with this", and then he pointed to his tongue.[1206] The Prophet ﷺ wept over the death of his son, Ibrāhīm, and said: "The eyes shed tears and the heart feels pain, but we utter only what pleases our Lord. O Ibrāhīm, We are grieved by your departure".[1207] He also wept when his granddaughter, Umāmah, daughter of Zaynab, died. At this Saᶜd ibn ᶜUbādah said: "O Messenger of Allāh ﷺ, are you weeping?" The Prophet ﷺ replied: "This weeping is the mercy that Allāh has placed in the hearts of His slaves. And surely Allāh bestows mercy upon those who are merciful among His slaves".[1208]

It is not permissible for a woman to mourn for more than three days on the death of a near relative, except in the case of her husband's death, when she will mourn for four months and ten days. Umm ᶜAṭiyyah narrated that the Messenger of Allāh ﷺ said: "A woman should not mourn for any deceased person for more than three days, except in the case of her husband's death, which she may mourn for a period of four months and ten days. A woman in mourning should not wear brightly coloured clothes, but rather a plain dress. During this period she should not use any adornment or eye makeup, nor wear any perfume, nor dye her hands and feet with henna, nor comb her hair, except at the end of her menstruation period, when she may use some cleaning or refreshing agents such as perfume, etc, to get rid of any offensive smell left over from her period".[1209]

[1205] al-Bukhārī, *k. al-janā'iz, b. mā yunhā ᶜan al-nawḥ wa al-bukā' wa al-zajr ᶜan dhālik.*

[1206] al-Bukhārī, *k. al-janā'iz, b. al-bukā' ᶜinda al-marīḍ.*

[1207] al-Bukhārī, *k. al-janā'iz, b. qawl al-nabī ṣallallāhu ᶜalayhi wa sallam innā bika lamaḥzūnūn;* Muslim, *k. al-faḍā'il, b. raḥmatihi al-ṣibyān wa al-ᶜiyāl.*

[1208] al-Bukhārī, *k. al-janā'iz, b. qawl al-nabī ṣallallāhu ᶜalayhi wa sallam yuᶜadhdhabu al-mayyitu bi baᶜḍ bukā'i ahlihi;* Muslim, *k. al-janā'iz, b. al-bukā' ᶜalā al-mayyit.*

[1209] al-Bukhārī, *k. al-ṭalāq, b. talbasu al-ḥāddah thiyāb al-ᶜaṣb;* Muslim, *k. al-ṭalāq, b. wujūb al-iḥdād.*

It is recommended that others should prepare food for the bereaved family and not leave them to do it for themselves. ᶜAbdullāh ibn Jaᶜfar reported that the Messenger of Allāh ﷺ said: "Prepare some food for the family of Jaᶜfar, for what has befallen them is keeping them preoccupied".[1210] It is disliked for the deceased's family to prepare food for people coming to express their condolences. Abū al-Bukhturī said: "The food at the house of the dead is from the custom of *jāhiliyyah*".[1211] This is also narrated from ᶜUmar ibn al-Khaṭṭāb, Saᶜīd ibn Jubayr and ᶜUmar ibn ᶜAbd al-ᶜAzīz.[1212]

Offering condolences to the family of the deceased is desirable.[1213] Al-Qāsim ibn Muḥammad narrated that the Prophet ﷺ used to console Muslims in their distress.[1214] ᶜAmr ibn Ḥazm narrated that the Prophet ﷺ said: "No believer consoles his brother in distress, but Allāh will attire him with an apparel of honour on the Day of Resurrection".[1215] It is recommended, however, that condolences be only offered once.[1216] The condolences may be offered up to three days after death. If the person either offering or receiving condolences was not present at the time of death, then they may be offered at a later period.[1217]

Condolences may be presented in any words; it is preferable, however, to use the wording narrated from the Prophet ﷺ.[1218] Usāmah ibn Zayd reported: "A daughter of the Prophet ﷺ sent him a message to come to her house, because a son of hers had died. In response he sent her a message with his regards saying إِنَّ لله مَا أَخَذَ وَلَهُ مَا أَعْطَى، وَكُلُّ شَيْءٍ عِنْدَهُ بِأَجَلٍ مُسَمًّى 'Surely to Allāh belongs what He has taken, and to Him belongs what

[1210] Abū Dāwūd, *k. al-janā'iz, b. ṣanᶜat al-ṭaᶜām li ahl al-mayyit;* al-Tirmidhī, *abwāb al-janā'iz, b. mā jā'a fī al-ṭaᶜām li ahl al-mayyit;* Ibn Mājah, *k. al-janā'iz, b. mā jā'a fī al-ṭaᶜām yubᶜathu ilā ahl al-mayyit.*

[1211] Ibn Abī Shaybah, *al-Muṣannaf, ii.* 486.

[1212] Ibid., *ii.* 487.

[1213] *See*: *al-Fatāwā al-hindiyyah,* i. 167.

[1214] ᶜAbd al-Razzāq, *al-Muṣannaf, iii.* 395.

[1215] Ibn Mājah, *k. al-janā'iz, b. mā jā'a fī thawāb man ᶜazzā muṣāban.*

[1216] *See*: *al-Fatāwā al-hindiyyah,* i. 167.

[1217] Ibid.

[1218] Ibid.

He has given. For everything He has set a time. So be patient and be content'."[1219]

If one gives condolences to a non-Muslim for a Muslim relative, one should say: "May Allāh give you the best of condolences and grant forgiveness to your beloved deceased". If both the deceased and the one to whom condolences are given are non-Muslims, then one should say: "May Allāh grant you a substitute".[1220]

[1219] al-Bukhārī, *k. al-janā'iz, b. qawl al-nabī ṣallallāhu ʿalayhi wa sallam yuʿadhdhabu al-mayyit.*

[1220] See: *al-Fatāwā al-hindiyyah*, i. 167.

Chapter 2: Washing

Washing the body of a dead Muslim is a communal obligation. It is reported that the Prophet ﷺ said "A Muslim has six rights over other Muslims". Then he counted them and included washing the deceased.[1221]

The body of a deceased Muslim, other than a *shahīd* (martyr), should be washed. If more than half of a Muslim's body, or half of the body with the head is found, then it should be washed and the funeral *ṣalāh* be offered on it; otherwise it should not be washed nor should any funeral *ṣalāh* be offered on it, and it should be wrapped in a piece of cloth and buried.[1222]

HOW THE BODY SHOULD BE WASHED

It is *wājib* to wash the entire body at least once. It is recommended that the body be placed on a raised table (or something similar) which has been scented. The clothing should be removed, keeping the *ʿawrah* covered at all times. A washer should begin by gently applying pressure on the stomach of the deceased in order to push out any remnants, and then wash away all impurities. It is forbidden to touch the private parts of the deceased; hence, the washer should be cautious and cover/wrap his or her hands with gloves or a cloth. The washer should then wash the deceased in the manner of *wuḍū'* for *ṣalāhs*. The Prophet ﷺ said: "Begin washing the dead by washing the right parts of the body, and those parts that are washed in *wuḍū*'".[1223] After that, the right side should be washed by laying the body on the left side, then the left side should be washed by laying the body on the right side. The body should be washed with soap and water three times. If the washer feels that three washes are not enough to cleanse the body properly, then they may wash it

[1221] Muslim, *k. al-salām, b. min ḥaqq al-muslim li al-muslim.*

[1222] *al-Fatāwā al-hindiyyah,* i. 159.

[1223] al-Bukhārī, *k. al-janā'iz, b. yulqā shaʿr al-mayyit khalfahā;* Muslim, *k. al-janā'iz, b. fī ghusl al-mayyit.*

five or seven times. Then the dead person should be made to sit and the stomach should be wiped gently; if any dirt comes out it should be cleaned, without repeating the *wuḍū'* and *ghusl*.[1224] Ḥasan al-Baṣrī used to say: "If something comes out after washing the dead, then wash that place".[1225] This has also been narrated from ʿĀmir al-Shaʿbī and Ḥammād ibn Abī Sulaymān.[1226]

The washing should be done an odd number of times. The Prophet ﷺ said: "Wash the dead body an odd number of times, that is, three, five, or seven".[1227]

Once the body is washed, it should be dried with a clean cloth to prevent the shroud from becoming wet. It is also recommended that some perfume be applied to it. The Prophet ﷺ said: "When you apply perfume to the corpse, apply it an odd number of times after washing it".[1228] Umm ʿAṭiyyah said: "The Prophet ﷺ came to our house when his daughter died, and said: 'Wash her three times, five times, or more than that if you consider it necessary, with water and lote-tree leaves (*sidr*), and after the last wash apply some camphor to the body, and inform me after you have done so'. So when we finished washing we informed him. He gave us a cloth that he wore around his waist, and told us to wrap her in it as the first sheet of the shroud".[1229]

It is disliked to clip a deceased's fingernails, or trim or shave his hair. Ibn Sīrīn did not like doing so. [1230] Shuʿbah said: "I mentioned to Ḥammād ibn Abī Sulaymān that Ḥasan advises clipping the nails of the dead. Ḥammād rejected this saying: 'Do you think if the dead is uncircumcised that he will be circumcised'."[1231]

WHO SHOULD PERFORM THE WASHING

Men should be washed by men, and women by women. It is, however,

[1224] *al-Fatāwā al-hindiyyah*, i. 158.

[1225] Ibn Abī Shaybah, *al-Muṣannaf, ii.* 452.

[1226] Ibid.

[1227] al-Bukhārī, *k. al-janā'iz, b. yulqā shaʿr al-mayyit khalfahā;* Muslim, *k. al-janā'iz, b. fī ghusl al-mayyit.*

[1228] al-Ḥākim, *al-Mustadrak, i.* 506.

[1229] al-Bukhārī, *k. al-janā'iz, b. ghusl al-mayyit wa wuḍū'ihi bi al-mā' wa al-sidr.*

[1230] Ibn Abī Shaybah, *al-Muṣannaf, ii.* 453.

[1231] Ibid.

permissible for a woman to wash the body of her dead husband. ʿĀ'ishah said: "Had I known then what I know now, I would not have allowed anyone, except his wives, to wash the Prophet's body".[1232] Imām Mālik narrated that Asmā' bint ʿUmays, the wife of Abū Bakr, washed him when he died. Imām Muḥammad said after narrating this ḥadīth: "We adhere to it; there is no harm for the woman to wash her husband's body when he dies".[1233] Jābir ibn Zayd put it in his will that his wife should wash him.[1234] ʿAṭā' ibn Abī Rabāḥ said: "The woman can wash her husband".[1235]

However, it is not permissible for the husband to wash the body of his dead wife. If there is no other woman available then he should give her *tayammum.* Imām Muḥammad narrated from Ibrāhīm al-Nakhaʿī saying: "The woman will be washed by her husband, and a man by his wife". Abū Ḥanīfah, however, said: "It is not allowed for a man to wash his wife". Imām Muḥammad said: "We adhere to the opinion of Abū Ḥanīfah. There is no *ʿiddah* (waiting period) on the man, and how can he wash his wife while it is permissible for him to marry her sister, and (even) her daughter [his step-daughter] if he had not had relations [with his wife before her death]".[1236] ʿĀmir al-Shaʿbī said: "The man does not wash his wife".[1237] This is also the opinion of Sufyān al-Thawrī.[1238] Masrūq narrated that a wife of ʿUmar died, he said: "I had more right over her when she was alive; now you have more right over her".[1239]

[1232] Abū Dāwūd, *k. al-janā'iz, b. fī shadd al-mayyit ʿinda ghaslihi.*

[1233] Muḥammad, *al-Muwaṭṭa', ii.* 98-99.

[1234] Ibn Abī Shaybah, *al-Muṣannaf, ii.* 455.

[1235] Ibid., *ii.* 456.

[1236] Abū Ḥanīfah, *K. al-āthār* 60.

[1237] Ibn Abī Shaybah, *al-Muṣannaf, ii.* 456.

[1238] Ibid.

[1239] Ibid.

CHAPTER 3: THE SHROUD

SHROUDING THE BODY OF THE DECEASED is a communal obligation on Muslims. ʿAbdullāh ibn ʿAbbās reported the Prophet ﷺ as saying: "Wear white clothes, for these are your best clothes, and enshroud your dead in them".[1240] This ḥadīth makes it clear that enshrouding the dead is an obligation; and it is a continuous tradition since the time of our father Ādam ﷺ.

It is recommended that the shroud should be white, as it is recorded in the above-mentioned ḥadīth from Ibn ʿAbbās. The shroud should also be nice, as has been narrated by Abū Qatādah that the Prophet ﷺ said: "If one of you is a guardian to his deceased brother, he should shroud him nicely".[1241] It is also recommended that the shroud be scented. The Prophet ﷺ said: "If you perfume a dead body, do it an odd number of times".[1242]

If the dead person leaves some money behind, then his shroud should be purchased with this money before settling his will and inheritance. If the deceased did not leave any money, then, whoever is responsible for taking care of his living expenses should provide the shroud. If the deceased left no money and those taking care of him have no money, then the shroud should be purchased by the Public Treasury.[1243]

THE SHROUD OF A MAN

The shroud should consist of three wraps for a man, as has been narrated from ʿĀ'ishah who said: "The Messenger of Allāh ﷺ was wrapped in three pieces of new white sheeting from Yemen, without a shirt or a turban".[1244] Imām Muḥammad narrated from Ibrāhīm al-Nakhaʿī saying: "The Prophet ﷺ was wrapped in Yamani sheets and a *qamīṣ*".

[1240] Ibn Mājah, *k. al-janā'iz, b. mā jā'a fī mā yustaḥabbu min al-kafan.*

[1241] Ibid.

[1242] al-Ḥākim, *al-Mustadrak, i.* 506.

[1243] al-Kāsānī, *Badā'iʿ al-ṣanā'iʿ, ii. 330.*

[1244] al-Bukhārī, *k. al-janā'iz, b. al-thiyāb al-bīḍ li al-kafan.*

Imām Muḥammad said: "We adhere to it. The wraps of the man should be in three cloths, though two will suffice. And this is the opinion of Abū Ḥanīfah".[1245]

It is disliked to enshroud a male body in a single cloth; however, if no other cloth is available then one can be used without any dislike. Khabbāb said: "We migrated with Allāh's Messenger ﷺ seeking Allāh's pleasure, and our reward has become firm on Allāh. Some of us died and received no reward in this life. One of them was Muṣʿab ibn ʿUmayr, who was killed during the Battle of Uḥud. We did not find anything to shroud him in except a piece of cloth. When we covered his head, his feet would show, and if we covered his feet, his head would show. Allāh's Messenger ﷺ ordered us to use the cloth to cover his head with it and to cover his feet with *idhkhar* (a kind of grass)".[1246]

THE SHROUD OF A WOMAN

The shroud should consist of five wraps for a woman. Laylā bint Qānif al-Thaqafīyyah said: "I was one of those women who washed Umm Kulthūm, the daughter of the Prophet ﷺ, at her death. The Prophet ﷺ first gave us a lower garment, then a long shirt, then head-wear, then a cloak, and then she was wrapped in another garment". She further stated: "The Messenger of Allāh ﷺ was sitting at the door and he had a shroud with him. He gave us the garments one at a time".[1247]

[1245] Abū Ḥanīfah, *K. al-āthār* 59.

[1246] al-Bukhārī, *k. al-janā'iz, b. idhā lam yajid kafanan illā mā yuwārī ra'sahu aw qadamayh ghaṭṭā ra'sahu.*

[1247] Abū Dāwūd, *k. al-janā'iz, b. fī kafan al-mar'ah.*

Chapter 4: The funeral *Ṣalāh*

The funeral *ṣalāh* for a deceased person is a communal obligation. It is reported that the Prophet ﷺ said: "A Muslim has six rights over other Muslims". Then he counted them and included the offering of the funeral *ṣalāh*.[1248] Abū Hurayrah reported that when the Prophet ﷺ was informed of someone's death, he used to ask: "Does the deceased owe anything to anyone?" If the answer was in the affirmative, he would then ask: "Has he left anything to settle his debt?" If he had left something to settle his debt, the Prophet ﷺ would do the funeral *ṣalāh*. Otherwise, he would say to the Muslims: "Do the funeral *ṣalāh* for your companion".[1249]

Abū Hurayrah also narrated that the Prophet ﷺ said: "Whoever follows a funeral procession and offers the *ṣalāh* for the deceased, will receive one *qīrāṭ* (a weight) of reward. And whoever follows it and remains with it until the body is buried, will receive two *qīrāṭs* of reward, the least of which is equal in weight to Mount Uḥud".[1250]

Conditions for the *Ṣalāh*

The prerequisites for a funeral *ṣalāh* are the same as for obligatory *ṣalāhs*. Anyone intending to offer the funeral *ṣalāh* must be in a state of purity, be free from all minor and major impurities, must cover his or her *ʿawrah*, stand facing the direction of the Kaʿbah and make their intention.[1251] ʿAbdullāh ibn ʿUmar used to say: "One should not pray a funeral *ṣalāh* unless one is in a state of purity".[1252] Imām Muḥammad said: "We adhere to it; one should not pray *Janāzah Ṣalāh* unless one is in the state of *wuḍūʾ*. If the *ṣalāh* is being established, and one does not

[1248] Muslim, *k. al-salāmu, b. min ḥaqq al-muslim li al-muslim.*

[1249] al-Bukhārī, *k. al-kafalah, b. al-dayn.*

[1250] al-Bukhārī, *k. al-janāʾiz, b. man intaẓara ḥattā yudfan;* Muslim, *k. al-janāʾiz, b. faḍl al-ṣalāh ʿalā janāzah wa ittibāʿihā.*

[1251] *al-Fatāwā al-hindiyyah,* i. 164.

[1252] Mālik, *al-Muwaṭṭaʾ* 123.

have time to do *wuḍū'*, then it is permissible to pray with *tayammum*. This is the opinion of Abū Ḥanīfah".[1253]

FARḌS FOR THE *ṢALĀH*

The *farḍ* elements in the funeral *ṣalāh* are four *takbīr*s; the imām says them aloud, and those following in the *ṣalāh* say them quietly. Jābir and Abū Hurayrah narrated: "Allāh's Messenger ﷺ informed the people about the death of al-Najāshī on the very day he died. He went towards the *muṣallā* and the people stood behind him in rows. He said four *takbīrs*".[1254] Al-Tirmidhī said: "Most of the learned Companions of the Prophet ﷺ, may Allāh be pleased with them, and others followed and acted in accordance with the Prophet's example above. They hold that four *takbīrs* should be said in a funeral *ṣalāh*. Among these scholars are Sufyān al-Thawrī, Mālik ibn Anas, Ibn al-Mubārak, al-Shāfiᶜī, Aḥmad, and Isḥāq.[1255] Ibrāhīm al-Nakhaᶜī narrated that ᶜUmar ibn al-Khaṭṭāb consulted the Companions and asked them what the last funeral was that the Prophet ﷺ prayed, and how many *takbīrs* he said. The response was that he had said four *takbīrs* in the last funeral that he prayed. Imām Muḥammad said: "We adhere to it; and this is the opinion of Abū Ḥanīfah".[1256]

The hands should not be raised during these *takbīr*s, except at the opening *takbīr*. ᶜAbdullāh ibn Masᶜūd and ᶜAbdullāh ibn ᶜAbbās used to raise their hands at the first *takbīr*, then they did not raise their hands.[1257] Ḥasan ibn ᶜUbaydullāh narrated that Ibrāhīm al-Nakhaᶜī used to raise his hands at the first *takbīr*, then he did not raise his hands.[1258]

DESCRIPTION OF THE FUNERAL *ṢALĀH*

After the first *takbīr*, one should praise Allāh in any wording such as:

سُبْحَانَكَ اللَّهُمَّ وَبِحَمْدِكَ وَتَبَارَكَ اسْمُكَ وَتَعَالَى جَدُّكَ وَلَا إِلَهَ غَيْرُكَ

[1253] Muḥammad, *al-Muwaṭṭa', ii.* 118.

[1254] al-Bukhārī, *k. al-janā'iz, b. al-rajul yanᶜā ilā ahl al-mayyit binafsihi;* Muslim, *k. al-janā'iz, b. fī al-takbīr ᶜalā al-janāzah.*

[1255] al-Tirmidhī, *k. al-janā'iz, b. mā jā'a fī al-takbīr ᶜalā janāzah.*

[1256] Abū Ḥanīfah, *K. al-āthār* 62.

[1257] ᶜAbd al-Razzāq, *al-Muṣannaf, iii.* 470.

[1258] Ibid.

"Glory be to You, O Allāh, and to You are the praise and thanks. Blessed is Your name and Most High is Your Honour. There is no god besides You".

After the second *takbīr*, a prayer for peace and blessings upon the Prophet ﷺ may be said such as the supplication one says in the *ṣalāh*:

اَللَّهُمَّ صَلِّ عَلَى مُحَمَّدٍ وَعَلَى آلِ مُحَمَّدٍ كَمَا صَلَّيْتَ عَلَى إِبْرَاهِيْمَ وَعَلَى آلِ إِبْرَاهِيْمَ، اَللَّهُمَّ بَارِكْ عَلَى مُحَمَّدٍ وَعَلَى آلِ مُحَمَّدٍ كَمَا بَارَكْتَ عَلَى إِبْرَاهِيْمَ وَعَلَى آلِ إِبْرَاهِيْمَ إِنَّكَ حَمِيدٌ مَجِيْد

"O Allāh, grant mercy to Muḥammad and his family as You did to Ibrāhīm and his family. O Allāh, bless Muḥammad and his family as You blessed Ibrāhīm and his family. Truly You are Most Glorious and Most Praiseworthy".

After the third *takbīr*, the congregation should supplicate for the deceased, themselves and for all the believers. The Prophet ﷺ said: "When you do a funeral *ṣalāh* for a deceased person, pray sincerely for him to Allāh".[1259] It is reported from Abū Hurayrah that the Prophet ﷺ did a funeral *ṣalāh* and said:

اَللَّهُمَّ اغْفِرْ لِحَيِّنَا وَمَيِّتِنَا وَشَاهِدِنَا وَغَائِبِنَا وَصَغِيْرِنَا وَكَبِيْرِنَا وَذَكَرِنَا وَأُنْثَانَا اَللَّهُمَّ مَنْ أَحْيَيْتَهُ مِنَّا فَأَحْيِهِ عَلَى الإِسْلَامِ وَمَنْ تَوَفَّيْتَهُ مِنَّا فَتَوَفَّهُ عَلَى الإِيْمَانِ اَللَّهُمَّ لاَ تَحْرِمْنَا أَجْرَهُ وَلَا تَفْتِنَّا بَعْدَه

"O Allāh, Forgive our living, our dead, those of us who are present, and those who are absent, our young, our old, our males and our females. O Allāh, whomever among us You grant to live, make him live in Islam, and whomever You cause to die, let him die in faith. O Allāh, do not deprive us of his reward, and do not put us on trial after him".[1260]

After the fourth *takbīr*, the two salutations saying اَلسَّلَامُ عَلَيْكُمْ وَرَحْمَةُ الله, one to the right and the other to the left, are required, but are not obligatory.[1261]

[1259] Ibn Mājah, *k. al-janā'iz, b. mā jā'a fī al-duʿā' fī al-ṣalāh ʿalā al-janāzah.*

[1260] Abū Dāwūd, *k. al-janā'iz, b. al-duʿā' li al-mayyit;* al-Tirmidhī, *k. al-janā'iz, b. mā yaqūlu fī al-ṣalāh ʿalā al-mayyit;* Ibn Mājah, *k. al-janā'iz, b. mā jā'a fī al-duʿā' fī al-ṣalāh ʿalā al-janāzah.*

[1261] See the description in al-Kāsānī, *Badā'iʿ al-ṣanā'iʿ, ii.* 339-45.

Ibrāhīm al-Nakhaʿī said: "The first *takbīr* praises Allāh, the second is a prayer of peace for the Prophet ﷺ, the third is a prayer for the deceased, and the fourth is a *salām*, and then you say *salām*". Imām Muḥammad said: "We adhere to it, and this is the opinion of Abū Ḥanīfah".[1262]

If the deceased is a child, then it is recommended to say in the prayer:

اَللَّهُمَّ اجْعَلْهُ لَنَا سَلَفًا وَفَرَطًا وَذُخْرًا

"O Allāh, Make him our forerunner and make him a means of reward for us and a treasure".[1263]

WHO LEADS THE *ṢALĀH*?

The most appropriate person to lead the funeral *ṣalāh* is the Muslim ruler if present at the funeral, then the *qāḍī* , then the imām of the locality, then the guardian of the deceased, then the nearest blood relative. Of the blood relatives, if both the father and son are present, the father should be given precedence.[1264]

THE IMĀM'S POSITION

The position of the imām should be such that he stands opposite the head of a male body, and opposite the middle of a female body.[1265] This is based on a ḥadīth reported from Anas that he did a funeral *ṣalāh* for a male standing opposite his head. After the body of the man was removed, a female body was placed in front for the funeral *ṣalāh*. He led the *ṣalāh* standing opposite the middle of the female body. Thereupon, he was asked: "Did the Prophet ﷺ stand where you stood in the case of a man and a woman?" He answered: "Yes."[1266] Imām al-Ṭaḥāwī preferred this position[1267] Sufyān al-Thawrī said: "This is the most preferred position, because it is supported by other reports from Allāh's Messenger ﷺ". Samurah ibn Jundub narrated: "I prayed behind the Prophet ﷺ over a

[1262] Abū Ḥanīfah, *K. al-āthār* 62.

[1263] al-Bukhārī, *k. al-janā'iz, b. qirā'at fātiḥat al-kitāb ʿalā al-janāzah.*

[1264] al-Samarqandī, *Tuḥfat al-fuqahā'* 118-119.

[1265] This is the opinion of Imām Abū Ḥanīfah as narrated by Abū Yūsuf. (al-Marghinānī, *al-Hidāyah*, i. 99).

[1266] Ibn Mājah, *k. al-janā'iz, b. mā jā'a ayna yaqūm al-imām idhā ṣallā ʿalā al-janāzah.*

[1267] al-Ṭaḥāwī, *Sharḥ maʿānī al-āthār, i. 491.*

female who had died in childbirth. The Prophet ﷺ stood opposite the middle of her body".[1268]

THE ROWS FOR THE *ṢALĀH*

It is recommended that the people should make three rows; the minimum number of people in a row while offering a funeral *ṣalāh* is two, and that these rows should be straight. Mālik ibn Hubayrah, who had enjoyed the honour of the companionship of the Prophet ﷺ, is reported to have said: "When the bier was brought to the Prophet ﷺ and those who followed it were considered small in number, he would divide them into three rows. Then he would do the funeral *ṣalāh*, and say 'Whenever three rows of Muslims do funeral *ṣalāh* over the deceased, they ensure Paradise for him'."[1269]

It is preferable to have a large congregation of people for the funeral *ṣalāh*. Abū Hurayrah reported: "The Prophet ﷺ said: 'Whoever's funeral *ṣalāh* is attended by a group of a hundred Muslims is forgiven'."[1270] ʿĀ'ishah narrated that the Prophet ﷺ said: "If a Muslim dies and his funeral *ṣalāh* is attended by a group of a hundred Muslims, and they all sincerely pray for his forgiveness, he is forgiven".[1271] ʿAbdullāh ibn ʿAbbās reported: "I heard the Prophet ﷺ saying: "If a Muslim dies and forty people, who do not associate anyone with Allāh, pray for him, their *ṣalāh* is accepted and he is forgiven".[1272]

ṢALĀH IN A *MASJID*

It is not liked for the funeral *ṣalāh* to be prayed in the *masjid*. The Prophet ﷺ said: "Whoever does a funeral *ṣalāh* in the *masjid* will have nothing (i.e. no reward)".[1273] The reason behind this is that it can bring impurity

[1268] al-Bukhārī, *k. al-janā'iz, b. ayna yaqūmu min al-mar'ah wa al-rajul.*

[1269] Abū Dāwūd, *k. al-janā'iz, b. fī al-ṣufūf ʿalā al-janāzah;* al-Tirmidhī, *abwāb al-janā'iz, b. mā jā'a fī al-ṣalāh ʿalā al-janā'iz;* Ibn Mājah, *k. al-janā'iz, b. mā jā'a fī man ṣallā ʿalayhi jamāʿah min al-muslimīn.*

[1270] Ibn Mājah, *k. al-janā'iz, b. mā jā'a fī man ṣallā ʿalayhi jamāʿah min al-muslimīn.*

[1271] Muslim, *k. al-janā'iz, b. man ṣallā ʿalayhi arbaʿūna shuffiʿū fīh*

[1272] Ibid.

[1273] Ibn Mājah, *k. al-janā'iz, b. mā jā'a fī al-ṣalāh ʿalā al-janā'iz fī al-masjid.*

into the *masjid.* However, if there is no other place available and if the people can ensure the purity of the *masjid,* for example, by placing the body outside the *masjid,* then people are permitted to offer the *ṣalāh* in the *masjid.* In this respect, the Messenger of Allāh ﷺ prayed over Suhayl ibn Bayḍā' in the *masjid.*[1274] Imām Mālik reported from Ibn ʿUmar that the funeral *ṣalāh* of ʿUmar was offered in the *masjid.* After narrating this from Mālik, Imām Muḥammad said: "The funeral *ṣalāh* should not be prayed in the *masjid.* This is what has come to our knowledge from Abū Hurayrah. The place of the funeral *ṣalāh* in Madīnah is outside the *masjid;* this is where the Prophet ﷺ used to lead the funeral *ṣalāh*".[1275]

THE *ṢALĀH* FOR MORE THAN ONE

If there are a number of bodies, they should be placed in separate rows, between the imām and the direction of the Kaʿbah. If the deceased include both males and females, then the males should be placed immediately before the imām followed by the females.

There is a ḥadīth that if a funeral *ṣalāh* is done for a male child and also for a woman, the child's body should be placed nearest to the imām, and the woman's body next in the direction of the *qiblah.*[1276] The funeral *ṣalāh* of Umm Kulthūm, daughter of ʿAlī and the wife of ʿUmar, and her son Zayd, was led by Saʿīd ibn al-ʿĀṣ, and among the people attending this funeral were Ibn ʿAbbās, Abū Hurayrah, Abū Saʿīd and Abū Qatādah. The little boy was placed before the imām. A man did not like this way, and looked towards Ibn ʿAbbās, Abū Hurayrah, Abū Saʿīd and Abū Qatādah, and said to them: 'What is this?' They said: 'This is the *Sunnah*'."[1277] Imām Muḥammad said: "This is the opinion of Abū Ḥanīfah and we adhere to it".[1278]

ON WHOM THE *ṢALĀH* IS OFFERED

The funeral *ṣalāh* is offered on every Muslim. It is reported that the

[1274] al-Nasā'ī, *k. al-janā'iz, b. al-ṣalāh ʿalā al-janāzah fī masjid.*
[1275] Muḥammad, *al-Muwaṭṭa', ii.* 115-116.
[1276] al-Nasā'ī, *k. al-janā'iz, b. ijtimāʿ janāzat ṣabī wa imra'ah.*
[1277] al-Nasā'ī, *k. al-janā'iz, b. ijtimāʿ janā'iz al-rijāl wa al-nisā'.*
[1278] Abū Ḥanīfah, *K. al-āthār* 63.

Prophet ﷺ said "A Muslim has six rights over other Muslims". Then he counted them and included the offering of the funeral *ṣalāh*.[1279]

If a child is born dead and no voice is heard from it, then it may not be washed, nor may a funeral *ṣalāh* be performed. It should be wrapped in a piece of cloth and buried. If the child was born alive and his or her voice was heard, then the body should be washed and a funeral *ṣalāh* done over it.[1280] Jābir ibn ʿAbdullāh narrated that the Prophet ﷺ said: "When a baby utters a sound after birth a funeral *ṣalāh* will be done for him, and he will inherit".[1281]

The funeral *ṣalāh* is not done over highway robbers or those who have rebelled against a righteous leader.[1282]

ṢALĀH FOR AN 'ABSENT' DECEASED

The funeral *ṣalāh* may not be performed for a deceased who is absent. The Prophet ﷺ and the Companions did not hold a funeral *ṣalāh* for those who were deceased but not present. As for the ḥadīth of Abū Hurayrah that the Prophet ﷺ informed people about al-Najāshī's death the day he died, and then took them out to do funeral *ṣalāh* for him,[1283] Imām Muḥammad said: "It is not appropriate to do *Janāzah Ṣalāh* once one has already been done. The Prophet ﷺ in this matter is not like others. He prayed for al-Najāshī in Madīnah while he had died in Ḥabashah. The *ṣalāh* of the Messenger of Allāh ﷺ is blessing and purification. It is not like other *ṣalāhs*. This is the opinion of Abū Ḥanīfah".[1284]

Following the janāzah

According to the Sunnah it is preferable to carry the bier from all sides. ʿAbdullāh ibn Masʿūd said: "Whoever follows a funeral procession should carry the bier from all sides, for this is the Sunnah of the Prophet ﷺ".[1285] Imām Muḥammad said: "We adhere to it... You should first put

[1279] Muslim, *k. al-salām, b. min ḥaqq al-muslim li al-muslim.*

[1280] al-Marghinānī, *al-Hidāyah*, i. 101.

[1281] Ibn Mājah, *k. al-janā'iz, b. mā jā'a fī al-ṣalāh ʿalā al-ṭifl.*

[1282] al-Samarqandī, *Tuḥfat al-fuqahā'* 116-117.

[1283] Because of this ḥadīth, some scholars allow offering a funeral *ṣalāh* for an absent deceased.

[1284] Muḥammad, *al-Muwaṭṭa', ii.* 124-125.

[1285] Ibn Mājah, *k. al-janā'iz, b. mā jā'a fī shuhūd al-janā'iz.*

the front right then the rear right of the deceased [bier] on one's right, then the front left on one's left, and the rear left on one's left, and this is the opinion of Abū Ḥanīfah".[1286]

A funeral procession must proceed at a brisk pace. Abū Hurayrah narrated that the Prophet ﷺ said: "Walk briskly while carrying a coffin, for if the deceased is righteous, you will be taking them to something better, and if he or she is evil, then you will be getting them off your backs."[1287] Imām Muḥammad said: "We adhere to it. Walking briskly is better in our view than walking slowly. And this is the opinion of Abū Ḥanīfah".[1288]

Walking behind a coffin is preferable, as is indicated from the words of the Prophet ﷺ. ʿAbd al-Raḥmān ibn Abzā reported that Abū Bakr and ʿUmar walked in front of a coffin, while ʿAlī walked behind it. When he was told that Abū Bakr and ʿUmar were walking in front, ʿAlī remarked: "They both know that walking behind is better than walking in front of it, just as the *ṣalāh* of a person in congregation is better than the *ṣalāh* alone. But Abū Bakr and ʿUmar did so in order to make it easy for others".[1289] Imām Muḥammad said: "We do not see harm in being ahead of the coffin as long as one is close to it; though walking behind it is preferable. This is the opinion of Abū Ḥanīfah."[1290] Imām Muḥammad affirms the same point elsewhere, saying: "Walking in front of the *janāzah* is good, though walking behind is more preferable, and this is the opinion of Abū Ḥanīfah".[1291]

[1286] Abū Ḥanīfah, *K. al-āthār* 61.

[1287] al-Bukhārī, *k. al-janā'iz, b. al-surʿah bi al-janāzah.*

[1288] Muḥammad, *al-Muwaṭṭa', ii.* 105.

[1289] al-Bayhaqī, *k. al-janā'iz, b. al-mashy khalfahā.*

[1290] Abū Ḥanīfah, *K. al-āthār* 64.

[1291] Muḥammad, *al-Muwaṭṭa', ii.* 107.

Chapter 5: Burial

Burying a dead body in its grave is a communal obligation; it is a continuous tradition since the time of our father Ādam ﷺ. Allāh says: "*Have We not caused the earth to hold within itself the living and the dead?*"[1292]

It is preferable to bury a person in the area (town) of their death; the body may be taken for a mile or two for burial, for that is the usual distance to a cemetery. The removal of a body from one place to another is not liked; similarly, after burial, removing the body without genuine reason is not permissible.[1293]

THE SUNNAH OF DIGGING THE GRAVE

There are two types of grave: *laḥd,* which is a grave with a cavity large enough to hold the body dug to one side facing the *qiblah.* This cavity is covered with unbaked bricks. The second type is a *shaqq,* i.e. a regular grave, which is a pit dug in the ground, with the body placed in it and then sealed off with unbaked bricks and covered to form a ceiling. Either of these two methods is permissible, but the first, *laḥd,* is Sunnah.[1294] The Prophet ﷺ said: "*Laḥd* is for us, and *Shaqq* is for others".[1295] Anas said: "When the Prophet ﷺ died, there were two grave diggers. One usually dug the *laḥd* and the other a regular grave. The Companions differed as to what to do and their voices became raised. ʿUmar said: '*Do not raise your voices near the Messenger of Allāh* ﷺ', then they summoned the two diggers: the one who usually dug the *laḥd* came first, so they buried the Prophet ﷺ in a *laḥd*".[1296]

It is recommended to make the depth of the grave equal to the height of an average man. Hishām ibn ʿĀmir said: "We complained to the Prophet ﷺ on the day of the Battle of Uḥud, saying: 'O Allāh's

[1292] *al-Mursalāt* 25-26

[1293] *See: al-Fatāwā al-hindiyyah, i. 167.*

[1294] al-Kāsānī, *Badāʾiʿ al-ṣanāʾiʿ, ii. 353-4.*

[1295] Abū Dāwūd, *k. al-janāʾiz, b. fī al-laḥd.*

[1296] Ibn Mājah, *k. al-janāʾiz, b. mā jāʾa fī al-shaqq.*

Messenger, digging a separate grave for every body is a very hard job'. The Prophet ﷺ said: 'Dig, dig deeper, dig well, and bury two or three bodies in each grave'. The Companions asked him: 'Who should be put in the graves first?' The Prophet ﷺ said: 'Put those most learned in the Qur'ān first'. My father, (the narrator added) was the third of three who were put in one grave".[1297]

THE SUNNAH OF BURIAL

It is Sunnah to place a body in the grave from the direction of the *qiblah*; that is to put the coffin in the direction of the *qiblah* from the grave, then to take the body from there and place it in the *laḥd* or the *shaqq*.[1298] ʿAbdullāh ibn ʿAbbās narrated that the Prophet ﷺ said: "The body should be entered into the grave from the direction of the *qiblah*".[1299] Ḥammād ibn Abī Sulaymān asked Ibrāhīm al-Nakhaʿī about which side the body should be entered into a grave. He answered: "From the side of the *qiblah*". Imām Muḥammad said: "This is the opinion of Abū Ḥanīfah".[1300]

The person placing the body in the grave should say: بِسْمِ اللهِ وَعَلَى مِلَّةِ رَسُوْلِ اللهِ, "In the name of Allāh, and in accordance with the tradition of Allāh's Messenger ﷺ". Then he should loosen the shroud. Ibn ʿUmar reported that when a body was placed in the grave, the Prophet ﷺ used to say بِسْمِ اللهِ وَعَلَى مِلَّةِ رَسُوْلِ اللهِ , or he would say بِسْمِ اللهِ وَعَلَى سُنَّةِ رَسُوْلِ اللهِ "In the name of Allāh, and in accordance with the tradition or practice of Allāh's Messenger ﷺ".[1301]

Those attending the burial should throw three handfuls of soil over the grave from near the deceased's head.[1302] The Prophet ﷺ once prayed a funeral *ṣalāh* and then went to the grave of the deceased and threw three handfuls of soil from near the deceased's head.[1303] When throwing the first handful one should say مِنْهَا خَلَقْنَاكُم , "*Of this (i.e. the earth) We created you*", and on the second one should say وَفِيْهَا نُعِيْدُكُم , "*And to it shall We cause you to return*", and on the third handful one should say وَمِنْهَا نُخْرِجُكُمْ تَارَةً أُخْرَى, "*And of it We shall cause you to be resurrected a second time*".

[1297] al-Nasā'ī, *k. al-janā'iz, b. mā yustaḥabbu min iʿmāq al-qabr.*

[1298] al-Kāsānī, *Badā'iʿ al-ṣanā'iʿ, ii.* 355.

[1299] al-Tirmidhī, *k. al-janā'iz, b. mā ja'a fī al-dafn bi al-layl.*

[1300] Abū Ḥanīfah, *K. al-āthār* 63.

[1301] Abū Dāwūd, *k. al-janā'iz, b. fī al-duʿā' li al-mayyit.*

[1302] *al-Fatāwā al-hindiyyah, i.* 166.

[1303] Ibn Mājah, *k. al-janā'iz, b. mā jā'a fī ḥathw al-turāb fī al-qabr.*

After the burial, one may pray for the deceased. ʿUthmān said: "After burial the Prophet ﷺ would stand by the grave of the deceased and say: 'Seek forgiveness for your brother and pray for his acceptance, because he is now being questioned'."[1304]

A little mound should be made over the grave. Sufyān al-Tammār said that he had seen the grave of the Prophet ﷺ with a mound over it.[1305] Imām Muḥammad said: "This is what we adhere to; the grave should be made like a mound, and it should not be made square. This is the opinion of Abū Ḥanīfah".[1306]

If a person dies while at sea, and if land cannot be found to bury him, then the deceased should be washed, shrouded, and the funeral *ṣalāh* performed over him. Then the body should be tied with a heavy weight, and be lowered into the water.

VISITING GRAVES

Visiting graves is a Sunnah, because the Prophet ﷺ used to visit the graveyard of Madīnah regularly, and he instructed people to do so. Buraydah reported that the Prophet ﷺ said: "I had forbidden you to visit graves, but now you may visit them. It will remind you of the Hereafter".[1307] Abū Hurayrah reported: "The Prophet ﷺ visited his mother's grave and he wept, and moved others around him to tears. Then the Prophet ﷺ said: 'I sought my Lord's permission to seek forgiveness for her, but He did not permit me, and I sought permission to visit her grave and He permitted me to do this. So visit the graves, for that makes you mindful of death'."[1308] Imām Muḥammad said: "There is no harm in visiting graves to pray for the dead, and for the remembrance of the Hereafter. This is the opinion of Abū Ḥanīfah".[1309]

Whoever visits a grave should face the deceased, greet him, and supplicate for him. Buraydah reported: "The Prophet ﷺ taught us that

[1304] Abū Dāwūd, *k. al-janā'iz, b. al-istighfār ʿind al-qabr li al-mayyit.*

[1305] al-Bukhārī, *k. al-janā'iz, b. mā jā'a fī qabr al-nabī ṣallallāhu ʿalayhi wa sallam.*

[1306] Abū Ḥanīfah, *K. al-āthār* 65.

[1307] Muslim, *k. al-janā'iz, b. isti'dhān al-nabī ṣallallāhu ʿalayhi wa sallam fī ziyārat qabr ummih.*

[1308] Ibid.

[1309] Abū Ḥanīfah, *K. al-āthār* 68.

when we visit graves we should say: 'Peace be upon you, O believing men and women, O inhabitants of this place. Certainly, Allāh willing, we will join you. You have preceded us and we are to follow you. We supplicate to Allāh to grant us and you security'."[1310] ʿAbdullāh ibn ʿAbbās reported: "Once the Prophet ﷺ passed by some graves in Madīnah. He turned his face toward them saying: 'Peace be upon you, O dwellers of these graves. May Allāh forgive us and you. You have preceded us, and we are following your trail'."[1311]

It is permissible for women to visit graves as long as they can observe calmness, because the purpose of visiting graves is to remember the Hereafter, which is something that both men and women need to do. There are a number of *aḥādīth* which suggest that it is allowed for women to visit graves. ʿĀ'ishah reported: "I asked: 'What should I say when I pass by a graveyard, O Messenger of Allāh ﷺ?' He replied, 'Say, peace be upon the believing men and women dwelling here. May Allāh grant mercy to those who have preceded us and those who are to follow them. Certainly, Allāh willing, we will join you'."[1312] Muḥammad al-Bāqir narrated that Fāṭimah, the daughter of the Prophet ﷺ used to visit the grave of Ḥamzah every Friday.[1313] ʿAbdullāh ibn Abī Mulaykah is reported to have said: "Once ʿĀ'ishah returned after visiting the graveyard. I asked, 'O Mother of the Believers, where have you been?' She said: 'I went out to visit the grave of my brother ʿAbd al-Raḥmān'. I asked her: 'Didn't the Messenger of Allāh ﷺ prohibit visiting graves?' She said, 'Yes, he did forbid visiting graves during the early days, but later on he ordered us to visit them'."[1314]

However if a woman cannot keep herself patient and calm, then she should not visit the grave. Anas reported: "The Prophet ﷺ passed by a woman crying by the grave of her son, and said to her, 'Fear Allāh, and be patient'. She replied, 'What do you care about my trouble?' When he went away, someone said to her: 'That was the Messenger of Allāh ﷺ'. The woman immediately went to the Prophet's house, where she did

[1310] Muslim, *k. al-janā'iz, b. mā yuqālu ʿinda dukhūl al-qabr.*

[1311] al-Tirmidhī, *k. al-janā'iz, b. mā yaqūlu al-rajul idhā dakhala al-maqābir.*

[1312] Muslim, *k. al-janā'iz, b. mā yuqālu ʿinda dukhūl al-qubūr wa al-duʿā' li ahlihā.*

[1313] ʿAbd al-Razzāq, *al-Muṣannaf, iii.* 572.

[1314] al-Ḥākim, *al-Mustadrak, i.* 532.

not find any guards. She called out: 'O Messenger of Allāh ﷺ, I did not recognise you'. The Prophet ﷺ said: 'Patience is at the first shock'."[1315]

It is not liked, however, for women to make frequent graveside visits as they are generally more emotionally inclined. The Prophet ﷺ said: "May Allāh curse those women who are frequent visitors of the graves".[1316]

[1315] al-Bukhārī, *k. al-janā'iz, b. ziyarat al-qubūr;* Muslim, *k. al-janā'iz, b. fī al-ṣabr ʿalā al-muṣībah ʿinda al-ṣadmat al-ūlā.*

[1316] Ibn Mājah, *k. al-janā'iz, b. mā jā'a fī al-nahy ʿan ziyārat al-nisā' al-qubūr.*

CHAPTER 6: *SHAHĪD*

ALLĀH SAYS IN THE QUR'ĀN: "*Think not of those who are killed in the way of Allāh as dead. Nay, they are alive with their Lord, and they have provision. They rejoice in what Allāh has bestowed upon them of His Bounty and rejoice for the sake of those who have not yet joined them but are left behind that on them no fear shall come, nor shall they grieve. They rejoice in a Grace and a Bounty from Allāh, and that Allāh will not waste the reward of the believers*".[1317]

Anas ibn Mālik narrated that the Prophet ﷺ said: "Nobody who enters Paradise would ever wish to return to this life again, even if he was to be given the whole world and everything in it, except a *shahīd*; for he would wish to return and get killed ten times due to the honour that he received in Paradise".[1318]

DEFINITION OF A *SHAHĪD*

The term *shahīd* needs to be defined in *fiqh*, because certain rulings follow from a death being declared *shahīd*. This is different from the judgement in the Hereafter, which is the prerogative of Allāh. In this world if a person has died as a *shahīd* in *fiqh* terms, he or she must not be given a *ghusl*.

1. The death must be caused intentionally.
2. The death must be an unjust killing.
3. The means or weapon used to cause the death must normally be understood to cause death (for example, normally a beating with a stick will not qualify in this respect).
4. The act that led to the death must not be followed by a period of survival, (for example, if someone has been shot and survives for some days, his death is not classified as *shahīd*).[1319]

[1317] *Āl ʿImrān* 169-171.

[1318] al-Bukhārī, *k. al-jihād wa al-siyar, b. tamannī al-mujāhid an yarjiʿa ilā al-dunyā.*

[1319] For detailed description of *shahīd* see: al-Kāsānī, *Badāʾiʿ al-ṣanāʾiʿ*, ii. 360-4.

WASHING

The body of a *shahīd* does not need to be washed unless it is in a state of major impurity. The *shahīd* should be shrouded in the clothes he wore when he died, as long as they are in reasonably good condition and suitable. If they are not suitable, alternative cloth may be used to shroud his body according to the Sunnah. The body (of the *shahid*) should be buried in its blood-stained state without washing or removing the blood. The Prophet ﷺ ordered the martyrs of the Battle of Uḥud to be buried in their bloodstained clothes.[1320] ʿAbdullāh ibn ʿAbbās narrated that the Messenger of Allāh ﷺ ordered "that the weapons and coats of the martyrs at Uḥud should be removed from them, and that they should be buried in their garments stained with their blood".[1321] ʿAbd al-Raḥmān ibn Abī Laylā narrated that Saʿīd ibn ʿUbayd al-Qārī said on the occasion of the Battle of Qādisiyyah: "Verily we are meeting the enemy tomorrow if Allāh wills, and we are going to be *shahīds*. So do not wash any blood from our bodies, and do not enshroud us except in our clothes". [1322] Ibrāhīm al-Nakhaʿī said: "If someone is killed on the battlefield, then he will be buried in his clothes and will not be washed".[1323]

If a *shahīd* died in a state of major impurity, then he will be washed, because of the ḥadīth about Ḥanẓalah: when he was killed, the angels washed him. The Messenger of Allāh ﷺ said: "Your Companion is being washed by angels. Ask his wife, what the matter is. She said: 'He was in the state of *janābah*, when he left home'. The Messenger of Allāh ﷺ said: 'That's why the angels washed him'."[1324]

THE FUNERAL *ṢALĀH*

The funeral *ṣalāh* should be performed for a martyr.[1325] The Prophet ﷺ so offered funeral *ṣalāhs* for martyrs. ʿUqbah ibn ʿĀmir reported that the Prophet ﷺ did a funeral *ṣalāh* for the martyrs of Uḥud.[1326]

[1320] Abū Dāwūd, *k. al-janā'iz, b. fī al-shahīd yughsalu.*

[1321] Ibn Mājah, *k. al-janā'iz, b. mā jā'a fī al-ṣalāh ʿalā al-shuhadā' wa dafnihim.*

[1322] Ibn Abī Shaybah, *al-Muṣannaf, ii.* 458.

[1323] Ibid., *ii.* 459.

[1324] al-Ḥākim, *al-Mustadrak, iii.* 225.

[1325] *See*: al-Kāsānī, *Badā'iʿ al-ṣanā'iʿ*, ii. 369.

[1326] al-Bukhārī, *k. al-janā'iz, b. al-ṣalāh ʿalā al-shahīd.*

Abū Mālik al-Ghifārī reported: "The bodies of the martyrs of Uḥud were brought in batches of nine and placed with the body of Ḥamzah, who served as the tenth. Then the Prophet ﷺ did a funeral *ṣalāh* over them. After that the nine bodies were removed leaving Ḥamzah undisturbed. Then a batch of another nine martyrs was brought and placed beside Ḥamzah. The Prophet ﷺ offered the funeral *ṣalāh* over them as well. This way the Prophet ﷺ offered the funeral *ṣalāh* over all of them". Saʿīd ibn ʿAbdullāh narrated that he heard Makḥūl asking ʿUbādah ibn Awfā al-Numayrī: "Is there a funeral *ṣalāh* for *shahids*?" ʿUbādah said: "Yes".[1327] This opinion is held by Sufyān al-Thawrī, the people of Kufah, and Isḥāq ibn Rāhwayh.[1328]

[1327] al-Ṭaḥāwī, *Sharḥ maʿānī al-āthār, i.* 507.
[1328] al-Baghawī, *Sharḥ al-sunnah, iii.* 254.

GLOSSARY

adā'	– performance of an act of worship on time
adhān	– the call to *ṣalāh*
arkān	– (pl. of *rukn*) lit; pillars, essential elements
ʿAṣr	– the afternoon *ṣalāh*
ʿawrah	– parts of the body that must be covered
āyah	– (pl. *āyāt*) a verse of the Qur'ān
ayyām al-tashrīq	– three days following the Day of Sacrifice
bāṭil	– void, nugatory
bidʿah	– an innovation
dīnār	– a gold coin
dirham	– a silver coin
duʿā'	– supplication
Fajr	– the dawn *ṣalāh*
faqīh	– (pl. *fuqahā'*) jurist, an expert in law
farḍ	– a definitive obligation proved by a firm evidence, as distinguished from a mere obligation or *wājib.*
farḍ ʿayn	– individual obligation
farḍ kifāyah	– communal obligation
fatwā	– (pl. *fatāwā*) a legal opinion issued by an authoritative jurist
fiqh	– lit; understanding; the science of law
ghalīẓah	– heavy; enhanced
ghusl	– ritual bath, the complete washing of the body which removes major impurity
ḥadath	– (pl. *aḥdāth*) impurity, which makes *wuḍū'* or *ghusl* obligatory

ḥadīth	– (pl. *aḥādīth*) lit; .; account of a saying, act or approval of the Prophet ﷺ or of a Companion.
ḥalāl	– lawful, licit
ḥarām	– prohibited, forbidden by law
ḥayḍ	– menstruation
ḥukm	– ruling, judgement
ᶜibādah	– a ritual act of worship
ijmāᶜ	– the consensus of all qualified jurists of an age
ijtihād	– lit; effort; the effort of an expert jurist to determine the ruling in a matter on which the revelation is not explicit or certain
ᶜillah	– lit; cause, the base for an analogy
imām	– (pl. *a'immah*) a leader, the leader in daily *ṣalāhs*, a great authority in religion
iqāmah	– the second call preceding the congregational *ṣalāh*
iqtidā'	– following
ᶜIshā'	– night *ṣalāh*
istiḥāḍah	– extended or chronic menstrual bleeding
istiḥsān	– doctrine allowing exception to a legal reasoning
istinjā'	– cleansing of the private parts
istinshāq	– cleaning the nose with water
istisqā'	– a *ṣalāh* for rain
jā'iz	– permissible
janābah	– major impurity, which makes *ghusl* obligatory
janāzah	– (pl. *janā'iz*) funeral
Jumuᶜah	– Friday
junubī	– (pl. *junub*) a person in a state of *janābah*
Kaᶜbah	– the house of Allāh built by Ibrāhīm in Makkah. It is the direction faced in *ṣalāhs*
kaffārah	– expiation
khafīfah	– light
khimār	– women's head cover
khuff	– leather sock
khuṭbah	– an address, like the one given before the Friday *Ṣalāh* or after the *ᶜĪd Ṣalāh*s.
laḥd	– a grave with a cavity large enough to hold the body dug to one side facing the *qiblah*.

madhhab – (pl. *madhāhib*) school of law
madhy – a white sticky fluid that flows from the private parts because of thoughts about desire, foreplay, and so on
maḍmaḍah – gargling the mouth
Maghrib – the *ṣalāh* at sunset
makrūh – disliked, not liked or detestable
manī – semen
masḥ – wiping
al-Masjid al-Ḥarām – the sacred *masjid* at Makkah
miswāk – a stick for brushing the teeth
mu'adhdhin – the one who says the *adhān*
muftī – a jurisprudent who issues fatwās
mujtahid – one who is competent to perform *ijtihād*
muqallid – one who follows a *mujtahid*
muṣallā – the ground for the ʿ*Īd Ṣalāhs*
muṭlaq – absolute, unmixed; *al-ma' al-muṭlaq* – water in its natural state of purity
nafl; nāfilah – (pl. *nawāfil*) supererogatory *ṣalāh*, a voluntary act
najāsah – impurity
najis – impure
nifās – postnatal bleeding
niyyah – intention
qaḍā' – performance of an act of worship after its prescribed time
qiblah – the direction of the Kaʿbah
qiyās – analogy
Qunūt – supplication in the *Witr Ṣalāh*, or at other times
rakʿah – (pl. *rakaʿāt*) a basic unit of *ṣalāh* consisting of standing, reciting the Qur'ān, bowing, and prostrating
rukūʿ – the lowering of the head in the *ṣalāh* after the act of standing so that the palms of the hands reach the knees and the back becomes depressed
ṣaḥīḥ – a sound ḥadīth
sajdah, sujūd – (pl. *sajadāt*) prostration
ṣalāh – (pl. *ṣalawāt*) prayer
shafaq – redness or whiteness in the horizon after the sunset

shahīd	– a martyr
Sharīʿah	– divine law based on the Qur'ān and the Sunnah
sharṭ	– *(pl. shurūṭ)* condition/prerequisite
siwāk	– tooth-stick
Sunnah	– the exemplary practice of the Prophet ﷺ; recommended practice versus *farḍ*
sūrah	– a chapter of the Qur'ān
sutrah	– lit; screen; a barrier put in the direction of the *qiblah* to prevent people from passing in front of the person praying
Tahajjud	– recommended night *ṣalāhs*
ṭahārah	– purity
ṭāhir	– pure
ṭahūr	– purifying
takbīr	– uttering *Allāhu Akbar*
takbīr al-taḥrīmah	– the utterance of *Allāhu Akbar* followed by *niyyah,* after which the *ṣalāh* starts
taqlīd	– following the authority of a *mujtahid*
tarāwīḥ	– supererogatory *ṣalāhs* during the nights of Ramaḍān
tasbīḥ	– saying *subḥānallāh*
tashahhud	– lit; witnessing; the sitting at the end of the second *rakʿah* and the end of the final *rakʿah. Tashahhud* also refers to the words uttered whilst in this sitting
taslīm	– uttering *al-salāmu ʿalaykum wa rahmatullāh* to mark the end of the *ṣalāh*
tayammum	– a substitute ablution by pure earth over one's face and hands
wady	– a thick white secretion discharged by some people after urination
wājib	– a compulsory act, less than a *farḍ*
Witr	– intervenient *ṣalāh* between *ʿIshā'* and *Fajr*
wuḍū'	– ablution
Ẓuhr	– midday/noon *ṣalāh* when the sun declines from the meridian

BIBLIOGRAPHY

Abū Ḥanīfah, al-Nuʿmān ibn Thābit (d. 150): *Kitāb al-āthār,* narration of Muḥammad ibn al-Ḥasan al-Shaybānī, Multan, Maktabah Imdādiyyah, n.d.

Abū Dāwūd, Sulaymān ibn al-Ashʿath (d. 275): *al-Sunan,* ed. Muḥammad ʿAbd al-ʿAzīz al-Khālidī, Beirut, Dār al-kutub al-ʿilmiyyah, 1416/1996.

Abū Yaʿlā, Aḥmad ibn ʿAlī al-Mawṣilī (d. 307): *al-Musnad,* ed. Ḥusayn Salīm Asad, Damascus, Dār al-thaqāfah al-ʿarabiyyah, 1412/1992.

Abū Zurʿah, ʿAbd al-Raḥmān ibn ʿAmr al-Dimashqī (d. 281): *al-Tārīkh,* ed. Shukrullāh ibn Niʿmatullāh al-Qawjanī, Damascus, n.d.

Aḥmad ibn Ḥanbal (d. 241): *al-Musnad,* al-Maṭbaʿah al-maymanīyyah, 1313; Maṭbaʿat al-maʿārif, 1365.

al-Baghawī, Abū Muḥammad al-Ḥusayn ibn Masʿūd (d. 516): *Sharḥ al-Sunnah,* Beirut, Dār al-kutub al-ʿilmiyyah, 1412/1992.

al-Bayhaqī, Abū Bakr Aḥmad ibn al-Ḥasan (d. 458): *al-Sunan al-kubrā,* ed. Muḥammad ʿAbd al-Qādir ʿAṭā, Beirut, Dār al-kutub al-ʿilmiyyah, 1414/1994.

al-Bukhārī, Muḥammad ibn Ismāʿīl (d. 256): *al-Jāmiʿ al-ṣaḥīḥ,* printed with its commentary *Fatḥ al-bārī,* Beirut, Dār al-kutub al-ʿilmiyyah, 1410/1989.

al-Dāraquṭnī, ʿAlī ibn ʿUmar (d. 385): *al-Sunan,* ed. Majdī ibn Manṣūr ibn Sayyid Shurā, Beirut, Dār al-kutub al-ʿilmiyyah, 1417/1996.

al-Dārimī, Abū Muḥammad ʿAbdullāh ibn ʿAbd al-Raḥmān (d. 255): *al-Sunan,* ed. Muṣṭafā Dīb al-Bughā, Damascus, Dār al-qalam, 1417/1996.

al-Dhahabī, Shams al-dīn Muḥammad ibn Aḥmad (d. 748): *Siyar aᶜlām al-nubalā'*, Beirut, Mu'assasat al-risālah, 1413/1993.

al-Dihlawī, Walīullāh Aḥmad ibn ᶜAbd al-Raḥīm (d. 1176): *Ḥujjatullāh al-bālighah*, ed. Dr ᶜUthmān Jumuᶜah, Riyadh, 1420/1999.

Encyclopaedia of Islam, 2nd edn. Leiden: E. J. Brill. Vol. 1, 1960; vols. 2-10, Supplement, 1965-2002.

al-Fatāwā al-hindiyyah (known as *al-Fatāwā al-ᶜālamgīriyyah*), Pakistan, 1403/1983.

al-Ḥākim, Abū ᶜAbdillāh Muḥammad ibn ᶜAbdillāh al-Naysābārī (d. 405): *al-Mustadrak ᶜalā al-ṣaḥīḥayn*, ed. Muṣṭafā ᶜAbd al-Qādir ᶜAṭā, Beirut, Dār al-kutub al-ᶜilmiyyah, 1415/1995.

al-Haythamī, Nūr al-dīn ᶜAlī ibn Abī Bakr (d. 807): *Majmaᶜ al-zawā'id*, ed. ᶜAbdullāh Muḥammad al-Darwīsh, Beirut, Dār al-Fikr, 1414/1994.

Ibn ᶜĀbidīn, Muḥammad Amīn (d. 1252): *Ḥāshiyat radd al-muḥtar ᶜalā al-durr al-mukhtār sharḥ tanwīr al-abṣār*, ed. Dr Ḥusām al-dīn Farfūr, Damascus, 1421/2000.

Ibn Abī Shaybah, Abū Bakr ᶜAbdullāh ibn Muḥammad (d. 235): *al-Muṣannaf*, ed. Muḥammad ᶜAbd al-Salām Shāhīn, Beirut, Dār al-kutub al-ᶜilmiyyah, 1416/1995.

Ibn Ḥibbān, Abū Ḥātim Muḥammad (d. 354): *al-Ṣaḥīḥ*, Beirut, Dār al-Fikr, 1417/1996.

Ibn Mājah, Muḥammad ibn Yazīd al-Qazwīnī (d. 273): *al-Sunan*, ed. Maḥmūd Naṣṣār, Beirut, Dār al-kutub al-ᶜilmiyyah, 1419/1998.

Ibn al-Nadīm, Muḥammad ibn Isḥāq (d. 380): *al-Fihrist*, Beirut, Dār al-kutub al-ᶜilmiyyah, 1416/1996.

Ibn al-Qayyim, Muḥammad ibn Abī Bakr (d. 751): *Zād al-maᶜād fī hady khayr al-ᶜibād*, ed. Shuᶜayb al-Arnāwūṭ and ᶜAbd al-Qādir al-Arnāwūṭ, Mu'assasat al-risālah, Beirut, 1409/1989.

al-Kāsānī, Abū Bakr ibn Masᶜūd (d. 587): *Badā'iᶜ al-ṣanā'iᶜ*, ed. al-Shaykh ᶜAlī Muḥammad Muᶜawwiḍ and al-Shaykh ᶜĀdil Aḥmad al-Mawjūd, Beirut, Dār al-kutub al-ᶜilmiyyah, 1418/1997.

Mālik ibn Anas (93-179): *al-Muwaṭṭa'*, narration of Yaḥyā ibn Yaḥyā al-Laythī, Beirut, 1425/2004.

al-Marghinānī, Burhān al-Dīn Abū al-Ḥasan ᶜAlī ibn Abī Bakr (d. 593): *al-Hidāyah*, Egypt, Maktabah Muṣṭafā al-Bābī al-Ḥalabī, n.d.

al-Mawṣilī, ᶜAbdullāh ibn Maḥmūd (683): *Kitāb al-ikhtiyār li taᶜlīl al-mukhtār*, Beirut, Dār al-maᶜrifah, 1419/1998.

Muslim ibn al-Ḥajjāj al-Naysābūrī (d. 261): *al-Jāmiᶜ al-ṣaḥīḥ*, printed with the commentary by Imām al-Nawawī, Beirut, Dār al-kutub al-ᶜilmiyyah. 1415/1995.

Nadwī, S. Abū al-Ḥasan ᶜAlī (1333-1420): *The Four Pillars of Islam*, translated into English by Mohammad Asif, Qidwai, Lucknow, 1978.

al-Nasā'ī, ᶜAbd al-Raḥmān ibn Aḥmad ibn Shuᶜayb (d. 303): *al-Mujtabā*, Beirut, Dār al-kutub al-ᶜilmiyyah. 1416/1995.

Raḥmānī, Khālid Sayfullāh: *Jadīd fiqhī masā'il*, Karachi, 2005.

al-Samarqandī, ᶜAlā' al-dīn Muḥammad ibn Aḥmad (d. 539), *Tuḥfat al-fuqahā'*, Beirut, Dār al-Fikr, 1422/2002.

al-Ṣanᶜānī, ᶜAbd al-Razzāq ibn Hammām (d. 211): *al-Muṣannaf*. ed. Ḥabīb al-Raḥmān al-Aᶜẓamī, 2nd edn. Beirut: al-Maktab al-islāmī, 1403/1983.

al-Shaybānī, Muḥammad ibn al-Ḥasan (d. 189): *al-Muwaṭṭa'* published with its commentary *al-Taᶜlīq al-Mumajjad*, Azamgarh, 1419/1999.

al-Ṭabarānī, Abū al-Qāsim Sulaymān ibn Aḥmad (d. 360): *al-Muᶜjam al-kabīr*; *al-Muᶜjam al-awsaṭ*; *al-Muᶜjam al-ṣaghīr*, Matbaᶜah al-anṣārī, Delhi, 1311.

al-Tabrīzī, Muḥammad ibn ᶜAbdillāh al-Khaṭīb (d. 741): *Mishkāt al-maṣabīḥ* ed. Muḥammad Nizar Tamīm and Haytham Nizār Tamīm, Beirut, Dār al-Arqam, n.d.

al-Ṭaḥāwī, Abū Jaᶜfar Aḥmad ibn Muḥammad (d. 321): *Sharḥ maᶜānī al-āthār*, Beirut, Dār al-kutub al-ᶜilmiyyah. 1416/1996.

al-Ṭayālisī, Abū Dāwūd (d. 204), *al-Musnad*, Dā'irat al-Maᶜārif, Hyderabad Deccan, 1321.

al-Tirmidhī, Muḥammad ibn ᶜĪsā (d. 279): *al-Sunan*, ed. Aḥmad Shākir, Beirut, Dār iḥyā' al-turāth al-ᶜarabī, 1415/1995.

INDEXES

Index of Qur'ānic Āyāt

A

B

C

D

E

F

G

H

I

O

P

R

S

T

V

W

Index of Aḥādīth

A

J

K

L

M

N

O

T

Index of Narrators and Persons mentioned

A

B

C

D

E

F

G

H

I

J

K

L

M

N

O, P

Q

R

S

V

W

Y